Contents

INTRODUCTION

What to see	6	Things not to miss	12
When to go	10	Itineraries	18
Author picks	11		

BASICS 20

Getting there	21	The media	29
Arrival	23	Festivals	29
Getting around	24	Culture and etiquette	31
City tours	28	Travel essentials	32

THE GUIDE 38

1 The Belváros	38	7 Gellért-hegy and the Tabán	108
2 Lipótváros and Újlipótváros	48	8 Óbuda and Margít-sziget	114
3 Terézváros and Erzsébetváros	59	9 The Buda Hills	121
4 The Városliget and the stadium district	70	10 The city limits	126
5 Józsefváros and Ferencváros	77	11 Excursions from Budapest	129
6 The Vár and central Buda	88		

LISTINGS 150

12 Accommodation	150	17 Shopping	188
13 Restaurants	158	18 Sports and activities	196
14 Cafés and patisseries	169	19 Baths and pools	199
15 Bars and clubs	175	20 Kids' Budapest	203
16 Arts and entertainment	182	21 Gay Budapest	207

CONTEXTS 210

History	211	Hungarian	228
Music	220	Glossary of Hungarian terms	236
Books	225		

SMALL PRINT & INDEX 238

OPPOSITE TRAM ON SZABADSÁG HÍD **PREVIOUS PAGE** ART NOUVEAU MOSAIC, SZERVITA TÉR

Introduction to

Budapest

With a wonderful natural setting straddling the River Danube, beautiful architecture and delicious Magyar cuisine, Budapest is one of the most rewarding cities in Europe to visit. Its magnificent bridges and boulevards and its grand riverside views invite comparisons with Paris, Prague and Vienna – as do many features of its cultural life, from coffee houses and a love of music to its restaurants and wine-producing tradition. Budapest has recently acquired a new modern edge all its own, too, with cool boutique hotels and hip bars springing up in artfully decaying buildings. The city is also distinctively Hungarian, its inhabitants displaying fierce pride in their Magyar ancestry. Their language, whose nearest European relative is Finnish, underlines the difference – this can represent a challenge to visitors, but is no barrier to enjoyment of this most cosmopolitan of European cities.

Fundamental to the city's layout and history, the **River Danube** (Duna) – which is seldom blue – separates **Buda** on the hilly west bank from **Pest** on the eastern plain. Until 1873 these were separate cities, and they still retain a different feel. Buda is older and more dignified: dominated by the Vár (Castle Hill), a mile-long plateau overlooking the Danube, it was the capital of medieval monarchs and the seat of power for successive occupying powers. Built during the city's golden age in the late nineteenth century, with boulevards of Haussmann-like apartment blocks sweeping out from the old medieval centre, **Pest** holds most of the capital's magnificent Art Nouveau edifices and has a noisy, bustling feel. Following construction of the first permanent bridge between the two cities in 1849, power gradually moved across the river, culminating in the building of the grandiose Parliament on the Pest side. The two halves of the city each preserve their distinctive feel, but as a whole Budapest is a vibrant place today, never in danger of being overwhelmed by tourism but nonetheless offering plenty for visitors to enjoy.

ABOVE MILLENNIUM MONUMENT, HŐSÖK TERE

TOP 5 FOODIE TREATS

Great Market Hall Splendid wrought-iron structure harbouring a terrific assemblage of food stalls – try the *lángos* kiosks upstairs, too. See p.83

Goulash A tasty stew of meat and vegetables, seasoned with paprika, Hungary's classic national dish must be tried at least once. See p.159

Borkonyha The pick of the city's three Michelin-starred restaurants, *Borkonyha* oozes class. See p.161

Espresso Embassy One of Budapest's hip, new-style coffee houses, whose interior is as impressive as its coffee. See p.170

Szimplakert Farmers' Market Head to *Szimpla* on a Sunday morning to find all manner of delectable foodstuffs. See p.190

Above all, Budapest is probably best known for its **spas**, which range from fabulous Ottoman-era bathhouses like the Rudas, to fine nineteenth-century Art Nouveau buildings such as the Gellért. Another of Budapest's strong suits is its **restaurants**, which have made the city one of the new gastronomic destinations of Europe. Fantastically innovative, contemporary Hungarian cooking is now firmly to the fore, alongside some brilliant international cuisine. Hand in hand with this gastronomic renaissance is Hungary's superb **wine**; though often overlooked abroad, its quality may come as a surprise to many visitors. Catering for a wide range of tastes, Budapest's **nightlife** is also very much of a draw. Generally trouble-free, welcoming and accessible, it ranges from the city's distinctive "ruin pubs" in decaying apartment blocks or courtyards to *táncház* (dance houses) where Hungarians of all ages perform wild stamping movements to the rhythms of darkest Transylvania, and internationally renowned artists such as Márta Sebestyén appear in an informal setting.

There's plenty to offer in terms of **classical music** and **opera**, too: world-class ensembles and soloists can be enjoyed in the Palace of Arts' state-of-the-art concert hall or the grander, older settings of the Music Academy and Opera House. Fans of **pop**, **rock** and **world music** can discover a wealth of local talent, especially on the folk scene, alongside big international names, but the biggest event of the year is the **Sziget Festival**, held on an island just north of the centre in August, and one of Europe's largest musical celebrations.

What to see

Pest is where you're likely to spend most of your time, enjoying the streetlife, bars and shops within the **Belváros** (Inner City) and the neighbouring districts. These surrounding areas are defined by two semicircular boulevards – the **Kiskörút** (Small Boulevard) and the **Nagykörút** (Great Boulevard) – and radial avenues such as Andrássy út and Rákóczi út. Exploring the area between them can easily occupy you for several days. In the financial and government centre of **Lipótváros**, interest lies in St Stephen's Basilica and the monumental Parliament building, which rivals the grand structures across the Danube; here, too, you'll find the city's most important monuments and statues of pre-eminent Hungarians, many of which are sprinkled

OPPOSITE FROM TOP FISHERMEN'S BASTION; GELLÉRT BATHS; VÁRKERT BAZÁR

OFFBEAT BUDAPEST

Chess on the water Watch old-timers ponder their moves while taking a soak at Széchenyi Baths. See p.76

Communist trainers Check out retro brand Tisza for some cult 1970s Hungarian footwear. See p.193

Escape rooms Fancy being locked up in a ruined Soviet-era apartment block? Thought so… See p.198

Odd medicine Dried bats and mummified skulls are just some of the exhibits in the Semmelweis medical collection. See p.112

Sleep in a work of art Full of antiques, bric-a-brac and witty drawings – the *Lavender Circus* is a fantastically eccentric place to stay. See p.152

around the vast expanse of Kossuth Lajos tér. In **Terézváros**, Andrássy út leads out past the grandiose Opera House and the House of Terror to Hősök tere (Heroes' Square), a magnificent imperial set piece where the Fine Arts Museum displays a first-rate collection of old European masters. Beyond, the **Városliget** (City Park) holds one of the finest zoos in Europe, both in terms of its animals and its architecture, as well as the hugely popular Széchenyi Baths, served by its own thermal springs.

Of Pest's remaining inner-city districts, **Erzsébetváros** and **Józsefváros** hold the most appeal. The former is Budapest's old Jewish quarter, with a rich and tragic history that's still palpable in the bullet-scarred backstreets behind the Great Synagogue on Dohány utca. But its old apartment blocks have also spawned a new genre of drinking spots, the "ruin bars", which have become a popular destination for younger Budapestis. From here, it's not far to the National Museum, a well-presented introduction to Hungarian history, and the Great Market Hall, further round in **Ferencváros**, whose hinterland harbours the Applied Arts Museum, Holocaust Memorial Centre and the Palace of Arts, one of Budapest's foremost cultural venues.

The **Vár** (Castle) on the **Buda** side was once the seat of Hungary's monarchs, and its palace, museums, churches and Baroque streets offer some absorbing sightseeing: notably the immense Hungarian National Gallery and the remarkable Hospital in the Rock. Down along the banks of the Danube, the historic Turkish baths – such as the Király and Rudas – are well worth experiencing, as is the remarkable Cave Church in **Gellérthegy**. There's more history to the north in **Óbuda**, with its clutch of worthwhile museums clustered around the old centre, and extensive Roman remains at nearby Aquincum. In fine weather, people flock to **Margít-sziget**, the large, leafy island mid-river between Buda and Pest, to swim and sunbathe at the enormous lido and party through the night. Encircling the city to the west, the **Buda Hills** have a different kind of allure, with fun rides on the Cogwheel and Children's railways and chairlift, and intriguing caves to be visited. **Further out**, the steam trains of the Hungarian Railway History Park and the redundant Communist monuments within the Memento Park rate as major attractions.

There is plenty to see on **excursions** from Budapest. Top of the list is **Szentendre**, a picturesque artists' colony with a superb open-air ethnographic museum. Further upriver, the **Danube Bend** offers gorgeous scenery, a Renaissance palace and citadel and an amazing treetop zip-ride at **Visegrád**, while **Esztergom** boasts its basilica and a remarkable Turkish relic; while on the east bank of the Danube sits **Vác**, with its well-preserved Baroque centre. Classical-music lovers, meanwhile, will also enjoy concerts in the former Habsburg palace of **Gödöllő**, to the east of Budapest.

TOP 5 SHOPS

Bortársaság Super-helpful staff who will help you find your way around the stocks of superb Hungarian wines.

Fakopáncs You'll find a wonderful collection of wooden toys here in the appropriately named "Woodpecker" shop.

Irók Boltja The "Writer's Bookshop" is the best place in the city to find translated Hungarian works, and it's cosy too.

Mai Manó Galéria Housed inside the gallery of the same name, this is a terrific place for picking up all manner of photography-related items.

MesterPorta If it's Hungarian folk music you're after, look no further than this friendly, well-stocked shop.

A TRIBAL NATION

As a small, landlocked country whose language sets it apart from its neighbours, Hungary is a tribal nation, whose citizens still identify with their ancestors, pagan **Magyar** tribes who conquered the Carpathian Basin in 896 AD. Since the epochal Christmas Day when the Magyar ruler Vajk was baptized and crowned as King Stephen by a papal envoy, Hungary has identified itself with Europe while simultaneously remaining aware of its "otherness" – a sentiment reinforced by successive foreign occupations and the loss of much of its territory to neighbouring states.

The symbol of statehood is **St Stephen's Crown**, whose bent cross – caused by it being squashed in the eighteenth century – is a cherished sign of the vicissitudes that Hungary has endured, and features on the national **coat of arms** that you'll see everywhere in Budapest. The shield beneath the crown bears a Catholic cross of Lorraine, and the red and white "Árpád stripes" of the early Magyar tribal kings; today, the latter signify far-right loyalties, having formerly been employed as the flag of the Fascist Arrow Cross. With the fall of Communism, St Stephen's Crown returned to the coat of arms, but not to the national **flag** – which is a simple red, white and green tricolour.

RISING FROM THE RUINS

Now synonymous with Budapest nightlife, the city's first **ruin bars** (*romkocsma*; see p.176) were guerrilla-like ventures, turning condemned buildings and crumbling courtyards into hip summer drinking spots. Decorated with graffiti and collages, the first wave of bars also put on entertainment in the form of music, film screenings and poetry readings. Once the authorities forced out a *romkocsma* it would simply take its name elsewhere: at the start of the summer word would spread where the latest incarnations of the popular bars would be. This purely nomadic existence began to change when councils started to realize the commercial potential of the bars, not least in attracting tourists. While this has caused some inevitable commercialization, most bars retain an undeniable wackiness, and places like *Rácskert*, for example, hint at a return to the anarchic spirit. The thirst for a touch of novelty has led to some bars setting up alternative markets at weekends, such as at *Anker't* (see p.177) and *Szimplakert* (see p.178).

When to go

The best times to visit Budapest are **spring** (late March to the end of May) and **autumn** (Sept–Oct), when the weather is generally pretty mild – though there are often long days of sunshine during these periods – and there are fewer tourists (though things tend to get busy during the Budapest Spring Festival in late March/early April). **Summers** can be extremely hot with prolonged periods of sunshine and temperatures regularly reaching the mid-30s (°C), and often higher. It is during this time that many residents decamp to Lake Balaton and those who remain flock to the city's pools and parks to escape the heat and dust. Though some concert halls are closed over summer, there are all kinds of outdoor events to compensate – and also major international events such as the Formula One Grand Prix at the end of July, and the Sziget Festival in mid-August.

Winters can be bitterly cold, and may be snowy, which can make for a wonderful sight around the festive season, particularly with the markets in full flow. But you can still enjoy all the city's sights and cultural attractions (as well as trying roasted chestnuts from street vendors), while the thermal baths take on an extra allure. It's wise to book accommodation in advance for Christmas, New Year, the Spring Festival and Grand Prix, though prices are ramped up considerably during these periods.

BUDAPEST CLIMATE

	Jan	Feb	Mar	Apr	May	Jun	Jul	Aug	Sep	Oct	Nov	Dec
AVERAGE DAILY TEMPERATURE												
Avg Min C°/Max F°	-4/25	-2/28	2/36	7/45	1/52	15/59	16/61	16/61	12/54	7/45	3/37	-1/30
Avg Min C°/Max F°	1/34	4/39	10/50	17/63	22/72	26/79	27/82	27/82	23/73	16/61	8/46	4/39
AVERAGE RAINFALL												
mm	37	44	38	45	72	69	56	47	33	57	70	46

Author picks

Our authors have scoured every corner of Budapest, seeking out everything from the quirkiest museums and coolest music to the finest coffee houses. Here are some of their favourite things to see, do, sip and savour.

Go flippin' crazy The Pinball Museum is the city's most unconventional attraction, offering some 130 lovingly restored machines, all of which you can have a bash at (p.58).

Ice cream Budapest's searing summer heat will have you yearning for something chilly, so make a beeline for one of the city's many enticing ice cream parlours; we love *Damniczki* (p.170), *Fragola* (p.171) and *Levendula* (p.173); wasabi hazelnut or wild garlic flavour perhaps?

Catch a concert The city rates some stellar performance spaces, but the beautifully decorated and acoustically brilliant Liszt Music Academy building takes some beating (p.63).

Caffeine kicks The third-wave coffee movement has hit Budapest with a vengeance: our top spots are *9Bar* (p.171), *Cube* (p.171) and *Kelet Kávézó* (p.173).

Going round the bend Take a leisurely cruise up to the Danube Bend, one of the grandest stretches of this mighty river; boat trips are also a great way to reach the historic towns of Szentendre (p.130), Visegrád (p.136), Vác (p.145) and Esztergom (p.141).

Retro Design Center Wallow in a little 1970s nostalgia with a visit to this entertaining retro museum in Szentendre, with its wonderful collection of Communist-era cars (p.133).

Super sleeps From the bohemian *Brody House* (p.154) to the leftfield *Lavender Circus* (p.152), Budapest is chock-full of truly idiosyncratic places to bed down for the night.

It's child's play Explore the city's many kid-centric entertainments, from the wonderful Zoo's carousel (p.75) and the Houdini Museum's magic displays (p.205) to the interactive Center of Scientific Wonders (p.128 & p.205) and the Railway History Park (p.127).

> Our author recommendations don't end here. We've flagged up our favourite places – a perfectly sited hotel, an atmospheric café, a special restaurant – throughout the Guide, highlighted with the ★ symbol.

FROM TOP RETRO DESIGN CENTER; PINBALL MUSEUM; DANUBE BEND

17

things not to miss

It's not possible to see everything that Budapest has to offer in one trip – and we don't suggest you try. What follows is a selective taste of the city's highlights: magnificent Art Nouveau treasures, unique thermal baths, and world-class concerts and festivals. All highlights have a page reference to take you straight into the Guide, where you can find out more. Coloured numbers refer to chapters in the Guide section.

13

1 THERMAL BATHS
Page 199

Bathe in splendour at the city's magnificent Ottoman-era and Art Nouveau spas, some fed by hot springs.

2 BUDAPEST ZOO
Page 75

Feed the giraffes, tickle the rhinos and marvel at the magnificent Art Nouveau buildings – the Elephant and Palm houses are particularly impressive.

3 BUDA HILLS
Page 121

Both children and adults will enjoy this delightful ride up into the verdant Buda Hills.

4 LIVE MUSIC
Page 184

The city's lively music scene offers everything from Gypsy fiddlers and Hungarian folk singers to world-class opera and classical performances.

5 #2 TRAM RIDE
Page 49

This route past Parliament and along the Pest embankment affords some wonderful views of Buda.

6 FISHERMEN'S BASTION
Page 92

Take a stroll along the Fishermen's Bastion for superlative views of the Danube and Pest beyond.

7 HUNGARIAN NATIONAL GALLERY
Page 99

Showcased in the imposing Royal Palace, this is Hungary's premier collection of home-grown art, from Gothic altarpieces to Art Nouveau and Abstract Expressionism.

8 DESIGN HOTELS
Page 150

Awash with colour, creativity and flair, Budapest possesses an impressive ensemble of superbly conceived design hotels.

9 SZIGET FESTIVAL
Page 183

Hungary's Glastonbury, this enormous mid-August bash draws some of the biggest bands on the planet.

10 COFFEE HOUSES
Page 169

Ponder the world over a coffee and cake – after all, it's an old Central European tradition.

11 MEMENTO PARK
Page 127

Re-live the city's Communist past in this atmospheric park on the outskirts of Budapest, where Lenin and his comrades now reside.

12 **RUIN BARS**
Page 176

Quartered within abandoned
apartment blocks and
courtyards, these wonderfully
ramshackle bars are terrific fun.

13 **GREAT SYNAGOGUE**
Page 65

Looming over the Jewish district,
this is Europe's largest and most
impressive synagogue.

14 **HOUSE OF TERROR**
Page 63

A dramatic memorial-museum
to the victims of state repression,
occupying the former
headquarters of the secret
police.

15 **HUNGARIAN RAILWAY
HISTORY PARK**
Page 127

Railway buffs are sure to get all
misty-eyed at this marvellous
collection of old locos; you can
even drive your own steam
engine.

16 **FOOD MARKETS**
Page 189

Stock up on sausages, cheeses
and other goodies at Budapest's
atmospheric market halls., and
refuel afterwards with a bowl of
goulash.

17 **BUDAPEST'S
CEMETERIES**
Pages 82, 83, 125 & 127

Take a wander through the
elaborate tombs in the city's
many atmospheric cemeteries.

A MI
POLITIKAI NYOMOZÓINK
LAMVÉDELMI HATÓS
DOLGOZÓI,

14

15

BLAHA LUJZA
1850 – 1926

ÉP LEGJOBBJAIBÓL K

16

17

Itineraries

Budapest is essentially two cities in one: Buda and Pest, but on both sides of the Danube, you'll find glorious architecture alongside remnants of the city's Communist past, not to mention all manner of superb music – and there are some fun ways to get around, too.

ARCHITECTURAL BUDAPEST

Museum of Applied Arts Lechner's flamboyantly designed Secessionist building is as much an exhibit as the voluminous displays inside. **See p.84**

Gellért Baths Soothe any aching limbs with a wallow in the hot pool and steam rooms of these magnificent Art Nouveau baths. **See p.110**

Centrál Kávéház If you only take coffee – alright then, cake too – in one place, then make it *Centrál*, which has retained its pre-World War II grandeur, when it was the meeting place of the Budapest literati. **See p.174**

Great Synagogue The crowning glory of the Jewish District is the Byzantine-inspired Great Synagogue, the largest in Europe; admire, too, Imre Varga's Holocaust Memorial, beautifully cast in the shape of a willow tree. **See p.65**

Budapest Zoo As famous for its architecture as its animals, the city's fabulous zoo will entertain kids and parents alike – don't miss the elephant house. Afterwards, take a stroll through Városliget Park. **See p.75**

Mátyás Church and Fishermen's Bastion At the heart of cobbled Castle Hill stands the glorious, colourfully patterned Mátyás Church, and just across the way, the Fishermen's Bastion with its sweeping views of Pest. **See p.91 & p.92**

ON THE RAILS AND ON THE WATER

Sikló Hop on the nineteenth-century funicular perched atop Castle Hill, and enjoy a great view of the city as you ride down to the riverside. **See p.103**

Millennium Line Completed in 1896 for Hungary's millennium celebrations – making it the second oldest metro in the world after London – a ride on yellow line #1 from Vörösmarty tér to Hősök tere is sure to conjure up images of a bygone era. **See p.41**

Tram ride Tram #2 along the Pest embankment offers the best views of Buda, so jump aboard at the southern terminus near the Palace of Arts, and take in the sights all the way up to the Parliament building and beyond. **See p.49**

River cruise What better way to appreciate the not always so blue Danube than on a lazy afternoon cruise. **See p.26**

Cogwheel and Children's railways Kids and adults alike will love this 3km climb up into the Buda Hills; and once you've reached the upper terminus, you can board the narrow-gauge railway, which runs for a further 11km through deep woods. **See p.122**

Castle Bus It might not be the most comfortable ride in the world, but as it rattles through the cobbled streets of the Vár, you'll get to see the pick of the sights hereabouts. **See p.89**

ABOVE KELETI STATION **OPPOSITE** APPLIED ARTS MUSEUM

RED BUDAPEST

House of Terror Housed in the former headquarters of the Secret Police, this gripping and often sobering museum commemorates the victims of the Communist regime. **See p.63**

Memento Park Head to the city outskirts and wander among Red Army soldiers and Communist dictators, then have your picture taken in the Trabant. **See p.127**

Soviet Army Memorial This typically stern Cold War-era memorial honours the soldiers killed during the liberation of the city from the Nazis. **See p.52**

Budapest Poster Gallery Pick up a piece of Communist chic at this fabulous poster shop, specializing in Soviet-era art. **See p.190**

Hospital in the Rock The Cold War comes to life in this fascinating former military-hospital-cum-nuclear-bunker located deep below Castle Hill. **See p.97**

MUSICAL BUDAPEST

Akvárium A semi-subterranean hub for live bands and DJs, plus an "underwater" restaurant – what's not to like? **See p.176**

Liszt Music Academy Get your classical kicks by attending a concert in the Grand Hall of the prestigious, and recently renovated, academy building, named after Hungary's most revered musician. **See p.63**

Music History Museum Learn more about Hungary's rich musical heritage at this engaging collection, from the irrepressible sounds of the Roma to the classical genius of Liszt and Bartók. **See p.93**

Cocoa concerts Themed, child-friendly concerts run by the Budapest Festival Orchestra are a fun way to introduce a bit of culture to the under-12s. **See p.205**

Opera House Take a backstage tour through one of central Europe's great opera houses, or, better still, take in a performance. **See p.61**

Jazz A strong jazz tradition prevails in Budapest, but for the very best, seek out the *Budapest Jazz Club* or the *Opus Jazz Club*, both of which feature a regular roster of high-class acts. **See p.185**

Folk music One of the most prominent aspects of Magyar culture is folk music, and one of the best places to appreciate these traditional sounds is a *táncház* (dance house); the Fonó Music Hall is a good place to start. **See p.186**

GETTING AROUND ON TWO WHEELS

Basics

21 Getting there

23 Arrival

24 Getting around

28 City tours

29 The media

29 Festivals

31 Culture and etiquette

32 Travel essentials

Getting there

Flying is the easiest way to reach Budapest, with several airlines operating direct from the UK. Flying from North America, Australasia or South Africa will entail one or more changes. Travelling overland from the UK is another option, though this inevitably takes much longer and usually works out far more expensive.

To get the cheapest flight deals, you'll need to book weeks, if not months, in advance, with the highest fares from June to September, Christmas and New Year. You'll get the best prices during the low season, November to February. As well as checking **fares** on airline websites and searching via sites such as ⓦ skyscanner.net, ⓦ kayak.co.uk or ⓦ momondo.co.uk, you may also be able to cut costs by going through a specialist flight agent, who in addition to dealing with discounted flights may offer student and youth fares and travel insurance. Other specialist **tour operators** can book you onto a variety of city breaks or themed tours in Budapest.

Flights from the UK and Ireland

Flying time to Budapest from the UK or Ireland is between two and a half and three hours, depending on your departure airport. There are currently several **budget airlines** flying **from the UK** to Budapest: easyJet (ⓦ easyjet.com) from London Gatwick; Norwegian Air (ⓦ norwegian .com) from London Gatwick; Wizz Air (ⓦ wizzair .com) from Luton, Liverpool, Birmingham and Glasgow; Ryanair (ⓦ ryanair.com) from Bristol, East Midlands, Manchester and Stansted; and Jet2 (ⓦ jet2.com) from East Midlands, Leeds Bradford, Manchester and Edinburgh. In addition, British Airways (ⓦ ba.com) has daily flights from Heathrow, though these tend to be more expensive than the budget airlines with a return costing £100–120. Book far enough in advance with one of the low-cost airlines and you can pick up a ticket for as

little as £60–70 return, even in summer; book anything less than three or four weeks in advance and this could triple in price.

From **Ireland**, both Aer Lingus (ⓦ aerlingus.com) and Ryanair (ⓦ ryanair.com) fly between Dublin and Budapest. Flights take around three hours and **fares** start at around €100 in low season.

Flights from the US and Canada

With no direct flights from North America to Budapest, your best bet is to fly with one of the major European-based airlines like Air France (ⓦ airfrance.com), British Airways (ⓦ ba.com) or Lufthansa (ⓦ lufthansa.com), where you'll probably be routed via their respective European hubs.

From the east coast of the **US**, **fares** average around US$650 in low season and US$1000 in high season; and from the west coast around US$950 in low season and US$1300 in high season. From **Canada**, expect to pay around Can$1200 in low season from Toronto (Can$1600 high season), and Can$1800 in low season from Vancouver (Can$2200 high season).

Flights from Australia, New Zealand and South Africa

There are no direct flights to Budapest from Australia, New Zealand or South Africa, so the best option is to fly to a western European gateway and get a connecting flight from there. A return **fare** to Budapest from eastern **Australia** costs around Aus$2200 in low season and Aus$2700 in high season. From **New Zealand**, a return fare costs around NZ$2400 in low season and NZ$3000 in high season. Flying from **South Africa**, you can get return flights for around ZAR9200 in low season and ZAR10,000 in high season.

City breaks and tours

Budapest is an extremely popular **city-break** destination and this is reflected in the number of operators offering the city as a destination in itself

---

A BETTER KIND OF TRAVEL

At Rough Guides we are passionately committed to travel. We believe it helps us understand the world we live in and the people we share it with – and of course tourism is vital to many developing economies. But the scale of modern tourism has also damaged some places irreparably, and climate change is accelerated by most forms of transport, especially flying. All Rough Guides' flights are carbon-offset, and every year we donate money to a variety of environmental charities.

or as part of a two- or three-centre trip, usually combined with Prague and Vienna.

AGENTS AND OPERATORS

Cox & Kings UK ☎ 020 3797 4759, ⓦ coxandkings.co.uk. Upmarket cultural trips to Budapest staying in five-star hotels such as the *Corinthia*: Three-night breaks start at around £400 including flights and transfers. There are also luxury and private group tours aboard the *Danube Express*, which stops off in Budapest.

Kirker Holidays UK ☎ 020 7593 1899, ⓦ kirkerholidays.com. Three-night cultural breaks in four- and five-star hotels from around £500 per person, including flights and transfers. They can reserve opera tickets and arrange walking tours of the city.

North South Travel UK ☎ 01245 608 291, ⓦ northsouthtravel .co.uk. Friendly, competitive travel agency, offering discounted fares worldwide. Profits are used to support projects in the developing world, especially the promotion of sustainable tourism.

Osprey Holidays UK ☎ 0131 243 8098, ⓦ ospreyholidays.com. Two-night breaks in one of several three-, four- and five-star hotels, from around £330 per person, including flights and transfers.

Regent Holidays UK ☎ 020 3811 3588, ⓦ regent-holidays.co.uk. Central and Eastern European specialist offering three-night city breaks in three-, four- and five-star accommodation from £345, including flights, as well as tailor-made itineraries.

Stag Republic UK ☎ 0845 686 0619, ⓦ stagrepublic.co.uk. A Budapest-based operation that arranges stag packages that can include Trabant treks, quad-biking, visits to the baths and stag dinners. Prices start at around £55 per person for a two-night hostel stay, on top of which you add flights and the various activities.

STA Travel UK ☎ 0333 321 0099, US ☎ 1 800 781 4040, Australia ☎ 134 782, New Zealand ☎ 0800 474 400, South Africa ☎ 0861 781 781; ⓦ statravel.co.uk. Worldwide specialists in independent travel; also student IDs, travel insurance, car rental, rail pass and more. Good discounts for students and under-26s.

Thermalia Spas UK ☎ 01843 864 688, ⓦ thermaliaspas.co.uk. Spa-holiday specialists offering stays centred around health and fitness at the four-star *Danubius Health Spa Resort Margitsziget*. Prices from around £450 for three nights, including flights.

Trailfinders UK ☎ 0207 368 1200, Ireland ☎ 016 777 888; ⓦ trailfinders.com. One of the best-informed and most efficient agents for independent travellers.

Trains

Getting to Budapest by **train** is likely to be considerably more expensive than flying, though it's a great deal more fun. First stop should be ⓦ seat61.com, an excellent website that provides route, ticket, timetable and contact information for all European train services.

The quickest and most straightforward option from the UK is to take the **Eurostar** from London's St Pancras International to Paris, and then continue from Gare de l'Est to Munich before catching the

night train to Budapest; the entire journey takes around twenty hours in total. A standard second-class **return ticket** on this route costs around £320. An alternative is to go via Brussels, Cologne and Vienna: it involves more changing of trains and takes up to twenty-four hours but the views along the Rhine Valley are delightful. There are discounts for students, and those under 26 or over 60.

A **train pass from** InterRail (ⓦ interrail.eu) or Eurail (ⓦ eurail.com) – both cover Hungary – makes it convenient to take in the country as part of a wider rail trip around Europe.

RAIL CONTACTS

European Rail UK ☎ 020 7619 1080, ⓦ traintours4u.co.uk.
Eurostar UK ☎ 08432 186 186, ⓦ eurostar.com.
Rail Europe UK ☎ 0844 848 5848, ⓦ uk.voyages-sncf.com.

By bus

Eurolines (ⓦ eurolines.co.uk) operates two **buses** a week directly from London to Budapest, which take around thirty hours. Otherwise, you can change in Vienna. A standard return **fare** costs around £140, though advance deals and special offers can bring this down considerably. Although by no means a particularly comfortable journey, buses are air-conditioned and have on-board toilets. The usual route is to take the ferry across the Channel to Calais and then on via Brussels and Vienna.

Driving to Budapest

Driving to Hungary from the UK can be a pleasant proposition, particularly if you want to make stops in other places along the way. It's about 1600km from London to Budapest which, with stops, takes two days to drive. To plan your route, try **motoring organizations** such as the AA (ⓦ theaa .com), the RAC (ⓦ rac.co.uk) and Via Michelin (ⓦ viamichelin.com).

The most common cross-Channel options are the **ferry** links between Dover and Calais or Ostend. However, the quickest way of crossing the Channel is to go via the **Eurotunnel** service (ⓦ eurotunnel .com), which operates drive-on drive-off shuttle trains between Folkestone and Calais/Coquelles. The 24-hour service runs every twenty minutes throughout the day.

Once across the Channel, the most direct route to Budapest is via Brussels, Aachen, Cologne, Frankfurt, Nürnberg, Linz and Vienna. To avoid the long queues at Hegyeshalom, consider entering Hungary from Deutsch-Kreutz, just south of Einstadt, instead.

The main cause for any queues is the need to buy an electronic motorway **vignette** (e-Vignette) – compulsory if you are driving on Hungarian motorways. The shortest vignette you can get is the ten-day one which costs 2975Ft (around €10); see Ⓦtoll-charge.hu for details. You can buy the *vignette* online ahead of travelling, or at one of the petrol stations in Austria before you cross the border, which should reduce any waiting. A system of mobile patrols and electronic number-plate readers enforces the scheme, and there are steep fines for travelling on a motorway without one.

FERRY CONTACTS

P&O Ferries UK Ⓣ 0800 130 0030, Ireland Ⓣ +353 1 686 9467; Ⓦ poferries.com.
Stena Line UK Ⓣ 0844 770 7070, Ⓦ stenaline.co.uk.

Arrival

Other than the airport, all points of arrival are fairly central and most within walking distance or just a few stops by metro from downtown Pest. Budapest's excellent public transport system ensures that few parts of the city are more than thirty minutes' journey from the centre; many places can be reached in half that time. Three of the city's four metro lines and three main roads meet at the major junction of Deák tér in Pest, making this the main transport hub of the city; there's a transport map at the back of this book.

By air

Liszt Ferenc International Airport (Ⓣ 1 296 7000, Ⓦbud.hu), 20km southeast of the centre in Ferihegy (which it is still sometimes known as), has two passenger terminals. Terminal 2A serves countries covered by the Schengen Agreement, while 2B serves all non-Schengen destinations (UK, the US etc). Before leaving, it is worth checking which terminal you're flying from, as the Schengen divide might be subject to revision. There are **ATMs**, exchange facilities, tourist information desks and car-rental offices in both terminal buildings.

The easiest – but most expensive – way to get into the centre is an **airport taxi**. Run by Főtaxi (Ⓣ 1 222 2222), these charge a fixed fee to different zones (you'll pay around 6500Ft or €22 to the centre). The next fastest option is the excellent

miniBUD **airport shuttle service** (Ⓣ 1 550 0000, Ⓦ minibud.hu), which will take you directly to any address in the city. Tickets (4800Ft/€15 for one person, 5900Ft/€19 for two) can be bought at their desk in arrivals, or you can make a reservation online. Travelling from the city centre to the airport, you can either reserve online or by phone.

Far cheaper is **public transport**; bus #200E departs every fifteen minutes from the stop between terminals 2A and 2B to Kőbánya-Kispest Station; from here, you switch to metro line #3 (blue) to get to the centre. Buses run between 4am and 11pm and the journey time to Kőbánya-Kispest is about forty minutes. To get to the centre you'll need a transfer ticket (530Ft); just remember to validate the second portion of the ticket before you board the metro. Buy your tickets (and collect a public transport map) from the **BKK** (**Budapest Transport Centre**; daily 9am–9pm) desk inside arrivals, next to the Budapest Information desk. Otherwise, you can buy **tickets** from the vending machine next to the bus stop (350Ft), or from the driver on board (450Ft); note that this is just for the bus leg of the journey – you will need to buy another ticket for the metro at Kőbánya-Kispest. With a Budapest Card (see p.32), available from the Budapest Information desk, it's free to travel on the bus from the airport.

By train

The Hungarian word *pályaudvar* (abbreviated "*pu.*" in writing) is used to designate a **train station**. Of the six in Budapest, only three are important for tourists, but note that their names, which are sometimes translated into English, refer to the direction of services handled rather than their location.

Most international trains terminate at Pest's **Keleti Station**, on Baross tér in the VIII district. Although the hawks and hustlers here are not nearly as prominent these days, if you are approached by anyone offering anything, it's best to simply ignore them. The best source of tourist information here is the Mellow Mood agency (June–Aug daily 7am–10pm; Sept–May Mon–Sat 8am–4pm; Ⓣ 1 343 0748, Ⓦ mellowmood.hu), whose office is to the right of the big glass doorways at the station entrance. The international ticket office is located in a passageway a little way along platform 6, which is to the left as you enter. You can get all local transport tickets and passes from the BKK public transport centre (daily 5.30am–10pm) located in the underpass. There are also 24-hour left-luggage lockers here (600Ft/800Ft for 24hr).

Nyugati Station, north of central Pest in the VI district, is the second most useful terminus. It has left-luggage lockers (400Ft/600Ft for 24hr) next to the international ticket office (daily 6.45am–6.45pm). To reach Deák tér, take the blue #3 metro line two stops in the direction of Kőbánya-Kispest. The third main station – though it's unlikely you'll need to use it – is **Déli Station**, near the Vár in Buda, and just four stops from Deák tér on the red #2 metro line. There are left-luggage lockers here but no tourist office.

Avoid all offers of a **taxi** at any of these stations – you'll almost certainly be ripped off. Instead, look out for taxis from companies such as Fótaxi (see p.26). Better still, call one.

By bus or hydrofoil

International buses and services from the Great Plain and Transdanubia terminate at **Népliget bus station**, 5km southeast of the centre at Üllői út 131 in the IX district. The international ticket counters are on the main concourse, where there's a travel centre, with domestic ticket counters located downstairs, which is where you'll also find the left-luggage office (daily 6am–9pm; 300Ft). An underpass links the bus station to metro line #3 (blue), from where it's just six stops to Deák tér in the centre.

Of the other bus stations, the **Újpest Városkapú** in the XIII district (on the blue #3 metro line) is the jumping-off point for buses to and from Szentendre and the Danube Bend; the **Stadion bus station** in the XIV district (on the red #2 metro line) serves the Northern Uplands and the **Etele tér bus station** in the XI district (take bus #7 or #7E to the centre) serves the Buda hinterland. None of the city's bus stations has any tourist facilities.

Hydrofoils (operated by Mahart; ☎1 484 4013, ⓦmahartpassnave.hu) from Vienna (June–Sept) dock at the **international landing stage**, on the Belgrád rakpart (embankment), near downtown Pest.

By car

Most drivers enter Budapest along the M1 motorway from Vienna via **Hegyeshalom**, which is a busy road, heavily policed to fine speeding foreigners. It approaches Budapest from the southwest, and goes straight through to Erzsébet híd in the centre, with turn-offs signed to Petőfi híd in the south of the centre, and Széll Kálmán tér and Margít híd to the north.

Getting around

Budapest's well-integrated transport system comprises the metro, buses, trams and trains, all of which reach most areas of interest to tourists, while the outer suburbs are well served by the overground HÉV rail network. Services operate generally between 5am and 11pm, and there are also night-time buses covering much of the city.

The local transport authority, the **Budapest Transport Centre** (**BKK**; ⓦbkk.hu), operates an increasing number of customer service points (Budapesti Közlekedési Központ), the most useful of which are located at Deák tér metro, Ferenciek tere metro, the Keleti station underpass, and on Széll Kálmán tér – these are all open daily from 5.30am to 10pm. The excellent website has full timetable and ticket information.

Tickets and passes

There is a whole array of **tickets** and passes available for use on public transport. Standard single **tickets** (*Vonaljegy*) valid for the metro, buses, trams, trolleybuses, the Cogwheel Railway (see p.122) and suburban HÉV lines (up to the edge of the city) cost 350Ft per journey and are sold at train and metro stations (via staffed counters and vending machines) as well as newspaper kiosks and tobacconists. There are also an increasing number of vending machines at bus and tram stops. Metro tickets also come in a variety of other types, depending on whether you are changing trains and how many stops you want to go: a short section metro ticket (*metrószakasz*; 300Ft) takes you three stops on the same line; a metro transfer ticket (*atszállójegy*; 530Ft) is valid for as many stops as you like with one line change. Tickets bought on board buses, trams and trolleybuses cost 450Ft. Books of ten standard single tickets (*tíz-darabos gyüjtőjegy*; 3000Ft) are also available – these are still valid if torn out of the book but cannot be used on night services.

Tickets must be **validated** when you use them. On the metro and HÉV you punch them in the machines at station entrances (remember to validate a new ticket if you change lines, unless you have a metro transfer ticket); on trams, buses and trolleybuses, you punch the tickets on board in the small red or orange machines.

Day **passes** (*napijegy*) cost 1650Ft and are valid for unlimited travel from midnight to midnight on

BUDAPEST ADDRESSES

Finding your way around Budapest is easier than the welter of names might suggest. Districts and streets are well signposted, and those in Pest conform to an overall plan based on radial avenues and semicircular boulevards.

Budapest is divided into 23 **districts**, numbered using Roman numerals. Except when addressing letters, a Budapest **address** always begins with the district number, a system used throughout this book. On letters, a four-digit **postal code** is used instead, the middle two digits indicating the district (so that 1054 refers to a place in the V district). For ease of reference, we list below the district numbers you're most likely to encounter, along with the areas within those districts that you'll probably spend most time in.

I	The Vár and Víziváros	IX	Ferencváros
II	Rószadomb and Hűvösvölgy	X	Kőbánya
III	Óbuda and Aquincum	XI	The area south and east of Gellért-hegy
IV	Újpest	XII	The area from the Vár west into
V	Belváros and Lipótváros		the Buda Hills
VI	Terézváros	XIII	Újlipótváros and Angyalföld
VII	Erzsébetváros	XIV	Városliget and Zugló
VIII	Józsefváros	XXII	Budafok and Nagytétény

As a rule of thumb, **street numbers** ascend away from the north–south axis of the River Danube and the east–west axis of Rákóczi út/Kossuth utca/Hegyalja út. Even numbers are generally on the left-hand side as you head outwards from these axes, odd numbers on the right. One number may refer to several premises or an entire apartment building, while an additional combination of numerals denotes the floor and number of individual **apartments** (eg Kossuth utca 14.III.24). Confusingly, some old buildings in Pest are designated as having a half-floor (*félemelet*) or upper ground floor (*magas földszint*) between the ground (*földszint*) and first floor (*elsőemelet*) proper – so that what the British would call the second floor, and Americans the third, Hungarians might describe as the first. This stems from a nineteenth-century taxation fiddle, whereby landlords avoided the higher tax on buildings with more than three floors.

the metro, buses, trams, trolleybuses, the Cogwheel Railway and suburban HÉV lines; three-day passes cost 4150Ft and weekly passes 4950Ft. **Season tickets** cost 6300Ft for two weeks and 9500Ft for a month, and are available from metro stations, but you'll need a passport photo for the accompanying photocard; there are photo booths inside the entrance of Deák tér and Széll Kálmán tér stations.

Children up to the age of 6 and EU citizens over the age of 65 travel free on all public transport, though in both cases some form of official documentation must be shown if challenged by inspectors.

As in any big city, **beware of pickpockets** on all forms of public transport. Gangs distract their victims by pushing them or blocking their way, and empty their pockets or bags at the same time.

The metro

The second oldest underground system in the world after London, the Budapest **metro** has four lines, usually referred to by their colour and shown

on the map at the end of this book. Line #1 (yellow) – also known as the Millennium Underground railway – was the first to be constructed in 1896, and in 2002 it was listed as a UNESCO World Heritage Site; it runs from Vörösmarty tér along the length of Andrássy út to Mexikói út beyond the Városliget. Line #2 (red) runs east–west from Déli station in Buda to Örs vezér tere, while line #3 (blue) runs north–south from Újpest Központ to Kőbánya-Kispest, from where buses continue to the airport; these three lines intersect at Deák tér in downtown Pest. Opened in 2014, line #4 (green) runs between Keleti and Kelenföld stations. There's little risk of going astray once you've learned to recognize the signs *bejárat* (entrance), *kijárat* (exit), *vonal* (line) and *felé* (towards). The train's direction is indicated by the name of the station at the end of the line. Trains run at two- to twelve-minute intervals on all lines.

Buses, trams and trolleybuses

There is a good **bus** (*autóbusz*) network across the city, especially in Buda, where Széll Kálmán tér (on

JUST THE TICKET

The myriad rules on Budapest's public transport system make it easy to catch foreigners out, and **inspectors** (who wear blue or purple armbands saying *jegyellenőr*) tend to be strict in levying 16,000Ft fines (8000Ft if you pay on the spot) for travelling without a valid ticket. Inspectors are plain-clothed, and only whip out their armbands once aboard. The easiest way to get fined is to fail to validate your ticket or when changing lines. If you feel you've been fined unfairly you can try taking your complaint to the BKK Customer Service Centre at Rumbach Sebestyén utca 19–21 (Mon, Tues & Thurs 9am–5pm, Wed 9am–7pm, Fri 9am–3pm; ☎1 258 4636).

the red #2 metro line) and Móricz Zsigmond körtér (southwest of Gellért-hegy) are the main terminals. Bus stops are marked by a picture of a bus on a white background in a blue frame, and have timetables underneath; most buses run every ten to twenty minutes (*utolsó kocsi indul …* means "the last one leaves …"). On busier lines, express buses – with an E at the end of the number – run along the same route making fewer stops: for example, the bus #7E that runs along most of the route of the #7. There is a comprehensive network of **night buses**, all of which have a three-digit number beginning with a 9, and which run every hour or half-hour from around midnight or whenever the service they replace finishes.

The network of yellow (or the newer orange) **trams** (*villamos*) is smaller, but they provide a crucial service round the Nagykörút and along the Pest embankment. **Trolleybuses** (*trolibusz*) mostly operate northeast of the centre near the Városliget. Interestingly, their route numbers start at 70 because the first trolleybus line was inaugurated on Stalin's 70th birthday in 1949. Trolleybus #83 was started in 1961, when Stalin would have been 83.

HÉV trains

The green overground **HÉV trains** provide easy access to Budapest's suburbs, running roughly three to five times an hour between 4.30am and 11.30pm. As far as tourists are concerned, the most useful line is the one from **Batthyány tér** (on the red #2 metro line) out to **Szentendre**, which passes through Óbuda, Aquincum and Rómaifürdő. The other lines originate in Pest, with one running northeast from **Örs vezér tere** (also on the red #2 metro line) to **Gödöllő** via the Formula One racing track at Mogyoród; another southwards from Boráros tér at the Pest end of Petőfi híd to Csepel; and the third from **Közvágóhíd** (bus #23 or #54 from Boráros tér) to **Ráckeve**.

Boats and other transport

Passenger boat services on the Danube make for an enjoyable way to see the Buda and Pest embankments. On weekdays, service D11 plies the route between Újpest and Haller utca (just beyond Petőfi híd towards the Palace of the Arts); while service D12 starts at Rómaifürdő and travels down to Boráros tér, near Petőfi híd. At weekends and on holidays, service D13 runs between Rómaifürdő and Haller utca. All services stop at Árpád híd, Margít-sziget, Batthyány tér, Petőfi tér and Szent Gellért tér, running roughly hourly between 7am and 7pm. Tickets (750Ft) can be obtained from kiosks (where timetables are posted) or machines at the docks.

In the Buda Hills, there's also the **Cogwheel Railway** (Fogaskerekűvasút; now officially designated as tram #60; see p.122), the **Children's Railway** (Gyermekvasút; see p.122), and the **chairlift** (*libegő*; see p.124) between Zugliget and János-hegy. Note that BKK tickets and passes are also valid for the Cogwheel Railway and BKK passes can be used on boats on weekdays – for the others, you'll need to buy tickets at the point of departure or on board.

Taxis

Though things have improved, Budapest's **taxis** still have a reputation for ripping off foreigners. Make sure your taxi has a meter that is visible and **switched on** when you get in, and that the rates are clearly displayed. **Fares** are fixed, though, with a starting fee of 450Ft, and a price per kilometre of 280Ft.

Taxis can be flagged down on the street, and there are **ranks** throughout the city. For a slightly cheaper rate, order a cab by phone. Avoid unmarked private cars, and drivers hanging around the stations and airport.

TAXI COMPANIES

Citytaxi ☎1 211 1111
Főtaxi ☎1 222 2222
Volantaxi ☎1 433 3322

USEFUL BUS, TRAM AND TROLLEYBUS ROUTES (LISTED WITH KEY STOPS)

BUSES

#7 Bosnyák tér–Keleti Station–Móricz Zsigmond körtér (via Ferenciek tere, Rudas Baths, *Gellért Hotel*).
#16A Dísz tér (Castle District)–Széll Kálmán tér.
#16 Deák tér–Dísz tér (Castle District)–Bécsi kapu tér–Széll Kálmán tér.
#26 Margít-sziget–Árpád híd metro station.
#65 Kolosy tér–Pálvölgyi Caves–*Fenyőgyöngye* restaurant at the bottom of Hármashatár-hegy.
#86 Southern Buda–Gellért tér–Batthyány tér–Margít híd–Flórián tér (Óbuda).
#105 Apor Vilmos tér–Lanchíd–Deák tér–Oktogon–Gyöngyösi utca.
#116 Fény utca market–Széll Kálmán tér– Dísz tér (Castle District).

NIGHT BUSES

#906 Széll Kálmán tér–Margít-sziget–Nyugati Station–Nagykörút (Great Boulevard)–Móricz Zsigmond körtér.
#907 Örs vezér tere–Bosnyák tér–Keleti Station–Erzsébet híd–*Gellért Hotel*–Etele tér (Kelenföld).
#914 and **#950** Kispest (Határ út metro station)–Deák tér–Lehel tér–Újpest, along the route of the blue #3 metro and on to the north and south.

TRAMS

#2 Margít Bridge (Jászai Mari tér)–Belgrád rakpart (along embankment)–Petőfi híd–Vágóhíd tér.
#4 Széll Kálmán tér–Margít-sziget–Nyugati Station–Nagykörút (Great Boulevard)–Petőfi híd–Október 23 utca.
#6 Széll Kálmán tér–Margít-sziget–Nyugati Station– Nagykörút (Great Boulevard)–Petőfi híd–Móricz Zsigmond körtér.
#19 Batthyány tér–the Vízíváros–Kelenföld Station.
#47 Deák tér–Szabadság híd–*Gellért Hotel*–Móricz Zsigmond körtér–Budafok.
#61 Móricz Zsigmond körtér–Villányi út–Déli Station–Széll Kálmán tér–Huvösvölgy.

TROLLEYBUSES

#72 Arany János utca metro station–Nyugati Station–Zoo–Széchenyi Baths–Hermina út.
#74 Dohány utca (outside the Main Synagogue)–Városliget.

Driving

If you're coming just to Budapest, it's unlikely you'll need, or want, to drive around the city, especially given the excellent public transport system. In any case, **driving** in Budapest can't be recommended: road manners are nonexistent, parking spaces are scarce and traffic jams are frequent – careering trams, bumpy cobbles, swerving lane markings and unexpected one-way systems make things worse. In addition, access to the Castle District and parts of the Belváros are strictly limited.

If you are driving, however, the most important **rules** to bear in mind are: you must give way to cars on your right if there are no road markings to indicate otherwise; at night, many traffic lights go into flashing orange mode, which means that priority is given to the right; drinking and driving is totally prohibited, as is the use of a hand-held mobile phone. The speed limit in built-up areas is 50kph (30mph), and 90kph (60mph) outside built-up areas. On main roads, it's 110kph (68mph), and on motorways 130kph (80mph).

In terms of **parking**, you might be better off leaving your car outside the centre and using public transport to travel in – there are park and ride facilities at most metro termini. If you must park in the centre, the best options are the underground car parks in Szent István tér by the Basilica and underneath Szabadság tér, both in Lipótváros. Parking on the street in the central districts typically costs 120–440Ft per hour – you get a ticket from the nearest machine. Alternatively, there are an increasing number of car parks that have been set up in areas where blocks of buildings have been knocked down.

Renting a car is easy, with prices inevitably cheaper the further in advance you book – expect to pay €40–45 for a day's rental (unlimited mileage) and upwards of €250 per week. When checking prices, make sure the price quoted includes the twenty-percent ÁFA (VAT). Before signing, check on mileage limits and any other restrictions or extras, as well as what you're liable for in the event of an accident.

CAR RENTAL COMPANIES

All these companies have offices at the airport.

Avis V, Szabadság tér 7 ☎ 1 318 4240, 🔗 avis.hu.
Budget Kassák Lajos utca 19–25 ☎ 1 214 0420 or ☎ 700 4859, 🔗 budget.hu.
Europcar V, Erzsébet tér 7–8 ☎ 1 505 4400, 🔗 europcar.hu.
Hertz V, Váci utca 135–139 ☎ 1 296 0998, 🔗 hertz.hu.
Sixt V, Váci utca 141 ☎ 1 451 4220, 🔗 sixt.hu.

Cycling

Cycling is finally catching on in Budapest, with rising numbers of cyclists and the emergence of dedicated cycle lanes (red with yellow lines on either side). That said, it isn't easy riding: drivers are generally oblivious and you also have to contend with sunken tramlines, bumpy cobbles and bad air pollution. **Cycle routes** are still patchy and don't link up to form a coherent network yet, so you're best off sticking to the city's green areas like Margaret Island and the City Park. There are also good routes out of town, such as along the Buda bank of the Danube to Szentendre and on up towards Slovakia. Bicycles can be carried on HÉV trains and the Cogwheel Railway for the price of a one-way ticket, but not on buses or trams. It's also possible to go trail-biking in the Buda Hills (see p.121).

There are several excellent **bike-rental** outfits in the city; expect to pay around 2000Ft for a half-day and 2500–3000Ft for a full day (same-day return), including a lock and helmet. Some bike shops offer repairs, including Nella Bikes, off Bajcsy-Zsilinszky út at V, Kálmán Imre utca 23 (☎ 1 331 3184, 🔗 nella.hu).

BIKE RENTAL

Bikebase VI, Podmaniczky utca 19 ☎ 070 625 8501, 🔗 bikebase .hu. Excellent operation near Nyugati Station, with friendly staff who dole out maps and advise on cycling routes. March to mid-Nov daily 9am–7pm.
BuBi Bike 🔗 molbubi.bkk.hu. Bike-sharing scheme with docking stations all over Budapest. Pre-registration is required; this costs 500Ft for 24hr, 1000Ft for 72hr and 2000 for a week; usage thereafter is 500Ft for 1hr, 1500Ft for 2hr.

Budapest Bike VII, Wesselényi utca 13 ☎ 30 944 5533, 🔗 budapestbike.hu. Bike rental and bike tours. Mid-March to mid-Oct daily 9am–6pm.

City tours

There is now a wide range of city tours available in Budapest; indeed you can't move these days without being accosted by someone offering a tour of some description. But if you're hard-pressed for time, you might appreciate one of the city's bus tours, which generally take you past the Parliament, along Andrássy út, across to the Várhegy and up to Gellért-hegy for panoramic photo opportunities.

That said, Budapest's backstreets and historic quarters are eminently suited to walking, and this is much the best way to appreciate their character. Moreover, traffic is restricted in downtown Pest and around the Vár in Buda, and fairly light in the residential backstreets off the main boulevards, which are the nicest areas to wander around. The Budapest Card (see p.32) entitles you to two free guided walks, one of Buda, one of Pest.

BIKE TOURS

Yellow Zebra VI, Lázár utca 16 ☎ 1 269 3843, 🔗 yellowzebra budapest.com. Excellent outfit offering both scheduled and private cycling tours of the city. Between April and October, there's a standard 4hr bike tour (€28), which departs at 11am daily (March & Nov Wed, Fri, Sat & Sun only), in addition to 3hr evening bike tours (€24) between April and September. They also offer 2hr Segway tours (€65).

BUS TOURS

Giraffe Hop-On Hop-Off VI, Andrássy útca 2 ☎ 1 374 7070, 🔗 citytour.hu. Red double-decker buses offering hop-on, hop-off bus tours taking in all the key sights. There are two lines, both of which depart every 30min; red from József Nádor tér, and yellow from Andrássy út 2. They also do a hop-on, hop-off cruise departing hourly from Vigadó tér, and a 90min night tour, also departing from Vigadó tér, at 9.15pm. A 24hr ticket (valid on all the above lines) costs 6000Ft (€21), while a 48hr ticket costs 7000Ft (€24). Budapest Card holders receive a twenty percent discount.

WALKING TOURS

Absolute Walking Tours VI, Lázár utca 16 ☎ 1 269 3843, 🔗 absolutetours.com. Run by the same team as Yellow Zebra (in the Discover Budapest office). Aside from the standard 3hr city walk (€34), Absolute offer a terrific range of themed tours, such as Hidden Budapest (€40), the Hammer & Sickle Communist tour (€54), and the Street Food Experience (€45).

Budapest 101 ☎ 30 449 8297, Ⓦ budapest101.com. Excellent private and tailor-made tours, based around food, coffee, design and even cemeteries. Their 101 tour is an introductory sightseeing tour of the city. Tours are priced per group, between one and six people (€25/hr for the group).

Free Budapest Tours ☎ 70 424 0569, Ⓦ freebudapesttours.hu. Aimed at backpackers, the 3hr walking tour departs from Deák tér daily at 10.30am; there is also a Jewish District tour, and a Communism, Faith and Terror tour on selected days (both 2hr 30min). All tours are free, though tips are welcome.

Jewish Heritage Tours ☎ 1 317 1377, Ⓦ jewish.hu. Tours of the Jewish quarter, including the 2hr 30min essential tour (€23) and the 4hr grand tour (€38); both include a guided visit to the Dohany synagogue. Advance booking required. Tours run Mon–Fri & Sun at 10am, plus May–Oct Mon–Thurs 2pm.

RIVER TOURS

RiverRide ☎ 1 332 2555, Ⓦ riverride.com. Jump aboard the floating bus for an unorthodox sightseeing tour; starting in Széchenyi tér, the bus takes in all the main sights in Pest before splashing into the Danube and continuing down to the Chain Bridge and winding up in Buda. Departures April–Oct daily at 10am, noon, 3pm and 5pm; Nov–March at 11am, 1pm and 3pm. (8500Ft/€28).

The media

Hungary's history of lively print media is counterbalanced by an enduring tradition of government control that has persisted into the post-communist era. Television differs little from that in other European countries, with foreign cable and satellite channels dominating the airwaves.

Newspapers and magazines

The number of Budapest-based English-language publications has dwindled in recent years. One survivor is the *Budapest Business Journal* (Ⓦ bbj.hu), which covers mainly business and politics, and can often be found for free in the lobbies of larger hotels, as can the occasional foreign newspaper. The best place to buy English-language newspapers and magazines are the newsagents (such as Relay) at stations and shopping malls, though bookshops such as Bestsellers (see p.192) have a good stock.

There are several sources of English-language **listings information**: the fortnightly *Budapest Funzine* (Ⓦ funzine.hu), distributed free in cafés and bars, is aimed at the expat market and has nightlife listings as well as information on other happenings in Budapest. The free monthly hotel magazine

Where Budapest has information on current events. The Hungarian-language listings bible *Pesti Est* (free in bars and cinemas) has extensive details of film and music events, and sometimes has an English section in the summer.

Television

Hungarian **television** is not particularly exciting, with state TV (MTV) screening a dreary diet of gameshows and low-budget soaps from morning to night. State influence extends to commercial channels, such as Duna TV, geared to Hungarian minorities abroad, though at the time of writing two channels, ATV and HirTV, do retain a critical voice. Many Hungarians subscribe to satellite channels, with whole apartment blocks sharing the cost of installation. The majority of hotels have satellite TV, though the programming is dominated by German channels or those from neighbouring countries. Most, though, will also feature the likes of BBC World, Sky or CNN.

Websites

You can find English-language **news** at Ⓦ budapest beacon.com, and news and entertainment **listings** at Ⓦ xpatloop.com. For a critical and liberal view of Hungarian politics, take a look at Ⓦ hungarian spectrum.org, while Ⓦ welovebudapest.com has up-to-the-minute restaurant, club and bar reviews. As for **blogs**, New York meets Eastern Europe in Ⓦ horinca.blogspot.hu, the entertaining musings of a long-term Budapest resident and klezmer player. Also worth looking at are Ⓦ disappearingbudapest .blogspot.com, which looks at undiscovered or disappearing features of the city; and the architectural blog Ⓦ budapest100.hu, which opens the doors of buildings and streets marking their 100th birthday.

Festivals

Whatever time of the year you visit Budapest, there's almost certain to be something happening. The two biggest events by far are the Spring Festival in March and the Café Budapest Contemporary Arts Festival in October, both of which feature world-class music, film and drama. Indeed, music is a constant theme throughout the festival year, with none bigger than the mega Sziget Festival in August.

Many theatres, concert halls and dance houses close down during the long, hot months of July and August, when open-air performances are staged instead. The city's population returns from the countryside for the fireworks on August 20, and life returns to normal as school starts the following week. The new arts season kicks off in the last week of September with a rash of music festivals and political anniversaries. Great fun, too, are the growing number of food and drink festivals during which stalls are often set up in Vörösmarty tér and in Varosháza Park, on Károly körút. Note, however, that festivals held in the Városliget and the Royal Palace may be moved if major construction projects slated for these two sites begin.

JANUARY AND FEBRUARY

Farsang Jan 6 to Ash Wednesday. Held in the run-up to Lent, this Hungarian carnival sees revellers taking to the streets in fancy dress, parading across the Lánchíd and down to Vörösmarty tér. Unfortunately the inclement weather at this time of year often dampens the event's spirit.

Mangalica Festival First weekend in Feb; ⓦ mangalicafesztival .hu. A pig-out in every sense of the word, as the nation's favourite curly-haired swine is celebrated in Szabadság tér; hog roasts aside, there are cooking competitions and a stack of other foodie treats.

MARCH AND APRIL

Declaration of Independence of 1848 March 15. A public holiday in honour of the 1848 Revolution, which began with Petőfi's declaration of the National Song from the steps of the National Museum. Budapest decks itself out with Hungarian tricolours (red, white and green), and there are speeches and gatherings outside the museum and by Petőfi's statue on Marcius 15 tér. The more patriotic citizens wear little cockades in the national colours pinned to their lapels.

Budapest Spring Festival (Budapest Tavaszi Fesztivál) Mid- to late March; ⓦ btf.hu. The city's most prestigious arts festival is an intensive two-week jamboree of classical music, with orchestral, chamber and operatic performances taking place in venues across Budapest. There's also theatre, cinema, exhibitions (including the World Press Photos show) and dance, including a big folk dance gathering and market (*Országos Táncháztalálkozó és vásár;* ⓦ tanchaztalalkozo.hu).

Easter (Húsvét) Late March/early April. Easter has strong folk traditions in Hungary. In the city this is limited to some processions in churches Easter Saturday, while on Easter Monday *locsolkodás* (splashing) takes place, when men and boys visit female friends to spray them with cologne in a tamer version of an older village tradition involving a bucket of water. Kids get a painted egg or money in return for splashing, while the men receive *pálinka* (schnapps). There is also an arts and craft fair in the Varkert Bazár, with traditional skills such as egg painting on display, accompanied by music and dancing. Look out too for lots of Easter stalls in Vörösmarty tér in central Pest, while folk skills are on display in situ at

the Hungarian Open-Air Museum in Szentendre (p.134). You can also catch performances of the Bach Passions in the big, yellow Lutheran church on Deák tér.

Titanic International Film Festival Mid-April; ⓦ titanicfilm fest.hu. Superb week-long programme of independent films from all over the world, with separately themed categories. The venues include the Uránia and Toldi cinemas. Most films have English subtitles. See p.186.

MAY, JUNE AND JULY

Labour Day May 1. These days, Budapest's citizens are no longer obliged to parade past the Lenin statue that once stood behind the Műcsarnok; instead, the major trade unions put on a big do in the park, with shows, games, talks – and food and drink in large quantities.

Book Week (Könyvhét) Early June. Established in 1929, and as popular as ever, Book Week sees Hungarian writers from all over the world gather around stalls on Vörösmarty tér and István tér. There are signings – politicians have now joined the book circus – as well as dancing on temporary stages in the two squares.

Judafest Street Festival Mid-June; ⓦ judafest.org. Kazinczy utca in the old Jewish quarter gets packed out for this weekend festival, which celebrates the history and culture of the area through music and food.

Beer Festival (Sörfesztivál) Mid-June; ⓦ sorfesztival.hu. The official beer festival moved from the Vár to the Belváros in 2017, offering 200 different brews for punters, accompanied by plenty of Hungarian-style street food. Look out also for the Craft Beer and Street Food Festival (Főzdefeszt; ⓦ fozdefeszt.hu), which celebrates Hungarian microbreweries. It usually takes place on the riverfront by the Technical University, below the *Gellért Hotel*, its timing oscillating between June and September.

Night of Museums (Múzeumok Ejszakája) Around June 21; ⓦ muzej.hu. Most of the city's big museums take part, opening their doors to visitors till late into the night with exhibitions, concerts and shows. The 1500Ft ticket gets you into all the sights and covers bus travel, as well – special bus services run till 2am.

Budapest Pride Late June–early July; ⓦ budapestpride.com. The largest event in the gay calendar, this is a week-long celebration of gay and lesbian culture, and includes a film festival. The week culminates in a march, which usually ends up in Kossuth tér. See p.208.

AUGUST

Sziget Festival Mid-Aug; ⓦ sziget.hu. A stamina-sapping eight days long, Sziget is now firmly established as one of Europe's biggest rock and pop festivals. Staged on Óbudai-sziget, an island north of the centre, it features a stellar line-up of rock, pop and world music acts, alongside dance, theatre, films and children's events. See p.183.

Festival of Crafts (Mesterségek Ünnepe) ⓦ mestersegek unnepe.hu; Mid- to late Aug. In the days leading up to Aug 20, the area around the Royal Palace is taken over by a huge festival of traditional crafts, accompanied by folk music and dancing.

St Stephen's Day Aug 20. A public holiday in honour of Hungary's national saint and founder, with day-long rites at his Basilica, and a spectacular fireworks display fired off between the Erzsébet and Margít bridges at 9pm, watched by over a million people who line the Danube; the traffic jam that follows is equally mind-blowing. Restaurants are packed that night, so book well ahead if you want to eat out.

Jewish Summer Festival End Aug; ⓦ jewishfestival.hu zsidokulturalisfesztival.hu. Vibrant week-long jamboree, attracting an international range of classical, jazz and klezmer music performances, films and exhibitions.

SEPTEMBER AND OCTOBER

Budapest Wine Festival (Budapest Bor Fesztivál) Early Sept; ⓦ winefestival.hu. The country's top producers set out their wares on the terrace of the Royal Palace in the Castle District: for the price of a day-ticket you get unrestricted access, a glass and a glass holder. Individual tasting tickets are available once inside.

Café Budapest Contemporary Arts Festival (Kortárs Művészeti Fesztivál) Mid-Oct; ⓦ cafebudapestfest.hu. The old Budapest Autumn Festival has been rebranded, but it is still strong on contemporary music and also features an excellent programme of film, dance and photography. A new edition to the programme is the Budapest Ritmo Festival (ⓦ budapestritmo.hu), a regional celebration of world music.

Anniversary of the Arad Martyrs Oct 6. Commemoration of the shooting of the thirteen Hungarian generals in 1849 in Arad (Nagyvárad) in present-day Romania, when the 1848 revolution was crushed by the Austrians with Russian help. Wreaths are laid at the Eternal Flame.

Commemoration of the 1956 Uprising Oct 23. A national holiday to mark the 1956 Uprising and the declaration of the Republic in 1990. Ceremonies take place in Kossuth tér, by the nearby Nagy Imre statue, and at Nagy's grave in the New Public Cemetery. Bear in mind that 1956 has left a divided inheritance and tempers can flare.

NOVEMBER AND DECEMBER

All Saints' Day (Mindenszentek napja) Nov 1. Cemeteries stay open late and candles are lit in memory of departed souls, making for an incredible sight as darkness falls.

St Nicholas's Day (Mikulás) Dec 5 & 6. On Dec 5, children clean their shoes and put them in the window for "Mikulás", the Santa Claus figure, to fill with sweets; naughty children are warned that if they behave badly, all they will get is *virgács*, a gold-painted bunch of twigs from Mikulás's little helpers.

Christmas (Karácsony) Dec 24 & 25. The main celebration is on Dec 24, when the city becomes eerily silent by late afternoon. Children are taken out while their parents decorate the Christmas tree (until then the trees are stored outside, and on housing estates you can often see them dangling from windows). When the kids return home, they wait outside until the bell rings, which tells them that "little Jesus" (Jézuska) has come. Inside, they sing carols by the tree, open presents, and start the big Christmas meal, which traditionally includes spicy fish soup. In the preceding weeks there are Christmas fairs in several locations around town, the best being in the Museum of Ethnography, where traditional crafts are demonstrated.

New Year's Eve (Szilveszter) Dec 31. Crowds gather on the Nagykörút during the evening, engaging in paper trumpet battles at the junction with Rákóczi út.

Culture and etiquette

Forty years of Communism swept away Hungary's archaic semifeudal society but you can still find remnants of the old ways, for instance in the language. As a foreigner, you are not obliged to know these details, but Hungarians will love it if you can get them right.

Hungarians preserve certain formalities in meeting and greeting. Young people will usually go straight into the informal form of address with each other (the Hungarian equivalent of the French "*tu*" is to use the second person), but with their elders or in the more formal settings of work or school they would use the formal mode, talking to people in the third person, until invited to use the **informal** mode. So "*Hogy vagy?*" is the informal "how are you?", "*Hogy van?*" is the **formal** – and then to be awfully polite, talking to someone's granny for instance, you can say "*Hogy tetszik lenni?*" (literally, "How does it please you to be?").

When introduced to someone you **shake hands** and say your name. You would usually shake hands when meeting people, though between friends, kissing on both cheeks is the norm – between men, too. Some older men still bow to kiss a woman's hand – but it looks rather affected when anyone else does it, so it is best not to try. You will hear an echo of this social convention in the greeting "*Csókolom*", which means "I kiss [your hand]". Adults will say it to elderly ladies and children will say this to adults – responding in kind is an easy error to make and will provoke much laughter.

The formal salutation – to say hello or goodbye – is "*Jó napot*" (or "*Jó reggelt*" before 9am) while with friends "*Szia*", "*Szervusz*" or even "*Helló*" is normal.

A sense of social formality is preserved in other ways too. When **visiting** someone at home, taking flowers is always acceptable: there are many complex rules and codes in flower-giving that you need not worry about – but do take an odd number of flowers (not 13, though).

Two other useful points when visiting: it is common to take off your shoes when you go into people's houses; and if eating at someone's house it is customary to compliment the host(ess) on the food early on after the first couple of mouthfuls.

Smoking is pretty universal in Budapest – though in someone's home, of course, it is polite to ask if it is permitted. The smoking ban in restaurants and bars is strictly enforced, but this does not apply to attached terraces and in gardens, where everyone lights up at will. Smoking is also banned on all public transport.

Religion

The majority of the Hungarian population is officially **Roman Catholic**, with the remainder comprising Calvinists, smaller numbers of Lutherans and Jews and even smaller groups such as Serb and Greek Orthodox. The 2012 constitution declared Hungary to be a "Christian" country, though official recognition initially left out Methodists, among others.

Churches may prohibit sightseeing during services and charge for entry. Visitors are expected to wear "decorous" dress – that is, no shorts or sleeveless tops. Several churches offer services in English: Anglican: Holy Communion service at 10.30am on the first and third Sunday of the month at XII, Eötvös út 35 in Buda, and the other Sundays at VII, Városligeti fasor 17–21 in Pest (☎06 20 269 5161, ⓦanglicanbudapest.com); Baptist: Sunday 10.30am, International Baptist Church, held in a school, the Móricz Zsigmond Gimnázium, at II, Törökvész út 48–54 (ⓦibcbudapest.org); Roman Catholic: Saturday 5 or 6pm at Pesti Jézus Szíve Templom, VIII, Mária utca 25 (☎1 318 3479).

Hungary has a rich **Jewish heritage** and Budapest boasts a sizeable and increasingly active Jewish community. The city is also the focus of huge donations aiming to restore buildings that were devastated in the Holocaust.

Travel essentials

Admission charges

The majority of the city's museums charge between 600Ft (€2) and 1200Ft (€4), though the showpiece ones, such as the Museum of Fine Arts and the House of Terror cost 1800–2200Ft (€6–7) and the Great Synagogue 4000Ft (€12.50). There's usually a reduction or free entrance if you show a student, youth or senior citizen card. If you're planning on visiting multiple museums, consider buying the Budapest Card (see p.32), which offers good savings. Admission to Budapest's baths (see p.200) is not cheap, and the price of tickets can be mystifying. Churches may charge a small fee to see their crypts and treasures.

Costs

Although Budapest is not the bargain destination it once was, it's still very good value, especially when compared to cities in Britain, France or Italy, for example.

If you're not staying in a hostel, the main drain on your resources will be hotel accommodation; while **room rates** fluctuate wildly according to season and demand, expect to pay around €70 a night for a double room in a three-star hotel, and somewhere in excess of €100 for a four-star. A two-course lunch or dinner with a glass of wine in one of the better restaurants should set you back around 6000Ft (€20). **Public transport** is cheap, with a one-day pass covering all modes of transport costing 1650Ft (€5.50).

Foreigners are easy targets for **overcharging**, so it is always worth checking the price of what you are buying ("*Mennyibe kerül?*" means "how much is it?"). One hidden extra is the ÁFA or **sales tax** (the equivalent of VAT in Britain) of up to 25 percent, which can hike up the cost of rental cars and hotels, for example: look out for the phrase "*az árak nem tartalmaznak Áfát*", meaning "prices do not include tax". There is also a three percent **tourist tax** on hotel prices, and it is worth checking that both taxes are included in any prices quoted. The simplest way to ask is "*Ez az ár bruttó vagy nettó?*" – "Is this price with or without tax?"

THE BUDAPEST CARD

If you're doing a lot of sightseeing, the **Budapest Card** (ⓦbudapest-card.com) represents great value. It's available for periods of 24hr (5500Ft), 48hr (8500Ft), 72hr (10,900Ft), 96hr (14,500Ft) and 120hr (17,500Ft), and grants free public transport in the city, free entrance to eight museums (Museum of Fine Arts, the Hungarian National Museum, the National Gallery and the Budapest History Museum), free entry to the Lukács Baths, and two free guided walking tours. In addition, there are discounts of between ten and fifty percent on lots of other attractions, including some of the baths, plus shops and restaurants. The card is available online, from tourist offices, hotels, central metro stations and at the airport, and comes with a booklet explaining where it can be used.

Crime and personal safety

Hungary is one of the safest European countries. Violent crime is extremely rare and there's little reason to worry about your personal security while visiting. However, **petty theft** is common, with downtown Budapest a prime area for pickpocketing, as well as scams directed at tourists such as luring them into rip-off restaurants. It is also advisable not to take valuables to the baths, as lockers are sometimes targeted by thieves.

The Hungarian **police** (*rendőrség*) have a milder reputation than their counterparts in other Eastern European states, and are generally keen to present a favourable image. During the summer, **tourist police** patrol the streets and metro stations mainly to act as a deterrent against thieves, and to assist in any problems visitors may encounter. Most Hungarian police have at least a smattering of German, but rarely speak any other foreign language. To contact the police, call ☎107, or ☎112, which is also the number for the ambulance and fire services. Alternatively, Tourinform has a 24-hour English-speaking service on ☎1 483 8080.

Electricity

The Hungarian system runs on 220 volts. Round two-pin plugs are used. A standard continental adapter allows the use of 13-amp square-pin plugs.

Entry requirements

Hungary is part of the Schengen Agreement, so citizens of the other Schengen states can enter Hungary with just an ID card and stay for up to ninety days. At the time of writing, citizens of the UK, Ireland, US, Canada, Australia and New Zealand, and most other European countries, can enter Hungary with just a passport and stay for the same period. However, the situation can change and it is advisable to check with the Hungarian embassy or consulate in your own country before departure. South African citizens will need to apply to their local Hungarian consulate for a visa, though note that visas valid for another Schengen country are also valid for Hungary.

FOREIGN CONSULATES IN BUDAPEST

Canada II, Ganz utca 12–14 ☎1 392 3360, ⓦ kanada.hu.
Ireland V, Szabadság tér 7, Bank Center, seventh floor ☎1 301 4960, ⓦ embassyofireland.hu.
South Africa II Gárdonyi Géza út 17 ☎1 392 0999.

UK II, Füge utca 5–7 ☎1 266 2888, ⓦ britishembassy.hu.
US V, Szabadság tér 12 ☎1 475 4400, ⓦ hungary.usembassy.gov.

Health

No inoculations are required for Hungary and standards of public health are good, although hospital services vary considerably and are probably best avoided, unless it's an emergency. The **European Health Insurance Card** gives EU citizens access to Hungary's national health service (OTBF) under reciprocal agreements. While this will provide free or reduced-cost medical care in the event of minor injuries or emergencies, it won't cover every eventuality – so **travel insurance** is essential (see below). At the time of writing, British citizens were still covered by the EHIC scheme, but it is advisable to check the situation online is before travelling.

Budapest has plentiful **pharmacies** (*gyógyszertár* or *patika*), which normally open Monday to Friday from 8am to 7 or 8pm, and on Saturday from 8am until noon or 1pm; signs in the window give the location or telephone number of the nearest all-night (*éjjeli* or *ügyeleti szolgálat*) pharmacy. There is one in Buda at XII, Alkotas utca 1/b, near Déli station, and in Pest at VI, Teréz körút 41.

In **emergencies**, dial ☎104 for the Mentok ambulance service (or ☎112, the central number for emergencies), or get a taxi to the nearest **hospital** (*kórház*). For non-urgent treatment, tourist offices can direct you to a local **medical centre** or doctors' surgery (*orvosi rendelő*), and your embassy in Budapest will have the addresses of foreign-language-speaking **doctors** and **dentists**, who will probably be in private (*magán*) practice.

Sunburn (*napszúrás*) and insect bites (*rovarcsípés*) are the most common **minor complaints** for travellers, so take plenty of sunscreen and repellent. Mosquitoes can be annoying, but the bug to beware of in the Buda Hills, and increasingly in the suburbs of Buda too, is the *kullancs*, a tick which bites and then burrows into human skin, causing inflammation of the brain. The risk of one biting you is fairly small, but if you get a bite that seems particularly painful, or are suffering from a high temperature and stiff neck following a bite, have it checked out as quickly as possible.

Insurance

You should take out a comprehensive **insurance policy** before travelling to Budapest, to cover against loss, theft, illness or injury. A typical policy

---

ROUGH GUIDES TRAVEL INSURANCE

Rough Guides has teamed up with WorldNomads.com to offer great travel insurance deals. Policies are available to residents of over 150 countries, with cover for a wide range of adventure sports, 24hr emergency assistance, high levels of medical and evacuation cover and a stream of travel safety information. Roughguides.com users can take advantage of their policies online 24/7, from anywhere in the world – even if you're already travelling. And since plans often change when you're on the road, you can extend your policy and even claim online. Roughguides.com users who buy travel insurance with WorldNomads.com can also leave a positive footprint and donate to a community development project. For more information go to ⓦroughguides.com/travel-insurance.

---

will provide cover for loss of baggage, tickets and – up to a certain limit – cash or travellers' cheques, as well as cancellation or curtailment of your journey.

If you need to make a **claim**, you should keep receipts for medicines and medical treatment, and in the event you have anything stolen, you must obtain an official statement from the police.

Internet

Budapest has excellent **wi-fi** coverage, with most hotels, youth hostels, cafés and bars offering free access for customers – you will need to log on with their password.

Kids

Budapest is a child-friendly city, with plenty to entertain young ones (see p.203). Hungarians tend to be welcoming to kids without making them the centre of attention as you might find in, say, Italy.

Facilities are a bit patchy, though; while the network of playgrounds is marvellous, nappy-changing facilities (*pelenkázó*) are hard to find – they're mostly concentrated in big shopping malls. Buildings don't tend to be very accessible if you're pushing a buggy, but help is usually quickly forthcoming when you're trying to negotiate stairs. On public transport people will readily give up seats to pregnant women and to parents with babies. They will also happily chat to children – the flipside is that old ladies may also loudly berate parents for not looking after their babies "properly", such as for not putting a hat on a baby even in the mildest of weather.

The malls are also the best bet for **nappies**, baby toiletries and clothes, while many also have indoor play areas. **Restaurants** usually have high chairs, and although there isn't a culture of whole families dining out in the evening, waiting staff (even in smart places) are usually accommodating. In many places you can ask for a small child's portion: *kisadag*.

Laundry

There are a few self-service **launderettes** (*mosoda*) in Budapest: Electric Café Laundry, near Blaha Lujza tér at VII, Dohány utca 37 (daily 9am–midnight); Liliom Szalon, IX, Liliom utca 7–9 (daily 8am–8pm; ⓦliliomszalon.hu); or a branch of the Bubbles chain (ⓦbubbles.hu), the most central one being at VI, Paulay Ede utca 3 (open 24hr). Expect to pay 1800Ft or more for a wash and dry. Otherwise, most youth hostels have laundry facilities, with a small fee payable; hotels will charge considerably more.

Living in Budapest

Teaching English has traditionally been the main opportunity for **work** in Hungary, and it remains a big business, with many native speakers working in Budapest and a number of schools in and around the capital. The most reputable **language school** is International House, whose Budapest branch is at I, Vérmező út 4 (☎1 212 4010, ⓦih.hu); its minimum requirement is a CELTA or TESOL qualification, and preferably one year's experience. It offers a range of teacher-training qualifications in Budapest. Other places to ask are the British Council, VII, Madách Trade Center, Madách Imre út 13–14 (☎1 483 2020, ⓦbritishcouncil.hu); and the Kathedra language schools (VI, Anker köz 1–3 ☎1 700 0137, ⓦkatedra.hu).

Study programmes

Several schools in Budapest cater for foreigners wishing to **learn Hungarian**. The best option is the Hungarian Language School at VIII, Bródy Sándor utca 4 (☎1 266 2617, ⓦmagyar-iskola.hu), which runs a comprehensive range of short- and long-term courses, from beginners to advanced, as well as organizing cultural programmes and workshops. The Debrecen Summer School at V, Váci utca 63. II/1, also runs year-round courses in Budapest (☎1 320 5751, ⓦsummerschool.hu/bp).

Lost property

For items left on **public transport** go to the BKV office at VII, Akácfa utca 18 (Mon 8am–8pm, Tues–Thurs 8am–5pm, Fri 8am–3pm; ☎1 258 4636). Lost or stolen **passports** should be reported to the police station in the district where they were lost.

Mail

Post offices (*posta*) are often pretty crowded and very few staff speak English. They are usually open Monday to Friday 8 or 9am to 5pm, though the main offices that follow keep longer hours: by Keleti Station at VIII, Baross tér 11c (24hrs); by Nyugati Station at VI, Teréz körút 51 (Mon–Fri 7am–8pm, Sat & Sun 8am–6pm); and at the Mammut Mall by Széll Kálmán tér (Mon–Fri 8am–8pm, Sat 9am–2pm). **Stamps** (*bélyeg*) can also be bought at tobacconists. Stamps for sending postcards and letters abroad cost the same. You'll do better choosing the slightly more expensive *elsőbbségi* ("priority" airmail) rate, 375Ft up to 20g within Europe, 435Ft for further afield, rather than the *nem-elsőbbségi* rate. If you are sending anything of value, it is worth forking out the 1705Ft or so for recorded delivery. The Magyar Posta website ⓦposta.hu has further details of post offices and mailing costs.

Maps

The maps in this guide, together with the small freebies supplied by tourist offices and hotels, should be sufficient to help you find your way around. Larger folding maps are sold all over the place, but their size makes them cumbersome. For total coverage you can't beat the wire-bound **Budapest Atlasz**, available in bookshops in a range of sizes (starting from the *Zsebatlasz* (Pocket Atlas); 1800Ft), which shows every street, bus and tram route, and the location of restaurants, museums and suchlike. It also contains enlarged maps of the Vár, central Pest, Margít-sziget and the Városliget, plus a comprehensive index.

Money

Hungary's unit of currency is the **forint** (Ft or HUF), with notes issued in denominations of 200, 500, 1000, 2000, 5000, 10,000 and 20,000 forints, and coins in denominations of 5, 10, 20, 50 and 100 forints. At the time of writing, the **exchange rate** was around 370Ft to the pound sterling, 310Ft to the euro and around 280Ft to the US dollar. You

HUNGARIAN NAMES

Surnames precede forenames in Hungary, to the confusion of foreigners. In this book, the names of historical personages are rendered in the Western fashion, for instance, Lajos Kossuth rather than Kossuth Lajos (Hungarian-style), except when referring to the names of buildings, streets, etc. The Hungarian order has a clear logic: in Hungarian the stress in any word always comes on the first syllable; since Hungarian, like most other languages, puts the main stress on the family name when saying a person's name, that means putting the family name first.

might be able to buy forints at some banks or exchange offices, or in the UK at post offices, but you will probably have to order them in advance. If taking cash, and you are not able to obtain forints in advance, a modest amount of low-denomination euros is advisable, although pound sterling and dollars are widely accepted. Avoid anyone who approaches you on the street or at stations offering to exchange money – you will almost certainly be fleeced.

By far the easiest way to get money once you are in Budapest is to use your bank **debit card** to withdraw cash from an ATM, found all over the city – although this often means paying a commission. However, you may well get a better exchange rate if you pay with a **credit card** – these are accepted in many hotels, restaurants and shops in the city. In addition, some credit cards do not charge a transaction fee, making them an even better deal – check with your card provider before you travel.

If you're **changing money**, the best option is generally one of the downtown banks, which are normally open Monday to Thursday from 8am to 4 or 5pm, and on Friday from 8am to 3pm, although the ubiquitous private exchange offices offer similar rates. Banks charge no commission, but you will need to show your passport; exchange offices do levy a commission, but no passport is required. Large hotels will change most hard currencies.

Opening hours and public holidays

Shops are generally open Monday to Friday from 10am to 6pm, and on Saturdays from 10am to 2pm; grocery stores and supermarkets open slightly

PUBLIC HOLIDAYS

January 1 New Year's Day
March 15 Independence Day
Good Friday
Easter Monday
May 1 Labour Day
Whitsun Monday
August 20 St Stephen's Day
October 23 National holiday
November 1 All Saints' Day
December 25 Christmas. (Since
celebrations start on Christmas Eve, many
shops will be closed the whole day, and
by the afternoon everything closes
down.)
December 26

longer hours at both ends of the day. The shopping malls are open Monday to Saturday 10am to 8pm or 9pm, and Sunday 10am to 6pm. There are also a growing number of 24-hour shops (signed "non-stop", "0–24" or "*éjjel-nappali*").

Museums are generally open Tuesday to Sunday 10am to 6pm, and in winter 9 or 10am to 4 or 5pm. Budapest's **thermal baths** are usually open daily from 6 or 7am to 8pm. Office hours are usually Monday to Friday from 8am to 4pm.

Most things in Hungary shut down on **public holidays** (see above). When these fall on a Tuesday or Thursday, the Monday before or the Friday after may also become a holiday, and the previous or next Saturday a working day to make up the lost day.

Phones

Telephone numbers in Budapest have seven digits, and the area code for all landline phone numbers is 1. To make a call to another part of Hungary, dial ☎06, followed by the area code and the subscriber's number. Hungarian mobile numbers have nine digits, and begin with ☎06 20, 06 30 or 06 70, depending upon the network.

If you want to use your home **mobile phone** in Budapest, check with your provider as to whether it will work in Hungary; US cell phones need to be tri-band to work. Following the **abolition of roaming charges** within the EU in June 2017, UK and Irish travellers can use their home mobile data and call allowance while in Hungary at no extra cost. However monthly data allowances when abroad may vary from those at home, so check with your provider. It's not yet known whether free roaming will still be in place if and when the UK leaves the EU. Travellers from other countries should check with their own network provider about the cheapest way to make mobile phone calls while abroad; roaming charges are likely to be high. If you plan on staying in Budapest for a while, you might want to consider buying a Hungarian pay-as-you-go **SIM card**; T-Mobile or Vodafone are the most ubiquitous outlets, and both have pay-as-you-go offers. Note that you may have to get your phone unlocked to use a local SIM. **Coverage** is generally good, even down in the metro.

To call Hungary from abroad, dial your international access code, then ☎36 for Hungary, then the area code (omitting the initial zero where present) and the number. If the Hungarian number begins with ☎06, omit these two digits. **Within Hungary**, directory enquiries is on ☎198, international directory enquiries on ☎199.

Time

Hungary is one hour ahead of GMT, six hours ahead of Eastern Standard Time and nine ahead of Pacific Standard Time. A word of caution: Hungarians express time in a way that might confuse the Anglophone traveller. As in German, 10.30am is expressed as "half eleven" (written 1/2 11 or f11), 10.45am is "three-quarter-eleven" (3/4 11 or h11), and 10.15am is "a quarter of eleven" (1/4 11 or n11).

Tipping

Tipping is standard practice in most restaurants; ten percent or thereabouts is fine, unless the service was not worth it. Note that ten, twelve or even fifteen percent may have quietly been added to the bill, though restaurant menus really should state whether a service charge is included. Otherwise, include the tip when you are paying the bill – say the amount you want to pay and they will give you the change – or give the tip to the staff rather than leaving it on the table. Taxi drivers usually get five to ten percent, more if they have helped you with bags or been similarly useful. It's also customary to tip bath attendants who unlock your cubicle (100–200Ft is usual). In all cases, when tipping be warned that if you expect change back, don't say *köszönöm* (thank you) when handing over payment, as it will be assumed that you want the change to be kept.

Tourist information

The official tourist office, Budapestinfo (🔘 budapest info.hu), has several branches in town, as well as desks at both airport terminals. There's also the independent Discover Budapest tourist office, providing similar information but with more enthusiasm. It may also worth looking at 🔘 gotohungary .com, which is aimed at arriving visitors. The website of the Hungarian Cultural Centre in London (🔘 hungary.org.uk) is a useful place to keep up Hungarian links after your visit.

INFORMATION OFFICES

Budapestinfo V, Sütő utca 2, by the Deák tér metro (daily 8am–8pm); and XIV, Hősök tere, in the City Park Ice Rink building (daily 9am–7pm); 🔘 1 438 8080, 🔘 budapestinfo.hu. Good for getting maps, brochures and the Budapest Card, but otherwise information is limited.

Discover Budapest VI, Lázár utca 16 (April–Oct daily 9am–8.30pm; Nov–March Mon–Thurs 9am–6.30pm, Fri–Sun 9am–7pm; 🔘 1 269 3842, 🔘 discoverbudapest.com). Handy office just behind the Opera House, with information on the city and on walking, cycle and Segway tours.

Travellers with disabilities

Hungary has been painfully slow to acknowledge the needs of the disabled traveller, and while progress is being made, don't expect much in the way of special facilities. However, the rapid growth of new hotels in Budapest has meant much better access for those with disabilities, with particular emphasis on specially designed rooms. Moreover, an increasing number of museums are providing ramps for wheelchairs.

The website of the **Hungarian Disabled Association** or Meosz, III, San Marco utca 76, 1032 Budapest (🔘 1 388 2387, 🔘 meosz.hu), has information about access to the main museums, cultural and historical sites – all in Hungarian, at the time of writing, but with English text expected soon. On **public transport**, there are a growing number of low-floor buses and trams in the city – for example most of the #4 and #6 trams on the Nagykörút. Access to the metro system is more limited: only the new fourth metro line has lifts at all stations. On bus and tram timetables, accessible services are underlined. If you want help finding a wheelchair-friendly route, go to the route planner 🔘 bkk.hu/en, which has an accessibility setting.

The Budapest Transport Centre operates three accessible buses in the city that you can book with at least a day's warning (🔘 70 390 3414, 🔘 bkk.hu). You can also contact Paralimo (🔘 70 606 5922, 🔘 paralimo.hu), a small private outfit that operates a 24-hour bus service.

CAFÉ CULTURE AT *GERBEAUD*, VÖRÖSMARTY TÉR

The Belváros

Abuzz with pavement cafés, street artists, vendors, boutiques and nightclubs, the Belváros or Inner City is the hub of Pest and, for tourists at least, the centre of what's happening. Commerce and pleasure have been its lifeblood as long as Pest has existed, first as a medieval market town and later as the kernel of a city whose *belle époque* rivalled that of Vienna. Unquestionably the focal point of the Belváros is pedestrianized Váci utca, running parallel to the Danube; the magnet for most first-time visitors to the city, this popular promenade is actually little more than a glorified shopping street, but you can still get a sense of the old atmosphere in the quieter backstreets south of Kossuth Lajos utca, where café life fans out in the shadow of some dramatic architecture.

The **Kiskörút** (Small Boulevard; comprising Károly körút, Múzeum körút and Vámház körút) that surrounds the Belváros follows the course of the medieval walls of Pest, showing how compact it was before the phenomenal expansion of the nineteenth century. However, little remains from further back than the eighteenth century, as the "liberation" of Pest by the Habsburgs in 1686 left the town in ruins. Some Baroque churches and the former Greek and Serbian quarters attest to its revival by settlers from other parts of the Habsburg empire, but most of the **architecture** dates from the era when Budapest asserted its right to be an imperial capital, between 1860 and 1918. Today, statues, domes and mosaics adorn the Neoclassical and Art Nouveau piles, which are reflected in the mirrored banks and luxury hotels that symbolize the post-Communist era. While restaurant prices in the Belváros are above average for Budapest, and there are few bargains to be had in the shops, one of the most enjoyable activities is people-watching from one of the many café terraces.

ARRIVAL AND GETTING AROUND

By public transport With three metro lines (#1, #2 and #3) converging at Deák Ferenc tér (line #1 continues to Vörösmarty tér), the Belváros is easily reached. Moreover, several trams and buses run the length of the Kiskörút, which skirts the Belváros, while tram #2 runs the entire length of the embankment, a worthwhile ride in itself (see p.49).

On foot Once in the Belváros, the best way to appreciate it is simply by wandering around, perhaps taking a stroll from Vörösmarty tér down through Váci utca, occasionally breaking off to admire the views of the Vár from the embankment.

Vörösmarty tér

Leafy **Vörösmarty tér** is a good starting point for exploring the Belváros. Crowds eddy around the food kiosks and craft stalls that fill the square, which is also the setting for the wonderful Christmas market, the Spring Fair in April and the Book Week in June (see p.30). While children play on the Lion fountain, teenagers lounge around the **statue of Mihály Vörösmarty** (1800–55), a poet and translator whose hymn to Magyar identity, *Szózat* ("Appeal"), is publicly declaimed at moments of national crisis. Its opening line "Be faithful to your land forever, Oh Hungarians" is carved on the statue's pedestal. Made of Carrara marble, the statue has to be wrapped in plastic sheeting each winter to prevent it from cracking. The black spot below the inscription is reputedly a "lucky" coin donated by a beggar towards the cost of the monument.

Gerbeaud patisserie

Gerbeaud cukrászda • V, Vörösmarty tér 7 • Daily 9am–9pm • ☎ 1 429 9000, ⌨ gerbeaud.hu

On the north side of Vörösmarty tér is the **Gerbeaud patisserie** (see p.170), Budapest's most famous confectioners. Founded in 1858 by Henrik Kugler, it was bought in 1884 by the Swiss confectioner Emile Gerbeaud, who invented the *konyakos meggy* (cognac-cherry bonbon) – still a popular sweet with Hungarians. He sold top-class cakes at reasonable prices, making the *Gerbeaud* a popular rendezvous for the middle classes. While the prices are now astronomical by Hungarian standards, and the service can be surly, it still has an undeniable appeal. Emile's portrait hangs in one of the rooms, whose gilded ceilings and china recall the *belle époque*.

HIDDEN GEMS: THE BELVÁROS
The Károlyi-kert park See p.42
Tram #2 along Pest Embankment See p.49
Pesti Vigadó See p.46
Underground Railway Museum See p.47
Old Father Danube statue in Erzsébet tér See p.47

Jacques Liszt bakery and café See p.160
Coffee and cake at Centrál Kávéház See p.170
Rózsavölgyi record shop See p.194

BELVÁROS

Lanchíd & Castle District

ACCOMMODATION

Astoria	5
Bohém Art	8
Boutique Hotel Zara	11
Buddha-Bar	4
Erzsébet City Center	6
Estilo Fashion	10
Gerlóczy	3
Lavender Circus	9
La Prima Fashion	2
Rum	7
Zenit	1

Gresham Palace

CEU

SZENT ISTVÁN TÉR

St Stephen's Basilica

ZRÍNYI UTCA

MÉRLEG UTCA

OKTÓBER 6. UTCA

SAS UTCA

JÓZSEF ATTILA UTCA

SZÉCHENYI ISTVÁN TÉR

DOROTTYA UTCA

JÓZSEF NÁDOR TÉR

Former Bus Station

ERZSÉBET TÉR

RÉVAY UTCA

ANDRÁSSY ÚT

Bajcsy Zsilinszky út

PAULAY EDE UTCA

BAJCSY-ZSILINSZKY ÚT

Opera & Városliget

Budapest Eye

Old Father Danube

SZENDE PÁL UTCA

Little Princess

VIGADÓ UTCA

Pesti Vigadó

VIGADÓ TÉR

Ferry Docks

APÁCZAI CSERE JÁNOS UTCA

DUNA-KORZÓ

JANE HANNING RAKPART

Vörösmarty tér

Vörösmarty

VÖRÖSMARTY TÉR

Bershka Store

DEÁK FERENC UTCA

Deák tér

Anker Palace

Underground Railway Museum

Gödör Klub

KIRÁLY UTCA

RUMBACH U.

MADÁCH ÚT

MADÁCH SÉTÁNY

Rumbach utca Synagogue

Lutz

SEBESTYÉN UTCA

Bank Palace Building

KRISTÓF TÉR

BÉCSI UTCA

FEHÉR HAJÓ UTCA

Fisher-girl

Lutheran Museum

Lutheran Church

SÜTŐ UTCA

DEÁK FERENC TÉR

VÁCI UTCA

Ferry Docks

Pest Theatre

Art Nouveau Mósaic

SZERVITA TÉR

BÁRCZY ISTVÁN UTCA

Városháza Park

MADÁCH IMRE TÉR

KÁROLY KÖRÚT (KISKÖRÚT)

DOB UTCA

Auction House

Rózsavölgyi building

RÉGI POSTA UTCA

PETŐFI SÁNDOR UTCA

Servite Church

VÁROSHÁZ UTCA

City Council

GERLÓCZY U.

SEMMELWEIS U.

WESSELÉNYI UTCA

Cathedral of the Dormition

Petőfi

GALAMB UTCA

PIARISTA UTCA

PETŐFI TÉR

Contra Aquincum

MÁRCIUS 15. TÉR

PARIZSI

HARIS KÖZ

PILVAX KÖZ

Katona József Theatre

Pest County Hall

VITKOVICS M. U.

RÖSER BAZÁR

Dohány utca Synagogue & Jewish Museum

HERZL TÉR

Belváros Parish Church

KÍGYÓ UTCA

Párisi Udvar

Klotild Palaces

SZABAD SAJTÓ ÚT

FERENCIEK TERE

KOSSUTH LAJOS UTCA

Puskin Cinema

Astoria

RÁKÓCZI ÚT

Buda

DUNA UTCA

IRÁNYI UTCA

Ferenciek tere

Franciscan Church

SZEP UTCA

University Library

REÁLTANODA UTCA

St Michael's Church

VÁCI UTCA

NYÁRI PÁL UTCA

MOLNÁR UTCA

VERES PÁLNÉ UTCA

KÁROLYI MIHÁLY UTCA

FERENCZY ISTVÁN UTCA

Petőfi Literary Museum

KÁROLYI-KERT

MAGYAR U.

Unger Ház

MÚZEUM KÖRÚT (KISKÖRÚT)

ELTE

PUSKIN UTCA

International Landing Stage

SÖRHÁZ

BELGRÁD RAKPART

PIN. U.

University Church

Budapest City Hall

ELTE Law Faculty

EGYETEM TÉR

BRÓDY SÁNDOR UTCA

PESTI ALSÓ RAKPART

HAVAS UTCA

Serbian Orthodox Church

SZERB UTCA

KECSKEMÉTI UTCA

Hungarian National Museum

POLLACK M. TÉR

Radio Building

River Danube (Duna)

SÓ UTCA

BÁSTYA UTCA

KIRÁLYI PÁL UTCA

LÓNYAY U.

FŐVÁM UTCA

FŐVÁM TÉR

Kálvin tér

Szabó Ervin Library

VÁMHÁZ KÖRÚT (KISKÖRÚT)

SZABADSÁG HÍD

Corvinus University

Great Market Hall

Buda & Gellért-hegy

0   250
metres

DRINKING AND NIGHTLIFE

Action	8
Akvárium	1
Castro	3
Csendes Társ	7
Csendes Vintage Bar	6
Habroló	4
Ibolya	5
Központ	2
Why Not?	9

N

1

● EATING				● SHOPPING			
QUICK BITES				BÁV	4	Központi Antikvárium	18
Belvárosi Disznótoros	13	Vapiano	2	Bio ABC	19	Ludovika	6
Beszálló	5			Emilia Anda	9	Magma	10
Igen	4	CAFÉS		Fabatka	13	Nanushka	3
Jacques Liszt	3	Azték Choxolat!	9	Fuga	15	Printa	8
Sonkapult	7	Centrál Kávéház	12	Gardrób Market	1	Retrock	2
Szimply	10	Fekete	11	Hababa Design Store	5	Rododendron	14
		Gerbeaud	1	Hecserli	21	Rózsavölgyi Music	7
RESTAURANTS				Holló Folk Art Gallery	12	Rózsavölgyi Chocolates	22
Al-Amir	6			Insitu	16	Valéria Fazekas	17
Gastro Bistro	14			Kodály Zoltán		Vass	11
Gerlóczy	8			Zeneműbolt	20		
Trattoria Toscana	15						

The Underground Railway

From the terrace outside the *Gerbeaud* patisserie on Vörösmarty tér you can observe the entrance to the **Underground Railway** (Földalatti Vasút, the yellow #1 metro line), whose vaguely Art Nouveau cast-iron fixtures and elegant tilework stamp it as decades older than the other metro lines. For its centenary in 1996, the line's stations were restored to their original decor. If you're curious to know more about its history, visit the Underground Railway Museum at Deák Ferenc tér (see p.47). The Underground Railway's route along Andrássy út is covered in Chapter 3, with Hősök tere described in Chapter 4.

Bershka store and former Bank Palace

V, Vörösmarty tér

Directly behind Vörösmarty's statue stands the **Bershka store**, its 1911 facade adorned with bronze panels with plant motifs. In the Communist era the Luxus Áruház, as it was then known, was *the* place to get your Western-style clothes. Now it sells the real thing: Western clothes as produced by the Spanish fashion company and aimed at the younger market.

Another early twentieth-century building, the former **Bank Palace**, stands at the southern end of Vörösmarty tér on the corner of Váci utca. When the Budapest **Stock Exchange** reopened its doors in 1990, this was its new home. Built in the heyday of Hungarian self-confidence by Ignác Alpár, who also designed the prewar Stock Exchange on Szabadság tér (see p.52), it has now been turned into a major retail centre.

Váci utca

Váci utca has been famous for its shops and **korzó** (promenade) since the eighteenth century. During the 1980s, its vivid street life became a symbol of the "consumer socialism" that distinguished Hungary from other Eastern Bloc states. It's now prime tourist territory, hence the endless souvenir shops, not to mention the myriad hawks and hustlers endeavouring to entice visitors into their restaurants and bars, or sell you some kind of tour or other. However, there are a few landmarks along the way that might catch your eye: heading south from Vörösmarty tér, there's the scantily clad **Fisher-girl fountain** on **Kristóf tér**; the **Pest Theatre** (no. 9) on the site of the *Inn of the Seven Electors*, where the 12-year-old Liszt performed in 1823 – note also the gorgeous Art Nouveau florist; and the former **Auction House** (no. 11a), with its Gothic Revival facade of majolica tiles and toothy wrought-ironwork.

An underpass further south brings you out on Március 15 tér, where a weird stone **monument** resembling a giant cactus flower commemorates the 125th anniversary of the unification of Buda and Pest. Beyond here, the pedestrianized continuation of Váci is infested with tourist-trap restaurants and shops, but retains some imposing architecture: worth a look are the prewar **Officers' Casino** (no. 38) guarded by statues of halberdiers (now a bank's headquarters), and the sculptural **plaque** on the wall of no. 43, commemorating the fact that the Swedish king Charles XII stayed here in 1714 during his lightning fourteen-day horseride from Turkey to Sweden. A little further

1

along, at no. 47, is the single nave **St Michael's church**, whose dull grey facade belies some interesting interior features, notably a fanciful altar with an image of St Dominic (founder of the Dominican order), and a superb stone balcony held up by Baroque sculptures – six giants with rippling muscles. Further along at nos. 62–64 looms the red-brick, griffon- and majolica-encrusted **Budapest City Hall**, where the city council still meets.

Petőfi Literary Museum

Petőfi Irodalmi Múzeum · V, Károlyi Mihály utca 16 · Tues–Sun 10am–6pm · 600Ft · ☎ 1 317 3611, ⓦ pim.hu

East of Váci utca, just beyond the University Law Faculty, stands the **Károlyi Palota**, birthplace of Count Mihály Károlyi, the liberal politician who briefly led the government after World War I. Today the palace houses the **Petőfi Literary Museum**, which has a permanent exhibition on the life of Sándor Petőfi, the nineteenth-century revolutionary poet (see box, p.46). It's a thoroughly enjoyable romp, thanks to some outstanding personal effects and to its excellent English captioning. Among the opening **exhibits** are Petőfi's first manuscript of poetry (and the publishing contract), his walking stick and billiard cue, an extravagant travelling chest, and the bonnet and engagement ring belonging to his wife of just two years, Júlia Szendrey – there are also several gifts exchanged between Petőfi and his lifelong friend, Arany János, the other pre-eminent poet of that time. Here, too, are the keys to the Petőfi family mausoleum (see p.83), though Sándor's body was, of course, never found. As one of the key figures in the 1848 Revolution, prominent coverage is given to Petőfi's role both here and as a soldier in the Hungarian Revolutionary Army, where he fought under the Polish general, Józef Bem; exhibits in this section include his captain's sword and a chess set that he and Bem supposedly used when in combat together in Szaszebes (today, Sebes in Romania), though the most poignant item is the warrant issued for his arrest by the Germans. In the garden to the rear stands a **statue of Petőfi** with sabre in hand, which is invariably adorned with wreaths in Hungarian colours.

Károlyi-kert

Fenced off from the Károlyi Palace – but accessible from Ferenczy István utca – **Károlyi-kert** is Budapest's oldest public park; a delightful green haven, this French-style park keeps a healthy array of colourful plants and flowers, and has a super children's playground. It was here too that Lajos Batthyány, head of the independent Hungarian government following the 1848 revolution, was arrested in 1849, and General Haynau, the "Butcher of Vienna", signed the death warrants of Batthyány and other rebel leaders after finishing his morning exercises.

Ferenciek tere

North of the Petőfi Literary Museum lies the **Centrál Kávéház** (see p.170), one of Pest's grand old coffee houses where, in the early twentieth century, writers and intellectuals lingered day and night, while to the right rises the coloured dome of the university library. Beyond here is **Ferenciek tere** (Franciscans' Square) – though it's more L-shaped than square, and is dominated by the network of roads approaching the Erzsébet bridge. Yet even the six-lane highway that runs across the top of the square cannot detract from the magnificence of the buildings.

Párisi Udvar

V, Ferenciek tere

The most notable building on Ferenciek tere is the **Párisi Udvar**, a flamboyantly eclectic shopping arcade constructed in 1915. Upon completion, its fifty naked statues above

1

the third floor were deemed incompatible with its intended role as the headquarters of the city savings bank, symbolized by images of bees throughout the building. After years of neglect the building was recently purchased by the Mellow Mood hotel group, with a five-star complex due, though this was still some way from completion at the time of writing. All things being equal, the ornate interior, with its hexagonal stained-glass dome designed by Miksa Róth, carved wooden statues, and majolica tiles from the Zsolnay factory, will be retained.

The Klotild Palaces
V, Ferenciek tere

Traffic roars into the western end of Ferenciek tere between a pair of imposing *fin-de-siècle* office buildings – designed by Flóris Krob and Kálmán Giergl, the same team behind the Bershka department store building (see p.41) and the Music Academy (see p.63). Named the **Klotild Palaces** after the Habsburg princess who commissioned them, the northern one is home to the luxury *Buddha-Bar* hotel (see p.152); slated for a major renovation, with a five-star hotel in the offing, the noticeably grimier southern palace once housed a restaurant owned by Egon Ronay's father – after it was nationalized in 1946, the young Ronay moved to London where he was appalled by cooking standards.

Kossuth Lajos utca

Ferenciek tere melds seamlessly into **Kossuth Lajos utca** at its eastern end, where the noise and the fumes deter the visitor from lingering. Immediately on the right is the **Franciscan Church** that gave the square its name. The relief on the church's wall recalls the great flood of 1838, in which over four hundred citizens were killed; it depicts the heroic efforts of Baron Miklós Wesselényi, who personally rescued scores of people in his boat.

Some 200m further along, the junction of Kossuth Lajos utca with the Kiskörút is named after the **Astoria Hotel** on the corner, a prewar haunt of spies and journalists that was commandeered as an HQ by the Nazis in 1944 and the Soviets after the 1956 Uprising. Today, its Neoclassical coffee lounge is redolent of Stalinist chic.

Szervita tér

A couple of blocks south of Vörösmarty tér, **Szervita tér** contains the best and the worst of twentieth-century architecture. Three remarkable buildings from the golden age of Hungarian architecture line its western side. No. 3, the former Turkish Bank House dating from 1906, has a gable aglow with a superb **Art Nouveau mosaic** of *Patrona Hungariae* (Our Lady) flanked by key figures from Hungarian history, one of the finest works of Miksa Róth (see p.69). No. 2 (1908) is one of the earliest Modernist buildings in Budapest, with its geometric motifs and its decorative screws; while at no. 5 the **Rózsavölgyi Building** (1911–12) was built by the "father" of Hungarian Modernism, **Béla Lajta**, whose earlier association with the National Romantic school is evident from the majolica bands on its upper storeys, typical of the style. The Rózsavölgyi music shop (see p.194) on the ground floor is one of the oldest, and best, in the city – sadly Lajta's interior fittings were lost in a fire in 1955.

Servite Church
Szervita Templom • V, Szervita tér 6 • Daily 10am–6pm • Free • Concerts March–Oct Wed noon, donations accepted

Szervita tér is named after the eighteenth-century **Servite Church** (otherwise known as St Anne's Church), built following liberation from Turkish rule, indeed on the site of a former mosque. The recently restored facade bears a relief of an angel cradling a dying horseman, in memory of the Seventh Kaiser Wilhelm Hussars killed in World War I. The interior, meanwhile, is standard Baroque exuberance, the pick of the paintings being those of the seven founders of the Servite order, located on the right-hand side of the nave. The attached monastery was damaged in World War II and in 1964 was replaced with the brutalist communications centre that now hems in the church.

Along the embankment

The riverbank bore the brunt of the fighting in 1944–45, when the Nazis and the Red Army exchanged salvoes across the Danube. As with the Vár in Buda, postwar clearances exposed historic sites and provided an opportunity to integrate them into the environment – but the magnificent **view** of the Royal Palace and Gellért-hegy is hardly matched by the row of modern hotels on the Pest side. While such historic architecture as remains can be seen in a fifteen-minute stroll between the Erzsébet híd and the Lánchíd, tram #2 enables you to see a longer stretch of the waterfront between Szabadság híd and Kossuth tér in the north, interrupted by a tunnel at the Lánchíd.

Erzsébet híd

The bold white pylons and cables of the **Erzsébet híd** (Elizabeth Bridge) are as dominant a feature of the panorama as the stone Lánchíd to the north or the wrought-iron Szabadság híd to the south. Of all the Danube bridges blown up by the Germans as they retreated to Buda in January 1945, the Erzsébet híd was the only one not rebuilt in its original form. In fact it was not replaced until 1964 – and even then had to be closed down immediately due to faulty engineering.

Március 15 tér

A largely nondescript square today, **Március 15 tér** nevertheless betrays strong military associations – in one corner you can peer down through the glass covers at the remains of **Contra-Aquincum**, a Roman fort that was an outpost of the settlement at Óbuda at the end of the third century. More pertinently to Hungarian history, the name of the square refers to March 15, 1848, when the anti-Habsburg Revolution began.

Belváros Parish Church

Belvárosi Főplébánia Templom • V, Március 15 tér 2 • Mon–Sat 9am–4.30pm, Sun 9am–10pm • 1000Ft • Mass in English Sun 6pm

Dominating Március 15 tér is the **Belváros Parish Church**, the oldest church in Pest. Founded in 1046 as the burial place of St Gellért (see p.110), it was rebuilt as a Gothic hall church in the fifteenth century (his remains had long been shipped off to Venice), turned into a mosque by the Turks and then reconstructed as a church in the eighteenth century. This history is reflected in the interior, and after Latin Mass at 10am on Sunday you can see the Gothic sedilia and Turkish *mihrab* (prayer niche) behind the high altar, which are otherwise out of bounds. The austere Gothic interior is largely devoid of ornamentation save for a few splashes of colour on the rib-vaulted nave.

Petőfi tér and Duna-korzó

To the northwest of Március 15 tér, **Petőfi tér** is named after Sándor Petőfi, whose poem *National Song* – the anthem of 1848 – and romantic death in battle the following year made him a patriotic icon (see box, p.46). Erected in 1882, the square's **Petőfi statue** has long been a focus for demonstrations as well as patriotic displays – especially on March 15, when the statue is bedecked with flags and flowers.

The concrete esplanade running north from Petőfi tér is a sterile attempt at re-creating the prewar **Duna-korzó**, the most informal of Budapest's promenades, where it was socially acceptable for strangers to approach celebrities and stroll beside them. The outdoor cafés here, which boast wonderful views, charge premium rates.

1

SÁNDOR PETŐFI

Born on New Year's Eve, 1822, to a Slovak mother and a southern Slav butcher-innkeeper father, **Sándor Petőfi** was to become obsessed by acting and by poetry, which he started to write at the age of 15. As a strolling player, soldier and labourer, he absorbed the language of working people and composed his lyrical poetry in the vernacular, to the outrage of critics. Moving to Budapest in 1844, he fell in with the young radical intellectuals who met at the *Pilvax Café* on Pilvax koz (the café is no more), and embarked on his career as a revolutionary hero. He declaimed his *National Song* from the steps of the National Museum on the first day of the 1848 Revolution, and fought in the War of Independence with General Bem in Transylvania, where he disappeared during the Battle of Segesvár in 1849. Though he was most likely trampled beyond recognition by the Cossacks' horses (as predicted in one of his poems), Petőfi was long rumoured to have survived as a prisoner. In 1990, a Hungarian entrepreneur sponsored an expedition to Siberia to uncover the putative grave, but it turned out to be that of a woman.

Cathedral of the Dormition

Nagyboldogasszony magyar ortodox székesegyház • V, Petőfi tér 2 • Wed 2–5pm, Fri 1–5pm, Sat 3–7pm, Sun noon–5pm • Free • Services Mon–Fri 5pm, Sat 6pm, Sun 8, 9 & 10am

On the eastern side of Petőfi tér looms the Greek Orthodox **Cathedral of the Dormition**, built by the Greek community in the 1790s and, more recently, the object of a tug-of-war between the Patriarchate of Moscow that gained control of it after 1945 and the Orthodox Church in Greece that previously owned it. One of the church's towers was lost in the siege of Budapest in 1944, and in its place there now sits an awkward-looking replacement. The cathedral has services in Hungarian, Church Slavonic and Greek, according to the make-up of the congregation, accompanied by singing in the Orthodox fashion. The big feast here is on August 28, the Dormition of Mary (the Assumption) in the Orthodox calendar.

Vigadó tér

Elegant **Vigadó tér** is named after the Pesti Vigadó concert hall (see p.185), whose name translates as "having a ball" or "making merry". On the opposite side of the square to the hall, look out for the statue of the impish **Little Princess**, which has been sitting on the railings by the tram line since 1990. After dusk, you'll hardly notice that she isn't a person, if you notice her at all. By day, she looks like a cross-dressing boy in a Tinkerbell hat. Prince Charles was so taken by her that he invited her creator, László Marton, to hold an exhibition of his work in Britain.

Pesti Vigadó

V, Vigadó tér 2 • Daily 10am–7pm • Guided tours 2900Ft • ☎ 1 328 3325, ⓦ vigado.hu

A Romantic pile by Frigyes Feszl, encrusted with statues of the Muses and plaques recalling performances by Liszt, Mahler and Wagner and other renowned artists, the **Pesti Vigadó** concert hall was inaugurated in 1865. Badly damaged in World War II, it didn't reopen until 1980, such was the care taken to re-create its sumptuous decor. Following another lengthy closure between 2004 and 2014, during which time the facade was cleaned up and the interior renovated, the magnificent main hall is once again staging classical concerts. The guided tours are very worthwhile.

Deák Ferenc tér

Three metro lines and several important roads meet at **Deák Ferenc tér** to form a jumping-off point for the Belváros and Lipótváros. However, finding local addresses can be confusing since Deák Ferenc tér merges seamlessly into the far larger **Erzsébet tér** to the north.

Anker Palace

The vast, mustard-coloured **Anker Palace** (Anker palota), to the east of Deák Ferenc tér, is one of several imposing edifices in the centre of Budapest built for a foreign insurance company, in this case the Viennese Insurance Company. Its design by Ignác Alpár, the man behind the former Stock Exchange and the National Bank on Szabadság tér, was widely admired for its clever use of an awkward plot. Not everyone was impressed: when it opened in 1910, Alpár's wife said, "Oh Ignác, aren't you ashamed of yourself? What have you done here?"

Lutheran Church and Museum

Deák téri Evangélikus Templom & Evangélikus Múzeum • V, Deák Ferenc tér 4 • **Church** Mon–Fri 9am–1pm • Free • **Museum** Tues–Sun 10am–6pm • 1200Ft • ☎ 1 317 4173, ⓦ evangelikusmuzeum.hu

The large, spireless **Lutheran Church**, which looms over the metro pavilion on the edge of the Belváros, was built in 1808 according to designs by Mihály Pollack. Both the exterior and interior exhibit typical early Neoclassical styles, exemplified by minimal ornamentation. More interestingly, the church hosts some excellent concerts that include regular free Sunday-evening organ recitals and Bach's *St John Passion* over the fortnight before Easter. Next door, the **Lutheran Museum** displays a facsimile of Martin Luther's last will and testament, and a copy of the first book printed in Hungarian, a New Testament from 1541.

Underground Railway Museum

Földalattivasút Múzeum • V, Deák Ferenc tér underpass by the entrance to the metro station • Tues–Sun 10am–5pm • 350Ft

Accessible via the upper sublevel of Deák tér metro, the enjoyable little **Underground Railway Museum** extols the history of Budapest's original metro. The exhibition is set up in a stretch of tunnel that was abandoned in 1955 when the line was altered, while the constant rumble of the trains close by adds another layer of authenticity. Sitting on the track are three old wooden carriages (one used up until 1973), while exhibits include construction diaries, models, and period fixtures and posters, which enhance the museum's nostalgic appeal.

The metro's genesis was a treatise by Mór Balázs, proposing a steam-driven tram network starting with a route along Andrássy út, an underground line being suggested as a fallback in case the overground option was rejected. Completed in under two years, it was inaugurated in 1896 – in time for the Millennial Exhibition – by Emperor Franz Josef, who agreed to allow it to bear his name, which it kept until 1918. The metro was the first on the European continent and the second in the world (after London's Metropolitan line), and originally ran from Vörösmarty tér as far as the Millennial Exhibition grounds at Hősök tere. The exhibition also recalls the role of women on the underground, more precisely their recruitment as conductors during World War I owing to male staff shortages.

Erzsébet tér

Once the site of a cemetery beyond the medieval city walls, **Erzsébet tér** has gone through many names since then, notably Sztálin tér from 1946 until 1953, when it became Engels tér, before getting its older name back. The statue in the middle of the park is of **Old Father Danube** with his three tributaries, the Dráva, Száva and Tisza, and was designed in 1880 by Miklós Ybl.

The long, low functionalist building on the square's eastern side is the former bus station, protected by a conservation order and so unable to be demolished, much to the ire of locals. However, it does now function as a cool alfresco bar in warmer months, while just a few paces from here, a glass-bottomed pool sits above a series of stepped terraces leading down to the hip *Akvárium* club (see p.176) – the whole area is one of the most popular places to gather on summer evenings, as the crowds spill out across the square.

Lipótváros and Újlipótváros

Lipótváros (Leopold Town), lying to the north of the Belváros, started to develop in the late eighteenth century, first as a financial centre and later as the seat of government. Several institutions of national significance are found here, including Parliament, St Stephen's Basilica, the National Bank and the Hungarian Television headquarters. Though part of the V District, as is the Belváros, Lipótváros has quite a different ambience, with sombre streets of Neoclassical buildings interrupted by squares flanked by monumental Art Nouveau piles. That said, the area has developed into quite a social hub, with bars sprawled across Szent István tér and Zrinyi utca, and some of the city's best restaurants sited along Sas utca. Across Szent István körút, Újlipótváros (New Leopold Town; the XIII district) is worth visiting for the entertaining Pinball Museum.

ARRIVAL AND GETTING AROUND

Lipótváros It makes sense to start a Lipótváros visit either with Széchenyi István tér, by the Lánchíd, or St Stephen's Basilica, two minutes' walk from Deák tér. Most of the streets between them lead towards the set-piece expanse of Szabadság tér, whence you can head on towards Parliament – though the Kossuth tér metro station or tram #2 along the river will provide quicker access.

Újlipótváros Although easily reachable on foot, the other way to get to Újlipótváros is either by tram #4 or #6 along the Nagykörút or on the blue #2 metro line.

Széchenyi Istvan tér

2

At the Pest end of the Lánchíd, **Széchenyi István tér** is named after "the greatest Hungarian", the man responsible for building the bridge (see p.103). Blitzed by traffic crowding on and off the bridge, it's also dominated by huge trees – including one propped-up acacia said to be the oldest tree in the city – that make it hard to get a feel for this historic square. It was here that the Austrian emperor Franz Josef was crowned King of Hungary in 1867 – paradoxically symbolizing Hungary's increasing independence within the Habsburg empire. Soil from every corner of the nation was piled into a Coronation Hill, on the site of the present square. The emperor flourished the sword of St Stephen and promised to defend Hungary against all its enemies – a pledge that proved almost as ephemeral as the hill itself. In 1947 the square was renamed **Roosevelt tér** in honour of the late US president – a rare example of Cold War courtesy that survived until 2011 when the mayor of the time set about sweeping away the old Communist names.

Gresham Palace

V, Széchenyi Istvan tér 5

Unquestionably the finest building on Széchenyi István tér, and one of Budapest's landmark hotels (see p.153), is the magnificent Art Nouveau **Gresham Palace** on its eastern side. Commissioned by a British insurance company in 1904, it's named after the financier Sir Thomas Gresham, the author of Gresham's law that bad money drives out good, whereby the circulation of coins of equal face value but different metals leads to those made of more valuable metal being hoarded and disappearing from use.

The building was in an awful state when it was acquired by the Four Seasons hotel chain in 2001, but fears of a crass refurbishment were dispelled by a loving restoration: authentic materials and even the original workshops were sought out to do the job. Today you can once again see Gresham's bust high up on the facade, and members of the public may walk in to admire the subtle hues of the tiled lobby and the **Páva Udvar** (Peacock Passage), a superb glass-roofed arcade with wrought-iron peacock gates and stained-glass windows by Miksa Róth. If you don't mind your wallet taking a bit of a bashing, stop by for an early evening cocktail in the gorgeous lobby bar.

Hungarian Academy of Sciences

Magyar Tudományos Akadémia • V, Széchenyi István tér 9 • ☎ 1 411 6489

Statues of Count Széchenyi (see box, p.103) and Ferenc Deák, another major nineteenth-century politician who helped to forge Hungary's agreement with the Austrians in 1867, stand at opposite ends of Széchenyi István tér. The statue of the former isn't far from the imposing **Hungarian Academy of Sciences**, founded after

---

HIDDEN GEMS: LIPÓTVÁROS AND ÚJLIPÓTVÁROS

Cocktails in the glass-roofed arcade of the Gresham Palace See p.49
St Stephen's Basilica Treasury See p.51
Hungarian State Treasury See p.53
Lunch in the Belvárosi market hall See p.53

Art Nouveau Bedő House See p.54
Museum of Ethnography See p.57
Dinner at Zeller Bistro See p.162
Coffee in Espresso Embassy See p.170
Bestsellers Bookshop See p.192

LIPÓTVÁROS AND ÚJLIPÓTVÁROS

EATING

QUICK BITES
Briós	2
Delibaba	16
Hummus Bar	17

RESTAURANTS
Babka	4
Borkonyha	22
Café Kör	20
Csarnok	10
Firkász	3
Govinda	18
Hilda	21
Kispiac	9
Mák Bistro	19
Pomo d'Oro	15
Pozsonyi Kisvendéglő	1
Stand 25	8
Zeller Bistro	13

CAFÉS
Artizán	11
Damniczki	12
Espresso Embassy	14
Europa	6
Gelarto Rosa	23
Madal	5
Smuz	7

ACCOMMODATION
Aria	2
Four Seasons	1
Starlight Suiten	3

DRINKING AND NIGHTLIFE
Drop Shop	1
Tokaji Borozó	2

SHOPPING
Bestsellers	4
Bortársaság	3
Malatinszky	5
Ōmama Bizsúja	1
Wladis Galéria	2

0   250
metres

Széchenyi pledged a year's income from his estates towards its establishment in 1825 – as depicted on a relief on the wall facing Akadémia utca.

St Stephen's Basilica

Szent István-Bazilika • V, Szent István tér 1 • **Basilica** Mon–Sat 9am–7pm, Sun 1–6pm • 200Ft • Mass on weekdays 7am, 8am & 6pm, Sun 8.30am, 10am, noon, 5pm & 6pm • **Chapel** April–Sept Mon–Sat 9am–4.30pm, Sun 1–4.30pm; Oct–March Mon–Sat 10am–4pm, Sun 1–4.30pm • Free • **Panorama Tower** Daily: Oct–June 10am–4.30pm; July–Sept 10am–6.30pm, closing earlier in bad weather • 500Ft • **Treasury** Same hours as tower • 400Ft • ☎ 1 311 0839, ⓦ bazilika.biz

2

St Stephen's Basilica took so long to build that Budapestis once joked, when borrowing money, "I'll pay you back when the basilica is finished." Work began in 1851 under the supervision of József Hild, continued after his death under Miklós Ybl, and was finally completed by Joseph Krauser in 1905. At the inaugural ceremony Emperor Franz Josef was seen to glance anxiously at the dome, whose collapse during a storm in 1868 had set progress back. At 96m, it is exactly the same height as the dome of the Parliament building – both allude to the putative date of the Magyars' arrival in Hungary (896 AD). After recent restoration work that seemed to take as long as the original construction, the basilica looks very grand today. Its beauty lies in the combined effect of the frescoes, marble and gilded stucco rather than in any particular works of art, though the mosaics by Károly Lotz in the cupola are worth admiring. The **organ**, too, is quite splendid, and put to good use every Thursday evening with a concert at 8pm (5700–8900Ft). In the second chapel to the right is a painting of King Stephen offering the Crown of Hungary to the Virgin (see box, p.57), while a statue of him haloed as a saint (but with a sword at his side) forms the centrepiece of the altar.

For most visitors, though, the chief attraction lies inside the **Holy Right Chapel**, where the gnarled **mummified hand of St Stephen**, Hungary's holiest relic, resides. Over the centuries, the relic was variously kept in Bihar (Transylvania), Ragusa (now Dubrovnik) and Vienna, before being returned to Buda in 1771. Each year, on August 20, the Szent Jobb (literally, "holy right") is paraded with great pomp through the surrounding streets, the anniversary of his death.

If you've time, make a beeline for the **treasury** (*kincstár*), reachable via a lift next to the entrance. As well as the usual chalices, monstrances and suchlike, there's a fascinating display on the life of Cardinal Mindszenty, the head of the Church who is much honoured for his challenge to the Communist regime (see box, p.141). Photos, robes and mitres, as well as various items garnered while in exile, including a suitcase (presumably the one he took with him), attest to his life's work. Finally, you shouldn't miss the grand view over the city from the **Panorama tower** (Körkilátó) reached by lift to the base of the cupola, or by climbing 302 stairs.

Bajcsy-Zsilinszky út

While Stephen is revered as the founder and patron saint of Hungary, the pantheon of national heroes includes a niche for **Endre Bajcsy-Zsilinszky** (1866–1944), after whom the avenue that runs past the Basilica is named. Originally a right-winger, he ended up an outspoken critic of Fascism, was arrested in Parliament and shot as the Russians approached. **Bajcsy-Zsilinszky út** is the demarcation line between the Lipótváros and Terézváros districts, running northwards to **Nyugati Station**, an elegant, iron-beamed terminal built in 1874–77 by the Eiffel Company of Paris.

Szabadság tér and around

For more than a century, Lipótváros was dominated by a gigantic barracks where scores of Hungarians were imprisoned or executed, until this symbol of Habsburg tyranny was demolished in 1897 and the site redeveloped as **Szabadság tér** (Liberty Square).

2

Invested with significance from the outset, it has become a kind of record of the vicissitudes of modern Hungarian history, where each regime added or removed **monuments**, according to their political complexion.

Stock Exchange building
V, Szabadság tér

In the early twentieth century, Hungary's burgeoning prosperity was expressed by two monumental temples to capitalism on opposite sides of Szabadság tér. To the west stands the former **Stock Exchange**, one of the grandest buildings in Budapest. Designed by Ignác Alpár, it has blended motifs from Greek and Assyrian architecture and is crowned with twin towers resembling Khmer temples. After the Communists closed down the Exchange in 1948, it became the **headquarters of Hungarian Television**, which it remained until 2009; it's now slated for redevelopment.

National Bank
V, Szabadság tér 8

Ignác Alpár, the man behind the former Stock Exchange, also designed the **National Bank** on the eastern side of Szabadság tér, which still functions as such and is notable for the bas-reliefs on its exterior, representing such diverse aspects of wealth creation as Magyars ploughing and herding, ancient Egyptians harvesting wheat, and Vikings loading longships with loot. The stones for its columns were hauled all the way from Transylvania by oxen. Unfortunately, the bank is generally off-limits, but if you happen to be here during European Heritage Days in September, you may get a peek; notable features include some fine stained-glass windows on the stairs.

US Embassy
V, Szabadság tér 12

The northern neighbour of the National Bank on the eastern side of Szabadság tér is the imposing **US Embassy**; for fifteen years, the latter sheltered Cardinal Mindszenty, the Primate of Hungary's Catholic Church, in the aftermath of the 1956 Uprising. Later, however, the US became embarrassed by his presence, as did the Vatican, which finally persuaded him to leave for Austria in 1971 (see box, p.141).

In front of the US Embassy, the stocky figure of **General Harry Bandholtz** commemorates the US general who intervened with a dogwhip to stop Romanian troops from looting the Hungarian National Museum in 1919. The statue was erected in the 1930s, removed after World War II, and reinstated by the Communists prior to President George Bush's visit in 1989.

German occupation monument
V, Szabadság tér

At the southern end of Szabadság tér stands its most recent memorial, the **German occupation monument**, this time marking the **Nazi takeover** on 19 March 1944. Depicting archangel Gabriel – representing Hungary – being menaced by a Germanic eagle, the monument has caused much debate. The government insists that it stands for all victims of the occupation, while Jewish groups see it as part of an official attempt to absolve Hungary of responsibility in the Holocaust, hence the plethora of photos and messages left by families of those killed during this episode. One hundred metres west of the monument, recessed in front of the Church of Homecoming (Hazatérés Temploma), stands a bust of **Admiral Horthy** – put up by a right-wing priest who belongs to the Jobbik party.

Soviet Army Memorial
V, Szabadság tér

The top end of Szabadság tér has seen its share of controversy. From 1921 to 1945 it was dominated by the Monument to Hungarian Grief in protest at the 1920 Treaty of

Trianon, which awarded two-thirds of Hungary's territory and a third of its Magyar population to the "Successor States" of Romania, Czechoslovakia and Yugoslavia. After World War II, this was replaced by a **Soviet Army Memorial** commemorating the liberation of Budapest from the Nazis, with bas-reliefs of Red Army troops and tanks advancing on Ferenciek tere and Parliament.

Statue of Ronald Reagan

V, Szabadság tér

Immediately behind Szabadság tér's Soviet Army Memorial is a statue of **Ronald Reagan**, put up to mark the 100th anniversary of the former US president's birthday in 2011. The 2m-high statue, which presents him striding from Parliament into the square (he never visited the city), was erected in recognition of his role in ending the Cold War.

Hungarian State Treasury

V, Szabadság tér

Right behind the US Embassy lies a fine example of Hungarian Art Nouveau. The tiled facade of the **Hungarian State Treasury** is patterned like a quilt, with swarms of bees symbolizing thrift – this was originally the **Post Office Savings Bank** (Postatakarékpénztár). The polychromatic roof with its beehives and dragon tails is the wildest part of the building. Its architect, Ödön Lechner, once asked why birds shouldn't enjoy his buildings too, and amazing roofs are a feature of his other masterpieces in Budapest, the Geological Institute (see p.76) and the Museum of Applied Arts (see p.84). The building is only open to the public on European Heritage Days, but in the foyer (accessible during banking hours), a small display of photographs of the interior gives you a taste of the design.

Belvárosi market hall

Vásárcsarnok • V, Hold utca 13 • Mon–6.30am–5pm, Tues–Fri 6.30am–6pm, Sat 6.30am–2pm

The wrought-iron **Belvárosi market hall** was one of five opened on a single day in 1896. Much less touristy than the Great Market Hall on Vámház körút (see p.83), it's really worth visiting for its array of food outlets (see p.162), which largely cater for office workers hereabouts; if you fancy a steaming bowl of goulash or smoked sausage with sauerkraut, this is a great place to come. Its rear entrance will bring you out on Vadász utca, not far from one of Budapest's least-known memorials to the Holocaust, the Glass House (see below).

Glass House Memorial Room

Üvegház Emlékszoba • V, Vadász utca 29 • Daily 1–4pm • Free, donations accepted • ☎ 1 242 6964, ⓦ uveghaz.org

The **Glass House Memorial Room** was named both for the extensive use of glass in its Modernist design and for its erstwhile role as a glass showroom. From 1944 to 1945, it was one of many properties in Budapest that was designated as neutral territory by the Swiss consul Carl Lutz (1895–1975), serving as a refuge for three thousand Jews and the underground Zionist Youth organization. An **exhibition** (to the right in the courtyard) explains how Lutz and other "Righteous Gentiles" managed to save thousands of Jews from the SS and Arrow Cross death squads by issuing Schutzpasses to Jews, attesting that they were Swiss or Swedish citizens – a ruse subsequently used by Wallenberg. After the war Lutz was criticized for abusing Swiss law and, feeling slighted, proposed himself for the Nobel Peace Prize. While their co-religionists from the provinces were transported en masse to Auschwitz, the Jews of Budapest faced random executions in the heart of the capital, within full view of Parliament (see p.55) and their Gentile compatriots, who seemed more offended by the bloodshed than outraged by their murder. Inside, **exhibits** include a letter to Lutz from Admiral Horthy, the trunk that Lutz brought with him from America, and the shattered marble tablet to Artur Weisz, the owner of the Glass House, who was shot in 1944: it stood on the wall outside until it was smashed by neo-Nazis a few years ago. There's little by way of English captioning, but do ask for the audio commentary.

Bedő House

Bedő Ház, or Magyar Szecesszió Háza • V, Honvéd utca 3 • Mon–Sat 10am–5pm • 2000Ft • ☎ 1 269 4622, ⓦ magyarszecessziohaza.hu

The pistachio facade of the **Bedő House** is another superb example of Hungarian Art Nouveau architecture, built by Emil Vidor in 1903. Restored to its original state after decades of neglect, it now holds the **Museum of Hungarian Art Nouveau**, an extensive but rather haphazard collection of furniture, ceramics, interior design and other knick-knacks; check out the toilets in the basement too. If you find the entrance price off-putting, settle instead for a browse around the shop, with its reproduction and original pieces, or enjoy a coffee in the café.

Batthyány and Nagy monuments

Two monuments off the northern corners of Szabadság tér recall very different historical figures. To the northeast at the far end of Aulich utca, in the centre of a small roundabout, a badly weathered lantern flickers with an **Eternal Flame** commemorating **Count Lajos Batthyány**. The Prime Minister of the short-lived republic declared after the 1848 War of Independence, Batthyány was executed by the Habsburgs on this spot on October 6, 1849. As a staunch patriot – but not a revolutionary – he is a hero for conservative nationalists, and his monument is the destination of marches on October 6.

To the northwest of Szabadság tér at the far end of Vécsey utca, a figure stands on a footbridge in Vértanuk tere (Martyrs' Square), gazing towards Parliament. This is a monument to **Imre Nagy**, the reform Communist who became Prime Minister during the 1956 Uprising and was shot in secret two years afterwards. With his raincoat, trilby and umbrella hooked over his arm, Nagy cuts an all-too-human, flawed figure – and is scorned by those who pay homage to Batthyány.

Kossuth Lajos tér

The apotheosis of the government district and Hungary's romantic self-image comes at **Kossuth Lajos tér**, with its colossal Parliament building and its memorials to national heroes. The square is named after **Lajos Kossuth**, the leader of the 1848 Revolution (see box, p.55), who is represented by a sculptural tableau showing him and his ministers downcast by their defeat in 1849. The Communists had replaced it with a more heroic version, but that has been removed as the square is returned to its pre-March 1944 state. Two restored statues stand to the north and south of Parliament: by the visitor centre is the grandiose monument to **István Tisza**, the prime minister of Hungary in 1914, while to the south is the equestrian statue of **Gyula Andrássy**, prime minister after the 1867 compromise. The equestrian statue on the grass in front of Parliament is of **Prince Ferenc Rákóczi II**, a hero of the struggle for Hungarian independence, whose plinth is inscribed: "The wounds of the noble Hungarian nation burst open!" This is a reference to the anti-Habsburg war of 1703–11, but also perfectly describes the evening of October 23, 1956, when crowds filled the square, chanting anti-Stalinist slogans at Parliament – the prelude to the Uprising that night.

1956 Memorial

V, Kossuth Lajos tér • March–Oct daily 10am–6pm • Free

Down the steps between Kossuth Lajos tér's two equestrian statues – inside one of the old ventilation tunnels – is the **1956 Memorial**, which pays tribute to those who died here on October 25, when ÁVO snipers opened fire on a peaceful crowd that was fraternizing with Soviet tank-crews. It's smartly presented, courtesy of large

LAJOS KOSSUTH

Lajos Kossuth was the incarnation of post-Napoleonic bourgeois nationalism. Born into landless gentry in 1802, he began his career as a lawyer, representing absentee magnates in Parliament. His Parliamentary reports, which advocated greater liberalism than the Habsburgs would tolerate, became widely influential during the Reform era, and he was jailed for sedition. While in prison, Kossuth taught himself English by reading Shakespeare. Released in 1840, he became editor of the radical *Pesti Hírlap*, was elected to Parliament and took the helm during the 1848 Revolution.

After Serbs, Croats and Romanians rebelled against Magyar rule and the Habsburgs invaded Hungary, the Hungarians proclaimed a republic with Kossuth as de facto dictator. After the Hungarians surrendered in August 1849, Kossuth escaped to Turkey and later toured Britain and America, espousing liberty and trying to win support for the Hungarian cause. So eloquent were his denunciations of Habsburg tyranny that London brewery workers attacked General Haynau, the "Butcher of Vienna", when he visited the city. One man who did his best to undermine Kossuth's efforts was Karl Marx, who loathed Kossuth as a bourgeois radical and wrote hostile articles in the *New York Herald Tribune* and the London *Times*.

As a friend of the Italian patriot Mazzini, Kossuth spent his last years in Turin, where he died in 1894. His remains now lie in the Kerepesi Cemetery (see p.82).

black-and-white photos, moving testaments from those who were present, and film footage beamed onto the bare brick walls – meanwhile, a 3D tank manoeuvres menacingly in front of the Parliament building. Exhibits include uniforms, weapons and ammunition from both the Soviet and Hungarian sides, and items of civilian clothing, including jackets, boots and caps.

Statue of Attila József

V, Kossuth Lajos tér

Immediately south of the Andrássy statue, close to the river, sits the brooding figure of **Attila József**, shirtsleeves rolled up and crumpled jacket beside him. One of Hungary's finest poets, József was expelled from the Communist Party for trying to reconcile Marx and Freud, and committed suicide in 1937 after being rejected by his lover, throwing himself under a train at Lake Balaton. His powerful, turbulent verse has never lost its popularity, and he earns his place here for his poem *By the Danube*.

Holocaust Memorial

V, Id. Antall József rakpart

Right on the riverbank 200m south of Parliament is a poignant **Holocaust Memorial**: dozens of shoes cast in iron, marking the spot where hundreds of Jewish adults and children were machine-gunned by the Arrow Cross, their bodies thrown into the Danube. Before being massacred, they were made to remove their coats and footwear, which were earmarked for use by German civilians.

Note that access from Parliament is dangerous as it means crossing the busy embankment road; the nearest crossing is down by the tram stop before the Lánchíd.

Parliament

Országház • V, Kossuth Lajos tér; entry is through the Visitor Centre (Látogatóközpont), down the steps at the northern end of the Parliament by the Tisza monument • Tours in English daily 10am, noon, 1pm, 2pm & 3pm (no tours on national holidays); tours in other major languages at different times • EU citizens with passport 2400Ft, otherwise 6000Ft; the ticket office opens at 8am and tickets sell fast, so you're best off purchasing online in advance at ⓦ jegymester.hu/parlament • ☎ 1 441 4000, ⓦ parlament.hu

The Hungarian **Parliament** building makes the Houses of Parliament in London look humble, its architect Imre Steindl having larded Pugin's Gothic Revival style with Renaissance and Baroque flourishes. Sprawling for 268m along the embankment, its symmetrical wings bristle with finials and 88 statues of Hungarian rulers, surmounted by a dome 96m high (alluding to the date of the Magyar conquest; see p.211). Though most people are impressed by the building, the poet Gyula Illyés once famously dismissed it as "no more than a Turkish bath crossed with a Gothic chapel" – albeit one that cost 38,000,000 gold forints. One weakness in the design was the white limestone of the exterior, which has been degraded by the elements and pollution; since 1925 it has required almost constant cleaning and replacement.

For centuries, Hungarian assemblies convened wherever they could, and it wasn't until 1843 that it was resolved to build a permanent "House of the Motherland" in Pest-Buda (as the city was then called). By the time work began in 1885, the concept of Parliament had changed insofar as the middle classes were now represented as well, though over ninety percent of the population still lacked the right to vote. Gains were made in 1918, but they were soon curtailed under the Horthy regime, just as the attainment of universal adult suffrage in 1945 was rendered meaningless after 1948 by a Communist dictatorship. The introduction of multiparty democracy in 1990 was symbolized by the removal of the red star from Parliament's dome and the replacement of Communist emblems by the traditional coat of arms featuring the crown of King Stephen – whose Coronation Regalia is now on show in the building's Dome Hall.

The interior

The **guided tour of the interior** feels a little rushed, and groups are quite big, but on balance it is worth the reasonably priced entry fee. Having passed through a security check, the extent to which the interior is accessible depends on Parliament's activities, but you can be sure of seeing the main staircase, the Dome Hall and the Lords Chamber, if nothing else.

Despite its archaic style, the building was high-tech for its time, being air-conditioned via blocks of ice in the basement that kept it at the constant temperature of 25ºC which the architect reckoned was most conducive to thought – since modern air conditioning was installed, MPs have complained of back pains. Statues, carvings, gilding and mosaics are ten-a-penny, lit by lamps worthy of the Winter Palace – but there are also cosy touches such as the individually numbered brass ashtrays where peers left their cigars smouldering in the lounge while they popped back into the chamber to hear someone speak; a good speaker was said to be "worth a Havana".

Following a procession along a series of grand corridors, you come to the **main staircase**, flanked by stained-glass windows by Miksa Róth and ceiling frescoes by Károly Lotz. From here, you're led towards the **Dome Hall**, where guards holding drawn sabres flank the **Coronation Regalia**, whose centrepiece, **St Stephen's Crown** (see box, p.57), has symbolized Hungarian statehood for over a thousand years. The hall, standing at 27m high, is concealed within an outer dome which, at 96m high, is exactly the same height as St Stephen's Basilica. Passing through the upper house lobby, you proceed to the **Lord's Chamber**, with seating for 453 members situated amidst a dazzling flourish of oak panelling, gold-plated decor and colourful murals.

Once back downstairs, you're left to your own devices to enjoy a small **exhibition**, which for the most part documents the building's principal architects, designers and artists, not least Steindl himself, who never actually lived to see Parliament's official completion – his death coming just one month prior to its opening in October 1902. Here, too, is the battered red star that once sat atop the dome (see above).

Museum of Hungarian Parliament

V, Kossuth Lajos tér • Daily April–Oct 8am–6pm; Nov–March 8am–4pm • Free

Housed inside the Parliament visitor centre, the **Museum of Hungarian Parliament** offers an illuminating insight into the country's parliamentary system, which is the longest-running in Europe after the UK. The roster of **exhibits** is impressive: Széchenyi's smoking cap and travelling inkwell, Kossuth's ceremonial sabre, Deák's writing implements, and Batthyány's ministerial chair and the gold-plated key to his

ST STEPHEN'S CROWN

The much revered **St Stephen's Crown**, the jewel of the Coronation Regalia on display in the Parliament building, consists in fact of two crowns joined together: the cruciform crown that was sent as a gift by Pope Sylvester II to Stephen for his coronation in 1000, and a circlet given by the Byzantine monarch to King Géza I. The distinctive bent cross was caused by the crown being squashed as it was smuggled out of a palace in a baby's cradle. At other times it has been hidden in a hay-cart or buried in Transylvania, abducted to Germany by Hungarian Fascists and thence taken to the US, where it reposed in Fort Knox until its return home in 1978, together with Stephen's crystal-headed sceptre, a fourteenth-century gold-plated orb and a sixteenth-century sword made in Vienna, used by his successors. Under the Dual Monarchy, Habsburg emperors ruled Hungary in the name of St Stephen, and travelled to Budapest for a special coronation ceremony, traditionally held in the Mátyás Church in the Vár.

2

coffin. Here too are several items of smashed-up furniture, the result of one particularly stormy session in the House of Representatives in 1904, following accusations by the minority party that the then ruling government had lost all authority; there's also some remarkable **footage** of the street riots that followed. The exhibition concludes with more footage, this time of the swearing-in ceremony of József Antall, Hungary's first democratically elected prime minister, in 1990.

Museum of Ethnography

Néprajzi Múzeum • V, Kossuth Lajos tér 12 • Tues–Sun 10am–6pm • 1000Ft • ☎ 1 473 2400, ⓦ neprajz.hu

The little-visited – but very worthwhile – **Museum of Ethnography** is housed in an extraordinary neo-Renaissance pile on the northeastern side of Kossuth Lajos tér. Originally built as the Palace of the Supreme Court, petitioners would have been overawed by its lofty, gilded main hall, whose ceiling bears a fresco, by Károly Lotz, of the goddess Justitia surrounded by allegories of Justice, Peace, Revenge and Sin. Thereafter the building functioned as the home of the Socialist Worker's Party, before the National Gallery took up residence, staying here until 1973.

The museum's **permanent exhibition** on Hungarian folk culture occupies thirteen rooms on the first floor (off the left-hand staircase) and helpfully is fully captioned in English. Exhibits from all over the Carpathian Basin, including musical instruments, bear traps, painted furniture and plentiful photos, are well presented under headings such as "Institutions" and "Peasant Work"; in particular look out for the selection of beautifully crafted wooden toys, including a train, bow and arrow, and a horse and cart. There is, though, only occasional reference to the range of ethnic groups who lived in Habsburg-ruled Hungary. Though few of the beautiful costumes and objects on display are part of everyday life in Hungary today, you can still see them in parts of Romania, such as Maramureş and the Kalotaszeg, which belonged to Hungary before 1920.

Temporary exhibitions (on the ground and second floors) cover anything from Hindu rituals to musical instruments from around the world, while over Easter and Christmas there are **concerts** of Hungarian folk music and dancing, and **craft fairs**.

Újlipótváros

Szent István körút, the section of the Nagykörút running from Nyugati Station to the Danube, marks the end of Lipótváros – but there are a few sights further out in **Újlipótváros** (the XIII District) that are worth a mention.

Holocaust memorials

Running up from the *körút* parallel to the river is Pozsonyi út, a bustling tree-lined street leading to **Szent István Park**, the prewar social hub of a wealthy Jewish

2

neighbourhood. The park is an apt site for a **monument to Raoul Wallenberg**, who gave up a playboy life in neutral Sweden to help the Jews of Budapest in 1944 (see p.67). The monument was constructed in the 1950s but "exiled" to Debrecen in eastern Hungary before being stashed away for decades, only taking its rightful place in Budapest in 1999.

There is another less-well-known Holocaust memorial some 100m north in the riverside Vizafogó Park at the end of Veső utca. The **Martyrs' Memorial**, by the Greek sculptor Agamemnon Makrisz, is a copy of the composition he made earlier for the Mauthausen concentration camp, and has nine figures standing with their arms upraised. Erected in 1986, this was the first major public memorial to the wartime murder of the Jews – and typically it was hidden away up here.

Lehel tér market hall
Lehel Csarnok • XIII, Lehel tér • Mon 6am–5pm, Tues–Fri 6am–6pm, Sat 6am–2pm
Heading 500m eastwards along Csanádi utca will take you to **Lehel tér**, notable for its picturesque 1930s reconstruction of the ruined Romanesque church at Zsámbék, west of Budapest. Beyond lies the **Lehel tér market hall**, which may look like a stylistic mishmash but it's a true locals' market and has a great set of stalls selling vegetables, fruit, meat and dairy products, and loads of freshly baked goodies.

Pinball Museum
Flipper Múzeum • XIII, Radnóti Miklós utca 18 • Wed–Fri 4pm–midnight, Sat 2pm–midnight, Sun 10am–10pm • 3000Ft • ☎ 030 900 6091, ⓦ flippermuzeum.hu
Budapest's most unusual – and unquestionably its most colourful – attraction is the **Pinball Museum**, a repository of some 130 gaming machines and the largest museum of its type in Europe. The private collection of fanatic Balazs Palfi, this bunker-like warren of rooms is crammed with machines from all over the world, though these are mostly American-made, including some vintage 1940s and 1950s wooden-framed versions, plus other games such as table hockey and air basketball. The light and sound sensation is such that you may need a break or two, so it's just as well that your entry ticket is valid on a come-and-go basis.

DOHÁNY UTCA SYNAGOGUE

Terézváros and Erzsébetváros

Terézváros (Theresa Town, the VI District) is home to the State Opera House, the Music Academy and several bar-filled squares, making it one of the most vibrant parts of the city. Its main thoroughfare, Andrássy út, is Budapest's longest, grandest avenue, running in a perfect straight line for two and a half kilometres up from Erzsébet tér to Hősök tere and the Városliget. With its coffee houses, high-end fashion shops and grey-stone edifices laden with dryads, not to mention the Opera House, the avenue retains something of the style that made it so fashionable in the 1890s, when "Bertie" the Prince of Wales drove its length in a landau, offering flowers to women as he passed.

● EATING

QUICK BITES

Bors	31
Kádár Étkezde	19
Montenegrói	
Gurman	27
PizzaMe	22

RESTAURANTS

Café Bouchon	5
Dang Muoi	3
Dobrumba	29
Fausto	36
Félix Hélix	20
Frici Papa	15
Funky Pho	8
Kazimír	26

Két Szerecsen	12
Kis Parázs	32
Klassz	11
Köles	16
Köleves	21
Krizia	6
M	17
Menza	9
Spinoza	28
Il Terzo Cerchio	30

CAFÉS

9 Bar	18
Cirkusz	25
Cube	4
Eco Café	2
Fragola	14
Fröhlich	23
Hisztéria Cremeria	7
London Coffee Society	33
Magvető	34
Mai Manó	10
Művész	13
New York	24
Podma Café	1
Sock's	35

■ DRINKING AND NIGHTLIFE

Alterego	2
Amigo Bar	15
Anker't	7
CoXx	18
Csak a Jó Sör	6
Doblo	16

Fekete Kutya	14
Kadarka	8
Kiadó	3
Kisüzem	12
Kuplung	5
Mazel Tov	9

Mika Tivadar	11
Most	4
Pótkulcs	1
Rácskert	13
Szimplakert	17
Szociális Helyiség	10

■ ACCOMMODATION

Benczúr	2
Casati	11
Caterina	6
Continental Hotel Zara	13
Corinthia Grand Royal	9
easyHotel	4
Home-Made Hostel	8

K&K Opera	10
Mamaison Hotel Andrássy	1
Marco Polo	14
Medosz	7
Radisson Blu Béke	3
Soho	12
Star Inn	5

● SHOPPING

Brush Shop	17
Budapest Poster Gallery	10
Deák Erika Galéria	2
Fókusz Könyváruház	19
Garden Studio	11
Herend	8
Irók Boltja	3
Játékszerek anno	1
Játék Udvar	13
Judaica	15

Knoll	4
Kóser piac	18
Mai Manó Galéria	6
Manier	5
Massolit Books	12
Sóos Fotó	16
Térképkirály	7
Tisza Shoes	20
Veritas	14
Wave	9

TERÉZVÁROS AND ERZSÉBETVÁROS

To the south of Király utca, the mainly residential **Erzsébetváros** (Elizabeth Town, the VII District) is composed of nineteenth-century buildings whose bullet-scarred facades, adorned with fancy wrought-ironwork, conceal a warren of dwellings and leafy courtyards. There is certainly no better part of Pest to wander around, soaking up the atmosphere. The old buildings have made the district popular for a distinctive form of nightlife in the "ruin gardens": bars set up in derelict plots or old houses that were previously awaiting development or demolition.

This is also the old **Jewish quarter** of the city, which was transformed into a ghetto during the Nazi occupation and almost wiped out in 1944–45, but has miraculously retained its cultural identity. Its current resurgence owes much to increased contacts with international Jewry, and a revival of interest in their religion and roots among the eighty-thousand-strong Jewish community of Budapest, which had previously tended towards assimilation, reluctant to proclaim itself in a country where anti-Semitic prejudices linger.

ARRIVAL AND GETTING AROUND

3

Terézváros The stretch of Andrássy út up to the Oktogon – where it meets the Nagykörút (Great Boulevard) – is within walking distance of Deák tér, and the whole length of the boulevard is served by metro line #1. Trams circle the Nagykörút night and day, and several trolleybus lines run through the two districts out to the Városliget.

Erzsébetváros The obvious starting point for exploring the area is the Dohány utca Synagogue, a short walk down the Kiskörút from the metro interchange at Deák tér.

Terézváros

Laid out in the late nineteenth century, **Terézváros** was heavily influenced by Haussmann's redevelopment of Paris, and at that time it was one of the smartest districts in the city. Under Communism, the area became pretty run-down, but the appeal of the old apartment blocks lining its streets has brought in the middle classes; luxury brands such as Gucci and Louis Vuitton have moved in, the villas near the park have recovered their value and café society flourishes around Liszt Ferenc tér.

Andrássy út was inaugurated in 1884 as the Sugár (Radial) út, but was soon renamed after the statesman Count Gyula Andrássy, and it was this name which stayed in popular use throughout the years when this was officially Stalin Avenue (1949–56) or the Avenue of the People's Republic (1957–89).

State Opera House

Állami Operaház • VI, Andrássy út 22 • English-language tours of the interior daily 2pm, 3pm & 4pm; tickets available from the shop to the left in the foyer • 2900Ft • ☎ 1 332 8197, ⓦ opera.hu (for programmes; see p.184), ⓦ operavisit.hu (for tours)

The **State Opera House** was founded by Ferenc Erkel, the composer of Hungary's national anthem, and occupies a magnificent neo-Renaissance pile built in 1875–84 by Miklós Ybl. It can boast of being directed by Mahler (who was driven out by the anti-Semitism he experienced in the city), hosting performances conducted by Otto Klemperer and Antal Doráti, and sheltering two hundred local residents (including Kodály) in its cellars during the siege of Budapest. The 1260-seat auditorium was the first in Europe to feature an iron fire curtain

HIDDEN GEMS: TERÉZVÁROS AND ERZSÉBETVÁROS

Robert Capa Photographic Center See p.62

Miksa Róth Múzeum See p.69

Dinner at Beszálló See p.162

Backgammon evening in Félix Hélix See p.165

Friday táncház at the Rácskert See p.178

Wine at Doblo See p.177

Concert at the Liszt Music Academy See p.184

Sunday farmers' market in Szimplakert See p.190

(installed after a blaze at the Vienna Opera House), underfloor heating and air-conditioning. Its chandelier weighs three tonnes, and 2.7 kilos of gold were used to gild the fixtures. To the left of the stage is the box used by Emperor Franz Josef's wife Sisi (see p.149), who loved Hungarian opera as much as he detested it. The upstairs reception rooms and downstairs foyer are equally lavish, festooned with portraits and busts of Hungarian divas and composers.

Nagymező utca

Northeast along Andrássy út from the Opera House, the first major junction is **Nagymező utca**, somewhat optimistically nicknamed "**Broadway**" because of its clutch of theatres and nightclubs. Outside the Operetta Theatre at no. 17, take a look at the **statue** of the composer **Imre Kálmán**, lounging on a bench; better known to the world as Emmerich Kalman, he penned such operetta favourites as *The Gypsy Princess* and *Countess Maritsa* – it's a genre that wins Hungarian hearts with its combination of music and melodrama; the bronze computer beside it lists his greatest works. Two blocks down from Nagymező utca, on Paulay Ede utca, take a peek at the **New Theatre**, whose blue-and-gold early Art Deco facade and foyer (by Béla Lajta in 1909) look superb.

Mai Manó House (Hungarian House of Photography)

Mai Manó Ház (Magyar Fotográfusok Háza) • VI, Nagymező utca 20 • Mon–Fri 2–7pm, Sat & Sun 11am–7pm • 1500Ft • ☎ 1 473 2666, Ⓦ maimano.hu

During the interwar years, the best-known club on Nagymező utca was the *Arizona* at no. 20: "the most glamorous nightclub I have ever visited," said Patrick Leigh Fermor, who went there on his way across Europe. It was run by Sándor Rozsnyai and his wife, Miss Arizona. However, he was sent to a concentration camp and she was murdered by the Arrow Cross in 1944 (which inspired Pál Sándor's 1988 film, *Miss Arizona*, starring Hanna Schygulla and Marcello Mastroianni). The bottle-green-tiled building was the former home of the Habsburg court photographer **Mai Manó**, who had this striking eight-storey studio-house constructed in 1894. On the first floor is an excellent photographic bookshop and gallery, while the two floors above host temporary exhibitions – the colourful café on the ground floor (see p.172) is a well-frequented haunt.

Robert Capa Contemporary Photographic Center

Robert Capa Kortárs Fotográfiai Központ • VI, Nagymező utca 8 • Mon–Fri 2–7pm, Sat & Sun 11am–7pm • 1500Ft • ☎ 1 413 1310, Ⓦ capacenter.hu

The **Robert Capa Contemporary Photographic Centre** is named after the renowned war photographer (and co-founder of Magnum Photos) who was born in Budapest in 1913. A fabulous space, it is the venue for the city's most important photographic exhibitions, including the annual Hungarian Press Photo Competition, which usually takes place in April and May; if your visit coincides, this is well worth attending. In any case, do take a peek inside to see the Art Nouveau features by József Rippl-Rónai and Ödön Lechner; it's worth nipping into the Art Deco lobby of the Tivoli Theatre next door, too.

Miklós Radnóti statue

VI, Nagymező utca

Outside the eponymous theatre at no. 11 Nagymező utca lounges a statue of one of Hungary's finest poets, **Miklós Radnóti**, whose most powerful poems were written while serving in a Jewish labour brigade in the war (see p.226). When his body was exhumed eighteen months after he was shot in 1944, a notebook of his last poems was discovered in his pocket; Radnóti now lies in Kerepesi Cemetery (see p.82). There are several more excellent sculptures of Radnóti in the Varga Museum in Óbuda (see p.117).

Paris Department Store

Párizsi Nagyáruház • VI, Andrássy út 39

With a glass facade that soars up five floors, it's impossible to miss the striking Art Nouveau frontage of the **Paris Department Store** which, when it opened in 1911, was the first department store in the city and boasted a roof terrace and even an ice rink. If it is open, it is worth having a look inside to see how the restoration has preserved the sweeping lines of the vast interior. There is a surprising contrast on the first floor at the back: the **Lotz terem**, which was a ballroom dating from 1885 in a neighbouring casino, is magnificently decorated in frescoes by Károly Lotz. And if the rooftop bar is open, it offers superb views over the city.

Liszt Music Academy

Liszt Zeneakadémia • VI, Liszt Ferenc ter 8 • Guided tours daily 1.30pm • 3500Ft • ☎ 1 462 4600, ⓦ zeneakademia.hu

Crammed with the terraces of bars and restaurants, **Liszt Ferenc tér** is named after the eponymous composer, a **statue** of whom stands in the middle of the square – the great man hammers an imaginary keyboard with his vast hands, blind to the drinkers and diners surrounding him. Presiding over the far end of the square is the **Music Academy** that bears his name. Founded by Liszt in 1875 – though it didn't move here until 1907, having originally been based in Liszt's apartment on Andrássy út (see p.64) – the entire building has been beautifully renovated, re-establishing the Academy's status as Budapest's most prestigious concert venue. The florid exterior is dominated by Stróbl's statue of a seated Liszt, while the magnificent Art Nouveau entrance hall, designed by Aladár Körösfői Kriesch, is flush with green Zsolnay tiles and golden mosaics. The two gilded auditoriums, meanwhile, manifest glorious decor that matches the quality of the music played here (see p.184). In any case, the guided tour is well worth fifty minutes of your time.

3

The Oktogon

Andrássy út meets the Nagykörút at the **Oktogon**, an eight-sided square flanked by eclectic buildings. With 24-hour fast-food chains, and trams and taxis running along the Nagykörút through to the small hours, the Oktogon never sleeps. During the Horthy era it rejoiced in the name of Mussolini tér, while under the Communists it was called November 7 tér after the date of the Bolshevik revolution.

House of Terror

Terror Háza • VI, Andrássy út 60 • Tues–Sun 10am–6pm • 2000Ft, audioguide 1500Ft • ☎ 1 374 2600, ⓦ terrorhaza.hu

With stern, dark-grey walls, blacked-out windows and an ominous black frame that surmounts the building, the **House of Terror** was once the dreaded headquarters of the state secret police. Dubbed the "House of Loyalty" by the Fascist Arrow Cross during World War II, it was subsequently used for the same purpose by the Communist **ÁVO**. After the reimposition of Soviet rule, the building was thoroughly sanitized before being handed over to the Communist Youth organization.

Before beginning, you might consider an audioguide, which will save you the trouble of reading the English-language sheets in each room, though the latter pack far more information, and you can also take them away. Upon entering the atrium, you are confronted with a Soviet tank sitting in a pool of water, alongside hundreds of images of ÁVO victims, before you proceed to the second floor (you take the lift, then work downwards).

To the sound of thumping, industrial-style music, the exhibition begins with "Double Occupation", which documents the respective Nazi and Soviet occupations, courtesy of some powerful video footage. The next couple of rooms deal with the reign of the feared Arrow Cross, before you get to the main subject of the museum: the Soviet "liberation" and the emergence of Communism with its associated themes of religious persecution, resistance, interrogation and

THE ÁVO

The **Communist secret police** began as the Party's private security section during the Horthy era, when its chief, **Gábor Péter**, betrayed Trotskyites to the police to take the heat off their Stalinist comrades. After World War II it became the 9000-strong Államvédelmi Osztály or **ÁVO** (State Security Department), its growing power implicit in a change of name in 1948 – to the State Security Authority or **ÁVH** (though the old acronym stuck). Ex-Nazi torturers were easily persuaded to apply their skills on its behalf, and its network of 41,000 informers permeated society. So hated was the ÁVO that any members caught during the Uprising were summarily killed, and their mouths stuffed with banknotes (secret policemen earned more than anyone else).

intimidation. The focus here is inevitably on the activities of the Soviet-style **PRO** (**Political Security Department**), which subsequently became the ÁVO and then the ÁVH, though all three organizations were headed up by Gábor Péter (see box above), whose desk and phone remain in situ. Throughout, there are moving testimonies from many of those arrested and detained on suspicion of anti-Bolshevik activities – tens of thousands of "class enemies" were interned in forced labour camps such as the notorious Recsk camp in northeastern Hungary. No less compelling is the Communist propaganda film of Nagy and his cohorts in court attempting to defend themselves against charges of counter-revolutionary activities.

From the first floor a lift descends, almost imperceptibly, to the darkened bowels of the building, and as it does so, a tape plays one prisoner's last moments before execution. Down in the **basement**, you'll find a reconstructed torture chamber and cells, alongside pictures of some of those who were kept here, as well as further and even more harrowing testimonies. There's coverage, too, of the events surrounding the 1956 Revolution, including some remarkable footage and a green, bullet-riddled overcoat.

Liszt Memorial Museum

Liszt Ferenc Emlékmúzeum • VI, Vörösmarty utca 35 • Mon–Fri 10am–6pm, Sat 9am–5pm • 1500Ft • Concerts every Sat at 11am 1500Ft, or 2200Ft for concert and museum • ☎ 1 413 0440, ◍ lisztmuseum.hu

The old Liszt Music Academy was also where the composer – who was the Academy's first president – lived from 1881 until his death in 1886. The three rooms that once comprised the first-floor apartment now harbour the **Liszt Memorial Museum**, the centrepiece of which is the drawing room and its extensive collection of pianos; the star exhibit is a Chickering Grand given to Liszt in 1880, atop which sits a silver music stand, complete with his portrait and a bust of Beethoven, among others. Among the wealth of personal memorabilia on display in the study-bedroom are letters, books and scores, items of clothing, and a bronze cast of Liszt's right hand by Stróbl; here, too, is his composing desk which, rather ingeniously, features a pull-out keyboard.

Kodály körönd

Kodály körönd, named after the composer Zoltán Kodály, is one of Budapest's most elegant squares, albeit flanked by four neo-Renaissance mansions in various states of disrepair. During World War II, the *körönd* (circus) was named Hitler tér, prompting the émigré Bartók to vow that he would not be buried in Hungary so long as anywhere in the country was named after Hitler or Mussolini. Curiously, there is no statue of Kodály here, but instead, there are statues of three military heroes who fought in the wars against the Ottomans, namely Miklós Zrinyi, János Botthány and György Szondy, in addition to a statue of the poet Bálint Balassa.

Kodály Memorial Museum

Kodály Emlékmúzeum • VI, Andrássy út 89 • Wed–Fri 10am–noon & 2–4.30pm, by prior appointment only on ☎ 1 352 7106; at least two days' notice is required • 900Ft • ⊕ kodaly.hu

In the northeast corner of Kodály körönd, the ground-floor flat where Zoltán Kodály lived until his death in 1967 now houses the **Kodály Memorial Museum**, preserving his library, dining room and salon, the last of which keeps his grand piano as well as a rich assemblage of folk art, which Kodály was particularly fond of collecting during his various trips. A fourth room is used for temporary exhibitions, often pertaining to Kodály himself.

Ferenc Hopp Museum of Asiatic Arts

Hopp Ferenc Ázsiai Művészeti Múzeum • VI, Andrássy út 103 • Tues–Sun 10am–6pm • 1000Ft • ☎ 1 322 8476, ⊕ hoppmuseum.hu

Lurking just northeast of the Kodály körönd, the **Ferenc Hopp Museum** presents temporary displays of works from the vast collection of more than twenty thousand items amassed by optician and art collector Ferenc Hopp (1833–1919) during his regular and extensive travels around Southeast Asia. It's also worth taking a look around the beautifully landscaped **oriental garden**, complete with a Jain shrine from India, a Brahma statue from Vietnam, and an imposing Chinese moon gate.

3

Post Office Museum

Posta Múzeum • VI, Benczúr utca 27 • Tues–Sun 10am–6pm • 500Ft • ☎ 1 269 6838, ⊕ postamuzeum.hu

Since being established in 1881, the wonderful **Post Office Museum** has had a somewhat nomadic existence, only moving to its current home here in the Benczúr House (with which the postal service has long had various associations) in 2012. The Hungarian Postal Service (Magyar Posta) itself was founded in 1867, following the country's separation from Austria, and its history since is surprisingly noteworthy. Indeed, it can boast a series of notable firsts: in 1869, it became the first country in the world (along with Austria) to introduce the postcard, while in 1881 it was one of the first to install a telephone exchange – thanks largely to the work of inventor and telephone pioneer Tivadar Puskás, a colleague of Thomas Edison. More impressive, though, were the technical innovations, from the manufacture and introduction of mechanically emptied mailboxes, to the use of petrol-driven vehicles for mail collection and delivery, at the end of the nineteenth century – as testified by the vintage delivery vehicles designed by engineer János Csonka.

Erzsébetváros

One of the centres of the new cool Budapest is **Erzsébetváros**, separated from **Terézváros** by the narrow **Király utca** (the main road through the area before Andrássy út was built). The vibrant "ruin garden" (*romkocsma*) movement that has spread through the city started among the decaying apartment blocks and empty plots of the old **Jewish quarter** (see box, p.66). The run-down stock of the district continues to attract big money in housing and retail developments such as the **Madách sétany**, cutting swathes through the old city, or doing up older parts such as the Gozsdu-udvar or Kazinczy utca.

Dohány utca Synagogue

Dohány utcai Zsinagóga • VII, Dohány utca 2–8 • March, April & Oct Mon–Thurs & Sun 10am–6pm, Fri 10am–4pm; May–Sept Mon–Thurs & Sun 10am–8pm, Fri 10am–4pm; Nov–Feb Mon–Thurs & Sun 10am–4pm, Fri 10am–2pm • 4000Ft including the Jewish Museum • ☎ 70 533 5696, ⊕ greatsynagogue.hu

One of the landmarks of Pest, the splendid **Dohány utca Synagogue** (also known as the Great Synagogue, Nagy Zsinagóga) is Europe's largest synagogue and the second biggest in the world after the Temple Emmanuel in New York, with 3600 seats and a total capacity for over five thousand worshippers. It belongs to the **Neolog** community,

THE JEWISH QUARTER

In the streets fanning out to the east of Károly körút lies Budapest's old **Jewish quarter**. After Josef II's reforms in 1783 allowed Jews back into Pest for the first time since the defeat of the Turks, they were invited to live in the grounds of Count Orczy's house between Király utca and Madách tér. Thereafter they flourished, and the Pest community grew from eight percent of the population in 1800 to twenty-three percent in 1920. In April 1944 this was chosen by the Nazis as the location of Budapest's Jewish **ghetto** – a sign on Wesselényi utca by the synagogue marks where the ghetto gate stood. All Jews living outside the ghetto were compelled to move in. As their menfolk had already been conscripted into labour battalions intended to kill them from overwork, the 70,000 inhabitants of the ghetto were largely women, children and old folk, crammed into 162 blocks of flats, with over 50,000 of them (in buildings meant for 15,000) around Klauzál tér alone. For **guided walks** around the Jewish quarter, contact Jewish Heritage Tours (see p.29).

3

a Hungarian denomination combining elements of Reform and Orthodox Judaism. Today, eighty percent of Hungarian Jewry are Neologs, but their numbers amounted to only twenty percent before the Holocaust, which virtually wiped out the Orthodox and Hasidic communities in the provinces. Neolog worship includes features that are anathema to other denominations, not least organ music during services.

Designed by a Viennese Gentile, Ludwig Förster, the building epitomizes the so-called Byzantine-Moorish style that was popular in the 1850s, and attests to the patriotism of Hungarian Jewry – the colours of its brickwork (yellow, red and blue) being those of Budapest's coat of arms. In the 1990s the synagogue was restored at a cost of over $40 million; the work was funded by the Hungarian government and the Hungarian-Jewish diaspora, notably the Emanuel Foundation, fronted by the late Hollywood actor Tony Curtis, who was born of 1920s emigrants.

The interior

The magnificent, cathedral-like **interior** was designed by Frigyes Feszl, the architect of the Vigadó concert hall. Arabesques and Stars of David decorate the ceiling, the balconies for female worshippers are surmounted by gilded arches, and the floor is inset with eight-pointed stars. The layout reflects the synagogue's Neolog identity, with the *bemah*, or Ark of the Torah, at one end, in the Reform fashion, but with men and women seated apart, according to Orthodox tradition. On Jewish festivals, the place is filled to the rafters with Jews from all over Hungary, whose chattering disturbs their more devout co-religionists. At other times, the hall is used for concerts of classical or klezmer music, as advertised outside.

Jewish Museum

Heading up to the second-floor **Jewish Museum** (Zsidó Múzeum), to the left of the main synagogue entrance, note a relief of Tivadar (Theodor) Herzl, the founder of modern Zionism, who was born and taught on this site. In the foyer is a gravestone inscribed with a menorah (seven-branched candlestick) from the third century AD – proof that there were Jews living in Hungary six hundred years before the Magyars arrived. The first three rooms are devoted to Jewish festivals, with beautifully crafted objects such as Sabbath lamps and Seder bowls for the Passover festival, some from medieval times. The final room focuses on the Holocaust in Hungary, with chilling photos and examples of anti-Semitic propaganda. Oddly, the museum says nothing about the huge contribution that Jews have made to Hungarian society, in every field from medicine to poetry.

The cemetery and Heroes' Temple

The **cemetery** beside the synagogue only exists at this spot because the Nazis forbade Jews from being buried elsewhere – one of many calculated humiliations inflicted on the Jewish quarter (by then a walled ghetto) by the local SS commander, Eichmann. Some 2281 Jews are interred beneath simple headstones, erected immediately after the Red Army's liberation of the ghetto on January 18, 1945. Beyond the cemetery looms the cuboid, domed **Heroes' Temple**, inaugurated in 1931 in honour of the ten thousand Jewish soldiers who died fighting for Hungary during World War I. It now serves as a synagogue for everyday use and so may not be open to tourists.

Raoul Wallenberg Memorial Park

Just beyond the cemetery, you enter the **Raoul Wallenberg Memorial Park**, named after the Swedish consul who saved twenty thousand Jews during World War II. Armed with diplomatic status and money for bribing officials, Wallenberg and his assistants plucked thousands from the cattle trucks and lodged them in "safe houses", manoeuvring to buy time until the Russians arrived. He was last seen alive the day before the Red Army liberated the ghetto; arrested by the Soviets on suspicion of espionage, he died in the Gulag. The park's centrepiece is a **Holocaust Memorial** by Imre Varga, shaped like a weeping willow, each leaf engraved with the names of a family killed by the Nazis. On the plinth are testimonials from their relatives living in Israel, the US and Russia. Behind it, glass panels by the artist Klára Szilárd commemorate the sixtieth anniversary of the neighbouring Goldmark Hall.

3

Goldmark Hall

Goldmark terem • VII, Wesselényi utca 7 • March–Oct Mon–Thurs & Sun 10am–5.30pm, Fri 10am–3.30pm; Nov–Feb Mon–Thurs & Sun 10am–3.30pm, Fri 10am–1.30pm • 800Ft

Named after Károly Goldmark, the composer of the opera *The Queen of Sheba*, the **Goldmark Hall** houses the fascinating small Jewish Quarter exhibition. This display of objects from the **Jewish Archives** includes the screenplay for a performance of *The Magic Flute* performed here in 1942; opened in 1931, the hall was the only place where Jews were able to perform in the city at that time. There's also a coffee grinder that was one family's sole possession to survive the Holocaust, and a pair of weighty scales from the *Fröhlich* patisserie on Dob utca (see p.171), which opened in 1953 and is still going strong today.

Monument to Carl Lutz

Northeast of the Dohány utca Synagogue, Rumbach Sebestyén utca crosses Dob utca, where you'll see a **monument to Carl Lutz**, the Swiss consul who saved many Jewish lives during the war (see p.53). His monument – a gilded angel swooping down to help a prostrate victim – is locally known, rather unimaginatively, as "the figure jumping out of a window".

Rumbach utca Synagogue

Rumbach utca zsinagóga • VII, Rumbach Sebestyén utca 11–13

In happier times, each Jewish community within the quarter had its own place of worship, with a *yeshiva* (religious school) and other facilities within an enclosed courtyard invisible from the surrounding streets – as epitomized by the **Rumbach utca Synagogue**. Built by Otto Wagner in 1872, for the so-called "Status Quo" or middling-conservative Jews, it now belongs to the Neolog community though is presently closed pending an extensive restoration project; it's unlikely to be finished before 2020, at the very earliest. As a plaque outside notes, the building served as a detention barracks in August 1941, from where up to 1800 Slovak and Polish refugees were deported to the Nazi death camps.

Király utca

The official boundary between Terézváros and Erzsébetváros runs down the middle of **Király utca**, once the main street here before Andrássy út was built. In the 1870s it contained fourteen of the 58 licensed brothels in Budapest, and as late as 1934 Patrick Leigh Fermor was told that "any man could be a cavalier for five pengöes" here. After decades of shabby respectability under Communism the street has undergone quite a revival, and is now flush with cafés, bars and restaurants, plus interior design and furniture boutiques.

Gozsdu-udvar

At Király utca 13, a grey stone portal leads into the **Gozsdu-udvar**, a 200m-long passageway built in 1904 and running through to Dob utca 16. Connecting seven courtyards, it was a hive of life and activity before the Holocaust; after many years of dereliction, it has been sensitively redeveloped and new restaurants, cafés and bars once again populate this atmospheric space; there's also a terrific Sunday flea market. As you walk down the Gozsdu-udvar, you cross the **Madách Walk** (Madách sétány), a controversial plan to modernize the district through the creation of new apartments, shops and restaurants. The Walk runs parallel to Király utca, stretching from Madách tér on the Kiskörút through to Kazinczy utca.

Dob and Kazinczy utcas

These two streets form the axis of Budapest's three-thousand-strong Orthodox Jewish community. At Dob utca 22 the *Fröhlich* patisserie (see p.171) is a popular haunt for locals and visitors, while further along there's a kosher butcher at no. 35. Down to the right on Kazinczy utca are a kosher baker and pizzeria, opposite the kosher *Carmel* restaurant. The recent pedestrianizing of this section of the street makes it all the more enjoyable to wander around.

Orthodox Synagogue

Kazinczy utcai Zsinagóga • VII, Kazinczy utca 29 • March–Oct Sun–Thurs 10am–6pm, Fri 10am–4pm; Nov–Feb Sun–Thurs 10am–4pm, Fri 10am–1pm • 1000Ft • ☎ 1 351 0524, ⓦ kazinczyutcaizsinagoga.hu

Looming over the middle of Kazinczy utca is the **Orthodox Synagogue**, built by Béla and Sándor Löffler in 1913 in the Art Nouveau style, with a facade melding into the curve of the street, and an interior with painted rather than moulded motifs. A smaller wood-panelled synagogue for winter use, a *yeshiva* and the *Hanna* Orthodox kosher restaurant are all contained within an L-shaped courtyard that can also be entered via an arcade on Dob utca.

Museum of Electrotechnology

Magyar Elektrotechnikai Múzeum • VII, Kazinczy utca 21• Tues–Fri 10am–5pm, Sat 10am–4pm • 800Ft • ☎ 1 342 5750, ⓦ elektromuzeum.hu

For something quite different from the rest of the sights in the Jewish quarter, visit the **Museum of Electrotechnology**, set in a former electricity substation. Its devoted curators can demonstrate the world's first dynamo (invented in 1859 by Áynos Jedlik, a Benedictine monk), tie irons and a child-proof plug from 1902 in rooms devoted to such topics as the history of light bulbs and the Hungarian section of the **Iron Curtain**, along the border with Austria. Other exhibits include spotlights that lit up the Fisherman's Bastion in the 1920s, wrought-iron street lamps, and a wonderfully nostalgic collection of vintage audio equipment, including radio transistors, tape decks and stereos. This museum is certainly one for diehards, and captions are in Hungarian only, but the beauty of early domestic electrical contraptions comes across anyway.

Dohány utca

Dohány utca takes its name – Tobacco Street – from the tobacco factory that once stood on the corner of Sip utca – close to the sadly neglected Art Deco **Metro Klub** that stands there today; now a hostel, the facade still bears a shallow, brightly coloured relief featuring a rocking horse flanked by toy soldiers. This narrow thoroughfare sweeps through the lower part of Erzsébetváros from the Kiskörút and out across the Nagykörút towards the Garment District.

Hungária Baths

VII, Dohány utca 44

Halfway between the two *körúts* you pass the magnificent Art Nouveau front of the ill-fated **Hungária Baths**. When the complex opened in 1908, its main selling point – its large number of private bathtubs – was its downfall, as the building of better-equipped apartments reduced demand. The baths closed in 1929, and were used after the war as a cinema and then as a theatre until 1965. By the 1980s the inside was crumbling fast and the baths were close to complete ruin – the little that could be saved can be seen on the facade and in the lobby of the *Continental Hotel Zara* (see p.153) that now stands in its place.

New York Palace

At the junction of Dohány utca and the Nagykörút is a piece of old Budapest that for many years lay derelict. Like the *Gresham Palace* on Széchenyi tér (see p.49), the **New York Palace** is a Budapest landmark also associated with an insurance company, in this case the New York, which commissioned the building in 1895 and included in the plans a magnificent coffee house – the *New York Café* (see p.172) – which became one of the great literary cafés of interwar Budapest. Under Communism the edifice housed a publishers, and its Beaux-Arts facade – with a small Statue of Liberty high up on the corner – survived being rammed by a tank in 1956. Now the luxury *Boscolo* hotel, its gilded and frescoed restaurant-cum-coffee-house is worth a look, even if you don't want to fork out to eat there.

Miksa Róth Museum

Róth Miksa Múzeum • VII, Nefelejcs utca 26 • Tues–Sun 2–6pm • 800Ft • ☎ 1 341 6789, ⓦ rothmuzeum.hu

Northeast of the New York Palace, among the backstreets near Keleti Station, the **Miksa Róth Museum** showcases the work of the eponymous artist, a leading figure in the Hungarian Art Nouveau movement. Formerly a furniture factory, Róth purchased the building in 1911, living here until his death in 1944. The museum reveals the wonderful diversity of his work – both in stained glass and in mosaics – which can also be seen in the Parliament, the *Gresham Palace*, the Music Academy and the Jewish Museum. Otherwise, three rooms – living room, bedroom and study – remain in their original state, complete with furnishings designed by Róth himself.

The Városliget and the stadium district

Both Hősök tere (Heroes' Square) and the Városliget (City Park) were created in the late nineteenth century to celebrate the thousand-year anniversary of the Magyar conquest of Hungary in 895 AD (though neither was ready on time, so the commemoration took place in 1896). The Városliget is currently undergoing major changes – extensive re-landscaping, renewed infrastructure, and the relocation of several museums here alongside the creation of some new ones – though works are unlikely to be completed much before 2020. The area's other chief attractions are the Museum of Fine Arts, Széchenyi Baths, Vajdahunyad Castle and Budapest's wonderful zoo. Further out lie the city's most important stadia, and one of Budapest's Art Nouveau masterpieces, the Geological Institute.

ARRIVAL

Városliget The best ways to reach the Városliget from the centre are on the yellow #1 metro line or bus #105, but trolleybus #74 from the Dohány utca Synagogue, #75 from the Margít híd and #72 from Arany János utca metro station

are also useful.

The stadium district To reach the stadium district, catch trolleybus #75 or the red #2 metro line from the centre of town to the Puskás Ferenc Stadion stop.

Hősök tere

The enormous ceremonial plaza of **Hősök tere** is flanked by two galleries resembling Greek temples. At its centre is the **Millennary Monument** – Budapest's version of Nelson's Column in London – consisting of a 36m-high column topped by the figure of the Archangel Gabriel who, according to legend, appeared to Stephen in a dream and offered him the crown of Hungary. Around the base are figures of Prince Árpád and his chieftains, who led the seven Magyar tribes into the Carpathian Basin. They look like a wild bunch; one of the chieftains, Huba, even has stag's antlers strapped to his horse's head. As a backdrop to this, a semicircular colonnade displays statues of Hungary's most illustrious leaders, from King Stephen to Kossuth.

During the brief Republic of Councils in 1919, when the country was governed by revolutionary Soviets, the square was decked out in red banners and the column enclosed in a red obelisk bearing a relief of Marx. In 1989, it was the setting for the ceremonial reburial of Imre Nagy and other murdered leaders of the 1956 Uprising (plus an empty coffin representing the "unknown insurgent") – an event which symbolized the dawning of a new era in Hungary. Today it's usually thronged with tourists, but also hosts the odd event such as the National Gallop in September.

Műcsarnok

XIV, Hősök tere • Tues, Wed & Fri–Sun 10am–6pm, Thurs noon–8pm • 1800Ft • ☎ 1 460 7000, 🌐 mucsarnok.hu

On the southeast side of the Hősök tere is the **Műcsarnok** (Exhibition Hall), also called the Palace of Art (not to be confused with the Palace of Arts, covered on p.87). A Grecian pile with gilded columns and a mosaic of St Stephen as patron of the arts, it was inaugurated in 1896 just in time for the Millenary celebrations. Its magnificent facade and foyer are in contrast to the four austere rooms used for **temporary exhibitions** (two or three at a time), often of modern art, though these are usually of a high quality – with anything from graphic art to multimedia and installation art.

VÁROSLIGET AND THE STADIUMS

Museum of Fine Arts

Szépművészeti Múzeum • XIV, Hősök tere • Tues–Sun 10am–6pm with late opening on alternate Thurs till 10pm • 1800Ft • ☎ 1 469 7100, ⓦ szepmuveszeti.hu

On the northwest side of Hősök tere, the **Museum of Fine Arts** is the pan-European equivalent of the Hungarian National Gallery, housed in an imposing Neoclassical building completed in 1906, though without the gilt of the Műcsarnok. Note that a major four-year renovation project, due to be completed in 2018, means that the content, and/or layout, of the pictures is likely to be radically different from that outlined here – check the website for updates.

Lower ground floor

In the museum's bowels, a hippopotamus-tusk wand carved with spells to protect a child presages the small but choice **Egyptian Collection**, chiefly from the Late Period and Greco-Roman eras of Egyptian civilization. The highlights of the first room are four huge painted coffins and a child-sized one from Gamhud in Middle Egypt; *shabti* figures, intended to perform menial tasks in the afterlife; and mummified crocodiles and other creatures from the Late Period, when animal cults reached their apogee. In the second room, look out for the sculpted heads of a priestess of Hathor and a bewigged youth from the New Kingdom, the painted coffin of a priestess of Amun, and a tautly poised bronze of the cat goddess Bastet.

Across the basement lobby, the section entitled **Art around 1900** starts with **Symbolist** and **Decadent** works such as Franz von Stuck's *The Kiss of the Sphinx*, Arnold Böcklin's *Spring Evening*, and Hans Makart's *Nessus Carries off Deianeira*. The remainder musters a few works by the Hungarian **Art Nouveau** masters József Rippl-Rónai and Károly Ferenczy, an Utrillo street scene, some Bonnards and two famous images by **Oscar Kokoschka**: *Veronica's Veil* and the poster *Der Sturm*.

Ground floor

The rooms to the right of the entrance lobby are devoted to **ancient Mediterranean cultures** from Etruria to Athens, mainly represented by jugs and vases. Highlights include a pair of bronze shin-guards decorated with rams' heads, terracotta tiles portraying bestial deities, a man's torso and head from the pediment of a Campanian temple, lifelike busts of Roman worthies, and an early fifth-century-BC Etruscan grave marker with reliefs of funerary games.

Across the ground-floor lobby is an excellent **bookshop**, leading to a wing used for **temporary exhibitions** (requiring a separate ticket). Before heading upstairs, visit the grand **Renaissance Hall**, used for hanging large allegorical or religious works on loan from other museums; the **Baroque Hall** (often used for televised events), and the **Prints and Drawings Room** at the far end on the right, mounting temporary displays drawn from the museum's holdings of works by Raphael, Leonardo, Rembrandt, Rubens, Dürer, Picasso and Chagall.

The first floor: the Spanish Collection

The museum's forte is its hoard of **Old Masters**, based on the collection of Count Miklós Esterházy, which he sold to the state in 1871. The room numbering can make navigation here confusing: the main rooms have Roman numerals and smaller ones down the sides have Arabic digits.

The **Spanish Collection** of seventy works is arguably the best in the world outside Spain. Located off to the right at the top of the stairs, it kicks off with vivid altarpieces by unknown Catalans, such as the *Bishop-Saint Enthroned* (whose bewilderment belies his magnificent attire) in room II. Room V, beyond, has seven **El Grecos** – including *The Disrobing of Christ*, *The Agony in the Garden*, *The Apostle St Andrew* and *The Penitent Magdalene* – and a superb *Adoration of the Magi* by Eugenio Cajes.

Murillo's *Flight into Egypt* and *Holy Family with the Infant St John the Baptist* hang beside a tender *Holy Family* by **Zurbarán** in room IV; across the room are two depictions of St Andrew, one by Zurbarán and the gory *Martyrdom of St Andrew* by **Ribera**, together with **Velázquez**'s *Tavern Scene*. Room III next door has five **Goyas** ranging from war scenes (*2nd of May*) to portraits of the rich (*Señora Ceán Bermudez*) and humble (*The Knife-Grinder*). Murillo's *Madonna and Child with Angels Playing Music* is a highlight of room VI, and there's an annexe of Habsburg court portraits by Juan Martínez (room 1).

The Flemish Collection

Entering the adjacent **Flemish Collection** in room VII, Snyders' gigantic *Hawk in the Barnyard* and Van Valckenborch's nocturnal *Pilgrims Before a Forest* are overshadowed by room VIII, where the serenity of **Van Dyck**'s *St John the Evangelist* contrasts with the melodrama of **Rubens**' *Mucius Scaevola before Porsenna* and **Jordaens**' *The Satyr and the Peasant*.

Room IX segues into the **Dutch Collection** with an array of **Brueghels**, from Pieter the Elder's *Sermon of St John the Baptist* to Pieter the Younger's *Blind Hurdy-Gurdy Player* and Jan's *Paradise Landscape* and *Garden of Eden with the Fall of Man*. A copy of **Bosch**'s *The Bacchus Singers* (featuring a man making himself vomit) hangs in room VII. The rest of the Dutch collection is on the floor above, reached by stairs (or a lift) off room IX. There you'll find the *Parable of the Hidden Treasure* by **Rembrandt** and his pupil Gerard Dou and other works from his studio in room XVIII to the right, with portraits by **Hals** and wildlife scenes by **Melchior de Hondecoeter** in rooms XXVII and XXVI, off to the left.

The German Collection

Back on the first floor, in room X, the **German Collection** opens with **Angelika Kauffmann**'s *The Wife of Count Esterházy as Venus* – a strumpet with her jewellery box – and darkly Gothic works by **Cranach the Elder**, such as *Christ and the Adulteress* and *The Lamentation, and the Holy Virgin in Prayer* by **Dürer**. In Cranach's *Salome with the Head of St John the Baptist,* Salome displays his head on a platter with the nonchalance of a hostess bringing out the roast. Every emotion from awe to jealousy appears on the faces in **Holbein**'s *Dormition of the Virgin*, at the far end of the room. Don't overlook **Dürer**'s *Young Man* with an enigmatic smile, sharing room XIV with pictures by **Altdorfer**.

From Romanticism to Postimpressionism

For a change of mood, cross the lobby and enter **From Romanticism to Postimpressionism**, where Room XII displays **Courbet**'s wild landscapes and life-sized *Wrestlers*, **Corot**'s *Remembrance of Coubrou* and **Rodin**'s sculpture *The Brazen Age*. In the small rooms alongside you'll find orchards and river-views by **Renoir** and **Monet** (room XIX), *Lady with a Fan* by **Manet**, a **Pissarro** Paris scene and **Toulouse-Lautrec**'s *These Ladies* (room XX), as well as a little-known **Gauguin**, *Black Pigs*, from his Tahitian period and more Monets (room XXII). Teutonic Romanticism rules in room XIII, with Von Lenbach's *The Triumphal Arch of Titus in Rome* and Böcklin's *Centaur at a Forge*.

English and French art

The single room (XIV) devoted to **English art** musters a dullish portrait apiece by Hogarth, Reynolds and Gainsborough, and a melodramatic theatre scene by Zoffany, while the highlight of **French art until 1800** in room XVI is *The Rest on the Flight into Egypt* by **Poussin**. However, both are totally outshone by the display of masters that follows.

Italian Collection

The superb **Italian Collection** occupies nine rooms and can be viewed in a very rough chronological order by entering from the lobby opposite the Spanish section, or in reverse from the English or French rooms; some backtracking is inevitable. A tradition of gilded altarpieces such as *The Mystic Marriage of St Catherine* (room XXIV) gave rise to **Boccacio**'s masterpiece *The Adoration of the Infant Christ*, usually displayed near **Titian**'s *Madonna and Child with St Paul* in the later rooms. **Bellini**'s pig-eyed *Queen of Cyprus* and a possible **Fra Angelico** landscape are the highlights of room XXIII.

Room XIX boasts **Raphael**'s exquisite *Esterházy Madonna* – a Virgin and Child with the infant St John – and two **Giorgione** paintings, one a self-portrait, leading to a powerful **Bronzino** portrait in room XX. The highlights of the neighbouring Room XVII are a couple of portrayals of Venetian doges, a friendly one by **Titian** and another, more watchful character by **Tintoretto**, who is also represented by *Hercules Expelling the Faun from Omphale's Bed*; and a couple of **Veronese** paintings, including one of a disagreeable grandee in an ermine-trimmed robe.

Room XVIII hosts the biblical epic *Jael and Sara*, by **Artemisia Gentileschi**. Finally, up by the English collection, room XV has two superb **Canalettos**: one of Vienna and the other of the Pantheon, though the latter is poorly displayed high above a door. Also on show are a handful of landscapes by **Guardi** and some paintings by **Tiepolo**.

Ötvenhatosok tere

Ötvenhatosok tere, 56ers' Square, the wide avenue running off alongside the Városliget, was called Parade Square in Communist times, as it was here that Party leaders reviewed marching soldiers. Up to 1956 they did so beneath a 25m-high statue of Stalin that was torn down during the Uprising and hammered into bits for souvenirs. Later, a statue of Lenin was erected in its place, which in turn was removed to the Memento Park (see p.127) in 1989. Today it serves as the setting for occasional **fairs** and **concerts**.

Ötvenhatosok tere monuments
XIV, Ötvenhatosok tere

Today, three monuments mark the distance that Hungary has travelled since 1989. The **Timewheel** is the world's largest hourglass, a metal canister 8m in diameter that rotates 180° on the last day of each year, symbolizing Hungary's accession to the European Union in 2004. Where the Stalin statue once stood, you now see the **Monument to the Uprising**, a forest of oxidized columns merging into a stainless steel wedge, beside a Hungarian flag with a circle cut out, recalling the excision of the hated Soviet symbol in 1956. Beyond this, a crucifix rises over the foundations of the **Virgin Mary Church** that the Communists demolished in 1951.

The Városliget

The **Városliget** (City Park) starts just behind Hősök tere, where the fairy-tale towers of **Vajdahunyad Castle** rear above an island girdled by an artificial lake that's used for **boating** in the summer and transformed into a splendid outdoor **ice rink** in winter. Between May and September, pedaloes can be rented out (1800Ft/1hr) from the lakeside building just down from the tourist office. Otherwise, the park is a great spot to take the kids, with numerous play areas and acres of space to run around.

Vajdahunyad Castle
XIV, Városliget • **Chapel at Ják** May–Oct daily 10am–4pm • 100Ft

Like the Városliget, **Vajdahunyad Castle** was created for the Millenary Anniversary celebrations of 1896, proving so popular that the temporary structures were replaced by permanent ones. Vajdahunyad is a catalogue in stone of architectural styles from the kingdom of Hungary, incorporating parts of two Transylvanian castles and a replica of the Romanesque **chapel at Ják**, with a splendidly carved portal and a Renaissance courtyard that makes a romantic setting for evening **concerts** from July to mid-August.

Next to the church sits the hooded **statue of Anonymous**. Completed in 1903, this nameless chronicler to King Béla is the prime source of information about early medieval Hungary, though the existence of several monarchs of that name during the twelfth and thirteenth centuries makes it hard to date him (or his chronicles) with any accuracy.

Agriculture Museum

Mezőgazdasági Múzeum • XIV, Vajdahunyad Castle • Tues–Fri 10am–4pm, Sat & Sun 10am–5pm • 1200Ft • ☎ 1 363 1117, ⓦ mezogazdasagimuzeum.hu

Filling the bulk of the castle these days are the extensive displays of the **Agriculture Museum**. It's generally a mixed bag, but what is certainly worth the entrance fee is the first section, which includes a superb hoard of archeological finds, including exquisitely produced items of pottery such as milk jugs and butter churns. The breeding of livestock became more extensive in the fourteenth and fifteenth centuries, particularly on the Great Plain, where **Hungarian breeds** such as the long-horned grey cattle and woolly Mangalica pigs were favoured. By the nineteenth century the **Great Plains** were one of Europe's most valuable grain-producing regions and by the time the Hungarian Ministry of Agriculture was established in 1889, only the US produced more maize.

The remainder of the exhibition, comprising displays on forestry, hunting and fishing, is eminently missable, though the craftsmanship in antique crossbows and rifles exquisitely inlaid with leaping hares and other prey is undeniably impressive, as is a 270-year-old dugout boat carved from a single piece of oak, which was found at Lake Balaton, southwest of the capital.

Apostles' Tower and Gatehouse Tower

XIV, Vajdahunyad Castle • **Gatehouse Tower** Daily 9am–8pm • 300Ft • **Apostles' Tower** Guided tours on the hour Tues–Sun 10am–5pm • 600Ft • Combined ticket for both towers 700Ft

The castle's **Gatehouse Tower** features a small exhibition on the history of the castle, though the main reason for climbing the 56 steps is to take a stroll along the battlements, from where there are splendid views of both the castle and the park laid out before you. Ascending the 150 steps of the nearby **Apostles' Tower** (which can only be visited on a guided tour) affords even finer views. Modelled on the famous Clock Tower in Sighisoara, Romania, this chunky Gothic structure features a lovely wood-carved Hungarian coat-of-arms on the exterior and, inside, stairways lined with frescoes depicting hunting scenes.

Budapest Zoo

Állatkert • XIV, Állatkerti körút 6 • Jan, Feb, Nov & Dec daily 9am–4pm; March & Oct daily 9am–5pm; April & Sept daily 9am–5.30pm; May–Aug Mon–Thurs 9am–6pm, Fri–Sun 9am–7pm; animal houses open 1hr later and close 30min before the zoo itself • 2800Ft, family 7900Ft • ☎ 1 273 4900, ⓦ zoobudapest.com

The delightful Elephant Gates welcome visitors to **Budapest Zoo**, which opened its doors in 1866, thus establishing itself as one of the world's oldest. The wonderful Art Nouveau pavilions, designed by Kornél Neuschloss and Károly Kós and originally dating back to 1912, seem like the last word in zoological architecture: the exotic **Elephant House**, resembling a Central Asian mosque, the **India House** with its big cats, and the **America Tropicana** (formerly the **Palm House**) with its magnificent **aquarium** below. In recent years, there have been some notable arrivals: 2007 saw the world's first birth of a rhino conceived by artificial insemination; and in 2013, the zoo welcomed Asha, the first elephant calf born here for more than fifty years. Look out too for **children's events**, evening concerts and exhibitions under the Great Rock.

Municipal Circus

Fővárosi Nagycirkusz • XIV, Állatkerti körút 12 • Showtimes Wed, Thurs & Fri 3pm, Sat 11am, 3pm & 7pm, Sun 11am & 3pm • 1500–4500Ft; children 1500–3100Ft • ☎ 1 343 8300, ⓦ fnc.hu

The highly regarded **Municipal Circus** traces its origins back to 1783, when the Hetz

Theatre played to spectators on what is now Deák Ferenc tér. Today the building has a changing programme featuring anything from tiger-taming and horse shows to musical clowns, ice shows, illusionists and Chinese and Cuban acrobats. It also hosts a big international circus festival every even-numbered year in January – check the website for details.

Széchenyi Baths

Széchenyi Gyógyfürdő • XIV, Állatkerti körút 11 • Daily 6am–10pm • ☎ 1 363 3210, ⓦ szechenyispabaths.com

The **Széchenyi Baths** (see p.202) could be mistaken for a palace, so grand is its facade – albeit one that's looking a little tired these days. Outside is a statue of the geologist Zsigmondy Vilmos, who discovered the thermal spring that feeds its outdoor pool and Turkish baths. This is perhaps the city's best venue for mixed-sex bathing, and in one of the large outdoor pools you can enjoy the surreal spectacle of people playing **chess** while immersed up to their chests in steaming water – so hot that you shouldn't stay in for more than twenty minutes. The best players sit at tables around the pool's edge (the late former world champion **Bobby Fischer** among them in the 1980s); bring your own set if you wish to participate.

The stadium district

The **stadium district**, 1km south of Vajdahunyad Castle, is chiefly notable for the **Puskás Ferenc Stadium** (Puskás Ferenc Stadion), which stages international football matches. The latest version of the stadium is currently under construction, pending completion in 2019, hopefully in time to host four matches of the pan-continental Euro 2020 Football Championships. Originally known as Népstadion (People's Stadium) and built in the early 1950s by fifty thousand Budapestis who "volunteered" their labour, on Soviet-style "free Saturdays", it was renamed in 2002 after the legendary footballer Ferenc Puskás (1927–2006), who captained the Mighty Magyars in their remarkable 6–3 victory over England at Wembley Stadium in 1953 (a team that went unbeaten for a world record of 32 consecutive games), before defecting to forge a second career at Real Madrid.

To the west of the stadium is the smaller **Kisstadion**, which is commonly used for ice sports, while to the east Stalinist statues of healthy proletarian youth line the court that leads to the indoor **Papp László Sportaréna** (or Aréna), a mushroom-shaped silver structure which hosts both concerts and sporting events – Papp was the first boxer to win three Olympic gold medals (1948, 1952 and 1956). The **Stadion bus station** completes this concrete ensemble.

Geological Institute

Földani Intézet • XIV, Stefánia út 14 • Visits by appointment only • Free • ☎ 1 251 0999, ⓦ mfgi.hu • Trolleybus #75 from Puskás Ferenc Stadion metro station or from City Park

The **Geological Institute** was one of the major edifices in Budapest designed by Ödön Lechner; indeed, much of the original design has been preserved simply because the institute has never had enough money to make major changes. The exterior is as striking as his Post Office Savings Bank (see p.53) and Museum of Applied Arts (see p.84), with a gingerbread facade, scrolled gables and steeply pitched Transylvanian roofs patterned in bright blue tiles, crowned by four figures supporting a globe on their backs. Lechner put numerous geological references into the design and originally planned to have dwarves holding up the globe. The institute has a small **Geological Museum**, but the helpful staff will happily show visitors round the building itself, with its gingerbread stucco and faux lapis lazuli stairways. (Ernő Rubik, the man behind the famous cube, left his mark here: he designed the museum's cataloguing system.) The little concrete turret on top of the rear of the building is said to be a 1950s machine-gun turret, though it never saw any action.

Józsefváros and Ferencváros

Separated from Erzsébetváros by Rákóczi út, which runs out to Keleti Station, Józsefváros (the VIII District) is an amalgam of high and low life. While the Hungarian National Museum, Eötvös Loránd University and the Ervin Szabó Library on Múzeum körút make for a lively student quarter, its seedier hinterland beyond the Nagykörút district – nicknamed "Chicago" between the wars – still has an association with vice and crime, though this is now largely redundant as the area around the old apartment blocks near the Rákóczi tér market hall has become increasingly gentrified. You can wander safely anywhere in Józsefváros by day, and between the Kiskörút and Nagykörút in the small hours, but elsewhere stick to main roads and avoid pedestrian underpasses after midnight – particularly around Keleti Station, where Kerepesi Cemetery and the Police History Museum are worth a visit by day.

JOZSEFVÁROS AND FERENCVÁROS

ERZSÉBETVÁROS

Stadium District

Keleti Station

Deák tér

Blaha Lujza tér

Erkel Theatre

II. János Pál papa tér

BAROSS TÉR

KEREPESI ÚT

Keleti pu

Police History Museum

Kerepesi Cemetery

Urânia Cinema

Astoria

Unger Ház

ELTE University

Italian Institute

National Museum

Radio Building

Szabó Ervin Library

Kálvin tér

Fővám tér

Great Market Hall

Corvinus University

Bálna Building

Nehru Part

A38

Egyetemisták Parkja

ELTE University

National Theatre

Közvágóhíd Station

Ludwig Museum

Palace of Arts

Budapest Park

Rákóczi tér

Rákóczi tér Market Hall

JÓZSEFVÁROS

Józsefváros Parish Church

Fountain of Hungarian Truth

Magnum Szauna

IF Kávézó

Budapest Music Center

Museum of Applied Arts

Corvin Film Palace

Paul Street Boys

Corvin Promenade

Corvin-negyed

Kilián Barracks

St Francis of Assisi Church

Trafó Centre

Holocaust Memorial Centre

Goethe Institute

Szauna 69

Boráros tér Station

Botanical Garden

Natural History Museum

Klinikák

FERENCVÁROS

River Danube (Duna)

● EATING

QUICK BITES

Butter Brothers	9
Caffé Torino	6
Club 93	2

RESTAURANTS

Borbíróság	8
Fülemüle	3
Kék Ló	4
Múzeum	7
Rosenstein	1

CAFÉS

Múzeum Café & Bistro	5
Nándori	12
Rengeteg RomKafé	11
Tamp & Pull	10

■ DRINKING AND NIGHTLIFE

Corvintető	1
Csiga	2
Élesztő	7
Grund	6
Jedermann	9
Jonás	8
Lumen	3
Monyó	4
Trapéz	5

● SHOPPING

Fakopáncs	3
Magyar Pálinka Háza	1
Szalamibolt	4
Tasting Table	2

■ ACCOMMODATION

Atrium Fashion	1
Brody House	4
Casa de la Musica	3
City Hostel Pest	6
Museum	2
Palazzo Zichy	5

0 _____ 300
metres

Üllői út – leading to the airport – marks the boundary of the adjacent **Ferencváros** (Franz Town, the IX District), once the most solidly working-class area of the inner city. Today, **Ráday utca** and the backstreets behind the wonderful **Great Market Hall** on Vámház körút are full of hip restaurants and bars; luxury condos rise where teenage insurgents once fought, and the district's historic far-right sympathies are challenged by a **Holocaust Memorial Centre**. Along the riverbank there is much ongoing development all the way down to the **Palace of Arts** complex, which is transforming the balance of the district. Children will enjoy the **Natural History Museum**, while football fans might want to see Fradi in action at the sparkling new **Groupama Aréna** (see p.197).

ARRIVAL	JÓZSEFVÁROS AND FERENCVÁROS
Public transport links for the two districts are excellent, and include metro lines #2, #3 and #4, trams #4 and #6	along the Nagykörút and tram #2, which runs down the Pest bank of the Danube to the Palace of Arts.

Józsefváros

Named after the heir to the Habsburg throne in 1777, Józsefváros has many faces. The grand but neglected apartment blocks speak of an old middle-class suburb that fell into decline. Rákóczi tér became the centre of the city's sex industry and cheap housing in the streets behind it attracted a big Roma population; the prostitutes have long since gone, however, and gentrification has spread rapidly throughout the district.

Múzeum körút

Part of the Kiskörút, **Múzeum körút** separates the Belváros and Józsefváros. Aside from being curved rather than straight, it resembles Andrássy út in miniature, lined with trees, shops and grandiose buildings. Immediately beyond the East–West Business Centre by the Astoria junction stands the old faculty of the **Eötvös Loránd Science University** (known by its Hungarian initials as ELTE). It's named after the physicist Loránd Eötvös, whose pupils included many of the scientists who later developed the US atomic bombs at Los Alamos, including Edward Teller, "Father of the Hydrogen Bomb". A few paces further along, at no. 12, you'll find the **Múzeum**, which was one of the earliest coffee houses in Pest (not to be confused with the 24-hour café at no. 10). Its original frescoes and Zsolnay ceramic reliefs dating from 1885 still grace what has long since become a restaurant (see p.167). Across the street, at no. 7, pop into the courtyard of the neo-Renaissance **Unger House** (Unger ház), built by Miklós Ybl in 1852. Now sadly neglected, it still features fabulous old wooden floor tiles and a glazed first-floor colonnade; meanwhile intricately carved capitals support the crumbling arches.

Bródy Sándor utca

Running along the garden of the Hungarian National Museum (see p.80), **Bródy Sándor utca** is named after the eponymous nineteenth-century writer. The Renaissance-style mansion at no. 8 housed the lower chamber of the Hungarian Parliament from 1867 until its present building was completed, and is now home to the **Italian Institute**. Next door is the *Brody House*, one of the city's coolest hotels (see p.154). Diagonally across the street at nos. 5–7, is the **Radio Building**, from which ÁVO guards fired upon

---

HIDDEN GEMS: JÓZSEFVÁROS AND FERENCVÁROS

Ervin Szabó Library reading room See p.81

Kerepesi Cemetery See p.82
Paul Street Boys statue See p.84
Holocaust Memorial Centre See p.86

Fűvészkert Botanical Garden See p.86
Craft beers on the Jonás riverside terrace See p.179
Jedermann jazz bar See p.179

5

students demanding access to the airwaves, an act which turned the hitherto peaceful protests of October 23, 1956 into an uprising against the secret police and other manifestations of Stalinism.

Hungarian National Museum

Magyar Nemzeti Múzeum • VIII, Múzeum körút 14–16 • Tues–Sun 10am–6pm • 1600Ft, audioguide 750Ft • ☎ 1 327 7773, ⓦ hnm.hu

Like the National Library in the Royal Palace, the **Hungarian National Museum** was the brainchild of Count Ferenc Széchenyi (father of István), who donated thousands of prints and manuscripts to form the basis of its collection. Housed in a Grecian-style edifice by Mihály Pollack, it was only the fourth such museum in the world when it opened in 1847, and soon afterwards became the stage for a famous event in the **1848 Revolution**, when Sándor Petőfi (see box, p.46) first declaimed the *National Song* from its steps, with its rousing refrain "Choose! Now is the time! Shall we be slaves or shall we be free?" ("Some noisy mob had their hurly-burly outside so I left for home", complained the museum's director at the time.) Ever since, March 15 has been commemorated here with flags and speeches.

The basement and first floor

The museum has two lower levels devoted to medieval and Roman **stonework** – the latter starring a second-century-AD mosaic floor from a villa at Nemesvámos-Baláca in western Hungary. The darkened room to the left of the foyer displays the **coronation mantle**, allegedly donated to the Basilica of Székesfehérvár by King Stephen in 1031. Beautifully embroidered with gold thread, this exquisite silk robe was considered too fragile to be transferred to the Parliament building when the rest of the Coronation Regalia was moved there in 2000.

To the right of the foyer is the archeological exhibition, entitled **Between East and West**, which covers the pre-Hungarian peoples of the Carpathian Basin. Highlights of this outstanding hoard, roughly in chronological order, include animal figurines and anthropomorphic urns from the Copper Age, two magnificent bronze spoked wheels and, from the Iron Age, a fine assortment of gilded helmets, many of which were unearthed from Március 15 tér (see p.45). No less impressive are the prestigious ninth-century finds from Blatnica, in Slovakia, not least a remarkable iron and silver-gilt double-edged sword, as well as some gold harnesses. Winding up with the period of the Hungarian conquest (895 AD onwards), look out for some gorgeous, and extremely rare, sabretache plates – silver-plated pouches used to hold tools and suchlike.

The second floor

The main exhibition upstairs traces **Hungarian history** from the Árpád dynasty to the end of Communism, via twenty rooms, starting to the left side of the rotunda at the top of the stairs. Room 1 contains Béla III's crown, sceptre and sword, though more eye-catching is a thirteenth-century silver-gilt crown encrusted with gemstones found on Margaret Island. Room 2 is dominated by a wall fountain from the royal palace at Visegrád (see p.138), while room 6 is similarly consumed by a single piece, this time a huge carved Renaissance pew, commissioned by the Báthori family. Turkish weaponry and the ornate tomb of Count György Apafi in room 7 speak of the 150 years when Hungary was divided and its destiny decided by intriguers and warlords, including the Forgáchs and Nádasdys depicted in the oldest **portraits** in Hungary, hung in room 8 – the portrait of their contemporary, the infamous "Blood Countess" Erzsébet Báthori, is kept in storage. As the widow of national hero Ferenc Nádasdy, charged with torturing six hundred women to death and reputedly bathing in their blood to preserve her beauty, Báthori was walled up in her castle and the atrocity hushed up.

On the other side of the rotunda, room 9 covers the Rákóczi War of Independence (1703–1711), its star exhibit being a surprisingly low (and extremely uncomfortable-looking) armchair, made by Rákóczi himself during his year of exile. Hungarian reform takes centre-stage in room 11, with personalities like István Széchenyi to the fore – personal effects include handwritten journals and a pair of pistol barrels presented to him by the Duke of Wellington; here too is a rock sample from the Chain Bridge alongside a note from its architect, Adam Clark, plus the ceremonial trowel used to lay the foundation stone. Room 13, meanwhile, is given over to **Beethoven's Broadwood piano**, which was subsequently acquired by Liszt, some of whose keepsakes are also on display, notably his flamboyant pearl and emerald encrusted baton. There's comprehensive coverage of World War II: look out for the diary and whip of General Bandoltz (see p.52) as well as Horthy's heavily decorated uniform, Browning pistol, and the monogrammed suitcase he took to Germany following his arrest in 1944.

The last room, given over to the **Communist** era, features some memorable items, not least the right hand and left ear from the statue of Stalin torn down in 1956 (see p.74), and the miniature chess set belonging to Imre Nagy which he used in prison prior to his execution in 1958. There are also kitsch tributes to János Kádár, who reimposed Communist rule with a vengeance, but later liberalized it to the point that his successors felt able to abandon it entirely.

Ervin Szabó Library

Szabó Ervin Könyvtár • VIII, Szabó Ervin tér 1 • Mon–Fri 10am–8pm, Sat 10am–4pm, closed July, reduced hours in Aug • 200Ft • ☏ 1 411 5011, 🖰 fszek.hu

It seems almost miraculous that the ornate reading rooms of the **Ervin Szabó Library**, on the corner of Baross utca, survived unscathed from the fighting in the surrounding streets in 1956. Built in 1887 by the Wenckheim family – who enjoyed a near-monopoly on Hungary's onion crop – the library has come through a thorough modernization in sparkling form. At the main entrance on Reviczky utca, you can ask at the information desk about visiting the fourth-floor reading rooms, reached by a lovely wooden staircase.

Fountain of Hungarian Truth

VIII, Szabó Ervin tér

Outside the Ervin Szabó Library stands one of the few surviving monuments marking the hated Treaty of Trianon (see p.215): the so-called **Fountain of Hungarian Truth** (Magyar Igazság kútja). Erected in 1928, it honours the British press magnate Lord Rothermere, whose campaign against the treaty in the *Daily Mail* was so appreciated that he was offered the Hungarian crown. On June 4, the anniversary of the treaty's signing, nationalist and neo-Nazi groups gather to pay their respects.

Rákóczi tér

Behind the Ervin Szabó Library lies an atmospheric quarter of small squares and parochial schools; formerly shabby, it's now buzzing with cafés and bars popular with students. Having given a face-lift to **Mikszáth Kálmán tér** and much of Krúdy utca, the process of gentrification has crossed the **József körút** – one of the sleazier arcs of the Nagykörút – to embrace **Rákóczi tér**, the focus of street prostitution until it was outlawed in 1999. Now smartened up, the square boasts both a shiny metro station and one of Budapest's finest market halls (see p.190).

II János Pal pápá tér

II János Pal pápa tér (Pope John Paul II Square) was formerly known as Köztársaság tér, long associated with lynchings that were carried out in front of the Communist Party HQ here in 1956. The addition of a new metro station, alongside the presence of the **Erkel Theatre** (see p.184), Budapest's "second" opera house (named after the composer of the national anthem, Ferenc Erkel), has lent this square a pleasant air of respectability. A couple of blocks away lies **Keleti Station**, where the grittier side of life still prevails, though this is also much improved thanks to spruced-up Baross tér and new underpasses.

5

Police History Museum

Rendőrség-Történeti Múzeum • VIII, Mosonyi utca 7 • Tues–Sat 9am–5pm • Free • ☎ 1 477 2183, ⓦ rendormuzeum.com

A couple of blocks from Keleti Station, and marked by a sentry box, the **Police History Museum** charts the history and evolution of the Hungarian police through documents, weaponry and uniforms – some of the mannequins are a hoot – though the most absorbing displays dwell on some of Hungary's more notorious characters such as nineteenth-century cattle rustler and highwayman Sándor Rózsa, whose skull cap is exhibited here, and serial killer Béla Kiss, who is alleged to have murdered 23 women between 1900 and 1914, pickling their bodies before disposing of them in metal drums – strangely, he was never captured and his fate remains unknown; photos displayed here provide evidence of his gruesome deeds.

Kerepesi Cemetery

Kerepesi temető • VIII, Fiumei út 16 • **Cemetery** Daily: April & Aug 7am–7pm; May–July 7am–8pm; Sept 7am–6pm; Oct–March 7.30am–5pm • Free • **Funerary Museum** (Kegyeleti Múzeum) Mon–Fri 9am–5pm • Free

The **Kerepesi Cemetery** (also known as Nemzet Sírkert and Fiumei úti Sírkert) is the Père Lachaise of Budapest, where the famous, great and not-so-good are buried. Vintage hearses and mourning regalia in the **Funerary Museum** near the main gates illuminate the Hungarian way of death and set the stage for the necropolis. In Communist times, Party members killed during the Uprising were buried in a special plot near the entrance and government ministers in honourable proximity to Kossuth, while leaders and martyrs who "lived for Communism and the People" were enshrined in a starkly ugly **Pantheon of the Working Class Movement**; some have been removed by their relatives since the demise of Communism, and all the old Communist sections are looking distinctly unkempt – in contrast to the area for 1956 insurgents. Party

NOT DRAWN TO SCALE

A	Party dead of 1956
B	János Kádár
C	Lajos Batthyány
D	Mór Jókai
E	Lujza Blaha
F	Petőfi family
G	Gerbeaud
H	Chess Grandmasters
I	József Antall
J	Ferenc Deák
K	Ferenc Erkel
L	Martyrs of 1848
M	Kossuth Lajos
N	Communist Ministers
O	1956 Insurgents
P	Antal Szerb

PLAN OF KEREPESI CEMETERY

5

leader János Kádár – who ruled Hungary from 1956 to 1988 – rates a separate grave, heaped with plastic wreaths from admirers.

The florid **nineteenth-century mausoleums** of Hungarian historical giants Kossuth, Batthyány and Deák are quite extraordinary, though no less ostentatious is the mausoleum of József Antall, the first post-Communist prime minister of Hungary, who is honoured by a bizarre allegorical monument with riders on horseback struggling out from under a sheet.

Many of Hungary's **literary greats** also rate spots here, including twentieth-century poets Attila József (see p.55) and Endre Ady, and the writer Antal Szerb (see p.94), who has a very humble grave on the southern edge of the cemetery. The cemetery also holds the family tomb of Petőfi, though his own body was never found (see box, p.46). Other notables include the composer Erkel, the confectioner Gerbeaud and three chess grandmasters whose tombs are engraved with the chess moves that won them their titles. Finally, don't miss the Art Nouveau funerary arcades, at the end of which (the novelist Jókai's mausoleums) is the tomb of the diva **Lujza Blaha**, the "Nation's Nightingale", whose effigy is surrounded by statues of serenading figures.

Jewish cemetery

Izraelita temető • VIII, Salgótarjáni út 6 • Mon–Fri & Sun 8am–2pm • Free • The cemetery gates are on Salgótarjáni út, a 10min walk from the main entrance to Kerepesi Cemetery

Immediately east of Kerepesi lies an overgrown **Jewish cemetery**, with some beautiful Art Nouveau tombs of artists, politicians and industrialists, several designed by the brilliant architect Béla Lajta. That of **Manfred Weiss**, founder of the Csepel ironworks that once dominated the industrial island south of the city centre, is still maintained by Csepel's council, in gratitude and by way of apology for the fact that Weiss had to sign his factory over to the government in return for being allowed to leave Hungary with his family in 1944.

Ferencváros

Ferencváros was developed to house workers in the latter half of the nineteenth century, on the same lines as the more bourgeois Józsefváros. During the 1930s and 1940s, its population confounded Marxist orthodoxy by voting for the extreme right, who returned the favour by supporting the local football team **FTC** – popularly known as "**Fradi**" – which became the unofficial team of the opposition under Communism, subsequently known for its hooligan "ultras" (see p.197).

Corvinus University

Budapesti Corvinus Egyetem • VIII, Fővám tér 8 • Trams #2, #47 and #49

Standing at the Pest end of Szabadság híd, the **Corvinus University of Budapest** makes a fine sight from Buda at night, reflected in the river, and adds to the liveliness of the area by day. The building was originally Budapest's main **Customs House** (Fővámház) – hence the name of the square and the adjoining section of the Kiskörút, **Vámház körút**. The university was named after Karl Marx during Communist times and is still sometimes called the Economics University.

Great Market Hall

Nagycsarnok • VIII, Fővám tér 1–3 • Mon 6am–5pm, Tues–Fri 6am–6pm, Sat 6am–3pm

The magnificent wrought-iron **Great Market Hall** was originally opened in 1897, though badly damaged in World War II and only properly restored in the late 1990s. Today, it's as famous for its ambience as for its produce, and ranks highly on many tourists' list of things to see in Budapest. Downstairs, you'll find fresh fish, meat, fruit, vegetables and baked goodies, while the right-hand side is called Hungarikum utca (aka "tourist row"), which tells you all you need to know; here you'll find a plethora of

5

vendors selling paprika, Tokaj, foie gras and the like, though you'll almost certainly get better value elsewhere. Upstairs you'll find cheap stand-up food stalls and the excellent *Fakanal* self-service restaurant.

Museum of Applied Arts

Iparművészeti Múzeum • IX, Üllői út 33–37 • Tues–Sun 10am–6pm • 2000Ft, 3500Ft including temporary exhibitions • ☎ 1 456 5107, ⊕ imm.hu

The **Museum of Applied Arts** is the most flamboyant creation of Ödön Lechner, who strove to create a uniquely Hungarian form of architecture emphasizing the Magyars' Ugric roots, but was also influenced by Art Nouveau. Inaugurated by Emperor Franz Josef during the 1896 Millennial celebrations, it was given a rough reception, derided by some as "the palace of the Gypsy kings", thanks to its green-and-yellow-tiled dome, and a portico with ceramic Turkic motifs on an egg-yolk-coloured background. By contrast, the arcaded, all-white interior, with its glazed roof and elegantly arching girders, is reminiscent of Mogul architecture: at one time it was thought that the Magyars came from India.

Most of the exhibits in the permanent collection, entitled **Collections and Treasures**, were bequeathed to the museum by distinguished individuals and noble families, such as Archduke Joseph August of Austria and the Esterházys, with other items purchased from the World Exhibitions in Paris (1873) and Vienna (1878). Among the highlights is *Statue of Equestrian Archer*, a marvellous example of Han Dynasty pottery, an oversized Zsolnay vase entitled *Dancers Under the Stars* (this just one of many Zsolnay pieces), and a beautiful pair of stained-glass windows by Miksa Róth that once adorned the old *Café Japan*, now the Irók Boltja bookshop.

Donations from the museum's first two directors, György Ráth and Jenő Radisics, comprise a large chunk of the collection, with a dazzling array of clocks and mirrors among those pieces given by the former, and a selection of fancy tableware from the latter. Nothing, though, comes close to the gilt-copper-and-silver **astronomical clock**, commissioned by Emperor Maximilian II in 1566.

In addition to the permanent exhibition there are typically two **temporary exhibitions** on at any one time, which are invariably excellent.

Corvin köz

On the northeast corner of the Corvin negyed junction, duck into **Corvin köz**, the grand oval passage separating the **Corvin Cinema** from the surrounding flats, from which teenage guerrillas (some as young as 12) sallied forth to battle Soviet tanks in 1956. Since the fall of Communism, they have been honoured by a statue of a young insurgent outside the cinema. Its auditoriums are named after illustrious Hungarian actors or directors such as Alexander Korda – one of many Magyars who made it in Hollywood (see p.186).

Just around the corner from Corvin köz, on Práter utca, you'll find a delightful statue of the **Paul Street Boys** – the heroes of Ferenc Molnár's eponymous 1906 novel – portraying the moment they are caught playing marbles in the yard of their enemies, the Redshirts. The most widely sold and translated Hungarian book ever, it's both a universal tale of childhood and a satire on extreme nationalism. Just behind here, and carving a path through the old blocks between Üllői út and Práter utca, is **Corvin Promenade** (Corvin sétány), a mall and luxury apartment complex.

Kilián Barracks

IX, Üllői út 51

The Hungarian garrison of the **Kilián Barracks** was the first to join the insurgents during the 1956 Revolution, organizing youths already aware of street-fighting tactics due to an obligatory diet of films about Soviet partisans. It was in Budapest that the Molotov cocktail proved lethal to T-54s, as the "Corvin Boys" trapped columns in the

HUNGARIAN NATIONAL MUSEUM (P.80) >

5

backstreets by firebombing the front and rear tanks. Memorial plaques honour Colonel Pál Maleter and others who directed fighting from the Corvin Cinema. These days the barracks stand empty, but head through the graffitied passageway into the courtyard and you'll find the *Food Truck Udvar*, one of a growing number of superb street-food enterprises dotted around the city.

Holocaust Memorial Centre

Holokauszt Emlékközpont • IX, Páva utca 39 • Tues–Sun 10am–6pm • 1400Ft • ☎ 1 455 3333, ⓦ hdke.hu

Located within the grounds of the **Páva Street synagogue**, the **Holocaust Memorial Centre** is arguably even more chilling than the House of Terror (see p.63); think twice about bringing children here. The courtyard is dominated by a vast black glass wall inscribed with the names of over half a million Hungarian Jews lost in the Holocaust, while the entrance itself is framed by angled stone blocks listing over 1440 settlements that once had a Jewish presence, but which sadly no longer do. Like Libeskind's Jewish Museum in Berlin, the building, designed by István Mányi, is distorted and oppressive; darkened ramps resounding to the crunch of jackboots and the shuffle of feet lead to artefacts, newsreels and audiovisual testimonies relating the slide from "deprivation of rights to genocide".

From 1920 onwards, Jews in Budapest were increasingly stripped of their assets by right-wing regimes with the participation of local citizens, and Gypsies forced into work gangs. Under Admiral Horthy (there are some chilling photos of the Hungarian regent with Hitler), the interwar period was a time of increasingly repressive anti-Jewish measures, and the fate of both groups was effectively sealed in March 1944 following the German occupation. The section on pseudo-medical experiments makes for particularly grim reading, while the family stories and newsreel footage of the death camps after liberation are truly harrowing. Visitors emerge from the bowels of hell to find themselves within the glorious and sunlit Art Deco synagogue, built by Leopold Baumhorn in the 1920s and now beautifully restored. There's a very pleasant on-site café here, and the bookshop is worth a quick browse too.

On your way back to the main road it's worth a detour on to Liliom utca to see another striking building – an old transformer plant turned into an outstanding contemporary arts centre, **Trafó** (see p.183).

Natural History Museum

Magyar Természettudományi Múzeum • VIII, Ludovika tér 2 • Daily except Tues 10am–6pm • 1600Ft, 400Ft for dinosaur garden, 2000Ft for temporary displays • ☎ 1 210 1085, ⓦ nhmus.hu • Metro #3 to Klinikak or tram #24

Though slightly out on a limb, the **Hungarian Natural History Museum** is – on balance – just about worth a visit, but really only if you have children. From the entrance hall, dominated by a whale skeleton, you walk through to an **underwater room**, which has colourful fish in sea- and freshwater aquariums – the (rather tacky) mock seabed under the glass floor makes you feel as if you're walking on water, sort of. Upstairs, **Underground Secrets** offers up a dazzling array of minerals and other geological treasures, the star exhibit being a giant amethyst from Brazil as well as some meteorites from the US. Elsewhere there are extensive sections on dinosaur fossils, Hungarian animals and their habitats, and a Noah's Ark that focuses on animals under threat and what Hungary is doing for the environment. You'd be wise, though, to give the Dinosaur Garden exhibition a wide berth; it's really rather rubbish.

Botanical Garden

Füvészkert • VIII, Illés utca 25 • Daily: April–Oct 9am–5pm; Nov–March 9am–4pm • 950Ft • ☎ 1 210 1074, ⓦ fuveszkert.org

A pleasant, cooling retreat from the hustle and bustle of the city, Budapest's well-tended **Botanical Garden** was established by the Eötvös Loránd University faculty of medicine as long ago as 1771, before moving to its present site in 1847. Delightfully jungle-like, its main features are greenhouses, a pleasantly landscaped Asian garden with ponds and streams, and a magnificent Palm House fronted by neatly arranged herb gardens.

National Theatre

Nemzeti Szinház • IX, Bajor Gizi Park • ☎ 1 476 6868, ⓦ nemzetiszinhaz.hu • Tram #2 to Vágóhíd utca, or take the Csepel HÉV one stop from Boráros tér

Like something resembling a Ceauşescu folly, the **National Theatre** could have been plucked straight out of Bucharest, its exterior and environs strewn with random architectural references and statuary. The Classical facade is a replica of the frontage of the original theatre on Blaha Lujza tér, torn down to build the metro in 1964 – a Communist plot to undermine Hungary's identity, many said – which condemned the company to a dump in the backstreets of Pest while the debate continued as to where this national institution should be housed. A proposed move to Erzsébet tér never materialized and the theatre moved here in 2002.

Palace of Arts and Ludwig Museum

Művészetek Palotája • IX, Komor Marcell utca 1 • **Palace of Arts** ☎ 1 555 3001, ⓦ mupa.hu • **Ludwig Museum** Kortárs Művészti Múzeum • Tues–Sun 10am–8pm • 800Ft for permanent collection, 1600–2000Ft for temporary exhibitions • ☎ 1 555 3444, ⓦ ludwigmuseum.hu

Facing the National Theatre, the similarly vast **Palace of Arts** is home to the excellent Philharmonic Orchestra. Resembling a dull office block by day, it comes alive each evening with spectacular lighting and events (see p.183), from classical and operatic works to popular and world music, jazz and dance. No expense has been spared to make this a top venue; particularly in the main Béla Bartók concert hall, whose acoustics are so sharp that some orchestras are said to dislike it, as you can hear their mistakes.

The Palace also encompasses the **Ludwig Museum**, or Museum of Contemporary Art, established in 1996 to build upon an earlier bequest by the German industrialist Peter Ludwig, prints and portraits of whom hang by the entrance to the main exhibition hall. Note that at the time of writing, a fairly extensive renovation project was underway, hence not everything outlined here might be on show. That said, there are a few big-hitters you can be guaranteed to see, such as **US pop artists** Warhol (*Single Elvis*) and Lichtenstein (*Vicki*), paintings by **Picasso**, including *Musketeer with a Sword* and *Matador*, and **Yoko Ono**'s glass-encased, pristine-white chess set entitled *Play it by Trust* – the artist's metaphor for the futility of war.

Native and Central/Eastern European artists are well represented too, typically in such styles as Hyper-Realism and Neo-Primitivism. Look out, too, for the occasional piece by **Judit Reigl**, perhaps Hungary's most famous contemporary artist, best known for her visceral surrealist/abstract works of art. The museum also hosts first-class **temporary exhibitions** – so the permanent collection is not always on view.

MÁTYÁS CHURCH

The Vár and central Buda

The Vár (or Várhegy – Castle Hill) is Buda's most prominent feature.
A 1500m-long plateau encrusted with bastions, mansions and a huge
palace, it dominates both the Víziváros below and Pest, over the river,
making this stretch of the river one of the grandest, loveliest urban
waterfronts in Europe. Often referred to as the Várnegyed (Castle District),
the hill is studded with interesting museums, from the National Gallery
and the Budapest History Museum in the Royal Palace to the Golden Eagle
Pharmacy and the Telephone Museum, but it's equally enjoyable just
walking the streets and admiring such florid creations as the Mátyás
Church and the Fishermen's Bastion, or exploring the World War II Hospital
in the Rock and the surrounding nuclear bunkers and labyrinth of caves
that lie beneath the hill.

Between the castle and the river, the **Víziváros** is something of a quiet residential backwater in the heart of Buda, with a distinctive atmosphere but few specific sights other than the Lánchíd (Chain Bridge) and the Sikló (funicular) at the southern end, the **Church of St Anne** on **Batthyány tér** in the middle, and the **Király** and **Veli Bej baths** further up.

The area to the **north of the Vár** has a variety of attractions in the backstreets off Margít körút, notably a lively **market** and the **Millenáris Park**, comprising an intriguing exhibition, concert venue and children's indoor and outdoor play areas. Further north, on the edge of the affluent Rózsadomb district, is **Gül Baba's tomb**, one of Budapest's most significant Turkish remnants.

6

ARRIVAL

THE VÁR

By funicular The simplest and most novel approach to the Vár is to ride up to the palace by the Sikló, a renovated nineteenth-century funicular that runs from Clark Ádám tér by the Lánchíd (see p.103).

By bus From Pest, the most direct approach is to get bus #16 from Erzsébet tér across the Lánchíd to the lower terminal of the Sikló, or straight up to the Vár. From Széll Kálmán tér (on the red metro line #2) you can take buses #16, #16A or #116 from the raised side of the square, which all run through to Dísz tér.

On foot From Széll Kálmán tér head up Várfók utca or Ostrom utca to the Vienna Gate at the northern end of the Castle District. Walking from Batthyány tér via the steep

flights of steps (*lépcső*) off Fő utca involves more effort, but the dramatic stairway up to the Fishermen's Bastion is worth the sweat. There are also stairs leading up from the southern end of the Vérmező on the western side of the hill.

Lift A passenger lift by the Lion Gateway of the Royal Palace provides direct access to and from Dózsa tér, on the western foot of the hill (Mon 6am–7pm, Tues–Sat 6am–9m, Sun 9am–6.30pm; 100Ft).

CENTRAL BUDA

By bus and tram The red metro line and bus #16 are the best approach to Víziváros. For Rózsadomb, trams #4 and #6 skirt the southern edge, running between Pest and Széll Kálmán tér.

The Vár

The Vár's striking location and its strategic utility have long gone hand in hand: Hungarian kings built their palaces here because it was easy to defend, a fact appreciated by the Turks, Habsburgs and other occupiers. The **Royal Palace** serves as a reminder of this past, rising like a house of cards at the southern end of the hill, as proud yet insubstantial as those who ruled there while Hungary's fate was determined by mightier forces.

The buildings here have been almost wholly reconstructed from the rubble of 1945, when the Wehrmacht and the Red Army battled over the hill while Buda's inhabitants cowered underground. This was the eighty-sixth time that the Vár had been ravaged and rebuilt over seven centuries, rivalling the devastation caused by the recapture of Buda from the Turks in 1686. It was this repeated destruction that caused the melange of styles characterizing the hill. Adding to the mix, the neo-Gothic **Mátyás Church** and **Fishermen's Bastion** are romantic nineteenth-century evocations of medieval glories, interweaving past and present national fixations. The plain exterior of the **Royal Palace**, an uninspiring reconstruction of the prewar behemoth that stood here, fails to evoke any such glory. Here, it's what is inside that matters: two major museums, the

---

HIDDEN GEMS: THE VÁR AND CENTRAL BUDA

Sunset walk along Tóth Árpád sétány
See p.96

A ride on the Sikló See p.103

Pastries at the Ruszwurm Patisserie
See p.173

Coffee in the Átrium Theatre's 1930s foyer See p.187

Mesterporta CD shop See p.194

Veli Bej Baths See p.107

THE VÁR AND CENTRAL BUDA

FELHÉVÍZ

Óbuda

Császár
Komjádi Pool

RÓZSADOMB

Veli Bej Baths

Turkish Ruin

Lukács
Baths

Elvis
Presley
Park

Gül Baba
Tomb

Margit híd

MARGÍT HÍD

Margit-sziget & Pest

BEM
TÉR

BEM UTCA

Invisible
Exhibition

Foundry
Museum

GANZ UTCA

Millenáris
Park

Atrium
Theatre

Király
Baths

Fogadó

Playground

KACSA UTCA

Feny utca
Market

Military Court
of Justice

NAGY
IMRE
TÉR

Mammut
Malls

VÁRSÁNYI IRÉN UTCA

Jurányi Ház

CSALOGÁNY UTCA

SZÉNA
TÉR

Szell
Kálmán
tér

Bus #16A
& #116 to
the Vár

BATTHYÁNY UTCA

BATTHYÁNY
TÉR

Church
of St Ann

Batthyány
tér

Vienna
Gate

Mátyás
Church

Hungarian
Heritage
House

VÁR

Institut
Français

Vérmező
Park

Déli pu
Déli
Station

KRISZTINA-
VÁROS

Krisztinaváros
Parish Church

Siklo
(funicular)

Royal
Palace

LÁNCHÍD

Pest & Belváros

Gellért-Hegy & The Tabán

Mom Park Mall

EATING
QUICK BITES
Finomító Kantin	5
Gusto's	2
KicsiZso	1

RESTAURANTS
| Csalogány 26 | 9 |
| Mandragora | 3 |

CAFÉS
Artigiana Gelati	11
Auguszt	6
Budai Pékség	12
Levendula	7
Steamhouse	10
Szelence Café	13
Szerelmeslevél	4
À Table	8

SHOPPING
Bio-piac	3
MesterPorta	2
Várfok Galéria	1

ACCOMMODATION
| Art'otel | 1 |
| Victoria | 2 |

DRINKING AND NIGHTLIFE
| Bambi | 1 |
| Szalonspicc | 2 |

SEE THE VÁR MAP FOR DETAIL

0   250
metres

N

River Danube (Duna)

River Danube (Duna)

Margit-sziget

Hungarian National Gallery, and the **Budapest History Museum**, as well as the **National Széchenyi Library**.

Szentháromság tér

The obvious starting point for exploring the Vár is **Szentháromság tér** (Holy Trinity Square), the historic heart of the district, named after an ornate **Trinity Column** erected in 1713 in thanksgiving for the abatement of a plague; a scene showing people dying from the Black Death appears on the plinth. To the southwest stands the former **Town Hall**, Buda having been a municipality until its unification with Pest and Óbuda in 1873; note the corner statue of Pallas Athene, bearing Buda's coat of arms on her shield.

Mátyás Church

Mátyás templom • I, Szentháromság tér • Mon–Fri 9am–5pm, Sat 9am–noon, Sun 1–5pm • 1500Ft, audioguide 500Ft • Tickets from the office across the road by the Fishermen's Bastion • Mass is celebrated daily at 7.30am and 6pm, and on Sun at 7am, 8.30am, 10am (in Latin with a full choir), noon and 6pm • ☎ 1 355 5657, ⓦ matyas-templom.hu

The Royal Palace aside, the Vár's most prominent feature is the neo-Gothic **Mátyás Church**, with its wildly asymmetrical diamond-patterned roofs and toothy spires. Officially dedicated to Our Lady but popularly named after "Good King Mátyás", the building is a late nineteenth-century re-creation by architect Frigyes Schulek, grafted onto those portions of the original thirteenth-century church that survived the siege of 1686. Ravaged yet again in World War II, the church was laboriously restored by a Communist regime keen to show its patriotic credentials, and the transition to democracy in 1989–90 saw the sanctity of this "ancient shrine of the Hungarian people" reaffirmed.

The church serves as a superb venue for **concerts** during the festival seasons, and for evening organ recitals throughout the year. These are listed on the website, and tickets are available at the church itself or from any booking agency (see p.183).

The nave

As you enter the church, the richness of its interior is overwhelming. Painted leaves and geometric motifs run up columns and under vaulting, while shafts of light fall through rose windows onto gilded altars and statues with stunning effect. Most of the **frescoes** were executed by Károly Lotz or Bertalan Székely, the foremost historical painters of the nineteenth century. Working your way around to the left side of the church, you can see the **coat of arms of King Mátyás**, either side of which are frescoes of two soldiers from his feared Black Army; his family name, Corvinus, comes from the raven (*corvus* in Latin) that appeared on his heraldry and on every volume in his famed Corvin Library. Close by is the so-called **Hunyadi capital**, which features three stone-carved heads, that of the great military leader himself alongside his two sons, Mátyás himself and László, whose head is lying sideways – well, he was beheaded after all. The church's oldest capital, however, is in the bay beneath the **Béla Tower**, and depicts a monk and a bearded figure reading a book. In between these two capitals is the **Loreto Chapel**, containing a Baroque black Madonna.

The **Béla Tower** is named after Béla IV, who founded the church, rather than his predecessor in the second chapel along, who shares a **double sarcophagus** with Anne of Chatillon. The tomb, originally located in the old capital, Székesfehérvár, 60km southwest of Budapest, was moved here after its discovery in 1848. Although Hungary's medieval kings were crowned at Székesfehérvár, it was customary to make a prior appearance in Buda – hence the sobriquet, the "Coronation Church".

The Treasury and St Stephen's Chapel

Up on the gallery, there's a small collection of **ecclesiastical treasures** and relics, offering up the usual array of glittering chalices, monstrances and vestments. From

6

KING STEPHEN

If you commit just one figure from Hungarian history to memory, make it **King Stephen**, for it was he who welded the tribal Magyar fiefdoms into a state and won recognition from Christendom. Born Vajk, son of Grand Duke Géza, he emulated his father's policy of trying to convert the pagan Magyars and develop Hungary with the help of foreign preachers, craftsmen and merchants. By marrying Gizella of Bavaria in 996, he was able to use her father's knights to crush a pagan revolt after Géza's death, and subsequently received an apostolic cross and crown from Pope Sylvester II for his coronation on Christmas Day, 1000 AD, when he took the name Stephen (István in Hungarian).

Though noted for his enlightened views (such as the need for tolerance and the desirability of multiracial nations), he could act ruthlessly when necessary. After his only son Imre died in an accident and a pagan seemed likely to inherit, Stephen had the man blinded and poured molten lead into his ears. Naming his successor, he symbolically offered his crown to the Virgin Mary rather than the Holy Roman Emperor or the pope; ever since, she has been considered the Patroness of Hungary. Swiftly canonized after his death in 1038, **St Stephen** became a national talisman, his mummified right hand a holy relic, and his coronation regalia the symbol of statehood. Despite playing down his cult for decades, even the Communists eventually embraced it in a bid for some legitimacy, while nobody in post-Communist Hungary thinks it odd that the symbol of the republic should be the crown and cross of King Stephen.

here, climb a spiral staircase to the **Royal Oratory** overlooking the stained-glass windows and embossed vaulting of the nave, and then on through to **St Stephen's Chapel**; here you'll find a **replica of the Coronation Regalia**, whose attached exhibition is more informative about the provenance of St Stephen's Crown than that accompanying the originals, on display in Parliament (see p.56). You exit the church through the beautifully carved **Mary Portal**, which is actually a copy of the glass-encased original next to it, itself superbly preserved given its age (around 1370) – albeit minus Mary's head.

Fishermen's Bastion

Halászbástya • Daily: mid-March to April 9am–7pm; May to mid-Oct 9am–8pm; mid-Oct to mid-March open 24hr • 800Ft to go to the upper level (free between mid-Oct and mid-March); tickets are sold at the office next door • ⓦ fishermansbastion.com

After the Mátyás Church, the most impressive sight in the Vár is the **Fishermen's Bastion**. An undulating white rampart of cloisters and stairways intersecting at seven tent-like turrets (symbolizing the Magyar tribes that conquered the Carpathian Basin), it looks as though it was dreamt up by the illusionist artist Escher, but the architect was Frigyes Schulek, who designed it as a foil for the adjacent Mátyás. Although fishermen from the Víziváros reputedly defended this part of the hill during the Middle Ages, the bastion is purely decorative. The **view** of Pest across the river, framed by the bastion, is only surpassed by the vistas from the terrace of Buda Palace, and the Citadella on Gellért-hegy. However, you might balk at paying the fee to climb to the upper level, as the free view from the ground level is just as good.

Statue of King Stephen

I, Szentháromság tér

Between the Fishermen's Bastion and the Mátyás Church, an equestrian **statue of King Stephen** honours the founder of the Hungarian nation, whose conversion to Christianity and coronation with a crown sent by the pope presaged the Magyars' integration into European civilization (see box, p.212). The relief at the back of the plinth depicts Mátyás' designer Frigyes Schulek offering a model of the church to Stephen. Like the church and the bastion, his statue is reflected in the copper-glass facade of the **Budapest Hilton**, incorporating chunks of a medieval

Dominican church and monastery on the side facing the river, and an eighteenth-century Jesuit college on the other, which bears a copy of the **Mátyás Relief** from Bautzen in Germany that's regarded as the only true likeness of Hungary's Renaissance monarch.

Ruszwurm patisserie

I, Szentháromság utca 7

The tiny **Ruszwurm patisserie** has been a pastry shop and café since 1827 and was a gingerbread shop in the Middle Ages. Its Empire-style decor looks much the same as it would have done under Vilmos Ruszwurm, who ran the patisserie for nearly four decades from 1884. Its two small rooms, and pavement terrace, are invariably packed to the gills, but its delectable pastries are most definitely worth sampling (see p.173).

Táncsics Mihály utca

In the fifteenth century, when both Ashkenazi and Sephardic Jews lived here, **Táncsics Mihály utca** was known as Zsidó utca (Jewish Street). The Ashkenazi community was established in 1251 in the reign of Béla IV, but was completely wiped out when Buda was captured from the Ottomans in 1686. The Jews, who had fared well under Turkish rule, assisted in the defence of Buda, and those who had not fled or died in the siege were carted away as prisoners by the victorious Christian army. After several name changes, the street was renamed in 1948 after **Mihály Táncsics**, a radical Hungarian politician of the 1848 uprising who was imprisoned here. As it happens, Táncsics, though not Jewish, joined a Jewish platoon of the National Guard in protest against anti-Semitism. On the wall at no. 1, a plaque denotes the former British legation building where **Carl Lutz**, the Swiss vice-consul (see p.53), lived between 1942 and 1945.

Music History Museum

Zenetörténeti Múzeum • I, Táncsics Mihály utca 7 • Tues–Sun 10am–4pm • 600Ft • ☎ 1 214 6770, ⓦ zti.hu

The absorbing **Music History Museum** occupies the Baroque Erdödy Palace where Beethoven was a guest in 1800, and where Bartók once had a workshop before he emigrated. Indeed, an entire room is given over to Bartók's achievements in the form of photos, documents, manuscripts and folk songs he collected on his travels and which informed much of his work.

No less fascinating is the assemblage of **folk instruments** from the eighteenth century onwards, including zithers, violins, trumpets and

● EATING		■ DRINKING	
RESTAURANTS		Lánchíd Söröző	1
21	1		
Alabárdos	3	■ ACCOMMODATION	
Vár: A Speiz	2	Baltazár	2
CAFÉ		Buda Castle	5
Ruszwurm	4	Burg	7
		Castle Garden	1
		Hilton Budapest	6
● SHOPPING		Lánchíd 19	8
Fian	1	Maison	3
Magma	2	St George's Residence	4

THE VÁR

6

ANTAL SZERB

"Best of all I loved the Castle District. I never tired of its ancient streets." So speaks Mihály, the antihero of one of Hungary's most popular novels, *Journey by Moonlight* (*Utas és Holdvilág*), by **Antal Szerb** (1901–45). As Mihály recalls his Bohemian past, this enchanting book captures very strongly the Mittel Europa feel of the Vár. Brought up a staunch Catholic in an assimilated Jewish family, Szerb was a highly respected writer in the interwar period, writing histories of Hungarian and world literature and penning a series of short stories and novels that have been brilliantly translated into English (see p.227). Yet he was classified as Jewish in 1942 by the Third Jewish Law, and was shot in Balf, western Hungary, on a forced march. Szerb turned down the chance to escape because he and two friends on the march had made a pact that they would either escape or die together. His grave can be found in Kerepesi Cemetery (see p.83).

Unfortunately Hungarians like their thinkers to be weighty, and the underlying seriousness of Szerb's books is all too often dismissed on account of their wit and lightness of touch.

that most Hungarian of instruments, the hammered dulcimer, or cimbalom, which was popularized in the mid-nineteenth century by Romani musicians.

Also on show is the reconstructed violin workshop of **Pilat-Sáránszky**, complete with a collection of exquisitely crafted bows; originally owned by Páty Pilat, the workshop was taken over by Pál Sáránszky in 1957, before it finally closed in 2007.

Medieval Jewish Prayer House

Középkori Zsidó Imaház • I, Táncsics Mihály utca 26 • Wed–Sun: May–Oct 10am–6pm; Nov–April 10am–4pm • 600Ft • ⊗ btm.hu

Evidence of Buda's Jewish past can be found at the **Medieval Jewish Prayer House**. Around 1470, King Mátyás allowed the Jews to build a synagogue and appointed a Jewish council led by Jacobus Mendel; part of Mendel's house survives in the entrance to the prayer house. All that remains of its original decor are two kabbalistic symbols painted on a wall, and though the museum does its best to flesh out the history of the community with maps and prints, all the real treasures are in the Jewish Museum in Pest (see p.66).

National Archives

Magyar Nemzeti Levéltár • I, Bécsi kapu tér 2–4 • Tours Mon & Thurs 10am, 11am & 2pm • 1200Ft • ☎ 1 225 2843, ⊗ mnl.gov.hu

Named after the **Vienna Gate** (Bécsi kapu) that was erected on the 250th anniversary of the recapture of Buda, **Bécsi kapu tér** is home to the forbidding-looking neo-Romanesque **National Archives** building, distinguished by wildly colourful pyrogranite roof tiles from the Zsolnay factory. The archive holds the most important national historical resources – charters, plans, maps and the like (the oldest document dates from 1109) – as well as records pertaining to some of Hungary's most prominent families, such as the Eszterházys and Széchenyis. While these are not available for public viewing, it is possible to have a **guided tour** of the building, though this involves little more than a nose around the corridors, whose walls are covered in fresco-seccos executed by Andor Dudits in the late 1920s, and which depict important moments and personalities in Hungarian history.

Kapisztrán tér

Kapisztrán tér is centred on the **Mary Magdalene Tower** (Magdolna-torony), whose accompanying church was wrecked in World War II. In medieval times this was where Hungarian residents worshipped (Germans used the Mátyás Church), so its reconstruction is occasionally mooted by nationalist politicians. Today the tower boasts a peal of ornamental bells that jingle through a medley composed by the jazz pianist György Szabados, including Hungarian folk tunes, Chopin études and the theme from *Bridge over the River Kwai*.

FROM TOP FISHERMEN'S BASTION (P.92); VIEW TOWARDS THE LÁNCHÍD (P.104) >

Beyond the tower is a statue of **Friar John Capistranus**, who exhorted the Hungarians to victory at the siege of Belgrade in 1456, a triumph which the pope hailed by ordering church bells to be rung at noon throughout Europe. The statue, showing Capistranus bestriding a dead Turk, is aptly sited outside the Military History Museum.

Tóth Árpád sétány

Running along the western edge of the Vár is **Tóth Árpád sétány**, a promenade lined with cannons and chestnut trees, looking across to the Buda Hills. Just to the east of its northern end, past a giant **flagpole** striped in Hungarian colours, you'll find the symbolic **grave of Abdurrahman**, the last Turkish Pasha of Buda, who died on the walls in 1686 – a "valiant foe", according to the inscription.

Military History Museum

Hadtörténeti Múzeum • I, Tóth Árpád sétány 40 • Tues–Sun: April–Sept 10am–6pm; Oct–March 10am–4pm • 1500Ft • ☎ 1 325 1600, Ⓦ militaria.hu

Housed in a former barracks, the **Military History Museum** has an exhaustive display on Hungarian military history, which for the most part is a pretty dry affair. Divided up by periods, coverage begins at 1815 with the birth of the Honvéd (national army), followed by the 1848–49 War of Independence; meanwhile, lovers of flags and uniforms will enjoy the "Under the Banners of Francis Joseph" display, which charts the period 1868–1914.

The one section that really does merit your time is "**Hungary in the Great War**", a sparkling overview that begins with the infamous assassination of Archduke Franz Ferdinand in Sarajevo, which of course sparked the outbreak of World War I; on display is his artillery *shako* (plumed cap), as well as some footage from the Bosnian capital. There are cabinets stuffed with medals and memorabilia belonging to some of the war's most celebrated generals, such as the sabre of Svetozar Borojevič (aka the Soča Lion), commander of the Austro-Hungarians during the savage campaigns along the Soča Front (the Italian/Slovenian border) between 1915 and 1917. Here, too, are items ingeniously crafted from battlefield waste by Hungarian prisoners of war (it's estimated that some 1.6 million were taken as POWs, mostly by Russians), plus some lovely birch postcards – pressed bark on which notes or drawings could be etched – alongside a hoard of hellish-looking weaponry, which includes the grenade shrapnel that blew the leg off ensign Lajos Szoczy; no less sobering is a horn medallion containing the ashes of Imre Bitskey, killed on the Russian Front.

Thereafter, there's coverage of the siege of Budapest at the end of World War II, and its aftermath – more misery for the Hungarians – before the exhibition stops abruptly

STREET LIFE

The **streets of the Vár** to the north of the palace still follow their medieval courses, with Gothic arches and stone carvings half-concealed in the courtyards and passages of eighteenth-century Baroque houses, whose facades are embellished with fancy ironwork grilles. For many centuries, residence here was a privilege granted to religious or ethnic groups, each occupying a specific street. This pattern persisted through the 145-year-long Turkish occupation, when Armenians, Circassians and Sephardic Jews established themselves under the relatively tolerant Ottomans. The liberation of Buda by a multinational Christian army under Habsburg command was followed by a pogrom and ordinances restricting the right of residence to Catholics and Germans, which remained in force for nearly a century. Almost every building here displays a stone *műemlék* (listed) **plaque** giving details of its history (in Hungarian), and a surprising number are still homes rather than embassies or boutiques – there are even a couple of schools and corner shops. At dusk, when most of the tourists have left, pensioners walk their dogs and toddlers play in the long shadows of Hungarian history.

at 1968. In the courtyard are post-Communist memorials to the POWs who never returned from the Gulag.

Országház utca

Running south from Kapisztrán tér towards Szentháromság tér, **Országház utca** was the district's main thoroughfare in the Middle Ages and was known as the "street of baths" during Turkish times. Its present name, Parliament Street, recalls the sessions of the Diet held in the 1790s in a former Poor Clares' cloister at no. 28, where the Gestapo imprisoned 350 Hungarians and foreigners in 1945. No. 17, over the road, consists of two medieval houses joined together and has a relief of a croissant on its keystone, from the time when it was a bakery. A few doors down from the old Parliament building, Renaissance graffiti survive on the underside of the bay window of no. 22 and a Gothic trefoil-arched cornice on the house next door, while the one beyond has been rebuilt in its original fifteenth-century form.

Úri utca

Úri utca (Gentleman Street) boasts historic associations, for it was at the former Franciscan monastery at no. 51 that the five Hungarian Jacobins were held before being beheaded on the "Blood Meadow" below the hill in 1795. As you walk down the street from Kapisztrán tér, notice the statues of the four seasons in the first-floor niches at nos. 54–56, Gothic sedilia in the gateway of nos. 48–50, and three arched windows and two diamond-shaped ones from the fourteenth and fifteenth centuries at no. 31. In the wall at no. 27 is a ventilation shaft for the secret hospital below.

Telephone Museum

Telefónia Múzeum • I, Úri utca 49, though the entrance is through the cloister at Országház utca 30 • Tues–Sun 10am–4pm • 500Ft • ☎ 1 201 8857, ⓦ postamuzeum.hu

The **Telephone Museum** is set in a wing of the former Poor Clares' cloister on Országház utca, which served as a telephone exchange after World War II. One of the earliest pioneers of the telephone exchange was Tivadar Puskás who, after having worked alongside Thomas Edison, set up Europe's first exchange (in Paris in 1879) – though it was actually his brother, Ferenc, who established the first one in Budapest, in 1881. Less well known is the involvement of the celebrated Serbian scientist Nikola Tesla, who made numerous improvements to the Pest exchange; alongside the noisy rotary one that's stood here since the 1930s is a quieter, more streamlined modern exchange, which still operates. Amid all the technical items, like meter relays, cables and capacitor joints (all stimulating stuff, for sure), you can indulge in some truly nostalgic pieces, including a marvellous selection of dial-up phones, as well as admire the personal telephones of Emperor Franz Josef (complete with royal insignia), Admiral Horthy and the Communist leader János Kádár.

Hospital in the Rock

Sziklakórház • I, Lovas út 4/c; the entrance is down the steps at the western end of Szentháromság utca and 50m to the right • Daily 10am–8pm; visits by guided tour only, every hour on the hour • 4000Ft • ☎ 70 701 0101, ⓦ sziklakorhaz.eu

Some six to fourteen metres beneath the Vár's streets lie 10km of galleries formed by hot springs and cellars dug since medieval times, though the system wasn't properly explored until 1935, by the Croatian speleologist Ottokár Kadić. Work then began on converting a section of it into a military hospital in readiness for World War II, though in fact it didn't open until 1944, doubling as an air-raid shelter during the Siege of Budapest. It was put to use as a hospital again during the 1956 Revolution, after which time it was repurposed as a **nuclear bunker**. The ventilation system is run by generators installed in the bunker, with charcoal air-filters, a laboratory for detecting toxins, atropine ampoules to be injected against nerve gas, and an airlock. To preserve its secrecy, fuel was delivered by trucks pretending to "water" flowerbeds on the surface,

6

A HISTORY OF THE ROYAL PALACE

As befits a former royal residence, the lineage of the **Royal Palace** (Királyi palota) can be traced back to medieval times, the rise and fall of various palaces on the hill reflecting the changing fortunes of the Hungarian state. The first fortifications and dwellings, hastily erected by Béla IV after the Mongol invasion of 1241–42, were replaced by the grander palaces of the Angevin kings, who ruled in more prosperous and stable times. This process of rebuilding reached its zenith in the reign of Mátyás Corvinus (1458–90), whose palace was a Renaissance extravaganza to which artists and scholars from all over Europe were drawn by the blandishments of Queen Beatrice and the prospect of lavish hospitality. The rooms had hot and cold running water, and during celebrations the fountains and gargoyles flowed with wine. After the Turkish occupation and the long siege that ended it, only ruins were left – which the Habsburgs, Hungary's new rulers, levelled to build a palace of their own.

From modest beginnings under Empress Maria Theresa (when there were a mere 203 rooms, which she never saw completed), the palace **expanded** inexorably throughout the nineteenth century, though no monarch ever dwelt here, only the Habsburg palatine (viceroy). After the collapse of the empire following World War I, Admiral Horthy inhabited the building with all the pomp of monarchy until he was deposed by a German coup in October 1944. The palace was left unoccupied, and it wasn't long before the siege of Buda once again resulted in total devastation. **Reconstruction** work began in the 1950s – you can see the contrast between the fancier prewar stonework in the Lion Courtyard and the tacky postwar version on the side overlooking the river. The interior also lacks the elegance of the prewar version, being designed to accommodate cultural institutions. However, one benefit of the reconstruction was that it revealed the medieval substrata beneath the rubble, which were incorporated into the new building.

via a concealed pipeline. A veritable time capsule from the Cold War, the bunker remained top secret until as recently as 2002.

Ramped throughout for wheelchairs and trolleys, this labyrinthine setup includes a handful of wards, bathrooms (there were just two showers), and operating theatres containing 1930s military field X-ray and anesthetic machines (one was used in the 1996 film *Evita*), not to mention a multitude of waxworks in various states of pose, including one chap straining on the loo. Two rooms have been given over to **exhibitions**, one on the Siege of Budapest, and another on Hiroshima, which horrifically demonstrates the effects of nuclear war.

Golden Eagle Pharmacy Museum

Arany Sas Patikamúzeum • I, Tárnok utca 18 • Tues–Sun 10.30am–5.30pm • 500Ft • ☎ 1 375 3533, ⊚ semmelweis.museum.hu

Established after the expulsion of the Turks, the **Golden Eagle Pharmacy** was the first in Buda, moving to its present site in the eighteenth century and operating until World War II. Its original murals and furnishings lend authenticity to dubious nostrums, including the skull of a mummy used to make Mumia powder to treat epilepsy; there's also a reconstruction of an alchemist's laboratory, complete with dried bats and crocodiles, and other obscure exhibits such as the small, long-necked Roman glass vessel for collecting widows' tears. Notice the portrait of the Dominican nun pharmacist – it was common practice for nuns and monks in the Middle Ages to double up as apothecaries. Next door but one, take a look at the *Tárnok* coffee house, which occupies a medieval building with a Renaissance graffiti facade of red and yellow checks and roundels and, like the street, is named after the royal treasurers who once lived here.

Dísz tér

Both Tárnok utca and Úri utca end in **Dísz tér** (Parade Square), whose cobbled expanses are guarded by a mournful Honvéd memorial to the dead of 1848–49. To the south lies the scarred hulk of the old **Ministry of Defence**, to the east of which stands the new Prime Minister's Office, housed in the former **Castle Theatre** Várszínház. This was originally a Carmelite church until the order was dissolved by Josef II; its conversion was supervised by Farkas Kempelen, inventor of a chess-playing automaton. It was here that the first-ever play in Hungarian was staged in 1790, and where Beethoven performed in 1800, as the plaque on the wall denotes. The last building in the row is the **Sándor Palace** (Sándor Palota), the pre-war prime minister's residence, where Premier Teleki shot himself in protest at Hungary joining the Nazi invasion of Yugoslavia. It is now the residence of the country's president, a figurehead who is elected by Parliament rather than the electorate.

6

Turul statue and around

Next door to Sándor Palace, the upper terminal of the **Sikló** (funicular; see p.103) is separated from the terrace of the Royal Palace by stately railings and the ferocious-looking **Turul statue** on Szent György tér – a giant bronze eagle clasping a sword in its talons, which is visible from across the river. In Magyar mythology, the Turul sired the first dynasty of Hungarian kings by raping the grandmother of Prince Árpád, who led the tribes into the Carpathian Basin. The Turul also accompanied their raids on Europe, bearing the sword of Attila the Hun in its talons. During the nineteenth century it became a symbol of Hungarian identity in the face of Austrian culture, but wound up being co-opted by the Habsburgs, who cast Emperor Franz Josef as a latter-day Árpád for the next millennium. Today, the Turul has been adopted as an emblem by Hungary's right-wing extremists.

From here, you can go through the wrought-iron gates and down some steps to the terrace of the Royal Palace, commanding a sweeping **view** of Pest and fine head-on views of Margít-sziget. Beyond the souvenir stalls prances an equestrian **statue of Prince Eugene of Savoy**, who captured Buda from the Ottomans in 1686. The smaller bronze statues nearby represent **Csongor and Tünde**, the lovers in the play of the same name, by Vörösmarty.

Hungarian National Gallery

Magyar Nemzeti Galéria • Royal Palace wings A, B, C and D • **National Gallery** Tues–Sun 10am–6pm, guided tour 2pm • 1800Ft for permanent display (audioguide 800Ft), 2200Ft for temporary shows • ☎ 1 201 9082, ⓦ mng.hu • **Habsburg crypt** Advance notice required – register online or ask at the desk or ring ☎ 06 20 439 7408 • 600Ft

The biggest attraction in the Royal Palace is the **Hungarian National Gallery**, which is devoted to Hungarian art from the Middle Ages to the present. It contains much that's superb, but the vastness of the collection and the confusing layout can be fatiguing; do not expect – or indeed attempt – to get through it all in one go. Though all the paintings are labelled in English, other details are scanty. It's therefore worth taking the free **guided tour** in English. Note that certain works are prone to being moved around, while others may be removed in order to accommodate other pieces, so displays may vary from that described here.

The gallery's main entrance is on the eastern side of Wing C, overlooking the river, behind the statue of Eugene of Savoy. You'll need to give a couple of days' notice to see the separate **Habsburg crypt**, containing the tombs of several Habsburgs who ruled as palatines of Hungary until 1849. On one Thursday each month, the gallery stays open till 10pm for an evening of themed events, which consist of talks, tours and concerts; consult the website for the latest information.

Ground floor

Through the shop to the left of the ticket office, a lovely **wooden ceiling** from a sixteenth-century church and marble reliefs of knightly tombs are the highlights of a **Medieval and Renaissance Lapidarium**. Between the two, doors on the left lead to the fantastic collection of fifteenth-century **Gothic altarpieces** and panels at the rear of Wing D. Salvaged from churches great and small that escaped destruction by the Turks, some are artful and others rustic, but all are full of character and detail: notice

6

HUNGARY'S GREAT PAINTERS

They were two of Hungary's finest painters, living in the same age, yet the lives they led could not have been more different. While **Mihály Munkácsy** (1844–1900) was fêted for his work and buried like a national hero, his funeral attended by government ministers and his body lying in state in Hősök tere, **Tivadar Kosztka Csontváry** (1853–1919) died alone and unrecognized.

Munkácsy spent much of his life in Paris, but always declared himself Hungarian. He painted large dusty landscapes and pictures of peasants and outlaws as well as grand portrayals of Christ before Pilate. His realist style sold very well, but that financial success was his downfall, and he died of syphilis at the age of 56. Time has not been kind to his work, either: many canvases have suffered from his use of bitumen in mixing paint, which has caused them to darken and crack.

Trained as a pharmacist, Csontváry was 27 when a voice told him: "You will be the world's greatest *plein-air* painter, greater than Raphael." When he began to study painting at the age of 41, he did not belong to any school, and his canvases, simple yet expressive, display an extraordinary use of colour and light. Most of his work was completed in just six years – he painted his last work in 1909, overwhelmed by lack of recognition and schizophrenia. When Picasso saw an exhibition of his works in the 1940s he remarked: "And I thought I was the only great painter of our century."

the varied reactions expressed within the *Death of the Virgin* from Kassa (Kosice, a Slovakian centre of altar-painting) and the gloating spectators in the Jánosrét *Passion* in the second room. From the same church comes a *St Nicholas* altar as long as a limo and lurid as a comic strip, whose final scene shows cripples being cured by the saint's corpse. Also strange to modern eyes are *The Expulsion of St Adalbert*, who seems blithely oblivious to the demolition of his church, and the woodcarving of *St Anthony the Hermit*, carrying a hill upon his back. The pointed finials on the high altar from Liptószentmária (Liptovská Mara in Slovakia) anticipate the winged altarpieces of the sixteenth century on the floor above. To get there without returning to the foyer, use the small staircase outside the doors to this section and turn left, left and left again at the top.

First floor: Gothic and Baroque art

The first floor covers the widest range of art and is likely to engage you the longest. It picks up where the ground floor left off in the former Throne Room, where **late Gothic altarpieces** with soaring pinnacles and carved surrounds are displayed. Most of them come from churches now in Slovakia or Romania, such as the *Annunciation* altarpiece from Csíkmenaság (now Armaseni in Romania) or the homely *St Anne* altarpiece from Kisszeben (Sabinov, Slovakia), which looks like a medieval playgroup. On an altar from Berki (Rokycany, Slovakia), Mary Magdalene is raptured by angels as bishops are impaled, while another piece from Liptószentandrás (Liptovsky Ondrej, Slovakia) shows St Andrew clutching the poles for his crucifixion. Also look out for **The Visitation** by the anonymous "Master MS", in the anteroom, and the coffered **ceiling** from Gogánváralija (Gogan-Varolea, Romania), in the room behind the *Kisszeben Annunciation* altarpiece.

Many of the works in the adjacent section on **Baroque art** once belonged to Count Miklós Esterházy (including his portrait), or were confiscated from private owners in the 1950s. The prolific Austrian **Anton Maulbertsch**, who executed scores of altars and murals reminiscent of Caravaggio, is represented here by works such as *The Death of St Joseph*. On the back of one panel running across the room, don't miss **Ádám Mányoki**'s portrait of Ferenc Rákóczi II from 1712, a sober study of a national hero that foreshadowed a new artistic genre of **National Historical art** in the nineteenth century.

Coming up the main stairs from the ticket office, you will find, at the rear of the mid-floor landing, two vast canvases by **Peter Krafft**. *Zrínyi's Sortie* depicts the suicidal sally by the defenders of Szigetvár against a Turkish army fifty times their number; not a drop of blood spatters the melee, as Count Zrínyi leads the charge across the bridge. The other shows Franz Josef being crowned King of Hungary in equally slavish detail. Facing you in the large first-floor atrium is **Gyula Benczúr**'s *Reoccupying of Buda Castle*, whose portrayal of Eugene of Savoy and Karl of Lotharingia suggests a mere exchange of Turkish rulers for Habsburg ones; while *The Bewailing of László Hunyadi* by **Viktor Madarász** (hung off towards Wing D) would have been read as an allusion to the execution of Hungarian patriots after the War of Independence. At the other end, near Wing B, you'll find **Sándor Lilzen-Mayer**'s *St Elizabeth of Hungary* offering her ermine cape to a ragged mother and child, and two iconic scenes by **Bertalan Székely**: *The Battle of Mohács*, a shattering defeat for the Hungarians in 1526; and *The Women of Eger*, exalting their defiance of the Turks in 1552.

6

First floor: Romanticism and Impressionism

The remainder of the first floor illustrates other trends in nineteenth-century Hungarian art, namely genre painting, **rural Romanticism** and Impressionism. On the Buda side of Wing C, *Thunderstorm on the Puszta* and *Horses at the Watering Place* evoke the hazy skies and manly world of the Hungarian "Wild West" – the Great Plain southeast of Budapest. Both are by **Károly Lotz**, better known for his frescoes around the city, such as in the Mátyás Church, Opera House and Parliament.

Wing B devotes an entire section to works by **Mihály Munkácsy**, Hungary's one painter of real international standing (see box, p.100). Munkácsy was renowned for his landscapes – standouts here include the superbly atmospheric *Storm on the Puszta* and lighter *Dusty Road* – character paintings, such as the gentle *Woman Churning Butter*, and pictures with a social message, notably the haunting *The Last Day of a Condemned Man*, considered his finest ever painting. Just off of here, one room is devoted to **nude sculptures**, an erotic series of works from the turn of the nineteenth century, the pick of which is Miklós Ligeti's rippling *Sitting Man*.

Impressionism was introduced to Hungary by **Pál Szinyei Merse**, whose models and subjects – such as in *A Picnic in May* – were cheerfully bourgeois. Nearby you'll find two mesmerizing landscapes by the prolific **László Mednyánszky** – *Watering-place* and *Fishing on the Tisza* – and paintings from the **Nagybánya school**, an influential artists' colony in what is now Baia Mare in Romania. The school's most adept pupil was **Károly Ferenczy**, to whom a whole room is given over; look out for the wonderful innocence of *Boys Throwing Pebbles*. The school's founder was **Simon Hollósy**, who quit during a spiritual crisis; his most luminous pieces here include *The Problems of the Country* and the *Rákóczi March*, while there's a more cheerful *Drying Clothes*, by **Béla Iványi Grünwald**, another leading member of the group.

Midway up the **stairs** hang three canvases by the visionary **Tivadar Kosztka Csontváry**, whose obsession with the Holy Land and the "path of the sun" inspired scenes such as *Pilgrimage to the Cedars in Lebanon* and the vast *Ruins of the Greek Theatre at Taormina*, with its magical twilight colours.

Second floor

There's more from the Nagybánya school, and Károly Ferenczy, up on the second floor, including a portrait of Ferenczy's twin children Noemi and Beni, themselves no slouches in the art world; Beni, in particular, was a distinguished sculptor and is represented here by *Atalanta* and *Young Man* – much more of the Ferenczy family's work can be seen in Szentendre (see p.130). Otherwise, this floor covers **twentieth-century Hungarian art up to 1945**, with the vibrant **Art Nouveau** movement off to the right of the atrium. Pictures by **János Vaszary** (*Golden Age*) and **Aladár Körösfői-Kriesch** (founder of the Gödöllő artists' colony – see p.149) are set in richly hand-carved frames, an integral part of their composition. **József Rippl-Rónai** was a pupil of Munkácsy whose portraits such as *Woman Holding a Rose* and *My Father and Uncle Piacsek with Red Wine* went mostly unrecognized in his lifetime – they're now regarded as Art Nouveau classics. Here you'll also find Csontváry's magically lit *Coaching in Athens at the Full Moon*.

Across the atrium, **István Szónyi**'s wintry *Funeral at Zebegény*, and **József Egry**'s watery *St John the Baptist* have simple lines and muddy colours in common. Both belonged to a generation of artists whose sympathies were on the left in largely right-wing times: Constructivists such as **Béla Uitz**, Cubists **János Kmetty** and **Gyula Derkovits**, the Expressionist **Vilmos Aba-Novák** and the "Hungarian Chagall", **Imre Ámos** (who died in a Nazi death camp), are all represented in Wing C off the stairs.

6

Third floor

On the third floor, **Tamás Lossonczy**'s abstract-surrealistic *Great Purifying Storm*, **Béla Kondor**'s whimsical *The Genius of Mechanical Flying* and a wire sculpture by **Tibor Vilt** portraying the awful fate of the peasant rebel leader Dózsa presage the section on **Hungarian art since 1945**. Exhibits are rotated to showcase the museum's collection of work by modern artists such as Endre Bálint, Attila Szűcs, Sándor Altorjai and Erzsébet Schaár. On fine days, visitors can ascend to the palace's **dome** for a **view** of the city.

Mátyás Fountain and the Lion Courtyard

An archway just before the entrance to the National Gallery leads through a square flanked on three sides by the palace overlooking Buda to the west. Against the wall on the left stands the flamboyant **Mátyás Fountain**, whose bronze figures recall the legend of Szép Ilonka. This beautiful peasant girl met the king while he was hunting incognito, fell in love with him, and died of a broken heart after discovering his identity and realizing the futility of her hopes. The man with a falcon is the king's Italian chronicler, who recorded the story for posterity (it is also enshrined in a poem by Vörösmarty).

Down to the left past the Mátyás Fountain, a gateway guarded by lions leads into the **Lion Courtyard**, totally enclosed by further wings of the palace. To the right of the gateway entrance a passage leading to the passenger lift down to Dózsa György tér is lined with photos that bear witness to the grandeur of the prewar palace.

National Széchenyi Library

Országos Széchenyi Könyvtár • Royal Palace Wing F; entrance on the right-hand side of the Lion Courtyard • Tues–Sat 9am–8pm, closed mid-July to late Aug • Reading room day-pass 1200Ft; passport or identity card required to apply • ☎ 1 224 3700, ⓦ oszk.hu

The **National Széchenyi Library** occupies the Royal Palace's nineteenth-century Ybl block, whose full size is only apparent from the far side of the hill, where it looms over Dózsa György tér like a mountain. The library was founded in 1802 on the initiative of Count Ferenc Széchenyi, the father of István (see box, p.103). A repository for publications in Hungarian and material relating to the country from around the world, by law it receives a copy of every book, newspaper and magazine that is published in Hungary. The library hosts regular exhibitions from its collection of books and newspapers; note that you can only visit the reading room with a reader's pass. During library hours, you can use the passenger **lift** in the adjacent building by the Lion Gateway (open to all), which provides direct access to and from Dózsa tér, at the foot of the Vár.

Budapest History Museum

Budapest Történeti Múzeum • Royal Palace Wing E; entrance on the far side of the Lion Courtyard • Tues–Sun: March–Oct 10am–6pm; Nov–Feb 10am–4pm • 2000Ft, audioguide 1200Ft • ☎ 1 487 8871, ⓦ btm.hu

The **Budapest History Museum** covers two millennia of history on three floors, and descends into original vaulted, flagstoned halls from the Renaissance and medieval palaces unearthed during excavations. It's worth starting with **prehistory**, to the left

COUNT SZÉCHENYI

Count István Széchenyi (1791–1860) was the outstanding figure of Hungary's Reform era. As a young aide-de-camp he cut a dash at the Congress of Vienna and did the rounds of stately homes across Europe. While in England, he steeplechased hell-for-leather, but still found time to examine factories and steam trains, providing Bernard Shaw with the inspiration for the "odious Zoltán Karpathy" of *Pygmalion* (and the musical *My Fair Lady*). Back in Hungary, he pondered solutions to his homeland's backwardness and offered a year's income from his estates towards the establishment of a Hungarian Academy. In 1830 he published *Hitel* (Credit), a hard-headed critique of the nation's feudal society.

Though politically conservative, Széchenyi was obsessed with **modernization**. A passionate convert to steam power after riding on the Manchester–Liverpool railway, he invited Britons to Hungary to build rail lines and the Lánchíd. He also imported steamships and dredgers, promoted horsebreeding and silk-making, and initiated the dredging of the River Tisza and the blasting of a road through the Iron Gates of the Danube. Alas, his achievements were rewarded by a melancholy end. The 1848 Revolution and the short-lived triumph of the radical party led by his *bête noire*, Kossuth, triggered a nervous breakdown, and Széchenyi eventually shot himself. Today he is often referred to as "the greatest Hungarian" – though curiously it was Kossuth who originally called him this.

6

on the top floor, to find out about Paleolithic inhabitants of the area. The Avars, the nomadic precursors of the Magyars who overran the Pannonian Plain after the Romans left, are represented by some impressive items retrieved from their burial mounds, such as a gold bridle and stirrup fastenings in a zoomorphic style. Owing to the ravages inflicted by the Mongols and the Turks, there's little to show from the time of the **Conquest** on the first floor, and only a few artefacts from Hungary's medieval civilization (there is more in the medieval palace below). From the Turkish period there are some fine pots and metalwork, as well as Jewish gravestones, but most of this floor is occupied by a display on **Budapest in Modern Times**, an exhibition giving insight into urban planning, fashions, trade and vices, from 1686 onwards. At the far end of the ground floor there is a fine display of **statues** from the late fourteenth century that were discovered in 1974.

The **remains of the medieval palace** are reached from the basement via an eighteenth-century cellar spanning two medieval yards on a lower level. A wing of the ground floor of King Sigismund's palace and the cellars beneath the Corvin Library form an intermediate stratum overlaying the cross-vaulted crypt of the **Royal Chapel** and a **Gothic Hall** where lute **concerts** are held. In another chamber are portions of red marble fireplaces and a massive portal carved with cherubs and flowers from the palace of King Mátyás. Emerging into daylight, bear left and up the stairs to reach yet another imposing hall, with a view over the castle ramparts.

The Sikló

Daily 7.30am–10pm, closed every other Mon • 1200Ft one-way, 1800Ft return; Budapest Card not valid

Between the Royal Palace and the Sándor Palace stands the upper station of the **Sikló**, a nineteenth-century **funicular** that takes you down to the river and the Lánchíd. Constructed on the initiative of Ödön Széchenyi, whose father built the bridge below, it was only the second funicular in the world when it was inaugurated in 1870, and functioned without a hitch until wrecked by a shell in 1945. The wooden carriages, replicas of the originals, are now lifted by an electric winch rather than a steam engine; they're divided into three sections at different heights to give as many people as possible a view (the bottom compartment gives the most unimpeded views). Capacity is limited, however, so in summer you can expect to queue to go up. In the small park at the foot of the Sikló stands **Kilometre Zero**, a zero-shaped monument from where all distances from Budapest are measured.

The Víziváros

Inhabited by fishermen, craftsmen and their families in medieval times, the **Víziváros** (Watertown), between the Vár and the Danube, became depopulated during the seventeenth century, and was resettled by Habsburg mercenaries and their camp followers after the Turks were driven out. The following century saw the neighbourhood gradually gentrified, with solid apartment blocks meeting at odd angles on the hillside, reached by alleys which mostly consist of steps rising from the main street, **Fő utca**. Some of these are still lit by gas lamps and look quite Dickensian on misty evenings.

6

Széchenyi Lánchíd

The majestic **Lánchíd** (Chain Bridge) has a special place in the history of Budapest and in the hearts of its citizens. As the first permanent link between Buda and Pest (replacing seasonal pontoon bridges and ferries), it was a tremendous spur to the country's economic growth and eventual unification, linking the rural hinterland to European civilization so that Budapest became a commercial centre and transport hub. The bridge symbolized the abolition of feudal privilege, as nobles (hitherto exempt from taxes) were obliged to pay the toll to cross it. It also embodied civic endurance, having been inaugurated only weeks after Hungary lost the 1849 War of Independence, when Austrian troops tried and failed to destroy it.

However, in 1945, the Wehrmacht dynamited all of Budapest's bridges in a bid to check the Red Army. Their reconstruction was one of the first tasks of the postwar era, and the reopening of the Lánchíd on the centenary of its inauguration (Nov 21) was heralded as proof that life was returning to normal, even as Hungary was becoming a Communist dictatorship. Today, the bridge is once again adorned with the national coat of arms rather than Soviet symbols.

The idea for a bridge came to **Count István Széchenyi** (see box, p.103) after he was late for his father's funeral in 1820 because bad weather had made the Danube uncrossable. Turning his idea into reality was to preoccupy him for two decades, and it became the centrepiece of a grand plan to modernize Hungary's communications. Owing to Britain's industrial pre-eminence and Széchenyi's Anglophilia, the bridge was designed by **William Tierney Clark** (who based it on his earlier plan for Hammersmith Bridge in London) and constructed under the supervision of a Scottish engineer, **Adam Clark** (no relation), from components cast in Britain. Besides the technical problems of erecting what was then the longest bridge in Europe (nearly 380m), there was also the attempt by the Austrians to blow it up – which Adam Clark personally thwarted by flooding its chain-lockers. He also dissuaded a Hungarian general from setting it alight in 1849.

Whereas Széchenyi died in an asylum, Clark settled happily in Budapest with his Hungarian wife. After his death, he was buried on the spot that now bears his name, though his remains were subsequently moved to Kerepesi Cemetery. Adam Clark also built the **tunnel** (*alagút*) under the Vár – another Széchenyi project – which Budapestis joked could be used to store the new bridge when it rained. A positive development in recent years has been the closing of the bridge to traffic for up to ten weekends over the summer for popular festivities. However, an extensive, two-year long renovation programme means that the bridge is likely to be closed until late 2019 at the earliest.

Szilágyi Dezső tér

North of the Chain Bridge, **Szilágyi Dezső tér** is infamous for the events that occurred here in January 1945. When Eichmann and the SS had already fled, the Arrow Cross massacred hundreds of Budapest's Jews and dumped their bodies in the river; an inconspicuous plaque commemorates the victims. From here, you can make a brief detour left up Vám utca, just north of the square, to see the **Iron Block**, a replica of a wooden block into which itinerant apprentices once hammered nails for good luck.

Batthyány tér

The main square and social hub of the Víziváros, **Batthyány tér** is named after the nineteenth-century prime minister, Lajos Batthyány, but it started out as Bomba tér (Bomb Square) after an ammunition depot sited here for the defence of the Danube. Today, it's busy with shoppers visiting the supermarket in an old market hall on the western side of the square, and commuters using the underground metro/HÉV interchange. On the southern side of the square is a **statue** of a stern-looking Batthyány standing on a bow of a ship. The sunken two-storey building to the right of the market, meanwhile, used to be the *White Cross* Inn, where Casanova reputedly once stayed. Many of the older buildings in this area are sunken in this way owing to the ground level being raised several feet in the nineteenth century to combat flooding. The views across to the Parliament building from the square are superb.

Church of St Anne

Szent Anna templom • II, Batthyány tér 7

The twin-towered **Church of St Anne**, on the southern corner of Fő utca, is one of the finest Baroque buildings in Budapest. Commissioned by the Jesuits in 1740, it wasn't consecrated until 1805 owing to financial problems, the abolition of the Jesuit order in 1773, and an earthquake. During Communist times there were plans to demolish the building, as it was feared that the metro would undermine its foundations, but these, fortunately, came to nothing. Figures of Faith, Hope and Charity hover above the entrance, and in the middle of the facade St Anne cherishes the child Mary, while God's eye surmounts the Buda coat of arms on its tympanum. The **interior** is ornate yet homely, the high altar festooned with statues of St Anne presenting Mary to the Temple in Jerusalem, accompanied by a host of cherubim and angels, while chintzy bouquets and potted trees welcome shoppers dropping in to say their prayers.

Military Court of Justice

II, Fő utca

North of Batthyány tér stands the hulking Fascist-style **Military Court of Justice** (Fővárosi Katonai Ügyészség), so big that it consumes an entire block. It was here that Imre Nagy and other leaders of the 1956 Uprising were secretly tried and executed in 1958, as indicated by the plaque on the wall facing Nagy Imre tér, opposite. Nagy's body lay in an unmarked grave in the New Public Cemetery for over thirty years, until his reburial in 1989 (see p.216).

Király Baths

Király gyógyfürdő • II, Fő utca 84 • Daily 9am–9pm • ☎ 1 202 3688, ⓦ kiralyfurdo.hu

Aside from its crumbling, muddy-green facade, you can identify the **Király Baths** by the four copper cupolas, shaped like tortoise shells, poking from its eighteenth-century facade. Together with the Rudas, this is the finest of Budapest's Turkish baths (see pp.199–202); the octagonal pool, lit by star-shaped apertures in the dome, was built in 1570 for the Buda garrison. The baths' name, meaning "king", comes from that of the König family who owned them in the eighteenth century.

Bem tér

Fő utca terminates at **Bem tér**, named after the Polish general Joseph Bem, who fought for the Hungarians in the War of Independence, and was revered by his men as "Father". A **statue of Bem** with his arm in a sling recalls him leading them into battle at Piski, crying "I shall recapture the bridge or die! Forward Hungarians! If we do not have the bridge we do not have the country." Traditionally a site for demonstrations, it was here that the crowds assembled prior to marching on Parliament at the beginning of the 1956 Uprising. In the northwest corner, at the junction of Frankel

6

Leó utca, stands a Budapest institution, the *Bambi* (see p.181), one of the few unreformed café-bars that retains its 1970s furnishings and no-nonsense waitresses.

Foundry Museum

Öntödei Múzeum • II, Bem utca 20 • March–Nov Tues–Sat 10am–4pm; Dec–Feb Thurs–Sat 10am–4pm • 800Ft • ☎ 1 201 4370, ⓦ mmkm.hu

A century ago, the neighbourhood surrounding Bem tér was dominated by a foundry established by the Swiss ironworker Abrahám Ganz, which grew into the mighty Ganz Machine Works. The original ironworks only ceased operation in 1964, when it was turned into a **Foundry Museum**, which sits rather incongruously amid the neighbouring flats and modern high-rises 200m up the hill from Bem tér. You can still see the old wooden structure and the foundry's huge ladles and cranes in situ, together with a quite superb collection of cast-iron stoves, tram wheels, lampposts and other exhibits.

Széll Kálmán tér and around

The area immediately north of the Vár is defined by the transport hub of **Széll Kálmán tér**. A former clay quarry that was turned into tennis courts between the wars, it was named in 1929 after Széll, a former finance and prime minister. Renamed **Moszkva tér** in 1951, it only regained its old name in 2011. To the north, the **Mammut mall** (fronted by a statue of the woolly beast) is a magnet for shoppers, as is the lively Fény utca **market**, while **Millenáris Park** lurks just beyond. Otherwise, Széll Kálmán tér is the place to catch buses to the Cogwheel Railway (see p.122) or the Farkasréti Cemetery (see p.125), as well as trams #4 and #6 to Pest.

Millenáris Park

Millenáris • II, Fény utca 20–22 • **Indoor play centre** Daily 10am–6pm • 1590Ft • ☎ 1 336 4000, ⓦ millenaris.hu

The main attraction of the area is the **Millenáris Park**, the site of the former Ganz Machine Works behind the Mammut mall. Set around a small lake, the converted factory buildings and the landscaped park between them host indoor and outdoor concerts and theatre, as well as an interactive playhouse and a **playground** themed around a Hungarian folk tale. The main **indoor play centre** is in building G, the Fogadó.

Invisible Exhibition

Láthatatlan Kiállítás • II, Kis Rókus utca 16–20, but the entrance is through Millenáris Park • Daily 10am–8pm • Mon–Fri 1700Ft, Sat & Sun 1990Ft • ☎ 0620 771 4236, ⓦ lathatatlan.hu

In Millenáris Park's building B, the marvellous **Invisible Exhibition** is one of Budapest's more unconventional attractions. Ostensibly aimed at educational groups, but open to individual visitors too, this was the first of several such centres to be opened (in 2007) throughout Central/Eastern Europe. Led by a blind or visually-impaired guide, the hour-long tour takes visitors on an interactive journey into darkness, with only touch, smell and sound to guide them. It's an experience that will unquestionably alter your perceptions of what it is to be blind.

Rózsadomb

The smoggy arc of **Margít körút** underlines the gulf between the polluted inner city and the breeze-freshened heights of Budapest's most affluent neighbourhood, **Rózsadomb**. Rózsadomb itself is as much a social category as a neighbourhood: a list of residents would read like a Hungarian *Who's Who*. During the Communist era this included the top Party *funcionárusok*, whose homes featured secret exits that enabled ÁVO chiefs to escape lynching during the Uprising. Nowadays, wealthy film directors and entrepreneurs predominate, and the sloping streets are lined with spacious villas and flashy cars.

Gül Baba's tomb

Gül Baba Türbe • II, Mecset utca 14 • Daily 10am–6pm • Free

Rózsadomb (Rose Hill) is named after the flowers that were reputedly introduced to Hungary by a revered Sufi dervish, Gül Baba, the "Father of the Roses", who participated in the Turkish capture of Buda but died during the thanksgiving service afterwards. **Gül Baba's Tomb** is located through a grubby park and up some steps at the end of Mecset utca (Mosque Street), five minutes' walk uphill from Margít körút via Margít utca. Its octagonal shrine is adorned with Arabic calligraphy and Turkish carpets, and is surrounded by a colonnaded parapet, marble fountains decorated with tiles, and rose bushes.

6

Rózsadomb baths

Lukács Baths Lukács Fürdő • II, Frankl Leó út 25–29 • Daily 6am–9pm • ☎ 1 326 1695, Ⓦ lukacsbaths.com • **Veli Bej Baths** Veli Bej Fürdő • II, Árpád fejedelem útja 7 • Daily 6am–noon & 3–9pm • ☎ 1 438 8400 • **Császár Komjádi Pool** Császár Komjádi Uszoda • II, Árpád fejedelem útja 8 • Daily 6am–7pm • ☎ 1 212 2750

Three noteworthy baths (see pp.199–202) dominate the Buda bank of the Danube, north of the Margít híd. First up are the Neoclassical **Lukács Baths**, entered via an atmospheric drinking hall, beyond which lies a large complex of indoor and outdoor pools, whirlpools and the like; the Lukács is also renowned for its popular and raucous bath party nights. A little further up stand the sixteenth-century **Veli Bej Baths**, the oldest and largest of the city's Ottoman spa houses. After a lengthy restoration project, the Veli Bej have been returned to something like their former majesty, featuring a superb central cupola surrounded by four smaller domed pools, in addition to steam chambers, saunas and jacuzzis. Next door is the **Császár Komjádi Pool**, the venue for the first European swimming and water polo championships in 1926, and which today is still a training pool for Hungary's world-class water polo players.

Gellért-hegy and the Tabán

A craggy dolomite hill rearing 130m above the Danube's embankment, Gellért-hegy is one area you'd be foolish to miss: it offers a fabulous view of the city from its imposing Citadella, and is as much a feature of Budapest's waterfront panorama as the Vár and the Parliament building. At its foot are two baths, the best known being the Gellért, with its Art Nouveau thermal baths and summer terrace, attached to the stately old hotel. North of Gellért-hegy is the Rudas, one of Budapest's most historic and magical Turkish baths. The second of these baths lies in the Tabán, Buda's former artisan quarter, though now with more roads than buildings; on its northern edge, however, you'll find the enlightening Semmelweis Medical Museum and the superbly restored Várkert Bazár.

ARRIVAL

By metro and bus Gellért-Hegy and the Tabán are fairly well served by public transport. The new green metro line (#4) has stations at Gellért tér and Móricz Zsigmond körtér, while bus #7 also serves these destinations. In terms of trams, the #18 from Széll Kálmán tér and tram #19 from Batthyány tér via the Tabán serve the same points.

By tram Lines #47 and #49 from Pest also serve Gellért tér and Móricz Zsigmond körtér, as do tram #18 from Széll Kálmán tér and tram #19 from Batthyány tér.

Gellért-hegy

Surmounted by the Liberation Monument and the Citadella, **Gellért-hegy** makes a distinctive contribution to Budapest's skyline. The hill is named after the Italian missionary Ghirardus (Gellért in Hungarian), who converted pagan Magyars to Christianity at the behest of King Stephen. After his royal protector's demise, vengeful heathens strapped Gellért to a barrow and toppled him off the cliff, where a larger-than-life **statue of St Gellért** now stands facing the Erzsébet híd, his crucifix raised as if in admonition to motorists.

Gellért Hotel and Baths

Gellért Gyógyfürdő • XI, Kelenhegyi út 4 • Daily 6am–8pm • ☏ 1 466 6166, ⓦ gellertbath.com

At the foot of Gellért-hegy, the graceful wrought-iron **Szabadság híd** (Liberty Bridge) links the inner boulevard of Pest to Szent Gellért tér on the Buda side, dominated by the Art Nouveau **Gellért Hotel** (see p.155). Opened in 1918, it was commandeered as a staff headquarters by the Reds, the Romanian army, and finally by Admiral Horthy, following his triumphal entry into "sinful Budapest" in 1920 – in his eyes it was a decadent, Communist and, above all, a Jewish city. During the 1930s and 1940s, the hotel's balls were the highlight of Budapest's social calendar, when debutantes danced on a glass floor laid over its pool. The ostentatious domed **drinking fountain** in front of the hotel symbolizes the eight springs of Budapest, though there's actually rarely any water emanating from it.

Entered from Kelenhegyi út to the right of the main entrance, the attached **Gellért Baths** (see p.201) are magnificently appointed with majolica tiles and mosaics, and a columned, Roman-style **thermal pool**, with lion-headed spouts. In the summer, visitors can also use the **outdoor pools**, including one with a wave machine, on the terraces behind the main baths.

Cave Church

Sziklatemplom (Pálos Fogadóközpont) • I, Szent Gellért rakpart 1 • Mon–Sat 9.30am–7.30pm, but closed during 5pm service • 600Ft, which includes an audioguide • Services daily 8.30am, 5pm & 8pm, plus Sun 11am

On the hillside opposite the *Gellért Hotel*, standing next to a **statue of St Stephen** with his horse, you'll find the **Cave Church**, where Mass is conducted by white-robed monks of the Pauline order. Founded in 1256, the Pauline is the only religious order indigenous to Hungary; its monks served as confessors to the Hungarian kings until Josef II dissolved the order in 1773, though it was re-established 150 years later.

The Cave Church itself was created in the 1930s to mark the return of the monks to Hungary, and functioned until the whole community was arrested by the ÁVO at midnight Mass on Easter Monday, 1951, whereupon the chapel was sealed up until 1989. Inside, a higgledy-piggledy warren of narrow corridors and small chambers eventually brings you to the nave, the most striking aspect of which is the **tiled altar** from the Zsolnay factory. Flickering candles and mournful organ music create a particularly eerie atmosphere during services.

To the rear of the nave, the tiny **Polish Chapel** is where Polish refugees sought sanctuary during World War II, while a relief commemorates St Maximilian Kolbe, who died at Auschwitz and was canonized as a saint in 1982.

HIDDEN GEMS: GELLÉRT-HEGY AND THE TABÁN

Cave Church See above
Wallow in the Rudas Baths See p.111
Várkert Bazár See p.112
View from the Citadella See p.111
Semmelweis Medical Museum See p.112
Lounge in the modernist Tranzit Art Café See p.173
Folk music at the Fonó See p.186

Liberation Monument and the Citadella

Felszabadulási emlékmű • Bus #27 from Móricz Zsigmond körtér to the Busuló Juhász stop, followed by a 10min walk, or 20min walk up
from the *Gellért Hotel* past the Cave Church

The **summit** of Gellért-hegy affords a stunning **panoramic view**, drawing one's eye
slowly along the curving river, past bridges and monumental landmarks, and then
on to the Buda Hills and Pest's suburbs, merging hazily with the distant plain. The
summit is very exposed, so to avoid the searing summer heat, and more pertinently the
murderously busy crowds that have usually arrived by mid-morning, get here as early as
you can – in any case, early morning is the best time to enjoy the view.

On the summit stands the **Liberation Monument**, a female figure brandishing
the palm of victory over 30m aloft. There is a famous tale that the monument
was originally commissioned by Admiral Horthy in memory of his son István
(who was killed in a plane crash on the Eastern Front in 1942), and that, by
substituting a palm branch for the propeller it was meant to hold and placing a
statue of a Red Army soldier at the base, the monument was deftly recycled to
commemorate the Soviet soldiers who died liberating Budapest from the Nazis.
While the story may not be true, the monument's sculptor, **Zsigmond Kisfaludi-
Strobl**, certainly succeeded in winning approval as a "Proletarian Artist", despite
having previously specialized in busts of the aristocracy – and was henceforth
known by his compatriots as "Kisfaludi-Strébel" (*strébel* meaning "to climb" or "step
from side to side"). The monument survived calls for its removal following the end
of Communism, but its inscription was rewritten to honour those who died for
"Hungary's prosperity", and the Soviet soldier was banished to the Memento Park
on the outskirts of Budapest (see p.127).

The **Citadella** behind the monument was built by the Habsburgs to dominate the city
in the aftermath of the 1848–49 Revolution; ironically, both its architects were
Hungarians. When the historic Compromise was reached in 1867, citizens breached
the walls to affirm that it no longer posed a threat to them – though in fact an SS
regiment did later hole up in the citadel during World War II.

7

The Tabán

The **Tabán** district, bordering the northern end of Gellért-hegy, chiefly consists of
arterial roads built in Communist times on land left vacant by the prewar demolition
of a quarter renowned for its drinking dens and open sewers. Traditionally this was
inhabited by Serbs (Rác in Hungarian), who settled here en masse after the Turks were
expelled, though in a typically Balkan paradox, some were present earlier, working in
the Ottoman gunpowder factories which may have been the origin of the name Tabán
(from *tabahane*, the Turkish for "armoury"). Thankfully, the slum clearance and
motorway building spared Tabán's historic Turkish baths, and its traditions of lusty
nightlife are kept alive by summertime concerts in the park.

Rudas Baths

Rudas Gyógyfürdő • I, Döbrentei tér 9 • **Baths** Daily 6am–8pm, plus night-swimming Fri & Sat 10pm–4am • **Wellness section and
sauna** Daily 6am–10pm • ☎ 1 356 1322, ⓦ rudasfurdo.hu

The relaxing and curative effects of Buda's **mineral springs** have been appreciated for
two thousand years, though it was the Turks who consolidated the habit of bathing and
built proper bathhouses which function to this day. The **Rudas Baths** (see p.202), in the
shadow of Gellért-hegy, harbour a fantastic octagonal pool constructed in 1556 on the
orders of Pasha Sokoli Mustapha. Bathers wallow amid shafts of light pouring in from
the star-shaped apertures in the domed ceiling, surrounded by stone pillars with iron
tie-beams and a nest of smaller pools for parboiling oneself or cooling down. A more
recent addition is a **Wellness section**, which incorporates five pools including a splendid
rooftop pool, and a sauna section.

Statue of Empress Elizabeth

I, Döbrentei tér

In the island of grass amid the swirl of roads leading to the Buda end of the bridge is a seated **statue of Empress Elizabeth** (1837–98; see p.149), after whom the Erzsébet híd (Elizabeth Bridge) is named. The Austrian empress – she was also the Queen of Hungary – endeared herself to Hungarians by learning their language and refusing to be stifled by her crusty husband, Franz Josef.

Semmelweis Medical Museum

Semmelweis Orvostörténeti Múzeum • I, Apród utca 1–3 • Tues–Sun: mid-March to Oct 10am–6pm; Nov to mid-March Tues–Fri 10am–4pm, Sat & Sun 10am–6pm • 700Ft • ☎ 1 375 3533, ⓥ semmelweis.museum.hu

Often overlooked by tourists, the **Semmelweis Medical Museum** contains a fascinating collection of artefacts relating to the history of medicine, with mummified limbs from ancient Egypt, and a shrunken head used by Borneo witchdoctors giving it an international dimension. Other exhibits – including a medieval chastity belt, trepanning drills, and a range of brutal-looking medical implements – bone saw, bullet extractor, dissection set – don't bear thinking about, frankly.

The museum is named after the eponymous nineteenth-century doctor who lived here until the age of five and is buried in the garden. Semmelweis helped save generations of women thanks to his work on puerperal fever (see box below). Along with the many family portraits on display, there's one of Vilma Hugonai, Hungary's first woman doctor, and another of Kossuth's sister, Zsuzsanna, who founded the army medical corps during the War of Independence. In the neighbouring room, the **Holy Ghost Pharmacy**, with its gorgeous, Baroque wood-carved fixtures and fittings, dates from 1786 and was transplanted here from Király utca.

Szarvas tér

Szarvas tér (Stag Square) is named after the eighteenth-century *Stag House* inn at no. 1, which today functions as the *Aranyszarvas* restaurant. In between the Semmelweis Museum and the restaurant stands a bust of **Dr József Antall** (1931–93), the first democratically elected prime minister of Hungary after the fall of Communism. For many years, while working as the director of the Semmelweis, he had been dreaming of the chance to emerge from the political shadows, and as prime minister he skilfully ran his centre-right coalition to give Hungary a stable start, though his social conservatism was loathed by his opponents. He died in office and is buried in the Kerepesi Cemetery (see p.83).

Várkert Bazár

I, Ybl Miklós tér 2–6 • **Garden** Daily 6am–midnight • Free • **Exhibitions** Tues–Sun 10am–5.30pm • 2000Ft • ☎ 1 225 0544, ⓥ varkertbazar.hu

Facing the riverbank on Ybl Miklós tér stands the grand facade and terraces of the superbly renovated **Várkert Bazár** (Castle Garden), designed by Miklós Ybl

---

DR IGNÁC SEMMELWEIS

Dr Ignác Semmelweis (1818–65) discovered the cause of puerperal fever – a form of blood poisoning contracted in childbirth, which was usually fatal. While serving in Vienna's public hospitals in the 1840s, he noticed that deaths were ten times lower on the wards where only midwives worked than on the ones attended by doctors and students, who went from dissecting corpses to delivering babies with only a perfunctory wash. His solution was to sterilize hands, clothes and instruments between operations – an idea dismissed as preposterous by the hospital, which fired him. Embittered, he wrote open letters to obstetricians, accusing them of being murderers, and was sent to an asylum where he died within a couple of weeks. Only after Pasteur's germ theory was accepted was Semmelweis hailed as the "saviour of mothers".

(1814–91), the man behind the Opera House and other major works. Designed as the grand entrance to the Várkert, the park running up to the palace, with shops either side of the steps, the Bazár was never in the right location to attract business and by 1920 was occupied by artists' studios. After suffering damage in the war, it reopened in 1961 as a "youth park" and was one of the few places offering entertainment for the younger generation. Its outdoor pop concerts became legendary, but the crumbling building was forced to close in the 1980s, and numerous plans for redevelopment came to nothing; after years of decay, the Bazár finally reopened in 2014 as a multicultural complex. At its heart is a neatly landscaped Renaissance **garden**, with lush, sloping lawns interspersed with rose flowerbeds. Flanking the gardens, the **Southern Palace** and **Guard's Palace** host temporary exhibitions, typically on a historic theme. Elsewhere, the foundry courtyard hosts various musical and theatrical events, while there's an information centre (also in the Guard's Palace), restaurant and food shop.

Across the road from the Várkert Bazár is the **Várkert Kioszk**, a former pumping station with an ornate interior and Miklós Ybl's statue standing in front.

7

MARGÍT-SZIGET

Óbuda and Margít-sziget

Óbuda is the oldest part of Budapest, though that's hardly the impression given by the industrial sites and high-rises that dominate the district today, hiding such ancient ruins as remain. Nonetheless, it was here that the Romans built a legionary camp and a civilian town, later taken over by the Huns. Under the Hungarian Árpád dynasty, this developed into an important town, but in the fifteenth century it was eclipsed by the Vár. The original settlement became known as Óbuda (Old Buda) and was incorporated into the newly formed Budapest in 1873. The small but spruce old town centre is not much visited by tourists, which is a shame as it rates a clutch of very enjoyable museums. But to find the best-preserved Roman ruins, you'll have to go to the Rómaifürdő district, further out.

To the west, there is a pair of striking **caves** near the valley of Szépvölgy, a visit to which can be combined with the **Kiscelli Museum**, with its interesting collection of furniture and interior furnishings in a former monastery.

In the middle of the Danube, leafy **Margít-sziget** is a haven from the noise and pollution of the city. One of Budapest's favourite parks and summer pleasure-grounds, the island is part of its grand waterfront panorama – unlike shabby **Óbudai-sziget** just north which, like Cinderella, gets but one chance to have fun, by hosting Hungary's equivalent of Glastonbury, the **Sziget festival**, each August (see p.183).

ARRIVAL

Public transport The HÉV from Batthyány tér (see p.105) provides easy access to riverside Óbuda (get off at Szentlélek tér for Fő tér and the museums), or take #1 tram from northern Pest. For Margít-sziget, trams #4 and #6 stop at the southern entrance to the island, while bus #26 runs the length of the island itself. You can also reach Rómaifürdő and Margít-sziget on one of the ferries that zigzag up the river from Haller utca (see p.26).

Óbuda

After its incorporation within the city, **Óbuda** became a popular place to eat, drink and make merry, with garden restaurants and taverns serving fish and wine from the locality. Some of the most famous establishments still exist around **Fő tér**, the heart of eighteenth-century Óbuda, with its ornate Trinity Column.

Vasarely Museum

Vasarely Múzeum • III, Szentlélek tér 6 • Tues–Sun 10am–5.30pm • 800Ft • ☎ 1 378 7551, ⓦ vasarely.hu

The **Vasarely Museum** displays eyeball-throbbing Op Art works by Viktor Vasarely (1906–97), the founder of the genre, who was born in Pécs in southern Hungary, emigrated to Paris in 1930 and spent the rest of his life in France. Arguably, his most productive period was the 1950s and 1960s, with his groundbreaking Black and White paintings, many of which are on display here (*Vega* and *Tau-Ceti* to name but two). You can also get a sense of his artistic development from earlier works, particularly as a graphic artist, when he gained numerous commissions from various publishing houses for his advertising graphics. Note that at the time of writing, the museum was undergoing a major renovation, so the displays described here may change.

Óbuda Museum

Óbudai Múzeum • III, Szentlélek tér 1 • Tues–Sun 10am–6pm • 800Ft • ☎ 1 250 1020, ⓦ obudaimuzeum.hu

The excellent little **Óbuda Museum** charts Óbuda's development through the ages; frustratingly, there's minimal English labelling, but you can borrow a booklet at the ticket desk. Particular emphasis is given to the city's growth in the seventeenth century, which was inextricably linked to the Zichy dynasty, whose domain stretched from Óbuda all the way up to Szentendre. In the nineteenth century, as well as the local shipyard and porcelain factory, there were as many as three brickworks here; don't miss the wonderful display of brick stamps. Look out, too, for the twelfth-century stone depicting an angel alongside a bearded man – a fine example of Romanesque art. Reconstructed shops and kitchens – including a pre-electric fridge – from the early twentieth century, as well as a living room from the 1950s, complete this enjoyable little romp.

HIDDEN GEMS: ÓBUDA AND MARGÍT-SZIGET

Varga Museum See p.117
Mosaics at Aquincum See p.117
Cycle around Margít-sziget See p.119
Cool down at the Palatinus Strand
See p.120

Chill out at Fellini Római Kultúrbisztró
See p.181
Sziget Festival See p.183
Test your wits in the Csopa PlayBar
See p.205

**Inset map labels:**

Hercules Villa
MEGYERI UTCA
RAKTÁR UTCA
SZÉL UTCA
KEREK UTCA
SZENTENDREI ÚT
Military Baths
Roman Remains
Varga Museum
BUDAI ALSÓ RAKPART
Kobuci
FŐ TÉR
Kassák Museum
FLORIÁN TÉR
SZENTLÉLEK TÉR
Óbuda Museum
Szentlélek tér (H)
PACSIRTAMEZŐ UTCA
MÓKUS UTCA
Museum of Trade & Tourism
Vasarely Museum
ÁRPÁD HÍD
Óbudai-sziget
River Danube (Duna)
Obuda Music Society ❶

0   250
metres

**Main map labels:**

Aquincum (H)
Civilian Amphitheatre
Aquincum Ruins and Museum
RÓMAIFÜRDŐ
SZENTENDREI ÚT
Kaszásdűlő (H)
Filatorigát (H)
Óbudai-sziget
SEE INSET FOR DETAILS
VÖRÖSVÁRI ÚT
SZENTENDREI ÚT
FLORIÁN TÉR
Szentlélek tér (H)
BUDAI ALSÓ RAKPART
ÁRPÁD HÍD
SZÉPVÖLGYI ÚT
KISCELLI UTCA
Kiscelli Museum
BÉCSI ÚT
SELMECI UTCA
PACSIRTAMEZŐ UTCA
ÓBUDA
Pálvölgyi Stalactite Cave
Tímár utca (H)
Military Amphitheatre
NAGYSZOMBAT U.
❸
❹
Görzenál
ÁRPÁD FEJEDELEM ÚTJA
BUDAI ALSÓ RAKPART
SZÉPVÖLGYI ÚT
Center for Scientific Wonders Playbar
FELSŐ ZÖLDMÁLI U.
Szemlőhegyi Cave
❺
BÉCSI ÚT
KOLOSY TÉR
LAJOS UTCA
SZÉCHENYI MARGIT
Szépvölgyi út
PUSZTASZERI ÚT
JÓZSEFHEGYI ÚT
Margít-sziget
River Danube (Duna)
PUSZTASZERI ÚT
TÖRÖKVÉSZI ÚT
VERHALOM UTCA
VERHALOM UTCA
FRANKEL LEÓ UTCA
ÚJLIPÓTVÁROS
BIMBÓ ÚT
BIMBÓ ÚT
ADY UTCA
Margít hid (H)
SEE MARGÍT-SZIGET MAP FOR DETAILS
MARGÍT HÍD
The Vár & Central Buda
N

Legend boxes:

● EATING
RESTAURANTS
Kéhli   1
Kerék   3
Stelázsi   4
CAFÉS
Cziniel   2
Daubner   5

■ ACCOMMODATION
Római Camping   1

■ DRINKING AND NIGHTLIFE
Fellini Római Kultúrbisztró   1

ÓBUDA AND MARGÍT-SZIGET

0   500
metres

Upstairs is a delightful exhibition on **toys** from the early twentieth century onwards: dolls, teddy bears, model railways, wooden vehicles, puzzles, board games and so on. Iconic (for Hungarians at any rate) were games like Gazdálkodj Okosan!, the Hungarian version of Monopoly whereby players were encouraged to save as opposed to spend; following the collapse of the Iron Curtain in 1989, Hungary became the first of the Eastern bloc countries to have an official Monopoly version in the native language. Look out too for Pebe, the East German equivalent of Lego, albeit a markedly inferior product.

Kassák Museum
Kassák Múzeum • III, Fő tér 1 • Wed–Sun 10am–5pm • 600Ft • ☎ 1 368 7021, ⍟ kassakmuzeum.hu

On the far side of the courtyard of the run-down Baroque Zichy mansion, the small but fascinating **Kassák Museum** features paintings, magazine designs, publications and possessions of the Hungarian Constructivist **Lajos Kassák** (1887–1967). A self-taught artist and publisher who devoted much of his younger life to the Socialist cause (publishing work by Cocteau and Le Corbusier), Kassák's avant-garde style fell foul of regimes on both the left and right. In a selective form of censorship typical of the post-1956 Communist years, he was recognized as a writer but was pretty much banned from exhibiting his art from 1948.

Varga Museum
Varga Imre Múzeum • III, Laktanya utca 7 • Tues–Sun 10am–6pm • 800Ft • ☎ 1 250 0274

Whatever the weather, you'll see four women sheltering beneath umbrellas just off Fő tér, as sculpted by Imre Varga, Hungary's best-known living artist (now well into his nineties), whose oeuvre is the subject of the nearby **Varga Museum**. Pathos and humour pervade his sheet-metal, iron and bronze effigies of famous personages, including Pope John Paul II, Liszt and Bartók; there's also a fine bust of Winston Churchill. Much of Varga's earlier work was informed by the time he spent in the Hungarian air force during World War II, manifest in sobering pieces like *Apocalypse* and *Forced March*, the title of a poem by Miklós Radnóti, of whom there is also a sculpture – this a cast of the statue on Nagymező utca (see p.62). Varga's career has spanned the eras of "goulash Socialism" and democracy – evinced by state-commissioned monuments to Béla Kun (in the Memento Park, see p.127) and Imre Nagy (near Parliament; see p.54).

Museum of Trade and Tourism
Magyar Kereskedelmi és Vendéglátóipari Múzeum • III, Korona tér 1 • Tues–Sun 10am–6pm • 1000Ft • ☎ 1 375 6249, ⍟ mkvm.hu

South of the bridgehead of the Árpád híd is another remnant of the old town that is even more isolated than Fő tér among the modern blocks. The **Museum of Trade and Tourism** was the world's first such museum when it opened in 1966, and today keeps a wealth of trade- and tourism-related relics, including shopfronts, merchandise and a series of nostalgia-inducing advertising boards promoting drink, food and tobacco products. A reconstructed sweet shop, stationer's and ironmonger's feature, as does a reconstructed prewar bedroom from the *Gellért Hotel* and specialized items of cutlery from the same period, such as asparagus clippers and a 25-bladed pocket knife, both made by a Hungarian firm.

Aquincum Museum and Archeological Park
Aquincumi Múzeum és Régészeti Park • III, Szentendrei út 135 • Tues–Sun: ruins April–Oct 9am–6pm, museum April–Oct 10am–6pm; Nov–March 10am–4pm • April–Oct 1600Ft, Nov–March 1000Ft • ☎ 1 430 1081, ⍟ aquincum.hu • HÉV to Aquincum and then a 10min walk south

North of Óbuda, the riverside factory belt merges into the **Rómaifürdő** (Roman Bath) district, harbouring a campsite, a lido and the vast ruins of Aquincum, the latter opened up to visitors as the **Aquincum Museum and Archeological Park**. Originally a settlement of camp followers spawned by the legionary garrison, Aquincum eventually became a *municipium* and then a *colonia*, the provincial capital of Pannonia Inferior. Enough of the foundation walls and underground piping survives to give a fair idea of

> ## ROMAN REMAINS
> Roman soldiers had been in the Transdanubian region since the first century AD, but the larger settlement only came a century later, lasting until the fourth century. While Aquincum was the main civilian centre, the Romans' **military garrison** was to the south, and today its remains lurk in the concrete jungle of Óbuda's centre. On Flórián tér, 500m west of Fő tér, weathered columns rise next to a shopping plaza, while the old **military baths** (*thermae maiores*) are exposed in the pedestrian underpass beneath the Szentendrei út flyover. You'll also find the odd Roman wall protruding between the apartment blocks near Fő tér. The largest ruin is a **military amphitheatre** (*amfiteátrum*) which once seated up to 13,000 spectators, at the junction of Pacsirtamező utca and Nagyszombat utca, 800m further south – accessible by bus #86 or by walking 400m from Kolosy tér, near the Szépvölgyi út HÉV stop. (The remains of a **civilian amphitheatre** are by the Aquincum HÉV stop.)
>   A more elusive relic is the **Hercules Villa**, Meggyfa utca 19–21, north of Florian tér, which contained the **mosaic floor** of the centaur Nessus abducting Deianeira that can now be seen in the Aquincum Museum (see p.117). A fragment of another mosaic remains in situ, featuring a delightfully rendered tiger and Hercules about to vomit at a wine festival.

the town's layout, with its forum and law courts, its sanctuaries of the goddesses Epona and Fortuna Augusta, and the *collegia* and bathhouses where fraternal societies met.

In the southeastern corner of the park, a **Tegularium** exhibition traces the production of **brickwork** during Roman times (nearby Kiscelli was rich in clay), which was put to a variety of uses, typically roofing, flooring and walling, and heating systems. The stamped bricks on display are remarkable, typically inscribed with the name of the manufacturer or workshop, or, when produced for military purposes, the name of the troop or commander.

Aquincum Museum

The park's bare bones are given substance by an excellent **museum**, with some beautifully presented artefacts from the proconsul's palace. The star exhibit is a **mosaic** from the third century AD of Nessus abducting Deianeira, whom Hercules had to rescue as one of his twelve labours. This originally consisted of sixty thousand stones, selected and arranged in Alexandria before shipment to Europe – there's also another equally fine mosaic, this one a sparkling seascape featuring a variety of marine life. Other highlights include a cult-relief of the god Mithras, a reconstructed water-organ, and a marble statue of the proconsul himself (minus his head). Meanwhile, down in the basement is a **virtual games** experience, where you can construct a Roman house, dig up artefacts, or partake in a sword fight – great fun for kids and adults alike. The **Floralia Festival** towards the end of May sees theatrical performances, craft-making displays, mock gladiator battles and other events staged here.

Pálvölgyi and Szemlőhegyi caves

Bus #86 from Flórián tér or Batthyány tér, or bus #6 from Nyugati tér in Pest, from where you catch bus #65 five stops to the Pálvölgyi Cave, or bus #29 four stops to the Szemlőhegyi Cave

The hills rising to the west of Óbuda feature a network of caves that are unique for having been formed by thermal waters rising up from below, rather than by rainwater. Two of the sites – **Pálvölgyi** and **Szemlőhegyi** – have been accessible to the public since the 1980s, on guided tours only. In both cases, the starting point is **Kolosy tér** in Óbuda. As the two caves are ten minutes' walk apart, it's possible to see them both within two and a half hours if you start with the Szemlőhegyi.

For refreshment after the caves you should schedule in a stop at the *Daubner* patisserie (at Szépvölgyi út 29, near Kolosy tér at the bottom of the hill), which does some of the most delicious cakes in the city and attracts huge queues at weekends (see p.174). Alternatively, you can combine a visit to the Szemlőhegyi Cave with the Bartók Memorial House (see p.124) or the Kiscelli Museum (see opposite).

Pálvölgyi Stalactite Cave

Pálvölgyi cseppkőbarlang • III, Szépvölgyi út 162 • 1hr tours hourly at quarter past the hour Tues–Sun 10am–4.15pm • 1400Ft, 2000Ft with Szemlőhegyi cave (see below) • ☎ 1 325 9505, ⊛ dunaipoly.hu

The **Pálvölgyi Stalactite Cave** is the more spectacular of the two labyrinths to the west of Óbuda; part of the longest of the cave systems in the Buda Hills, at around 29km, it is still being explored by speleologists. It was discovered in 1904 by a quarryman searching for a sheep that disappeared when the floor of the quarry fell in. Tours, on which you negotiate hundreds of steps and dank constricted passages, start on the lowest level, which boasts rock formations such as the "Organ Pipes" and "Beehive". From "John's Lookout" in the largest chamber, you ascend a crevice onto the upper level, there to enter "Fairyland" and finally "Paradise", overlooking the hellish "Radium Hall" 50m below.

Szemlőhegyi Cave

Szemlőhegyi barlang • III, Pusztaszeri út 35 • 40min tours hourly on the hour daily except Tues 10am–4pm • 1300Ft, 2000Ft with Pálvölgyi cave (see above) • ☎ 1 325 6001, ⊛ dunaipoly.hu

Quite different from the nearby Pálvölgyi Stalactite Cave is the **Szemlőhegyi Cave**, with less convoluted and claustrophobic passages and no stalactites. Instead, the walls are encrusted with cauliflower- or popcorn-textured precipitates. Discovered in 1930, the cave has exceptionally clean air, and its lowest level is used as a respiratory sanatorium. After the tour you can view a museum of cave finds and plans from all over Hungary.

Kiscelli Museum

Kiscelli Múzeum • III, Kiscelli utca 108 • Tues–Sun: April–Oct 10am–6pm; Nov–March 10am–4pm • 1200Ft • ☎ 1 250 0304, ⊛ kiscellimuzeum.hu • Bus #165 from Kolosy tér or bus #160 from Batthyány tér

On a hillside above Óbuda, fifteen minutes' walk north of the Szemlőhegyi Cave, the **Kiscelli Museum** occupies a former Trinitarian monastery in a beautiful wooded setting. The museum's wide-ranging collection includes Baroque sculptures, craftsmen's tools, antique printing presses and the 1830 Biedermeier furnishings of the Golden Lion pharmacy, which used to stand on Kálvin tér. The blackened shell of the monastery's Gothic church makes a dramatic backdrop for exhibitions of contemporary art, classical **concerts**, animated film shows and other events.

Margít-sziget

Trams #4 and #6 stop at the southern entrance on the Margít híd, and bus #26 runs down the middle of the island to and from the Árpád híd station on the blue metro line #3; Motorists can only approach from the north of the island, via the Árpád híd, at which point they must leave their vehicles at the car park (525Ft/hr)

There's a saying that "love begins and ends on **Margít-sziget**", for this verdant island has been a favourite meeting place for lovers since the nineteenth century (though before 1945 a stiff admission charge deterred the poor). A royal game reserve under the Árpáds and a monastic colony until the Turkish conquest, today Margít-sziget has two public baths fed by thermal springs, an outdoor theatre and other amenities, and in 2017 much of the park was smartened up for the staging of that year's World Swimming Championships.

The island was named at the end of the nineteenth century after Princess **Margít** (Margaret), the daughter of Béla IV. Legend has it that he vowed to bring her up as a nun if Hungary survived the Mongol invasion, and duly confined the nine-year-old in a convent when it did. She apparently made the best of it, acquiring a reputation for curing lepers and other saintly deeds, as well as for never washing above her ankles. Beatification came after her death in 1271, and a belated canonization in 1943, by which time her name had already been bestowed on the **Margít híd**, built by a French company in the 1870s. Linking Margít-sziget to Buda and Pest, it's an unusual bridge in the form of a splayed-out V, with a short arm joined to the southern tip of the island. In November 1944, it was blown up by the Nazis, killing hundreds of people including the German sappers who had detonated the explosives by mistake.

Margít-sziget swimming pools

Walking down from the tram stop on Margít híd, you are greeted by a **Millennial Monument** and a **fountain** that emits bursts of grand music. Further on, behind trees to the left, is the **Hajós Alfréd Pool** (known as the "Sport"; see p.201), named after the winner of the 100m and 1200m swimming races at the 1896 Olympics – hence the first modern Olympic swimming champion. Hajós (1878–1955) was also an architect and designed the indoor pool, but the main attractions here are the all-season outdoor 50m pool, where the national swimming team trains. Another swimming venue, the **Palatinus Strand** (see p.202), lies nearly a kilometre further north. With a monumental entrance from the 1930s, this lido can hold as many as ten thousand people at a time in numerous open-air thermal pools, complete with a water chute, wave machine and segregated terraces for nude sunbathing.

Ruins, zoo and gardens

Turning right off the road that runs northwards up Margít-sziget before you get to the Palatinus, you'll come to the ruins of a **Franciscan church** from the late thirteenth century and, beyond that, the **petting zoo** (April–Oct daily 10am–6pm; free), part of the Budapest Zoo (see p.75) where kids can enjoy llamas, deer, peacocks and numerous types of waterfowl. You'll also find several birds of prey, including a magnificent white-tailed (sea) eagle, all here as part of the Hungarian Bird Rescue Foundation which cares for birds too badly injured to be released back into the wild.

Walking north up the middle of the island takes you through the immaculately manicured **Rose Garden** and on up to the ruined **Dominican church and convent**. Just beyond here, in the shadow of the enormous Art Nouveau **water tower**, which rises some 66m, the **Outdoor Theatre** (Szabadtéri Színpad) hosts plays, operas, fashion shows and concerts during summer. A short way northeast of the tower is a **Premonstratensian Chapel**, whose Romanesque tower dates back to the twelfth century, when the order first established a monastery on the island. The tower's fifteenth-century bell is one of the oldest in Hungary. Heading towards the northern tip, you can't miss the island's two hotels, the original, late nineteenth-century *Grand* and its ugly twin sister, the *Thermal*. Beside the latter is a pretty **Japanese Garden** with plants donated by the botanical gardens of Hokkaido University, and warm springs that sustain tropical fish and giant water lilies.

ON BOARD THE COGWHEEL RAILWAY

The Buda Hills

A densely wooded arc around a sixth of Budapest's circumference, the Buda Hills are as close to nature as you can get within the city limits. The hills are a favourite place for walking in all seasons, with trails marked with the distance or the duration ("ó" stands for hours; "p" for minutes). While some parts can be crowded with walkers and mountain-bikers at the weekend, it's possible to ramble for hours during the week and see hardly a soul. The most rewarding destinations for those with limited time are the "railway circuit", using the Cogwheel and Children's railways and the chairlift, and the Bartók Memorial House. Further south is the Farkasréti Cemetery, noted for its architecture as well as the celebrated personages buried here.

9

ARRIVAL AND GETTING AROUND

By public transport Széll Kálmán tér is the easiest starting point for all the destinations in the hills, including all points along the railway circuit. The Cogwheel Railway is two stops away on tram #59 or #61 or bus #155 or #156; alight opposite the cylindrical *Budapest Hotel*; bus #155 goes on to the bottom of the chairlift while tram #61 goes on to Hüvösvölgy. Bus #21 and #21A go up to Normafa; the #21 goes on to Csillebérc.

By bike Exploring the Buda Hills by trail-bike is a more ambitious option, if you've got a day to spare and the stamina. Velo-Touring (XI, Előpatak utca 1; ☎ 1 319 0571, ⓦ velo-touring.hu) rents 21-gear bikes (from €14/day; €100 deposit) and can advise on routes; its office is about 1km from Farkasréti Cemetery. Bikes can be carried on the Cogwheel (validate an extra ticket) and Children's railways (200Ft fee).

The railway circuit

The **railway circuit** is an easy and enjoyable way to visit the hills that will especially appeal to kids. The whole trip can take under two hours if connections click, but you're better off taking your time and completing it over the course of a leisurely half-day.

Cogwheel Railway

Fogaskerekűvasút, also designated tram #60 • Daily 5am–11pm • BKK fares and passes (see p.24) apply

The railway circuit begins at the lower terminal of the **Cogwheel Railway**, which was the third such railway in the world when it was inaugurated in 1874, and steam-powered until its electrification in 1929. Running every ten minutes or so, its cogs fitting into a notched track, the train climbs 300m over nearly 4km through the villa-suburb of **Svábhegy**; for the best view on the way up, take a window seat on the right-hand side, facing backwards.

Children's Railway

Gyermekvasút • Tues–Sun (plus Mon June–Aug), trains go every 45–60min 9am–5pm • 600Ft to any mid-station, 700Ft from terminus to terminus • ☎ 01 397 5394, ⓦ www.gyermekvasut.hu

From the Cogwheel Railway's upper terminal on **Széchenyi-hegy**, it's a minute's walk to the **Children's Railway**. A narrow-gauge line built by Communist youth brigades in 1948, it's almost entirely run by 13- to 17-year-old members of the Scouts and Guides movement, enabling them to get hands-on experience if they fancy a career with MÁV, the Hungarian Railways company. Watching them wave flags, collect tickets and salute departures with great solemnity, you can see why it appealed to the Communists. The forty-minute ride along the full 11km length of the line is a delightful run through the wooded hills. In summer, they sometimes run heritage trains, pulled by a steam engine or vintage diesel loco, for which a 200Ft supplement is charged.

Normafa

The first stop along the Children's Railway route, **Normafa**, is a popular excursion centre with a modest **ski-run** (see p.198) and sledging slopes. Its name comes from a performance of the famous aria from Bellini's *Norma* given here by the actress Rozália Klein in 1840. A popular destination at the top of the slope is the *Rétes Büfé* (see p.174), a wooden shack that sells a range of delicious *rétes* strudel.

Csillebérc treetop adventure course

Kalandpálya XII, Konkoly Thege Miklós út 21 • April–Sept daily 10am–6pm; Nov–March Sat & Sun 10am–4pm • 3500Ft, children 3000Ft • ☎ 1 274 5705, ⓦ kalandpalya.com

Right by the second Children's Railway stop, **Csillebérc**, there's a large wooded **adventure course**, with tree-top walkways and a series of zip-wires of varying difficulty, though anyone attempting these must be over 100cm in height. Although not as challenging as the tree-top canopy at Visegrád (see p.140), it's tremendous fun for all ages. Moreover, on a hot day, the trees offer a refreshing shelter from the sun.

BUDA HILLS

N

Hüvösvölgy Bus Terminus
NAGYKOVÁCSI ÚT
HÜVÖSVÖLGY
Children's Railway
Hárshegy

Szépjuhászné

BUDAKESZI ÚT

ALSÓVÖLGYI UTCA
HÜVÖSVÖLGY ÚT
NAPRA FORGÓ ÚT
SZERB UTCA
CSALÁN UTCA
Bartók Memorial House
CSALÁN UTCA
CSÉVI UTCA
KAPY UTCA
Napraforgó Housing Estate
SZÉHER ÚT

PASARÉTI TÉR
PASARÉTI ÚT
PASARÉT
1

JÁNOS-HEGY
Erzsébet Lookout Tower
Chairlift (Libegö)
BUDAKESZI ÚT
ZUGLIGETI ÚT
2

Jánós-hegy

SZARVAS GÁBOR ÚT
KISS ÁRON ÚT
2
KÚTVÖLGYI ÚT
4

3 & Széll Kálmán tér

ZUGLIGET

Children's Railway

Virágvölgy
JÁNOSHEGYI ÚT
NORMAFA
3

SVÁBHEGY
BÉLA KIRÁLY ÚT
Cogwheel Railway

Normafa
Csillebérc
EÖTVÖS ÚT
Csillebérc Adventure Course
5
Children's Railway
Svábhegy

Széchenyi-hegy
Széchenyi-hegy

KONKOLY THEGE MIKLÓS ÚT
CSILLEBÉRC

Széll Kálmán tér & Erzsébet híd

Farkasréti Cemetery

Velo-Touring office

0 —— 500
metres

■ **ACCOMMODATION**
Beatrix Panzió	1
Buda Villa Panzió	4
Budapest	3
Csillebérci Camping	5
Zugligeti Niche Camping	2

● **EATING**
RESTAURANTS
| Alessio | 1 |
| Vendeglő a Kisbiróhoz | 2 |
CAFÉ
| Normafa Rétes | 3 |

9

János-hegy

Alighting from the Children's Railway at **János-hegy**, two stops on from **Csillebérc**, you can either strike out down through woods to the town of **Budakeszi**, from where bus #22 takes you back to Széll Kálmán tér, or make the steep twenty-minute climb from the station to the top of **János-hegy** (527m), the highest point in Budapest. The Romanesque-style **Erzsébet lookout tower** (daily 8am–8pm; free) on the summit offers a panoramic view of the city and the Buda Hills. The tower was designed by Frigyes Schulek, also the architect behind the Vár's Fishermen's Bastion (see p.92) – the similarity is clear. It takes its name from Empress Elizabeth, the Queen of Hungary (see box, p.149), who visited this spot in 1882 and came back on two other occasions.

By the buffet below the summit is the upper terminal of the **chairlift** or **Libegő** (daily: March & Oct 10am–5pm; April & Sept 10am–6pm; May–Aug 10am–7pm; Nov–Feb 10am–3.30pm; closed every other Mon; 1000Ft), meaning "floater" in Hungarian, which wafts you down over trees and gardens to the unremarkable suburb of **Zugliget**.

Hárshegy and Hűvösvölgy

Wild boar, which prefer to roam during the evening and sleep by day, are occasionally sighted in the forests above **Hárshegy**, one stop before the Children's Railway terminus at Hűvösvölgy. This is also a great place for finding **mushrooms** – most big markets, such as the Fény utca market by Széll Kálmán tér (see p.189) have stalls where you can get your mushrooms checked (*gombavizsgáló*). **Hűvösvölgy** (Cool Valley) is a vast suburb spreading into the hills and valleys beyond. It has always been a popular destination for Budapestis, trundling out on the old tram #56. Wicked tongues say that after the riots of 2006, the Socialist Party decided to change the numbering of the tram (with its connotations of 1956) to #61. The **Arts and Crafts bus terminus**, with its covered stairways leading to the train station, has been restored to its original elegance.

Bartók Memorial House

Bartók Béla Emlékház · II, Csalán utca 29 · Tues–Sun 10am–5pm, closed for three weeks in Aug · 1500Ft · ☎ 1 394 2100, ⓦ bartokmuseum.hu · Chamber music concerts 2000–3000Ft (includes entry to museum) are held here from Sept until June · Bus #29 from the Szemlőhegyi Cave to the Nagybányai út stop, or bus #5 from Ferenciek tere in Pest or Széll Kálmán tér to the Pasaréti tér terminus, and then a 10min walk uphill along Csévi utca (follow it round to the left at the first corner)

The **Bartók Memorial House**, located in a leafy suburb below Látó-hegy, was the residence of Béla Bartók, his wife and two sons from 1932 until their emigration to America in 1940, by which time Bartók despaired of Hungary's right-wing regime. Now a museum, it keeps an extensive range of Bartók memorabilia, though there's very little by way of English translation or information: the three rooms on the second floor are much as they would have looked when Bartók lived here, with his piano, cupboards and writing desk, as well as the phonograph he used to make field recordings during his ethno-musical research trips to Transylvania with Zoltán Kodály. In the attic, you can also see folk handicrafts Bartók collected on his travels and the shirt cuff on which he wiped his pen-nibs when composing scores, many of which were completed here and are on show. The shop, meanwhile, sells CDs, books and scores of Bartók's music.

Napraforgó utca housing estate

II, Napraforgó utca · Signposted from Pasaréti tér, the terminus of bus #5: follow Pasaréti út until you reach a playing field and cross the bridge on the left

Before you return to Széll Kálmán tér from the Bartók Memorial House, it's worth a brief detour to see the delightful **Napraforgó utca housing estate**, built in 1931. Its 22 houses – designed by as many architects – embody different trends in Modernist architecture, from severe Bauhaus to folksy Arts and Crafts style. The houses are all occupied – you can't go in – but they have pretty much preserved their original look.

For refreshment afterwards, head for the café in the listed 1930s **bus shelter** on Pasaréti tér. The shelter's curving horizontal form contrasts with the slender vertical lines of the Franciscan Church of St Antal across the road – both were designed by the architect Géza Rimanóczy as a single project for the square.

Farkasréti Cemetery

Farkasréti temető • XII, Németvölgyi út 99 • Daily 7.30am–5pm • Free • Tram #59 from Széll Kálmán tér or bus #8 from Astoria in Pest

Two kilometres west of Gellért-hegy in the hilly XII district is the **Farkasréti Cemetery**, where a mass of flower stalls and funerary masons indicate that you've arrived. Among the ten thousand graves in the "Wolf's Meadow Cemetery" are those of **Béla Bartók** (whose remains were ceremonially reburied in 1988 following their return from America, where he died in exile in 1945); his fellow composer **Zoltán Kodály**; and the conductor **Georg Solti**, who left Hungary in 1939 to meet Toscanini and thus escaped the fate of his Jewish parents.

Less well known abroad are the actress Gizi Bajor, Olympic-medal-winning boxer László Papp and some infamous figures from the Communist era: Hungary's Stalinist dictator **Mátyás Rákosi** (as a precaution against vandalism, only the initials on his grave are visible), his secret police chief Gábor Péter (see box, p.64), and András Hegedüs, the Politburo member who asked the Soviets to crush the Uprising. Also look out for the many wooden grave markers inscribed in the ancient runic Székely alphabet – the Székely people now form roughly half of the Hungarian population of the Székely region in Transylvania, Romania.

However, the real attraction is the amazing **mortuary chapel** by architect Imre Makovecz – one of his finest designs, dating from 1975, which was used for his own funeral in 2011. Its wood-ribbed vault resembles the inside of a human ribcage, with a casket for corpses where the heart would be. Be discreet, as the chapel is in constant use by mourners. Visitors keen to see more of Makovecz's work should pay a visit to Visegrád (p.140), an hour's journey north of the capital.

MEMENTO PARK

The city limits

While the centre of Budapest is hardly short of attractions, it would be a shame to overlook some others out towards or just beyond the city limits. In Pest, the Railway History Park – where visitors can drive steam trains – is popular with Hungarian tourists, while the New Public Cemetery completes the roll call of illustrious Hungarian dead begun at Kerepesi. In Buda, the Memento Park, with its exiled Communist memorials, is the prime destination for foreigners, while children will enjoy both the Center for Scientific Wonders and the Tropicarium, the former a "scientific playhouse", the latter with its sharks and rainforest creatures – leaving the Nagytétényi Castle Museum to devotees of stately homes. You can reach any of these places from the city centre within an hour.

Railway History Park

Magyar Vasúttörténeti Park · XIV, Tatai út 95 · April–Oct Tues–Sat 10am–6pm, Sun 10am–5pm · 1700Ft · ☎ 1 450 1497,
ⓦ vasuttortenetipark.hu · Bus #30 from Keleti Station or Hősök tere to the Rokolya utca stop, a short walk from the gates · See map p.5

The engagingly hands-on **Hungarian Railway History Park**, or Hungarian Railway
Museum, lurks in the freight yards of the XIV district. Its roundhouse and sidings
house over seventy locomotives and carriages from 1870 onwards, including the Árpád
railcar that set the 1934 speed record from Budapest to Vienna in just under three
hours, and a 1912 teak dining carriage from the *Orient Express*. Many of the museum's
staff are ex-employees of MÁV (Hungarian State Railways), proud of a tradition
inherited from the Royal Hungarian Railways. Here you can **drive** a steam train
(1200Ft), luggage cart (600Ft) or engine simulator (800Ft), as well as operate a model
railway (300Ft), and a turntable used for turning locomotives around (free). Worth
looking out for are the special event days, when further activities are laid on, including
the chance to ride a horse-drawn tram.

New Public Cemetery

Új köztemető · X, Kozma utca 8–10 · Daily 8am–dusk · Free · Tram #28 or #37 from Népszínház utca, by Blaha Lujza tér · See map p.5

The **New Public Cemetery** is located in the X district of Pest beyond the breweries of
Kőbánya, near the end of one of the longest tram rides in town. This is Budapest's
largest cemetery – reflecting the city's growth in the latter half of the nineteenth
century – and it was in a remote corner that **Imre Nagy** and 260 others, executed for
their part in the 1956 Uprising, were secretly buried in unmarked graves in 1958. Any
flowers left at **Plot 301** were removed by the police until 1989, when the deceased
received a state funeral on Hősök tere. The plot is 2km from the main gates on Kozma
utca – but note that the minibuses that shuttle back and forth every twenty minutes
only run between 9am and 3pm Tuesday to Friday. Near the graves, an ornate wooden
gateway and headposts mark a mass grave now designated as a **National Pantheon** – as
opposed to the Communist pantheon in Kerepesi (see p.82).

Jewish Cemetery

Izraelita temető · X, Kozma utca 6 · Mon–Fri & Sun 8am–2pm · Free · Last stop on tram #28 or #37 · See map p.5

The **Jewish Cemetery**, some 700m up the road from the New Public Cemetery, is the
burial place of Ernő Szép (author of *The Smell of Humans*, a searing Holocaust memoir),
as well as many rabbis and industrialists. Beside the wall on Kozma utca stand the grand
crypts of the Goldberger and Kornfeld manufacturing dynasties, and the dazzling
blue-and-gold-tiled Art Nouveau tomb of shopkeeper **Sándor Schmidl**, designed by Ödön
Lechner and Béla Lajta (who later became supervisor of Budapest's Jewish cemeteries).

Memento Park

Szoborpark · XXII, Balatoni út · Daily 10am–dusk · 1500Ft; guided tours cost an extra 1200Ft · ☎ 1 424 7500, ⓦ mementopark.hu ·
A Memento Park bus (May–Oct daily, March & April Sat–Mon; Nov–Feb Sat & Mon) departs from Deák tér bus stop by the old bus station
at 11am, returning at 1pm for 4900Ft (tickets include entry and a guided tour, and are purchased on the bus); by public transport, take
metro line #4 to Kelenföld Station, and then bus #101E, #101B or #150 · See map p.5

Fifteen kilometres southwest of the city centre, but easily the most popular sight on the
city's outskirts, the **Memento Park** (sometimes still known as the Statue Park) brings
together 42 of the monuments that glorified Communism in Budapest, to celebrate its
demise. Built in stages (1994–2004) as an "unfinished project" by architect Ákos Eleőd,
the complex is an anti-temple to a bankrupt ideology. Visitors are greeted by a replica
of the **Stalin grandstand**, from which Party leaders reviewed parades; the giant boots
recall the 8m-high Stalin statue toppled in 1956. Beyond lies Witness Square,
representing all those squares in Eastern Europe where people defied Communism; it's

10

flanked by two **barracks** buildings, one of which is used to screen *Life of an Agent*, a montage of ÁVO training films on how to bug or search premises and recruit informers; in the adjacent room, there's an exhibition on the 1956 Revolution and later events leading to the fall of the Berlin Wall.

The park proper lies behind a bogus Classical facade framing giant statues of **Lenin**, **Marx** and **Engels**. Lenin's once stood beside the Városliget, while Marx's and Engels' are carved from granite quarried at Mauthausen, a Nazi concentration camp in Austria, later used by the Soviets. Inside the grounds, you'll encounter the **Red Army soldier** that guarded the foot of the Liberation Monument on Gellért-hegy, and dozens of other statues and memorials, large and small. Here are prewar Hungarian Communists such as Béla Kun (secretly shot in Moscow on Stalin's orders) and Jenő Landler (afforded a place in the Kremlin Wall); Georgi Dimitrov, hero of the Comintern; and the Lenin statue from outside the Csepel ironworks. Artistically, the best works are the **Republic of Councils Monument** – a giant charging sailor based on a 1919 revolutionary poster – and Imre Varga's **Béla Kun Memorial**, with Kun on a tribune surrounded by a surging crowd of workers and soldiers (plus a bystander with an umbrella).

The ticket office sells Communist pins, Soviet-era postcards, Lenin and Stalin candles and a CD of revolutionary songs, which can be heard playing from a 1950s' radio set.

Tropicarium and Center of Scientific Wonders

Campona Shopping Centre, XXII, Nagytétényi út 37–43 • **Tropicarium** Daily 10am–8pm • 2500Ft, children 1800Ft • ☎ 1 424 3053, ⓦ tropicarium.hu • **Center of Scientific Wonders** Mon–Fri 9am–7pm, Sat & Sun 10am–8pm • 2500Ft, children 1900Ft • ☎ 1 814 8050, ⓦ csopa.hu • Bus #33 from Móricz Zsigmond körtér, or #114 and #214 from Kosztolányi Desző tér; a quicker alternative is the mainline train from Déli Station to Budatétény • See map p.5

A must-see for kids, Budapest's **Tropicarium** is the largest aquarium-terrarium in Central Europe, covering three thousand square metres. Its saltwater section has an 11m-long glass tunnel for intimate views of sand, tiger and brown **sharks**, clownfish, triggerfish and wrasses; not to be missed is the shark feeding, which takes place every Thursday at 3pm. The freshwater part has piranhas, mouth-breeding cichlids from Africa's Great Lakes, and an outdoor pool to show fish lying dormant when it freezes over. Even better is the **mini-rainforest**, complete with macaws, marmoset monkeys, iguanas and alligators, kept steamy by a downpour with thunder and lightning effects every fifteen minutes.

The Campona Shopping Centre also holds the **Center of Scientific Wonders** (Csopa), another big draw for those with kids. With over a hundred interactive installations, this enormous playhouse is the brainchild of two Hungarian physicists and aims to explain scientific principles to 6- to 12-year-olds, using devices such as optical illusions, a bed of nails and a simulated low-gravity "moonwalk". The hands-on physics show is held four times a day. There are also 4D cinema screenings, which cost an extra 600Ft.

Nagytétényi Castle Museum

Nagytétényi Kastélymúzeum • XXII, Kastélypark utca 9 • Tues–Sun 10am–6pm • 1500Ft • ☎ 1 207 0005, ⓦ imm.hu • Bus #33 from Móricz Zsigmond körtér (30–45min) or the Tropicarium (15min) to the Petőfi utca stop; cross the road and follow Hugonnay utca down past the children's playground to the *kastély*; or mainline train from Déli Station to Nagytétény (20min) and then a 15min walk • See map p.5

The last of the sights in the XXII district is the **Nagytétényi Castle Museum**, though this is strictly one for lovers of antique furniture. Though rendered as "castle" in English, "*kastély*" generally signifies a manor house or chateau without fortifications, which Hungarian nobles began building after the Turks had been expelled – in this case by converting an older, ruined castle into a Baroque residence. Nowadays, its 27 rooms display an extensive range of furniture from the Gothic to the Biedermeier epochs, owned by the Museum of Applied Arts; the most outstanding exhibit is a walnut-veneered refectory table from Trencsen Monastery. Elsewhere, there are tapestries, tiled stoves and paintings to admire.

ESZTERGOM

Excursions from Budapest

The attractions in this chapter are all within an hour or so of the city.
Foremost are three sites on the picturesque Danube Bend to the north of
Budapest. Szentendre is a historic Serbian settlement and artists' colony with
a superb open-air ethnographic museum. Further north, Visegrád boasts
medieval ruins, splendid scenery, "organic" buildings and a tree-top zip-slide,
while across the Danube from Slovakia, the cathedral town of Esztergom is
steeped in history. While each site merits a full day (though don't go on a
Monday, when most attractions are closed), you could cram two into one
long day. On the other side of the Danube, Vác has a magnificent Baroque
centre and some fascinating museums, or there's the former Habsburg
palace at Gödöllő, where classical concerts are held all year round.

Szentendre

SZENTENDRE (St Andrew), 20km north of Budapest, is both the most popular tourist destination in the vicinity of the capital and the easiest to reach. Despite a rash of souvenir shops, the centre remains a delightful maze of houses in autumnal colours, with secretive gardens and lanes winding up to hilltop churches, and plenty of museums and craft stalls; you should also allow at least a couple of hours for the open-air village museum outside town. Szentendre's location on the lower slopes of the Pilis Hills is not only beautiful, but ensures that it is one of the sunniest places in Hungary, making it a perfect spot for painters and artists – indeed, it was here, in the 1920s, that the town became a working **artists' colony**, and the links are just as strong today. Otherwise, Szentendre retains a strong Serbian identity, thanks to the waves of refugees who settled here from the fourteenth century onwards.

The heart of town is triangular **Fő tér**, which swarms with horse-drawn carriages and sightseers milling around an ornate **Plague Cross**, erected by the merchants' guild after Szentendre escaped infection in 1763.

11

Ferenczy Károly Museum

Ferenczy Károly Múzeum • Kossuth utca 5 • Tues–Sun 10am–6pm • 1200Ft • ☎ 0620 779 6657, ⓦ femuz.hu

North along Kossuth utca from the HÉV and bus stations, the splendid **Ferenczy Károly Museum** houses the oeuvre of the extraordinarily prolific Ferenczy family. A leading figure from the Nagybánya school, founded in 1896, Károly Ferenczy (1862–1917) pioneered Impressionism and *plein air* painting in Hungary, as beautifully demonstrated in works like *On Hilltop*, which has a figure standing under a tree looking out to a lustrous blue sky. His elder son Valér swung towards Expressionism (*A Street at Nagybánya*), while his two younger children – daughter Noemi and son Beni – branched out into tapestries and sculpture respectively; Noemi's Communist-leaning tendencies are reflected in such works as *Bricklayers* and *Shingle Maker*, both cardboard on canvas pieces. Among Beni's many wonderful creations, look out for the delightful *Playing Boys* and the suggestive *Genius*, supposedly his wife.

Kovács Ceramic Exhibition

Kovács Margit Kerámia Kiállítás • György utca 1 • Daily 10am–6pm • 1000Ft • ☎ 1 26 310 244, ⊕ kovacsmargit.com

Unjustly overlooked in the National Gallery, the sculptor and ceramicist Margit Kovács (1902–77) is instead celebrated in the wonderful **Kovács Ceramic Exhibition**. Her expressive, big-eyed statues are not particularly well known abroad, but in Hungary Kovács is honoured as one of the country's finest ceramicists – indeed, the themes of legends, dreams, religion, love and motherhood give her graceful sculptures and reliefs universal appeal.

Christianity is the dominant theme, with an entire room devoted to the subject – *Christ Holding the Lamb* and a wildly colourful *St George and the Dragon* are two typically sublime pieces – though she was also heavily inspired by folk-poetry, manifest in large-scale decorative compositions such as *Peasant Wedding*. Her last phase (she was still working in her 70s) was characterized, inevitably perhaps, by themes of ageing, most movingly in the colourless *Which is the Mother and Which is the Daughter Now?* Here too is a collection of her personal belongings, including powders, paintbrushes, potter's wheel and original furnishings from her home.

Blagovestenska Church

Fő tér 4 (entrance on Görög utca) • Tues–Sun 10am–5pm • 400Ft

Looming over the north side of Fő tér, the **Blagovestenska Church**, or Church of the Annunciation, is the most accessible of Szentendre's Orthodox churches. Painted by Mihailo Zivkovic of Buda in the early eighteenth century, its icons evoke all the richness and tragedy of Serbian history. Look out for the tomb of a Greek merchant of Macedonian origin to the left of the entrance, and the Rococo windows and gate facing Görög utca (Greek Street). Next door to the church, a portal carved with emblems of science and learning provides the entrance to a former Serbian church school.

Templom tér

Off the opposite side of Fő tér to the Blagovestenska Church, an alley of steps ascends to **Templom tér**, a walled hilltop with a great view of Szentendre's rooftops and gardens. This is the location for the Catholic **Parish Church** (Szent János templom; Tues–Sun 10am–5pm, but opening times not reliable), originally of medieval origin with Romanesque and Gothic features, but rebuilt in the Baroque style after falling derelict in Turkish times. The frescoes in its sanctuary were collectively painted by members of

---

SZENTENDRE'S ART GALLERIES

Szentendre has numerous **art galleries**, though these are of varying quality. There are two in particular worth venturing to: the **Barcsay Museum** at Dumtsa Jenő utca 10 (Barcsay Múzeum; Wed–Sun 10am–5pm; 600Ft) is named after the Transylvanian-born Jenő Barcsay (1900–88), a long-standing resident and teacher at Szentendre's artists' colony; exhibitions here veer towards abstract works. On the east side of Fő tér, the **Szentendre Gallery** (Szentendrei Keptár; Wed–Sun: May–Sept 10am–6pm, Oct–April 2–6pm; free) mainly holds temporary contemporary art exhibitions, but sometimes features names such as István Szőnyi, the twentieth-century Hungarian painter much loved for his Danube Bend landscapes.

SZENTENDRE

N

Hungarian Open-air Museum

MEHÉSZ UTCA
HOLD UTCA
DARU PIAC
DEZSMA UTCA
ZRINYI UTCA
ISKOLA UTCA
ANGYAL UTCA
BOGDÁNYI UTCA
KANCSÓ DUNAKORZÓ

Vinegrowers' Cross

Retro Design Center

RÉV UTCA

River Danube (Duna)

DUNAKANYAR KÖRÚT
MARTINOVICS UTCA
RÁKÓCZI UTCA

Preobraženska Church

SZERB UTCA

Blue Dye Shop

Art Mill

Skanzen Ház

Szentendre II

Serbian Orthodox Ecclesiastical Art Collection

Belgrade Church

Szántó Memorial House

LÁZÁR TÉR

Lázár Cross

RÁKÓCZI UTCA

Czóbel Museum

TEMPLOM TÉR

ALKOTMÁNY UTCA

Parish Church

Blagovestenska Church

GYÖRGY UTCA

Town Hall

FŐ TÉR

Plague Cross

Kovács Ceramic Exhibition

Szentendre Gallery

Szentendrei sziget

Peter-Paul Church

KUCSERA UTCA

PÉTER-PÁL UTCA

Barcsay Collection

DUMTSA JENŐ UTCA

BÜKKÖS PART

PAPRIKABÍRÓ UTCA

Bükkös Stream

DUNAKORZÓ

Požarevačka Church

KOSSUTH UTCA

Ferenczy Károly Museum

RÓMAI SÁNC KÖZ

PETŐFI UTCA

NAGY LAJOS
ORTORONY UTCA
ATTILA UTCA
DUNAKANYAR KÖRÚT

KERTÉSZ UTCA

VASÚTI VILLASOR

KOSSUTH UTCA

HÉV Terminal

BOLGÁR UTCA

Budapest

Bus Station

Budapest

EATING

Aranysárkány	2
Corner	1
Mjam	3
Múzeum Cukrászda	5
Palapa	4

0   200
metres

the town's artists' colony – among them Béla Czóbel (1883–1976), whose Bonnard-like portraits hang across from the church in the **Czóbel Museum** (Czóbel Béla Múzeum; Tues–Sun 9am–5pm; 600Ft).

Belgrade Church
Belgrád templom • Pátriáka utca 5 • April–Oct Tues–Sun 10am–6pm, but opening times not reliable • 600Ft

The rust-red spire of the Orthodox cathedral or **Belgrade Church** rises above a walled garden on Alkotmány utca. Built during the late eighteenth century, it has a lavishly ornamented interior with icons depicting scenes from the New Testament and saints of the Orthodox Church. The old tombstones with Cyrillic inscriptions in the churchyard bear witness to a tale of demographic decline.

Serbian Orthodox Ecclesiastical Art Collection
Szerb Ortodox Egyháztörténeti Gyüjtemény • Pátriarka utca 5 • Mid-March to Oct Wed–Sun 10am–4pm; Nov to mid-March Fri–Sun 10am–4pm • 800Ft

It's worth looking into the **Serbian Orthodox Ecclesiastical Art Collection** in the Episcopal palace, which holds a rich hoard of icons, vestments and crosses that come from churches in Hungary that fell empty after the Serbs returned to the Balkans and the last remaining parishioners died out.

11

Szántó Memorial House and Synagogue
Szanto Emlékház és Imaház • Hunyadi utca 2 • Tues–Sun 11am–5pm • Donations accepted

The **Szántó Memorial House** was set up by the grandson of a Jewish couple who were among a 250-strong Jewish community in the town that was almost completely wiped out in the Holocaust. While Budapest has the second largest **synagogue** in the world (see p.65), this one is reputed to be the smallest; the documents and relics inside are few, but they make a moving display.

Bogdányi utca and around
Sloping gently downhill north from Fő tér, **Bogdányi utca** is packed with craft stalls and folk-costumed vendors – it's souvenir heaven if you like that kind of thing, though there are also some more interesting sights along the street's length. The street opens onto a Lázár tér where the small iron **Lázár Cross** honours the eponymous Serb king, whom the Turks beheaded after the Battle of Kosovo. Lázár's body was buried here by the Serbs, before being taken back to Serbia in 1774.

Beyond the Skanzen ház bakery at Bogdányi utca 28, which sells delicious produce made in the Open-Air Museum (see p.134), is the **Art Mill** at no. 32 (Művészeti-Malom; Tues–Sun 10am–6pm; 1000Ft), a converted watermill hosting installations and performance art events. A couple of doors up, at no. 36, admire the deep blue hues of clothes, tablecloths and bedspreads at the Kovács **Blue Dye Shop**, showcasing a traditional style of folk dyeing.

Retro Design Center
Rév utca 4 • Mon–Wed & Fri–Sun 10am–5pm, Thurs noon–5pm • 1000Ft • ☏ 0630 823 5875

For a nostalgic trip back to the 1970s, pay a visit to the **Retro Design Center**. This fun, vintage collection embraces toys, telephones, cameras, vinyl album covers and a host of household appliances, in addition to a mock-up lounge (with obligatory brown furnishings) and kitchen. But the real stars are the **cars** (around 25 of them) from the old Eastern bloc, with names that are sure to raise a wry smile, at least among those of a certain age: Dacia (Romania), Lada (Russia), Skoda (Czechoslovakia) and Zastava (Yugoslavia), to name just a few. Perhaps the most iconic of all is the Trabant from East Germany, which became one of the symbols of the fall of the Wall in 1989, when thousands of East Germans piled into their Trabbis and crossed the borders of Czechoslovakia and Hungary en route to West Germany.

THE SERBIAN CONNECTION

Before artists moved in during the first decades of the twentieth century, Szentendre's character had been forged by waves of refugees from **Serbia**. The first followed the catastrophic Serb defeat at Kosovo in 1389; the second, the Turkish recapture of Belgrade in 1690, causing 30,000 Serbs and Bosnians to flee. Six thousand settled in Szentendre, which became the seat of the eighteenth-century Serbian Church in exile. Prospering through trade, they replaced their wooden churches with stone ones and built handsome townhouses, but as Habsburg toleration waned and phylloxera (vine-blight) and floods ruined the local economy they trickled back to Serbia, so that by 1890 less than a quarter of the population was Serb; it's estimated that there are around 150 Serbs in Szentendre now. The most tangible sign of prior Serbian presence is the handful of churches scattered around town. Sadly, though, most are no longer open, such as the slender **Požarevačka Church** on Kossuth utca, which was built from stone in the late eighteenth century to replace an older wooden structure in a grove of trees. The **Preobraženska Church**, on Vujicsics Tihamér tér, was erected by the tanners' guild in 1741–76, its stoutness enhanced by a Louis XVI gate the following century; the most likely chance of seeing the interior of this church is during the Serbian festival on August 19, when it hosts the Blessing of the Grapes ceremony.

11

Hungarian Open-Air Museum

Szabadtéri Néprajzi Múzeum • April–Oct Tues–Sun 9am–5pm • 2000Ft, mini-railway 500Ft • ☎ 26 502 537, ⊕ skanzen.hu • Buses (7 daily) leave from stand 7 at the Szentendre bus station

Set in rolling countryside 4km north of Szentendre, the amazing **Hungarian Open-Air Museum** is the country's largest outdoor museum of peasant architecture; it's termed a *skanzen*, after the first such museum, founded in a Stockholm suburb in 1891. This naturalistic village was transported here from eight ethnographic regions of Hungary, representing rural life from the nineteenth century up until the 1920s, complete with dwellings, demonstrations of cottage industries and traditional breeds of livestock in barns. The various areas are connected by a **mini-railway**, which makes it easier to cover the large site; even so, give yourself at least two hours to get around.

Demonstrations of **crafts** such as pottery, weaving and boot-making occur in each section at weekends and during **festivals**, of which there are several throughout the year; these include the Heritage Festival (June), a dance festival (Aug 11), and a big wine festival (Nov).

Upper Tisza

Downhill to the right from the entrance, a village from the isolated **Upper Tisza** region in the northeast corner of the country reveals that the homes of the poorest squires were barely superior to those of their tenants, yet rural carpenters produced highly skilled work, such as the circular "dry mill", the wooden bell tower, and the Greek Catholic church (on a hilltop beyond). Past the Calvinist graveyard with its boat-shaped grave-markers, signs point you to the scant remains of a Roman village and on to the next region.

Northern Hungary

The following region takes you to the region northwest of Budapest: **Northern Hungary** includes an original stone house furnished in nineteenth-century style and re-creates cave dwellings typical of the poorer parts of the region. You can also taste or get re-cipes for "Palóc" delicacies – the Palóc people being an ethnic Hungarian group retaining its own traditions, with a distinctive dialect to match.

The Uplands

Next comes the **Uplands** region, which on the map of Hungary is sandwiched between the two previous sections. This region includes the wine-growing area of Tokaj, where vineyards brought considerable privileges – and wealth, evident in the proud stone buildings from these market towns, with their stoves, well-stocked kitchens and, of course, wine cellars.

Bakony and Balaton Uplands

A short walk from the Uplands region brings you to a water-powered mill and grape-press; a washhouse and a fire station comprise the "centre" of a village from the **Bakony and Balaton Uplands**, where stone and hornbeam were used for building. The four neatly aligned dwelling houses reflect the varying financial standings of those living in the region in the early twentieth century.

Western Transdanubia

Across the stream and to the right, **Western Transdanubia** – on the Austrian border – was a poor region of clay soil and heavy rainfall, where houses were linked by covered verandas. Here, a schoolroom is equipped with benches, slates for writing on, a towel and basin for washing, and homespun schoolbags. The teacher's living quarters are at the other end of the building, separated by a kitchen with an apron chimney, where the smoke goes out of a hole in the roof.

11

Southern Transdanubia

Large adobe dwellings were typical of the wealthier, predominantly Protestant German and Hungarian villages in **Southern Transdanubia**, in the southwest of the country – their carved gateways big enough for haywains – but there are also wooden-framed thatched buildings typical of the more isolated areas. The region has a strong tradition of wine-making – it includes the areas of Szekszárd, which made the first Bull's Blood, and Villány – and you can see evidence of that here.

The Small Plain

The section representing the ethnic German communities of the **Small Plain**, in northern Transdanubia, seems far more regimented: neatly aligned whitewashed houses filled with knick-knacks and embroidered samplers bearing homilies like "When the Hausfrau is capable, the clocks keep good time". The village layout here is designed to show the diversity of the region: on one side of the street are stately brick buildings, while on the other are more humble dwellings with earth walls and thatched roofs.

The Great Plain

Large adobe dwellings were also typical of the market towns on the **Great Plain**. A Baroque cottage from Sükösd has its visitors' room or "clean room" laid out for Christmas celebrations with a nativity crib and a church-shaped box. Beyond the houses are stables and pastures for long-horned cattle and Rácka sheep, and a windmill built in 1888, its sails still operating.

ARRIVAL AND INFORMATION | **SZENTENDRE**

By train Szentendre is easily accessible by HÉV train from Batthyány tér metro station (every 20min 4.30am–11.30pm; 40min). BKK tickets (and Budapest Cards) are valid as far as the city limits (HÉV station: Békásmegyer), so you will need to buy a supplementary ticket to cover the remaining part of the journey, or show a BKK pass when buying a ticket at the station. The station is a 10min walk south of Szentendre town centre: cross Dunakanyar körút by subway and continue along Kossuth utca.

By bus Buses run from Budapest's Újpest-Városkapu bus

station to Szentendre's bus station (30min), next to the HÉV station.

By boat Excursion boats (2200Ft, return 3300Ft; ☎ 1 484 4013, ⓦ mahartpassnave.hu) make the 1hr 30min journey from Budapest, departing from Vigadó tér at 10.30am then calling at Batthyány tér at 10.40am (April & Oct Sat; May, June & Sept Tues–Sun; July & Aug daily); there's an extra boat at 2pm (Tues–Sun) in July & Aug. Boats dock at the landing stage near Lázár tér in the heart of town. From Szentendre, boats back to Budapest depart at 5pm (there's another boat at 7pm in July & Aug).

Information Tourinform is at Dumsta Jenő utca 22 (May–Aug Mon–Thurs 10am–6pm, Fri–Sun 10am–8pm; Sept–April Tues–Sun 10am–4pm; ☎26 317 965, ⓦiranyszentendre.hu); there's limited info in English, but you can obtain a map of town and information on concerts and festivals.

EATING

Szentendre has stacks of **restaurants**, though you'd do well to steer clear of those on and around Fő tér, which are heavily frequented by coach parties, and hence relatively pricey by Hungarian standards. You'll do better in the backstreets or on Dunakorzó (though it's no less crowded in summer), or in **cafés** on the periphery of the centre.

Aranysárkány Alkotmány utca 1a ☎26 301 479, ⓦaranysarkany.hu. The longstanding and popular "*Golden Dragon*" serves Hungarian nouvelle cuisine in traditional, folksy surrounds; try the honeyed goose steak with steamed red cabbage, mashed potatoes and wasabi (3400Ft). Three-course menu 3800Ft. Booking advisable. Daily noon–10pm.

Corner Kancsó Dunakorzó 4 ☎26 301 524. Occupying a super position near the waterfront, this is the best of several Serbian restaurants in town, serving classic Balkan dishes like *pljeskavica* (oversized beef burgers) and *cevapi* (lamb or beef or rissoles with diced onion, served in thick, soft pittas; 2000Ft). Nothing posh or fancy, but you will leave stuffed. Daily noon–midnight.

★**Mjam** Városház tér 2 ☎70 377 8178. Szentendre's standout restaurant offers an innovative fusion menu of South American, Asian and Caribbean cuisine; try the excellent Curacao burger, or the fish sausage and tempura (1600Ft). The weekday two-course lunch menu (1200Ft) is great value. Tues–Thurs 11am–10pm, Fri & Sat 11am–11pm, Sun 11am–5pm.

Múzeum Cukrászda Dumsta Jenő utca 14 ☎26 311 931. For afters or mid-morning refreshment, head to this chintzy café where coffee, cakes and ices have been served in the beautifully tiled salon since 1889. Cakes and confectionery to take away too. Daily 9am–8pm.

Palapa Dumsta Jenő utca 14a ☎26 302 418. Dazzlingly colourful Mexican bar-restaurant with all the usual suspects (fajitas, enchiladas, tacos; all from 2100Ft), though often with a local twist, such as catfish quesadilla; great cocktails too (1500Ft). The entrance is on Batthyány utca. Mon–Thurs & Sun noon–10pm, Fri & Sat noon–midnight.

Visegrád

Approaching **VISEGRÁD** from Szentendre, the hillsides start to plunge and the river twists shortly before you catch first sight of the citadel and ramparts of the ancient fortified site whose Slavic name means "High Castle". The view hasn't changed much since 1488, when János Thuroczy described its "upper walls stretching to the clouds floating in the sky, and the lower bastions reaching down as far as the river". At that time, courtly life in Visegrád was nearing its apogee and the palace of King Mátyás and Queen Beatrice was famed throughout Europe. The papal legate Cardinal Castelli described it as a "paradiso terrestri", seemingly unperturbed by the presence of Vlad the Impaler, who resided here under duress between 1462 and 1475. Today, Visegrád is a mere village, where the ferry docks and a few bars and restaurants round the church are the hub of local life. Tourists tend to focus on the historic sites north of the centre: the **Royal Palace** and **Solomon's Tower** near the river, and the hilltop citadel. All the river sites are in easy walking distance of each other but you might prefer taking a bus up to the **Citadel**, thus saving your energy for gung-ho activities in the **Visegrád Hills**.

The layout of the **ruins** dates back to the thirteenth century, when Béla IV began fortifying the north against a recurrence of the Mongol invasion, while the construction of a royal palace below the hilltop citadel was a sign of greater security during the reign of the Angevins. However, its magnificence was effaced by the Turkish conquest, and later mud washing down from the hillside gradually buried the palace entirely. Subsequent generations doubted its existence until archeologist János Schulek had a lucky break after searching in vain for years. At a New Year's Eve party in 1934, the wine ran out and Schulek was sent to get some more from the neighbours. An old woman told him to go down to the wine cellar, and there he found clues in the stones that convinced him the palace was there, beneath the surface.

FŐ TER, SZENTENDRE (P.130) >

Royal Palace

Királyi Palota • Fő utca 23 • Tues–Sun: March–Oct 9am–5pm; Nov–Feb 10am–4pm • 1300Ft • ☎ 26 597 010

Now excavated and tastefully reconstructed, Visegrád's **Royal Palace** spreads over four terraces. Founded in 1323 by the Angevin king Charles Robert, it was the setting for the Visegrád Congress of 1335, attended by the monarchs of Central Europe and the Grandmaster of the Teutonic Knights. Although nothing remains of this palace, the **Court of Honour** constructed for his successor Louis, which provided the basis for additions by kings Sigismund and Mátyás, is still to be seen on the second terrace.

A pilastered **Renaissance loggia** surrounds a replica of the famous **Hercules Fountain**, which cools the tiled, gilded uppermost storey, overlooking the court. The surrounding rooms house a voluminous display of exhibits, mainly ceramic vessels, weaponry and glazed stove tiles. On the third terrace, where Mátyás and Beatrice resided, stands a copy

VISEGRÁD

N

Szentendrei sziget   ▲ *Budapest*

Szentendre (20km) & Budapest (45km)

FŐ UTCA

MOGYORÓHEGY

11

River Danube (Duna)

Forest Educational Centre

▲ Sibrik Hill

Water Bastion ⊗ ⚓ Visegrád Gate

Zsitvay lookout tower
▲ Nagy-Villám (337m)

FŐ UTCA

SALAMON-TORONY UTCA

⚓

Solomon's Tower

Fun Extreme Canopy

● Bobsleigh

P

Citadel

P

Royal Palace

Calvary Path

ⓘ

PANORÁMA ÚT

FEKETE-HEGY

VISEGRÁD HILLS

Esztergom

Sports Hall

FŐ UTCA

N. LAJOS KIRÁLY UTCA

RÉV UTCA

Nagymaros

MÁTYÁS KIRÁLY UTCA

SZÉCHENYI UTCA

FŐ UTCA

PANORÁMA ÚT

Esztergom

● EATING	
Don Vito	2
Gulyás Csárda	4
Renaissance	1
Rigoletto Cukrászda	3

0   500
metres

of the **Lion Fountain**, bearing his raven crest and standing on leg-rests in the form of sleepy-looking lions and dogs. The reconstructed chapel is chiefly notable for housing the red marble *Visegrád Madonna*, a Renaissance masterpiece that shows many similarities to the works of Italian Tomaso Fiamberti. The renovated royal suites, meanwhile, remain mostly bare, save for some superb-looking stoves complete with dark green ceramic tiles depicting various coats-of-arms. The bathhouse, with its underfloor heating, and the palace herb gardens, further contribute to the impression of courtly life.

If you've got kids, you can bet that they'll make an immediate beeline for the wonderfully colourful, medieval-themed **playground** directly opposite the palace.

Solomon's Tower

Salamon-torony • Salamon-torony utca • May–Sept Wed–Sun 9am–5pm • 700Ft

Named after an eleventh-century Hungarian king once thought to have been imprisoned here after being deposed, **Solomon's Tower** is a mighty hexagonal keep buttressed on two sides by unsightly concrete slabs. Inside, various **exhibits** can be found from the Royal Palace, including a copy of the white Anjou Fountain of the Angevins. From the top of the tower you can see ramparts plunging down from the Citadel to the riverside **Water Bastion**, a squat, long-derelict structure with a fortified arch spanning the highway.

11

Citadel

Fellegvár • March, April & Oct daily 9am–5pm; May–Sept daily 9am–6pm; Nov daily 9am–4pm; Dec–Feb Fri–Sun 10am–4pm • 1700Ft • You can walk up from the rear gate of Solomon's Tower (40min), or there's an easier route (20min) via the Calvary footpath behind Visegrád's church

Dramatically sited on a crag above Solomon's Tower, Visegrád's thirteenth-century **Citadel** served as a repository for the Hungarian crown jewels until they were stolen by a treacherous maid of honour in the fifteenth century. Following the last major rebuilding work later that same century, the castle was occupied by the Turks, then the Habsburgs, before falling into decay. It's now only partly restored but mightily impressive nonetheless, commanding a superb view of the Börzsöny Mountains across the Danube. Come for this and not the two rather dull **museums** devoted to medieval hunting, fishing, punishment and torture; in fact, so comical are the waxworks, they probably are actually worth visiting. Otherwise, there are outdoor displays of **archery** and **falconry** in the summer.

Visegrád Hills

A popular rambling spot with fantastic views, the densely wooded **Visegrád Hills** offer great walks and views, and for thrill-seekers there is the chance to zip through the tree tops or go bobsleighing.

Zsitvay lookout tower

Zsitvay-kilátó • 10am–6pm: May–Oct daily; Nov–April Sat & Sun • 400Ft

Four hundred metres up the road from the Citadel car park, paths radiate from another car park. One leads up to the **Zsitvay lookout tower** on the top of the highest hill on the Danube Bend, Nagy-Villám (Great Lightning; 377m), with wonderful views as far as Slovakia.

Bobsleigh

Bobpálya • March Mon–Fri 11am–4pm, Sat & Sun 10am–5pm; April, Sept & Oct Mon–Fri 10am–5pm, Sat & Sun 10am–6pm; May–Aug Mon–Fri 9am–6pm, Sat & Sun 9am–7pm; Nov–Feb daily 11am–4pm • 500Ft for one run, 2500Ft for six runs • ☎ 26 397 397, ⓦ bobozas.hu

Next to the Bobpálya car park are the Buda Hills' two **bobsleigh** runs, where kids of all ages (and adults) can whizz down a couple of 1km-long chutes on either the summer bobsled or the Alpine Coaster; note that these may be closed on rainy days, when the sleds' brakes are ineffective, so it's best to call ahead if the weather's looking dodgy.

VISEGRÁD FESTIVALS

Each year (usually on the second weekend in July), Visegrád hosts the **International Palace Games** (⊕ palotajatekok.hu), an orgy of medieval pageantry featuring jousting and archery tournaments, craft workshops, a street fair, and plenty of eating and drinking, most of which is held in the grounds of the Royal Palace and surrounding streets; daily tickets cost 1000Ft, with tickets for the jousting events around 2000Ft. During the second half of June, the **Danube Bend Summer Games** see sports, musical and cultural events in all the villages between Szentendre and Visegrád; visit the Visegrád tourist office (see below) or their website, ⊕ visitvisegrad.hu, for more information.

Fun Extreme Canopy

Canopy pálya • March–Oct Tues–Sun 10am–6pm • 3900Ft • Trips require a minimum of four people, max twenty; individuals who turn up can be put with a group, but it's wiser to book ahead; ages 12 and over only • ☎ 20 661 7873, ⊕ canopy.hu

Inspired by the tree-top walkways in Costa Rica's Monteverde Cloud Forest National Park, the **Fun Extreme Canopy** comprises eleven platforms, 14m high, linked by wires to form an amazing zip-ride through the Buda Hills forest, which takes about forty minutes to complete, sliding at speeds of up to 50km an hour. Guides, safety harnesses and helmets are provided; nerve rather than strength is needed. The zip-wire's upper terminus is by the restaurant, *Nagyvillám Vendéglő*, on the far side of the car park from the bobsleigh run. Riders end up on a lower hill, Mogyoróhegy, from where you can return by minibus or walk up through the woods to Nagy-Villám.

Imre Makovecz buildings

Two hundred metres from the lower terminus of the Fun Extreme Canopy stand a couple of striking wooden buildings by **Imre Makovecz** (1935–2011), the Hungarian guru of "organic architecture". After creating the breathtaking crypt at Farkasréti Cemetery (p.125), he was branded a troublemaker for his outspoken nationalism and "exiled" to Visegrád's forestry department, where he acquired a following by teaching summer schools on how to construct buildings using low-tech methods and materials such as branches and twigs. In the 1980s he built here a campsite **restaurant** with a roof like a nun's wimple, and the yurt-like, turf-roofed **Forest Education Centre** (in the centre of town, he also built a **Sports Hall** resembling a Viking church), before being allowed to work elsewhere and given the honour of designing the Hungarian Pavilion at the 1992 Seville Expo. Though Makovecz's work was by this point widely acclaimed, his lavish use of wood vexed some environmentalists, and his dabbling in right-wing politics made his call for a return to a "real" Hungarian style of building somewhat suspect.

ARRIVAL AND INFORMATION   VISEGRÁD

By bus Bus #880 leaves from stand 7 at Budapest's Újpest-Városkapu terminal (hourly; 1hr 25min) and stops at various points along the main road between the town and the river, including in front of the tourist office and by the local ferry stop (at the bottom of Rév utca), before running on to Esztergom.

By boat Given the majestic scenery of the Danube Bend, arriving by river is far more scenic. The boat leaves Budapest's Vigadó tér at 9am and Batthyány tér at 9.10am (May–Aug Tues–Sun, Sept Sat only; 3hr 20min; 2750Ft, return 4125Ft; ☎ 1 484 4013, ⊕ mahartpassnave.hu) and

docks by the pier at the end of Rév utca. The return boat to Budapest departs at 5.30pm.

By hydrofoil A much quicker way (just 1hr) is the hydrofoil, which leaves Vigadó tér at 10am (May–Sept Tues–Sun; 4000Ft, return 6000Ft). The landing stage is by the highway, just below Solomon's Tower. The return to Budapest is at 6pm.

Tourist office The excellent local tourist office is located at Duna-parti út 1, in front of the Royal Palace (Tues–Sun 10am–4pm; ☎ 26 397 188, ⊕ visitvisegrad.hu); this is by far the best place to go for any information on sightseeing on the Danube Bend.

EATING

Don Vito Fő utca 83 ☎ 26 397 230. The town's most enjoyable restaurant, this stylish pizzeria features three

brightly decorated rooms and a long wooden bar themed on *The Godfather*, with wood-fired pizzas (1900Ft) named

accordingly: Pizza Michael Corleone and Pizza Consigliere to name but two. It's also the best place in town to drink, with occasional live music to boot. Daily noon–11pm.
Gulyás Csárda Nagy Lajos király utca 4 @ 26 398 329. This 1980s-style inn right in the centre of Visegrád does hearty, traditional Hungarian and German dishes at very affordable prices (mains 1700Ft), and also has a sunny beer garden. Daily noon–11pm.
Renaissance Fő utca 11 @ 26 398 081, @ renvisegrad

.hu. A medieval-themed restaurant popular with coach parties, where diners can feast on the likes of roasted goose leg steamed in red wine (3500Ft) served in ceramic bowls while wearing a cardboard crown and being serenaded by a lute-player. Daily noon–11pm.
Rigoletto Cukrászda Rév utca 13 @ 20 590 4970. Sweet and welcoming little daytime café doling out strong coffee, cakes and cookies alongside a delicious selection of ice creams. Tues–Sun 8am–6pm, Mon 10am–6pm.

Esztergom

Beautifully situated in a crook of the Danube facing Slovakia, **ESZTERGOM** is dominated by its basilica, whose dome is visible for miles around – a richly symbolic sight, as it was here that Prince Géza and his son Vajk (the future king and saint Stephen) brought Hungary into the fold of Christendom. Even after the court moved to Buda following the Mongol invasion, Esztergom remained the centre of Catholicism until the Turkish conquest, and resumed this role in the 1820s – as the poet Mihály Babits (who lived here) remarked, "This is the Hungarian Rome". Persecuted in the Rákóczi era but increasingly tolerated by the regime from the 1960s onwards, the Church regained much of its former property and influence under Christian governments in the post-Communist era, making Esztergom an obligatory stop for politicians in election year.

Esztergom makes an ideal day-trip, combining historic monuments and small-town charm in just the right doses, with the bonus of being within strolling distance of the Slovak town of Štúrovo (Párkány in Hungarian). It consists of an upper town beside the basilica, the waterfront Víziváros below it with its magnificent Turkish remains, and a sprawling lower town separated from the island of Prímás-sziget by a tributary of the Danube.

Esztergom basilica

Szent István tér 1 • **Cathedral** (Bazilika) Daily 8am–6pm • Free • **Crypt** (Kripta) Daily: March–Oct 9am–5pm; Nov–Feb 10am– 4pm • 200Ft • **Cupola** (Kupola) April–Oct daily 9.30am–5pm (closed in bad weather) • 700Ft • **Treasury** (Kincstár) Daily: March–Oct 9am–5pm; Nov to mid-Jan 10am–4pm • 900Ft • @ 33 402 354, @ bazilika-esztergom.hu

Built upon the site of the first cathedral in Hungary, where Vajk was crowned as King Stephen by a papal envoy on Christmas Day 1000 AD, Esztergom's **basilica** is the largest in the country, measuring 118m in length and 40m in width, and capped

CARDINAL MINDSZENTY

When the much-travelled body of **Cardinal József Mindszenty** was finally laid to rest with state honours in 1991, it was a vindication of his uncompromising heroism – and the Vatican realpolitik that he despised. As a conservative and monarchist, Mindszenty had stubbornly opposed the postwar Communist takeover, warning that "cruel hands are reaching out to seize hold of our children, claws belonging to people who have nothing but evil to teach them". Arrested in 1948, tortured for 39 days and nights, and sentenced to life imprisonment for treason, Mindszenty was freed during the Uprising and took refuge in the US Embassy, where he remained for the next fifteen years – an exile in the heart of Budapest.

When the Vatican struck a deal with the Kádár regime in 1971, Mindszenty had to be pushed into resigning his position and going to Austria, where he died in 1975. Although his will stated that his body should not return home until "the red star of Moscow had fallen from Hungarian skies", his reburial occurred some weeks before the last Soviet soldier left, in preparation for Pope John Paul II's visit. Nowadays the Vatican proclaims his greatness, without any hint of apology for its past actions.

by a dome 100m high. Representing a thousand years of faith and statehood, it was begun in 1822, and completed by József Hild in 1869, an occasion for which Liszt composed *Gran Mass* (Gran being the German name for Esztergom).

Its nave is on a massive scale, clad in marble, gilding and mosaics, while the main altarpiece was painted by the Venetian Michelangelo Grigoletti, based on Titian's *Assumption* in the Frari Church in Venice. More architecturally impressive, though, is the lavish, red-and-white marble **Bakócz Chapel** (below the relief of Christ on a donkey), whose Florentine altar was salvaged from the original basilica that was destroyed by the Mongols. Off to the right is the **treasury** (*kincstár*), an overpowering collection of bejewelled crosiers, vestments and kitsch papal souvenirs.

The spooky **crypt** (*krypta*), with its 17m-thick walls, bears the tomb of Cardinal Mindszenty (see box p.141), among other grand mausolea; another stairway from the nave leads up to the **cupola**, reached by three hundred steps and offering a superb view of Esztergom.

ESZTERGOM

EATING
Csülök Csárda	2
Központi Kávéház	4
Padlizsán	3
Prímás Pince	1

DRINKING
Trafó	1

Castle Museum

Vármúzeum • Tues–Sun: April–Oct 10am–6pm; Nov–March 10am–4pm • 1500Ft • ☏ 33 415 986, ⓦ varmegom.hu

On higher ground 30m south of the basilica are the red-roofed, reconstructed remains of the palace founded by Prince Géza, now presented as the **Castle Museum**. A royal seat for almost three hundred years, it was here that Béla III entertained Philip of France and Frederick Barbarossa on their way to the Third Crusade, while the Renaissance prelate János Vitéz made it a centre of humanist culture, where Queen Beatrice spent her widowhood. Despite being sacked by the Turks and twice besieged before they were evicted in 1683, enough survived to be excavated in the 1930s.

The main entrance is round to the left on the courtyard: past archeological finds and visualizations of the palace in various epochs, you reach the best part of the museum, the **royal suite**. Traces of the frescoes that once covered every wall can be seen in the vaulted living hall from Béla III's reign, from which stairs ascend to the study of Archbishop Vitéz – known as the **Hall of Virtues** after its allegorical murals. Beyond lies the **royal chapel**, whose Gothic rose window and Romanesque arches were executed by craftsmen brought over by Béla's French wives, while the reconstructed tower offers a panoramic view of Esztergom and the river. Returning to the courtyard, there is a lapidarium and a further section of the museum, where you can see archeological finds and a less enthralling collection of weapons.

From the basilica, you can walk down the slope that descends to the Kisvonat terminus, or take the steps at the side down to the former primate's wine cellars – now the *Prímás Pince* restaurant (see p.145) – and the monumental **Dark Gate**. This imposing tunnel was built in the 1820s as a short cut between church buildings on either side of the hill.

The Víziváros

At the northern end of the basilica's parapet overlooking the Danube is the striking **white statue** of the crowning of St Stephen. Nearby, the stairs of the precipitous **Cat Way** (or Cat Stairs – Macskaút or Macskalépcső) offer a dramatic way down from the heights, and provide a splendid view of the river and Štúrovo. At the bottom lies the **Víziváros**, a Baroque enclave of churches and seminaries – and the most magnificent Turkish relic.

Oziceli Hacci Ibrahim Djami

Ozicseli Hadzsi Ibrahim Dzsami • Berényi utca 18 • Tues–Sun 10am–5pm • Free • ☏ 33 315 665, ⓦ esztergomidzsami.hu

The fascinating, seventeenth-century **Oziceli Hacci Ibrahim Djami** mosque was built on what was then the northern edge of the Ottoman Empire, and is a rare example of a two-storey *djami* – the only other ones are in Bosnia. The mosque was later turned into a granary, and many of its original features – including a partly restored minaret – have been very well preserved, though it's no longer a place of worship. The lower floor is even more remarkable than the minaret: squeezed between the city wall and the castle hill, the *djami* was built over the medieval road that led to the gate in the city walls. You can walk down the excavated road and out of the gate, on the outside of which stands a tablet commemorating the victory of Suleiman I: when the Turks besieged Esztergom in 1543 they broke through this gate and discovered that the well inside supplied water for the castle. With their water cut off, the Hungarians surrendered. There's a sweet little café here too.

Christian Museum

Keresztény Múzeum • Mindszenty tér 2 • March–Nov Wed–Sun 10am–5pm • 900Ft • ☏ 33 413 880, ⓦ christianmuseum.hu

South of the Oziceli Hacci Ibrahim Djami mosque past the Cat Way lies the wedge-shaped plaza named after Cardinal Mindszenty. Next to the Italianate Baroque **Víziváros Parish Church** stands the old Primate's Palace, which now houses the **Christian Museum**. This is Hungary's richest hoard of religious art, featuring the largest collection of Italian prints outside Italy; Renaissance paintings and woodcarvings by German, Austrian and Hungarian masters; and some beautiful Orthodox icons from Russia and Serbia. Don't miss, either, the unique wheeled, gilded catafalque once used in Easter Week processions.

Prímás-sziget

From Mindszenty tér, a bridge runs over the narrow Kis-Duna (Little Danube), connecting the mainland to **Prímás-sziget** (Primate's Island), a popular recreation spot. Lined with chestnut trees and weeping willows, Gesztenye fasor and Kis-Duna sétány form a lovely shady promenade frequented by lovers and anglers.

Mária Valéria híd

At the western end of Táncsics Mihály utca, the reconstructed **Mária Valéria híd** links Esztergom with Slovak Štúrovo (also signposted as Párkány, its Hungarian name), five minutes' stroll across the river. Blown up by retreating Germans at the end of World War II, the bridge was left in ruins until an agreement to rebuild it was finally signed in 1999 after years of bilateral negotiations, with the European Union footing the bill. It seems only fair that EU citizens can **walk into Slovakia** with barely a flourish of their passports – other nationalities may need visas. Bring your passport anyway.

11 The lower town

From Prímás-sziget, it's an easy walk into Esztergom's lower town, which is largely devoid of life. The area's civic focus is the sprawling, pedestrianized **Széchenyi tér**, framed by an imposing **Town Hall** with Rococo windows that once belonged to Prince Rákóczi's general, János Bottyán. It's markedly quieter than nearby **Rákóczi tér**, the hub of everyday life with its supermarkets, banks and outdoor **market** running off along Simor János utca. Stop for cake and coffee at the Art Nouveau *Központi Kávéház* (see p.145) on the corner of Vörösmarty utca before exploring the backstreets beyond.

Danube Museum

Duna Múzeum • Kölcsey utca 2 • Daily except Tues: May–Oct 9am–5pm; Nov–April 10am–4pm; closed Jan • 700Ft • ☎ 33 500 250, ⓦ bit.ly/DunaMuzeum

The **Danube Museum** mounts a visitor-friendly exhibition on the history and hydrology of Hungary's great rivers, the Danube and the Tisza. Interactive models, videos and a children's section explain the principles of fluid hydraulics, regulating rivers and disaster relief during floods, which are not uncommon on this stretch of the Danube; the most recent floods occurred in 2013, comfortably beating previous record levels.

Szent Tamás-hegy

To get an overview of the lower town, walk northwest up Imaház utca from Kölcsey utca past a flamboyant, Moorish-style edifice that was once Esztergom's synagogue and is now a **Cultural Centre** (Művelődési Ház) with a variety of programmes. Shortly afterwards you'll find a flight of steps leading to **Szent Tamás-hegy** (St Thomas's Hill), a rocky outcrop named after the English martyr Thomas à Becket. A **chapel** was built here in his honour by Margaret Capet, whose English father-in-law, Henry II, prompted Thomas's assassination by raging "Who will rid me of this turbulent priest?" Even after her husband died and Margaret married Béla III of Hungary, her conscience would not let her forget the saint. The existing chapel (postdating the Turkish occupation) is fronted by a trio of life-size statues representing Golgotha.

ARRIVAL AND INFORMATION   **ESZTERGOM**

By train Trains from Budapest (every 30min; 1hr 10min–1hr 25min) arrive at the train station, 1km south of town; the station is linked to the centre by bus #1 and #5, or it's a 15min walk.

By bus Buses run from Budapest's Újpest-Városkapu terminal via Szentendre and Visegrád (#880 hourly from stand 7; 2hr) or from the Árpád híd terminal via Dorog, west of the Pilis Hills (#800 every 30min from stand 6; 1hr

15min), a less scenic but faster route (both routes cost 950Ft). Arriving from Visegrád, get off near Basilica Hill rather than riding on to the bus station in the south of town.

By boat The boat to Esztergom (May–Aug Tues–Sun, Sept Sat only; 3300Ft, return 4950Ft; ☎ 1 484 4013, ⓦ mahartpassnave.hu) leaves Budapest's Vigadó tér at 9am and makes the journey in just over 5hr, docking at

Prímás-sziget, a 15min walk south of the centre. The return boat to Budapest departs at 4pm.

By hydrofoil Departing at 10am from Vigadó tér, the hydrofoil (May–Sept Tues–Sun; 5000ft, return 7500Ft; ☎ 1

484 4013, ⓦ mahartpassnave.hu) takes 1hr 30min to get to Esztergom from Budapest, and also ties up at Prímás-sziget. The return to Budapest departs at 5.30pm.

EATING

Csülök Csárda Batthyány utca 11–13 ☎ 33 412 420, ⓦ csulokcsarda.hu. Popular with tourists and locals alike, the reasonably priced "Knuckle Inn" serves hearty Hungarian, Czech and German food, including a myriad of knuckle-contrived dishes (2500Ft), as well as the likes of goose-liver pie and smoked ox tongue. Daily noon–10pm.

Központi Kávéház Vörösmarty utca 2 ☎ 33 520 570. A stylishly revamped Art Nouveau patisserie-cum-chocolatier in the centre of town, whose fabulous coffee and delectable cakes you'll find difficult to resist; there's a chocolate museum upstairs too. Daily 9am–7pm.

Padlizsán Pázmány Péter utca 21 ☎ 33 311 212. A hive

of activity in the otherwise quiet Víziváros district, this well-regarded restaurant offers crisp, modern cooking, like pork fillet with onion cake and roast potatoes (2500Ft); dine out on the pleasant stone-cobbled courtyard. Daily noon–10pm.

Prímás Pince Szent István ter ☎ 33 541 965, ⓦ primaspince.hu. Despite being completely hammed up for the tourist hordes, the cavernous bowels of the former primate's wine cellars – all brick-vaulted ceilings and neat rows of thick tables – are an enjoyable place to tuck into solid national grub (mains 2500–3000Ft). Mon–Sat noon–10pm, Sun noon–5pm.

DRINKING

Trafó Vörösmarty utca ☎ 33 403 980. Popular little bar in an old electrical substation on a small triangular square across the road from the Danube Museum: the terrace

under the trees is a particularly lovely spot to kick back with a coffee or glass of wine. Mon–Sat 7am–2am, Sun 8am–midnight.

Vác

The town of **VÁC**, 40km north of Budapest, has a worldlier past than its sleepy atmosphere suggests, allowing you to enjoy its architectural heritage in relative peace. Its bishops traditionally showed a flair for self-promotion, like the cardinals of Esztergom, endowing monuments and colleges.

Under Turkish occupation (1544–1686), Vác assumed an oriental character, with seven mosques and a public *hammam*, while during the Reform Era it was linked to Budapest by Hungary's first rail line (the second continued to Bratislava). In 1849 two battles were fought at Vác, the first a victory for the town over the Austrian army, followed a few months later by a defeat in July 1849 when the town was captured; the battles are commemorated by a bright green **obelisk** by the main road from Budapest, shortly before you enter the town. More recently Vác became notorious for its prison, which has one of the toughest regimes in the country and was used to incarcerate leftists under Admiral Horthy and "counter-revolutionaries" under Communism.

Március 15 tér

One of the most eye-catching squares in the entire country, **Március 15 tér** is a perfect triangular wedge framed by a handsome melange of sunny, pastel-coloured Baroque and Rococo buildings. At the heart of the square are the excavated ruins of **St Michael's Church**, developed piecemeal since its thirteenth-century origins. What you see now – foundation walls, sections of nave and parts of a crypt – date mainly from the eighteenth century. During the summer, you can take a look around the **crypt** itself (Szent Mihály Altemplom; April–Oct Thurs & Fri 10am–2pm, Sat & Sun 10am–6pm; 500Ft).

Memento Mori (Tragor Ignác Museum)

Marcius 15 tér 19 • April–Oct Tues–Sun 10am–6pm, Nov–March 10am–5pm • 1200Ft • ☎ 30 555 7620

The Baroque style evolved into a fine art in Vác, as evinced by the gorgeous decor of the **Dominican church** on the south side of Március 15 tér. During renovation work in 1994, the church crypt was rediscovered, unearthing some remarkable finds, not least

262 corpses (166 of which were positively identified) that had been preserved in a state of mummification owing to the crypt's microclimatic conditions. Three of the mummified corpses (a male, female and infant) – dating from the eighteenth century – can be seen in the **Memento Mori (Tragor Ignác Museum)** display in a chilly medieval wine cellar near the church.

Also retrieved from the bodies (and now displayed in the museum) were an immaculately preserved assortment of clothes and other burial accessories (including crucifixes, which were traditionally placed in the hands of the deceased), alongside their colourfully painted wooden coffins – typically, the adult coffin would be painted brown or dark blue, and the child's coffin green and white.

Diocesan Treasury

Székesegyházi kincstár • Március 15 tér 4 • May–Oct Wed–Fri 2–6pm, Sat & Sun 10am–6pm • 500Ft • ☎ 27 319 494

On the northeast side of Március 15 tér, the **Diocesan Treasury** is housed in the former Bishop's Palace (Nagypréposti palota). It was built for Bishop Kristóf Migazzi (1714–1803) who erected Vác's cathedral and the Baroque **Town Hall** across the square, its gable adorned with two prostrate females bearing the coats of arms of Hungary and of Migazzi himself. During his years as Bishop of Vác (1762–86), this ambitious prelate was the moving force behind the town's eighteenth-century revival, impressing Empress Maria Theresa sufficiently to make him Archbishop of Vienna. Meanwhile his former palace was converted into Hungary's first Institute for the Deaf and Dumb in 1802. Downstairs is a collection of church treasures and displays on local diocesan history and architecture. But it is worth persevering and going upstairs, where restoration work has

VÁC

EATING	
Choco Café	2
Mihályi Cukrászda	1
Remete Pince	3

Triumphal Arch
Town Prison
Round Tower
Synagogue
Museum Hall
Diocesan Treasury
Town Hall
MÁRCIUS 15 TÉR
St Michael's Church & Crypt
Memento Mori (Tragor Ignác Museum)
Market
Dominican Church
Modern Art Collection
Cathedral
Bus Station
Train Station
River Danube (Duna)
Car ferry to Szentendrei sziget
KONSTANTIN TÉR
Budapest

0   200
metres

uncovered fabulous Rococo **frescoes** from two periods of the eighteenth century in four of the rooms, one with a winter garden scene, another decorated with fruit and flowers.

Museum Hall

Értéktár • Köztársaság út 19 • May–Oct Thurs & Fri 10am–2pm, Sat & Sun 10am–6pm • 400Ft, joint ticket with the St Michael's church crypt (see p.145) 500Ft

The northwest corner of Március 15 tér feeds seamlessly into Köztársaság út, where it's worth taking a quick look into the **Museum Hall** to see a delightful display of works by the popular Hungarian children's illustrator Gyula Hincz (1904–86).

The cathedral and around

Beyond Vác's lively **market** (Mon–Sat 8am–2pm), selling flowers, fruit and vegetables, you come to the back of the town's **cathedral** on Konstantin tér (Székesegyház; April–Nov Mon–Sat 10am–noon & 1.30–6pm, Sun 7.30am–7pm). Chiefly impressive for its gigantic Corinthian columns, Bishop Kristóf Migazzi's church is a temple to self-esteem more than anything else. Its Neoclassical design by Isidore Canevale was considered revolutionary in the 1770s, the style not becoming generally accepted in Hungary until the following century. Migazzi himself took umbrage at one of the frescoes by Franz Anton Maulbertsch, and ordered *The Meeting of Mary and Elizabeth*, above the altar, to be bricked over. His motives for this are unknown, but one theory is that it was because Mary was depicted as being pregnant. The fresco was only discovered during restoration work in 1944. From the cathedral you can head along Múzeum utca to Géza király tér, the centre of Vác in medieval times, where there's a Baroque **Franciscan church** with a magnificent organ, pulpits and altars.

Along the waterfront

From the Franciscan church you can follow the road down to the **riverside promenade**, József Attila sétány, where the townsfolk of Vác walk on summer weekends and evenings. The northern stretch of the promenade, named after Liszt, runs past the **Round Tower**, the only remnant of Vác's medieval fortifications.

The prison

Köztársaság út 62

North of the dock for ferries to Budapest and Esztergom rises the forbidding hulk of the Vác's **prison** (*fegyház*). Ironically, the building was originally an academy for noble youths, founded by Maria Theresa. Turned into a barracks in 1784 – you can still see part of the older building peering awkwardly above the blank white walls of the prison – it began its penal career a century later, achieving infamy during the Horthy era, when two Communists died here after being beaten for going on hunger strike to protest against maltreatment. In October 1956 a mass escape occurred. Thrown into panic by reports from Budapest where their colleagues were being "hunted down like animals, hung on trees, or just beaten to death by passers-by", the ÁVO guards mounted guns on the rooftop, fomenting rumours of the Uprising among prisoners whose hopes had been raised by snatches of patriotic songs overheard from the streets. A glimpse of national flags with the Soviet emblem cut from the centre provided the spark: a guard was overpowered, locks were shot off, and the prisoners burst free.

Triumphal Arch

Köztársaság út

The **Triumphal Arch** (Kőkapu or Diadalív) flanking the prison was another venture by Migazzi and his architect Canevale, occasioned by Maria Theresa's visit in 1764. Migazzi initially planned theatrical facades to hide the town's dismal housing (perhaps inspired by Potemkin's fake villages in Russia, created around the same time), but settled for the Neoclassical arch, from which Habsburg heads grimace a stony welcome.

11

ARRIVAL AND INFORMATION   VÁC

By train There are regular services from Nyugati Station to Vác – the *zonázó* trains are the faster ones. From the train station, at the northern end of Széchenyi utca, it's a 10min walk down to Március 15 tér.

By bus Buses go from Ujpest-Városkapu bus station in Budapest every 30min and take 55min. They arrive at the terminus on Szent István tér, a few minutes closer to the main square than the train station.

By hydrofoil The hydrofoil leaves Budapest's Vigadó tér at

9am (May–Sept Tues–Sun; 3000Ft, return 4500Ft; ☎ 1 484 4013, ⓦ mahartpassnave.hu) and takes 40min to make the journey upriver (the return to Budapest is at 6.20pm). Disembarking at the landing stage for ferries from Budapest, you can see the prison and triumphal arch to the north; head south along the promenade and the town centre is on the left.

Tourist office The helpful Tourinform, at Március 15 tér 17 (daily 9am–5pm; ☎ 27 316 160, ⓦ turizmusvac.hu), has all the information you need.

EATING

Choco Café Március 15 tér 20 ☎ 27 305 839. Cosy café in which you can mull over a long menu of chocolate drinks in every conceivable flavour, from almond and cinnamon to and orange and nutmeg. Mon–Thurs & Sun 9am–8pm, Fri & Sat 9am–9pm.

Mihályi Cukrászda Köztársaság út 21 ☎ 20 390 3367. László is the award-winning confectioner who produces a toothsome selection of the most perfectly formed cakes in this tiny, salon-like place; the best coffee in town too.

Outdoor terrace in summer. Daily 9am–8pm.

Remete Pince Fürdő lépcső 3 ☎ 27 302 199. Located out by Vác's lido, this is the town's best restaurant, an elegant but not too pricey brick-vaulted cellar with candle-topped tables and wrought-iron chairs, while the flower-bedecked terrace is lovely in warmer weather. The food, meanwhile, ranges from roast goose with braised red cabbage (3300Ft) to grilled pike-perch with king prawns (3650Ft). Daily noon–10pm.

Gödöllő

The small town of **GÖDÖLLŐ** boasts a former Habsburg summer palace and a famous artists' colony, but being 30km northeast of Budapest rather than on the Danube Bend, it gets far fewer tourists than Szentendre, despite a reliable HÉV service from Örs Vezér tere (the terminus of the red metro line #2) that means you can enjoy an evening concert and return easily to the capital afterwards.

Royal Palace

Királyi Kastély • Daily: April–Oct 10am–6pm; Nov–March 10am–5pm • 2600Ft, guided tour 6500Ft (up to nine people); last entry tickets sold 40min before closing; audioguide 800Ft • ☎ 28 410 124, ⓦ kiralyikastely.hu

Gödöllő's **Royal Palace** was commissioned by a confidante of Empress Maria Theresa's, Count Antal Grassalkovich, and designed by András Mayerhoffer, who introduced the Baroque style of mansion to Hungary in the 1740s. The palace suffered as a result of both world wars, being commandeered as a headquarters first by the Reds and then by the Whites in 1919–20, and pillaged by both the Nazis and the Red Army in 1944. One wing was later turned into an old people's home, while the rest was left to rot until 1985, when restoration finally began; this was finally completed in time for Hungary's hosting of the EU presidency in 2011.

The formal **state rooms**, reached by a grand staircase, precede the private apartments used by Emperor Franz Josef and his wife Elizabeth – his decorated in grey and gold, hers draped in her favourite colour, violet. Sisi, as she was known, stayed two thousand nights here, preferring it to the palace in Vienna. While her possessions are reverentially displayed – right down to a horseshoe from her stallion – there's no sign to identify the secret staircase that she had installed as a means of getting some privacy in a relentlessly public life.

Temporary exhibitions are held in the Rudolf and Gizella wings, while the **Riding Hall** (Lovárda), which hosted the EU presidency, is used for exhibitions and concerts. The **Baroque Theatre** (Barokk színház) that Count Grassalkovich established in a side-wing (used for only two weeks each year when he was in residence), the **Royal Hill Pavilion** (Királydombi pavilion) and **Baths** (Fürdő) in the large park that stretches behind the Palace are occasionally open to individual visitors. The baths were last enjoyed by

SISI, THE FRIEND OF HUNGARY

One of the most popular historical figures in Hungary today is **Empress Elizabeth** (1837–98), the beautiful wife of the Austrian Emperor Franz Josef. She might seem a strange choice, given that her husband crushed the Hungarians in 1848, but that may be the clue to the bond that developed between the empress and Hungary. She loathed life in the Viennese court and was none too attached to the emperor either, and Budapest came to represent a refuge for her. She also avoided staying in the empty Royal Palace in Budapest, preferring to spend her time in the palace in Gödöllő and a villa in the Buda Hills near the János-hegy (see p.124). The Hungarians called her Sisi (pronounced see-see) and she pleaded their cause in Vienna. There were even rumours of affairs with the Hungarian statesman Count Gyula Andrássy.

Sisi's later years were blighted by tragedy – the death of her siblings and the suicide of her son Rudolf at Mayerling – before she herself was stabbed to death by an anarchist in 1898 in Switzerland. Mourned throughout Hungary, she became the focus of a cult that outlasted all attempts to stifle it under Communism.

Admiral Horthy, who used Gödöllő as a holiday home from 1920 till 1944, installing a swimming pool and an air-raid shelter; this can only be visited on the guided tour, though these are normally available only for groups. Musical and cultural programmes are staged within the palace throughout the year.

Gödöllő Town Museum

Gödöllői Városi Múzeum • Szabadság tér 5 • Wed–Sun 10am–4pm • 800Ft • ☎ 28 421 997

Right in the centre of town, the delightful **Gödöllő Town Museum** focuses on the **Gödöllő Artists' Colony**. Founded in 1901, the colony was inspired by the English Pre-Raphaelites and the Arts and Crafts movement of William Morris and John Ruskin, whose communal, rural ethos it took a stage further. Members included Aladár Körösfői-Kriesch, who wrote a book about Ruskin and Morris, and Sándor Nagy, whose home and workshop may eventually become a separate museum. There was a strong tradition of weaving in the artists' colony – here at least the lack of English captions is no obstacle to enjoyment. The museum's displays include good exhibitions of regional history, including mock-up rooms illustrating the life of the Gödöllő estate; the sections on hunting and the Gödöllő scout troop should not detain you too long.

ARRIVAL AND INFORMATION   GÖDÖLLŐ

By train HÉV trains from Örs Vezér tere (every 30min) take about 50min to reach Gödöllő; get off at the Szabadság tér stop, bang opposite the palace. BKK tickets (and Budapest Cards) are valid as far as the city limits, so you will need to buy a supplementary ticket to cover the remaining part of the journey, or show a BKK pass or ticket when buying a ticket at the station or on the train.

Tourist office There's a Tourinform booth inside the palace (Tues–Sun: Nov–March 10am–4pm; April–Oct 10am–5pm; ☎ 28 415 402, ✆ gkrte.hu).

EATING

Solier Café Dózsa György utca 13 ☎ 20 396 5512. Set in a modern block on the corner of Kossuth Lajos utca, some 300m north of the HÉV station, *Solier* serves up the best meals and cakes in town; the wide repertoire of food includes duck breast with sesame tempura (3100Ft). Daily 11.30am–10pm.

Sulyán Cukrászda Szabadság tér 8 ☎ 28 416 536. In the big square behind the Gödöllő Town Museum, this is a popular place for cakes, ices and coffee. Outside tables in summer. Daily 9am–7pm.

GELLÉRT HOTEL

Accommodation

Budapest's accommodation is improving all the time, both in terms of availability and quality, though the downside is that prices are in many cases on a par with most Western European capitals. The city is flush with high-end hotels, typically around the Belváros and up in the Vár (Castle District), which includes the burgeoning trend for flashy boutique hotels where style is big but the rooms are often small. That said, there's still a decent spread of affordable three-star hotels out beyond the main downtown areas. Pensions are an even cheaper alternative, often with much the same facilities as small hotels, while the city is bursting with hostels. If you're on a tight budget, your best bet is a private room or a self-contained studio flat or apartment rented through internet-based companies.

All hotels are **star-rated**, though this is not always an accurate guide to the standard or ambience of a place. Some of the newer, smaller hotels have facilities that belie their star rating, while some of the more luxurious establishments can be disappointingly bland with an impersonal feel. Budapest is awash with well-run and well-equipped **youth hostels**, many of which now offer smart en-suite private rooms to go alongside the traditional large dorm. You'll see them all over the place, though you're best off avoiding any that advertise themselves just as "hostel" and stick to those listed in this guide. Some represent the cheapest form of accommodation in the city, while others are more expensive than private rooms. While it's unlikely that you'll come to Budapest to **camp**, there are a couple of year-round possibilities over on the Buda side.

ESSENTIALS

Reservations It's advisable to book a room during high season (roughly May–Oct). Otherwise, rooms are most in demand at Christmas, New Year, and during the Spring and Autumn festivals in March/October respectively, when many hotels ramp up the rates; unless you're here for the Grand Prix in early August, you may wish to avoid the city then, as most hotels double their prices. Also during August, many hostels get booked up months in advance for the Sziget Festival, and up their rates, too. Even so, it should always be possible to find somewhere that's reasonably priced, if not well situated.

Booking a room Aside from booking a room directly (either by phone or online), there are several online accommodation sites: ⓦ hotelinfo.hu lists the city's hotels and pensions and has information about Hungary Card discounts, but doesn't allow you to make bookings. To book online, try ⓦ budapesthotelreservation.hu. Agencies in Budapest that can arrange accommodation include: Ibusz V, Aranykéz utca 4–6 (Mon–Fri 9am–5pm; ☎ 1 501 4910, ⓦ ibusz.hu), and Vista Visitor Center VI, Paulay Ede utca 7–9 (Mon–Fri 9am–5.30pm; ☎ 1 429 9784, ⓦ vistahungary.com).

Prices Accommodation rates are usually quoted in euros; where prices are given in forints, we have followed suit, but note that you can always pay in forints. Rates given in our reviews reflect the typical cost of a double or twin room in high season. That said, rates fluctuate wildly according to both season and demand, and you can find some terrific deals, particularly in some of the top-end hotels – indeed, book early enough and out of season, and you'll often find prices much lower than the ones given here. The cheapest rooms in a three-star hotel or pension go for €50–70, while you'll typically pay upwards of €100–120 for a room in a four-star or design hotel. Beyond this, in many of the five-star establishments, you're often entering the realms of the stratospheric. Hostel dorm beds vary between €10 and €15, with a double room (with shared facilities) going for €35–40, while a private double room in a hostel costs about €45. Note that some hotels do not include twenty percent VAT (*Áfa*) and three percent tourist tax in quoted prices, so check before you commit yourself.

Internet Nearly all the hotels listed here have wi-fi; access is usually free, although a handful of places still charge. In any case, it's always best to check first.

12

PRIVATE ROOMS AND APARTMENTS

The best budget option in town is a **private room**, bookable through the agencies listed below or the likes of airbnb, booking.com, etc. You'll also find people touting rooms outside the metro station on Deák tér and the nearby Tourinform office, and at the train stations. However, while this may be cheaper, the chances are that you'll be located further out from the centre, and it doesn't offer any security.

Depending on location and amenities, **prices** for a double room start at around 7500Ft a night, while apartments cost upwards of 10,000Ft. For stays of less than four nights, there's usually a thirty-percent surcharge, though this is sometimes only applicable on the first night. These days most of the rooms and apartments are inside or near the Nagykörút – or in Buda close to the Vár. Families might enjoy the Szent István Park area (the inner XIII district just beyond the Nagykörút), which has plenty of playgrounds and green space.

Self-contained **studio** flats or **apartments** are available to rent through agencies such as Ibusz, Vista or the small To-Ma at V, Nádor utca 20 (daily 9am–6pm, in winter open Sat & Sun by arrangement; ☎ 1 353 0819, ⓦ tomatour.hu) and internet-based companies such as Budapest Lets (☎ 0670 557 6880, ⓦ budapestlets.com), a UK–Hungarian venture managing about two hundred well-equipped properties, from one-room studio flats on Ráday utca to three-bedroom luxury apartments in the city centre. Some hotels, such as *Brody House* (see p.154) and *Lavender Circus* (see p.152), also have apartments on their books.

HOTELS AND PENSIONS

The greatest choice of accommodation, particularly hotels and hostels, is in **Pest**, which is where you'll also find the greatest concentration of restaurants and bars – though you will have to contend with more traffic noise. The grand hotels that lined the riverbank were all destroyed during World War II, and while their replacements – such as the *Marriott* and *InterContinental* – offer fantastic views, they don't have quite the same elegance. Going in the other direction, there are plenty of hotels along and beyond the Nagykörút (the larger ring road) and up towards City Park. Across the water, **Buda** offers more restful possibilities, especially within the Castle District where there are several first-rate hotels, with more along the riverfront. It's on this side of the river, too, that you'll find Budapest's most appealing pensions, notably up in the **Buda Hills**, which is within easy reach of Széll Kálmán tér. In this city of baths, it's no surprise that several of the big hotels offer **spa packages**: the *Gellért* and the *Danubius* (on Margít-sziget) hotels were built next to springs, while several other five-star hotels in the centre have luxury spa complexes.

THE BELVÁROS

Astoria V, Kossuth Lajos utca 19–21 ☎1 889 6000, ⓦdanubiushotels.com; map p.40. Four-star vintage hotel that has given its name to the major junction in central Pest on which it's located, though fortunately all the windows are soundproofed. The two categories of room available (standard and deluxe, the latter €120) differ little by way of facilities, but the latter are larger and markedly more pleasing on the eye. The hotel's coffee house and bar is a popular meeting point. €110

Bohém Art V, Molnár utca 35 ☎1 327 9020, ⓦbohemarthotel.hu; map p.40. Hip four-star boutique hotel in a former paper factory close to the Danube. Bright and cosy, the sixty rooms squeezed into the building come in different sizes, from apartments and family suites to superior rooms with baths (the latter are €180), to the very compact classic rooms with showers. All are dominated by large prints covering whole walls. €125

Boutique Hotel Zara V, Só utca 6 ☎1 920 2100, ⓦboutiquehotelbudapest.com; map p.40. Four-star boutique hotel off the bottom of Váci utca, close to the Main Market Hall. Although by no means large, the rooms are impressive, with light, design-papered walls and smart, dark furniture set against hardwood flooring. Double and twin-bedded rooms in equal measure, and all with showers. €110

Buddha-Bar V, Váci utca 34 ☎1 799 7302, ⓦbuddha barhotel.hu; map p.40. If you thought the exterior of *Buddha-Bar* was grand enough, step through the doors and see the striking black and red decor inside. Pest's luxury chill-out zone is housed in one of the palaces that form the gateway to the Erzsébet bridge, and the 102 rooms have high ceilings and state-of-the-art fittings, from heated mirrors to remote control toilet-bidets,

while the corner apartments have huge family-size baths. The windows are well soundproofed, though you may prefer a room away from the main road. The bar has a DJ continuing the chill-out theme, and the restaurant also gets good marks. €200

Erzsébet City Center V, Károlyi utca 11 ☎01 889 3700, ⓦdanubiushotels.com; map p.40. Buzzy, always busy hotel whose slap-bang central location makes it a great choice for a couple of days; rooms (all standard) are functional in the main but are perfectly agreeable and very clean. Breakfast is taken in the adjoining restaurant. €110

Estilo Fashion V, Váci utca 83 ☎01 799 7170, ⓦestilohotel.hu; map p.40. Although sited along the city's busiest pedestrianized street, this smart retreat is surprisingly restful, while the bold blue-, red- and white-striped colour theme running throughout the hotel is rather more tasteful than it sounds. €100

★**Gerlóczy** V, Gerlóczy utca 1 ☎1 501 4000, ⓦgerloczy.hu; map p.40. Above the café of the same name (see p.160), the nineteen elegant *Gerlóczy* rooms all lead off a spiral staircase topped by a coloured glass skylight. The rooms are colour themed according to floor (grey, blue, red and yellow-green from the bottom upwards), though all have similar fixtures and fittings: high doors and ceilings, parquet flooring and gorgeous, brass-fitted bathrooms, some with clawfoot tubs, some with showers only. Two rooms have small balconies looking out over the square (€119). Free minibar. One of the best value-for-money places in the city, especially if you can nab one of the slightly cheaper attic rooms. €105

★**Lavender Circus** V, Múzeum körút 37 ☎0670 417 7763, ⓦlavendercircus.com; map p.40. Opposite the National Museum, this eccentric little "hostel" (it has no dorms but the simple foam mattresses give it a hostel feel) has a very individual touch: the owner Ádám has spent the past six years designing the rooms – expect vintage furniture, goldfish tanks and satirical artwork gracing the walls. The pricier rooms on the second floor have en-suite bathrooms and kitchenettes. Reception is on the third floor (no lift). You can also book one of the three apartments they have behind the Opera House. No breakfast. Doubles from €39

TOP 5 COOL HOTELS

Aria see p.50
Baltazár see p.93
Brody House see p.78
Gerlóczy see p.40
Rum see p.40

La Prima Fashion V, Piarista utca 6 ☎1 799 0088, Ⓦlaprimahotel.hu; map p.40. A stone's throw from Erzsébet bridge, this sparkling fashion hotel oozes sophistication, from the smart lobby to the plush rooms decorated in fetching turquoise and chocolate-brown colours. The cool factor extends to the oversized wall mirrors embedded with TVs, and designer bathrooms with walk-in showers. €150

★**Rum** V, Királyi Pál utca 4 ☎01 424 9060, Ⓦhotelrumbudapest.com; map p.40. Fabulous conversion of an old Pest apartment block, now concealing 38 sleek, differently configured rooms which come in one of four cleverly-titled categories, from Light Rums (small) to Black Rums (large plus; €100), some of which have Nespresso machines; stylish though not always practical furnishings include tree-trunk bedside stools, small armchairs and rainforest showers. €80

Zenit V, Apáczai Csere János utca 7 ☎1 799 8400, Ⓦbudapest.zenithoteles.com; map p.40. Four-star Spanish-run hotel, close to the river in the shadow of the *Marriott*. Most of the rooms overlook either the glass-roofed reception area in the block's central courtyard or the quiet sidestreet running down one side of the hotel. The pleasantly furnished rooms all have wooden floors, and connecting rooms or extra beds are available for families. The restaurant has a vaulted ham bar, hung with magnificent Spanish hams. €120

LIPÓTVÁROS AND ÚJLIPÓTVÁROS

★**Aria** Hercegprímás utca 5 ☎01 445 4055, Ⓦariahotelbudapest.com; map p.50. Enchanting music-themed hotel whose rooms are designed according to four genres (jazz, opera, classical and contemporary), each one paying homage to a different artist, be it Beethoven or the Beatles. Art Nouveau, Neo-Baroque and Pop Art furnishings are complemented by musically themed ornaments, Blecha-inspired caricatures and large flatscreen smart TVs with a comprehensive selection of DVDs. With complimentary wine and cheese each afternoon, a music library, rooftop bar and a stunning basement pool, it doesn't get any better than this. €240

★**Four Seasons** V, Széchenyi tér 5–6 ☎1 268 6000, Ⓦfourseasons.com/budapest; map p.50. A magnificent restoration of this Budapest landmark, also known as the *Gresham Palace*, has produced an unprecedented level of luxury in the city; the rooms have Art Nouveau-style fittings (even down to the beautiful radiators) and are superbly equipped; those overlooking the Danube naturally have the best aspect. The *Gresham* restaurant, which also acts as a coffee house, is excellent – drinks are also served in the bar in the wonderful glass-roofed Peacock Passage – and the service throughout the hotel is superlative. €350

Starlight Suiten V, Mérleg utca 6 ☎1 484 3700, Ⓦstarlighthotels.com; map p.50. Amazingly good value given its location near the Lánchíd (right behind the *Four Seasons*), with 54 immaculate and incredibly roomy suites. Each has a kitchenette with a microwave, two televisions (one in each room), a sofa and a writing desk. Facilities include a sauna, steam bath and fitness rooms. €210

TERÉZVÁROS AND ERZSÉBETVÁROS

Benczúr VI, Benczúr utca 35 ☎1 479 5650, Ⓦhotelbenczur.hu; map p.60. Large, modern and functional hotel on a leafy street off Andrássy út offering two categories of room; boxy economy rooms, and bigger, brighter superior rooms (€90) which come with showers – several also have a balcony. Some of the superior rooms are anti-allergen and have disabled access. There are also some apartments for families. Breakfast included. €70

Casati VI, Paulay Ede utca 31 ☎1 343 1198, Ⓦcasatibudapesthotel.com; map p.60. The appealing transformation of this historic apartment block into a hotel has preserved old features such as the eighteenth-century bared walls in the bar area. The lively decorations by young Hungarian artists in the public spaces might not be to all tastes, but the 25 generously sized, gracefully furnished rooms themselves are calmer, coming in four styles, from the dark-walled "Classic" to the light and airy "Heaven"; all face inwards over a balconied courtyard covered in greenery, which is also where breakfast is served. No children under 14. Gym and sauna in the basement. €125

Continental Hotel Zara VII, Dohány utca 42–44 ☎1 815 1000, Ⓦcontinentalhotelbudapest.com; map p.60. Occupying the old Hungária baths, this towering Secessionist edifice has been stylishly renovated. From the restored exterior and the shiny lobby, which incorporates details of the original building, to the sumptuous Art Deco rooms, the place oozes class. The spa centre, meanwhile, is as swish as any in Budapest, though its real selling point is the rooftop garden with a sparkling little pool offering views across the city. €130

Corinthia Grand Royal VII, Erzsébet körút 43–49 ☎1 479 4000, Ⓦcorinthia.com; map p.60. Opened as the *Grand Hotel Royal* in 1898, the *Corinthia* and its concierges enjoy the idea that this is the inspiration for Wes Anderson's celluloid *Grand Budapest Hotel*. The imposing building was used as offices for some forty years, and it took a major rebuilding project – only the facade is original – to turn out four hundred or so rooms with such unbridled luxury. Many look out onto the main boulevard, though a good number face inwards, overlooking the splendid, marble-tiled atrium. The centrepiece of the hotel's Royal Spa complex is a stunning pool. €140

easyHotel VI, Eötvös utca 25/a ☎1 411 1982, Ⓦeasyhotel.com; map p.60. Decent location near

12

Oktogon with the same approach as easyJet, where cheapness and simplicity rule. The a/c rooms have one bright orange wall and come in two sizes: small (7–9 square metres, enough room for a bed and your bag, as long as it's not too big); and standard, which has slightly more space and even a couple of hooks. The en-suite shower/toilets have the feel of an airplane cubicle, and, in true Easy style, you pay for everything else, such as TV, internet and breakfast. There are two larger rooms with disabled access on the ground floor. Bookable online only; prices vary according to demand, but usually average €65–75. From €33

K&K Opera VI, Révay utca 24 ☎ 1 269 0222, ⓦ kkhotels .com; map p.60. Opulent and expensive four-star hotel that really trades on its location right by the Opera House. Most of its two-hundred-plus rooms are of average size, but they are supremely comfortable; around half have baths, the others showers, some walk-in. €215

★**Mamaison Hotel Andrássy** VI, Andrássy út 111 ☎ 1 462 2100, ⓦ mamaison.com; map p.60. Housed in a fine Bauhaus building up near the Városliget (but with easy access to the Belváros), *Mamaison* offers luxury accommodation without the corporate feel. The rooms, some of which have a balcony, are beautifully appointed in silvery-grey tones offset with splashes of red, while bathrooms feature turquoise and cream patterned tiles. Try and bag one of the rooms away from busy Andrássy út. The tree-shaded terrace is a lovely spot to take in the first meal of the day (€15). €95

Medosz VI, Jókai tér 9 ☎ 1 374 3001, ⓦ medoszhotel .hu; map p.60. Overlooking a leafy square near Oktogon, the location, good prices and the helpful staff make this three-star hotel a popular choice. Operating till 1989 as a trade union hostel – its exterior betrays its past – the *Medosz* still has simply furnished but pleasant rooms. Most have baths and those with showers benefit from overlooking the quieter courtyard. The lower floors have family rooms sleeping up to six people, while the ninth-floor rooms have small balconies. The four rooftop Panorama apartments (€119) have terraces with breathtaking views. €79

Radisson Blu Béke VI, Teréz körút 43 ☎ 1 889 3900, ⓦ radissonblu.com/hotel-budapest; map p.60. Large, vintage hotel in a handy location on the Nagykörút near Nyugati Station. The rooms are smooth without being spectacular, though other facilities include a pool, sauna and gym, underground garage and an agreeable café on the ground floor. If you're passing, take a look at the corner facade, which is distinguished by a nineteenth-century mosaic of St George and the Dragon. €120

Soho V, Dohány utca 64 ☎ 1 872 8292, ⓦ sohohotel .hu; map p.60. The visual assault begins in the Pop Art-inspired lobby, and continues through to the small but snappily designed rooms, decked out in cool reds, greys

and blacks, and sporting Swedish hardwood flooring, bamboo-covered walls and glass-partitioned bathrooms. A filling American-style buffet breakfast rounds things off. €140

Star Inn VI, Dessewffy utca 36 ☎ 1 472 2020, ⓦ starinnhotels.com; map p.60. This rather nondescript glass and brick building does little to inspire, but the rooms concealed within are fresh and contemporary, with deep-red walls, white armchairs and low-slung beds. The location and price makes this a fair option. €100

JÓZSEFVÁROS AND FERENCVÁROS

Atrium Fashion VIII, Csokonai utca 14 ☎ 1 299 0777, ⓦ hotelatrium.hu; map p.78. This otherwise glum-looking street has been given a welcome dollop of colour, thanks to this cleverly conceived hotel. The focal point of the building is a gloriously light atrium, encircled by state-of-the-art rooms with floor-to-ceiling windows, built-in flatscreen TVs, and bits of artwork; some rooms have tubs, others have showers. €80

★**Brody House** VIII, Bródy Sándor utca 10 ☎ 1 266 1211, ⓦ brodyhouse.com; map p.78. A fabulously hip and award-winning retreat accommodating eleven individually styled rooms in the former home of the wartime Hungarian prime minister. The relaxed, shabby-chic style of the reception and lounges (at the top of the hotel, on the second floor – no lift) is continued throughout – the recycling of fittings in the furniture is great fun. It also has fourteen apartments (€100) in a house nearby on Paulay Ede utca, and a members' club, the *Brody Studios*, not far from Oktogon, which stages concerts and shows, and where guests can have lunch. Breakfast €8. €100

Museum VIII, Trefort utca 2 ☎ 1 485 1080, ⓦ museumhotel.hu; map p.78. Having established itself in an imaginatively transformed Pest apartment block on a quiet street behind the National Museum, the *Museum* has expanded into the next-door block. The rooms, which have a mix of baths and showers, aren't big, but it's a friendly place and in a good location. There's a small wellness centre in the basement and the hotel also has its own permanent art gallery. €130

★**Palazzo Zichy** VIII, Lőrinc pap tér 2 ☎ 1 235 4000, ⓦ hotel-palazzo-zichy.hu; map p.78. Lying on a quiet street in the Palace district, at the junction of Krudy utca and Mária utca, the hotel combines nineteenth-century grandeur with four-star twenty-first-century comfort. Its eighty slick and tastefully decorated rooms lie round the courtyard of the former Zichy palace, which now forms the glass-roofed reception area. Guests can use the fitness rooms and sauna. €130

THE VÁR AND THE VÍZIVÁROS

Art'otel I, Bem rakpart 16–19 ☎ 1 487 9487, ⓦ artotels.com; map p.90. Boutique hotel that combines eighteenth-century buildings – comprising beautiful, spacious rooms with original doors and high ceilings – with a modern wing overlooking the river, offering marvellous views; here, too, the rooms are well equipped and come with funkily designed bathrooms, most with shower. **€130**

★**Baltazár** I, Országház utca 31 ☎1 300 7051, ⓦbaltazarbudapest.com; map p.93. In a superb location next to the National Archives at the northern end of the Vár, this stylishly presented, family-run boutique hotel has become a firm favourite with travellers since it opened in 2013. Its eleven showy rooms – inspired by the likes of Vivienne Westwood, Andy Warhol and Keith Haring – are kitted-out with antique furniture and luxury products, and its restaurant specializes in steaks, cooked on an Argentinian Josper grill. Breakfast €10–15. **€155**

Buda Castle I, Úri utca 39 ☎1 224 7900, ⓦbudacastle hotelbudapest.com; map p.93. Located midway along one of the quieter streets in the Vár, this fifteenth-century merchant's house has been converted into a handsome design hotel. The rooms – which are essentially mini suites – are of the highest order, constructed around a small grassy courtyard, which is where guests can also take breakfast. The place is impeccably staffed, too. **€150**

Burg I, Szentháromság tér 7–8 ☎1 212 0269, ⓦburghotelbudapest.com; map p.93. Anonymous white-brick building right in the heart of the Castle District, opposite the Mátyás Church. The 26 rooms are nothing out of the ordinary, but most of them have a great view, overlooking the bustling main square and church. **€115**

★**Castle Garden** I, Lovas út 41 ☎1 224 7420, ⓦhotelcastlegarden.hu; map p.93. Friendly, modern four-star just below the Castle walls, a short walk down from the Bécsi kapu. The 39 rooms are light and airy; the superior rooms (€105) have terraces and great views, and there are also connecting rooms for families, and one with disabled access. The hotel's restaurant is excellent, and there's also a wellness centre with a jacuzzi. It's a refreshingly understated place, and it offers unbeatable value. Breakfast €10. **€85**

★**Hilton Budapest** I, Hess András tér 1–3 ☎1 889 6600, ⓦdanubiushotels.com; map p.93. In a prime location looking across the Danube, the remains of a medieval monastery, the *Hilton* is luxurious to a fault. All rooms – guest, plus superior (€230) and executive (€295) – are refreshingly light, with ample furnishings, a/c and fabulous walk-in showers; it's well worth paying €40 extra for a room with river view. Consummate service too. **€200**

Lánchíd 19 I, Lánchíd utca 19 ☎1 419 1900, ⓦlanchid19hotel.hu; map p.93. Located by the Chain Bridge, as its name suggests, this award-winning design hotel includes such features as an exterior facade of moving panels and suspended glass walkways leading to

artfully conceived rooms, each of which has been individually themed – for example on a wedding or a film. Breakfast €6–13. **€150**

Maison I, Országház utca 17 ☎1 405 4980, ⓦmaison budapest.hu; map p.93. This boutique hotel at the northern end of the Castle is a welcome addition to the area. Its seventeen well-equipped rooms – four with baths, and all with tasteful, if whimsical, decor – lie around a pleasant courtyard where you can sit out in warm weather. **€90**

★**St George's Residence** I, Fortuna utca 4 ☎1 393 5700, ⓦstgeorgehotel.hu; map p.93. Variously a medieval inn, art school and law court, this fabulous building has been tastefully restored to become one of the city's most characterful hotels; the 26 sumptuously decorated suites, all furnished in Grand Empire style, are priced according to size but all essentially comprise a bedroom, bathroom (some with jacuzzi), and living room with a study corner and kitchenette. A fine location and cheerful, obliging staff make this a first-class stopover. **€110**

★**Victoria** I, Bem rakpart 11 ☎1 457 8080, ⓦvictoria .hu; map p.90. Small, super-friendly hotel on the embankment directly below the Mátyás Church. The neat, a/c rooms are handsomely furnished and there are big windows through which you can soak up the excellent views of the Lánchíd and the river. **€110**

GELLÉRT-HEGY AND THE TABÁN

★**Ábel Panzió** XI, Ábel Jenő utca 9 ☎1 209 2537, ⓦabelpanzio.hu; map p.109. There are few more enjoyable pensions in Budapest than this graceful, early-1900s villa situated in a quiet, leafy street 20min walk from the Belváros. It boasts ten rooms of charming simplicity (none has TV, but they do at least have wi-fi), plus a drawing room where you can watch TV or listen to music, and a delightful garden and terrace for further relaxation. Two of the rooms also have a balcony. A popular place, so advance booking is essential. **€50**

Charles XI, Hegyalja út 23 ☎1 212 9169, ⓦcharles hotel.hu; map p.109. On the hill up from the Erzsébet híd on the main road to Vienna, this friendly apartment hotel was one of the first of its kind in the city. It has a wide range of studios (with double or twin beds, bath or shower), all of which come with a decently equipped kitchen; those facing the inner yard are better, as the road is very busy. Bikes available for rent. **€75**

Gellért XI, Szent Gellért tér 1 ☎1 889 5500, ⓦdanubiushotels.com; map p.109. There's no escaping the magnificence of this Art Nouveau building, which also incorporates one of the city's largest, most popular bath complexes. Once inside, there's a rather stiff atmosphere about the place, though the rooms are impressive enough, if overpriced; try and bag one facing

12

the river, some of which also have a balcony. Hotel guests receive one free entry to the pools, and a 50 percent discount after that. **€140**

Orion Várkert I, Döbrentei utca 13 ☎1 356 8583, ⓦ hotelorion.hu; map p.109. Small, modern block in the Tabán district, at the foot of the Vár. The thirty rooms are simply furnished (with space for a small writing desk) and the bathrooms are pretty cramped, but it's reasonably priced and in a useful location, across the river from the Belváros and a tram ride from the baths. Guests can also make use of the sauna. **€99**

MARGÍT-SZIGET

Danubius Grand and Danubius Health Spa Resort XIII, Margít-sziget ☎1 889 4752, ⓦ danubiushotel .com; map p.120. Located at the northern tip of the island, this mini-complex comprises the *fin-de-siècle Grand*, with rooms featuring period furniture and high ceilings, and the big modern *Health Spa Resort*, with balconies offering views over the Danube. Rates for both include access to the thermal baths, pool, sauna and gym, the two hotels linked by an underground passage. Other services include massages, pedicures and a host of other medical treatments. Grand €200, Health Spa Resort €150.

THE BUDA HILLS

★**Beatrix Panzió** II, Szehér út 3 ☎1 275 0550, ⓦ beatrixhotel.hu; tram #61 and #56 or bus #129; map p.123. Friendly pension in the villa district northwest of Széll Kálmán tér, keeping 22 good-sized rooms with modern amenities. There's a bar on the ground floor, while you're quite likely to find yourself attending one of the grill and goulash parties held in the landscaped garden. **€70**

Budapest II, Szilágyi Erzsébet fasor 47 ☎1 889 4200, ⓦ danubiushotels.com; map p.123. Cylindrical tower facing the Buda Hills, opposite the lower terminal of the Cogwheel Railway, 500m from Széll Kálmán tér. The three hundred a/c rooms are functional as opposed to fancy, but there's lots of window space and the views over the city from the upper floors are excellent. Smoking rooms available. There's a sauna, fitness room and business centre too. **€85**

★**Buda Villa Panzió** XII, Kiss Áron utca 6 ☎1 275 0091, ⓦ budapansio.hu; bus #155; map p.123. Up in the hills above Széll Kálmán tér, this comfortable and friendly pension has ten personable rooms, a bar in the lounge on the first floor, and a small garden that's perfect for relaxing in after a day's sightseeing. **€52**

HOSTELS

Most **hostels** offer a combination of same- and mixed-sex dorms, in addition to private rooms (singles or doubles) at much the same price as hotel or pension accommodation. As well as the year-round *Marco Polo Hostel*, the Mellow Mood group (☎1 413 2555, ⓦ hostels.hu) runs a couple of summer-only hostels and also handles some of the university accommodation open during the summer. Staff at the office in Keleti Station (see p.23) can make bookings and organize transport to their hostels from the station. You can't be sure of getting a bed in the hostel of your choice in summer without **booking** in advance. Note that many of Pest's hostels are in residential blocks – exceptions being *Marco Polo* and *City Hostel Pest* – therefore rowdy guests are generally frowned upon. Most hostels have wi-fi, as well as laundry facilities (for which there's usually a charge of around €5).

PEST

★**Casa de la Musica** VIII, Vas utca 16 ☎0670 373 7330, ⓦ casadelamusicahostel.com; map p.78. Colour is the watchword at the sparky *Casa*, located in a super spot and within easy walking distance of the Belváros and the Seventh District bars. Brightly painted stripes adorn the exterior walls, a theme echoed in the retro-styled dorms, which sleep four to twelve people, and in the double rooms, some with en-suite bathrooms. The reception is up on the second floor (no lift), and the

> ### TOP 5 HOSTELS AND CAMPSITES
> **Casa de la Musica** see above
> **Home-Made** see p.157
> **Marco Polo** see p.157
> **Shantee House** see p.157
> **Zugligeti Niche Camping** see p.157

rooms are on the second and third floors. The complex is arranged in a U-shape looking down onto a smart wood-decked terrace, where you'll find a bar and an inflatable swimming pool (in summer). Breakfast €3. Dorms **€9**, doubles **€28**

Caterina VI, Teréz körút 30 ☎1 269 5990, ⓦ caterinahostel.com; map p.60. Long-established hostel located above the Művész cinema near the Oktogon, and although it's on the third floor with no lift, the small setup gives it a friendly feel. There are rooms of four beds, as well as doubles and singles – the best ones are those looking onto the courtyard rather than the main road. It also has a couple of small apartments, a 5min walk from the hostel. Price includes breakfast. Dorms **€10**, doubles **€28**

City Hostel Pest IX, Ráday utca 43–45 ☎0620 443 2883, ⓦ cityhostels.hu; map p.78. One of six summer-only hostels run by the City Hostel group, this large building on a lively street has rooms of two to seven beds – you pay for rooms rather than beds – with and without shower facilities. Open July & Aug. Doubles €51

★**Home-Made Hostel** VI, Teréz körút 22 ☎1 302 2103, ⓦhomemadehostel.com; map p.60. As homely as its name suggests, this is a gem of a hostel, and its first-floor location near Oktogon isn't bad either. The brilliantly conceived, rustically styled dorms (four-, six- and eight-bed) feature household accoutrements (radios, typewriters, sewing machines) stuck to the walls, alongside patchwork rugs, paper lamps and random scattered suitcases. There are also two cosy double rooms, one with a loft space, the other with a bathroom, and a cute little kitchen which guests are free to use. Dorms €15, doubles €55

Marco Polo VII, Nyár utca 6 ☎1 413 2555, ⓦmarcopolohostel.com; map p.60. Very large, busy and popular hostel close to Blaha Lujza tér, with simply furnished four- and twelve-bed dorms with bunks, as

well as triple, twin and single rooms; all rooms except dorms are en suite and have a TV. Breakfast €3. Dorms €13, doubles €40

BUDA

Shantee House XI, Takács Menyhért utca 33 ☎1 385 8946, ⓦshanteehouse.com; tram #49 or bus #7 to Karolina út stop; map p.109. A charming forty six-bed hostel about 20min from the centre, with perky rooms holding four to twelve beds, as well as doubles, some en suite (€42). The cool vibe continues in the common-room area and garden, where guests can chill out in one of the hammocks or under the gazebo. You can also sleep in the yurt or in a hammock (€10) in the garden, or you can camp there. The staff also provide lots of information on the city, and organize trips into the hills and to the caves. Camping €20, dorms €12, doubles €40

CAMPING

Budapest's **campsites** are generally well equipped and pleasant, with trees, grass and sometimes even a pool. They can get crowded between June and September, when smaller places might run out of space. It is illegal to camp anywhere else, and the parks are patrolled to enforce this. The campsites listed here are all in Buda, since the Pest ones are not very inviting; camping rates cover a tent and two people.

12

Csillebérci Camping XII, Konkoly Thege Miklós út 21 ☎1 395 6527, ⓦcsilleberc.eu; bus #21 from Széll Kálmán tér to the Csillebérc stop, or bus #21A to Normafa then a short walk; map p.123. Large, well-equipped site up in the Buda Hills, with space for over a thousand campers and small blocks with double and triple rooms. Camping May–Sept only. Camping €10, doubles €35

Rename: Római Camping III, Szentendrei út 189 ☎1 388 7167, ⓦromaicamping.hu; HÉV train from Battyány tér; map p.5. Huge site beside the road to Szentendre in Rómaifürdő, 25min from the centre by train,

with space for 2500 campers, as well as wooden bungalows. It's perfectly placed for children's activities, lying next to the lido and Challengeland. Open all year round. Camping €20, bungalows €22

Zugligeti Niche Camping XII, Zugligeti út 101 ☎1 200 8346, ⓦcampingniche.hu; bus #291 from Nyugati Station; map p.123. Located next to the chairlift up to János-hegy, this is a small, terraced ravine site in the woods with space for thirty tents as well as camper vans. Good facilities, including a pleasant little restaurant occupying the former tram station at the far end. A substantial breakfast is included in the pitch price. Camping €20

BORKONYHA

Restaurants

The Budapest dining scene is developing at a hectic pace, with new restaurants opening all the time; there has also been a general rise in standards, and Hungarian chefs are now winning European awards. In a welcome change, where fine dining meets street food, top names are serving bistro-style takes on meaty Magyar classics, such as in the Belvárosi market hall. But vegetable lovers need not despair: the growing number of vegetarian and even vegan restaurants shows how much broader the Budapest palate is now. Despite the occasional tourist trap in the Vár, Buda offers some terrific eating possibilities, with a number of world-class restaurants: *21*, *Vendéglő a KisBiróhoz* and *Csalogány 26*, to name but three. Inevitably, Pest has a much wider range of places, with the largest concentration to be found within the Nagykörút, and the likes of *Mák*, *Café Kör* and the Michelin-starred *Borkonyha* leading the way.

Many offer terrific value for money and Budapest rates well when compared to dining out in capital cities elsewhere in western Europe. Even in the more expensive places, it is always worth looking out for the lunchtime *napi menüs*, which can offer real bargains. While **meat** is still king – lots of new restaurants have the word "meat" in their names – there is a new focus on quality and ingredients, and vegetables are partners, rather than afterthoughts.

Hungarians have welcomed the **street food** revolution with open arms, whether it is magnificent burgers – locally made, not industrial fast-food – or small authentic Thai and Vietnamese eateries, which have greatly increased the choice for **vegetarians**. Of course the other joy of street food is that you can eat quickly and informally. The emphasis on quality is nowhere more apparent than in the new **sandwich bars**, which pride themselves both on their bread and the interesting combinations they put inside. Another feature is a growing awareness of **allergens**, and an increasing number of places in central Budapest will alert you to gluten-free and other diet-sensitive foods.

The renaissance in Hungarian **wine** is now being reflected in Budapest's restaurants, and you'll find superb wine lists in many places – indeed, some restaurants deem the quality of the wine to be as important as the food. Another sign of the times has been the proliferation of lemonades on the menu – there seems to be a rivalry for the most unusual flavours.

ESSENTIALS

Prices and payment While Budapest is not the bargain gastronomic destination it once was, you can still eat out handsomely here without breaking the bank. Generally speaking, a two-course meal in most half-decent restaurants will set you back anywhere between 3000Ft and 4000Ft (€10–13) a head, while dining at the very top end will cost somewhere in the region of 5500–7000Ft (€18–23). A number of the smarter restaurants also offer tasting menus which, if you have the time and inclination, are a great way to sample a range of varied dishes; however, they usually start from around 7500Ft (€24). Credit and debit cards are now widely accepted (*Café Kör* and *M* being notable exceptions) though not necessarily in cheaper places, so check in advance if this is how you wish to pay.

Reservations While few restaurants in Budapest require you to make a reservation, it's best to do so at the more

---

HUNGARIAN CUISINE

For foreigners, the archetypal Magyar dish is still goulash – historically the basis of much **Hungarian cooking**. The ancient Magyars relished cauldrons of this *gulyás* (pronounced "gou-yash"), a soup made of potatoes and whatever meat was available, which was later flavoured with paprika and beefed up into a variety of stews, modified over the centuries by the various foreign influences which helped diversify the country's cuisine. Hungary's Slav visitors probably introduced native cooks to yoghurt and sour cream – vital ingredients in many dishes – while the influence of the Turks, Austrians and Germans is apparent in a variety of sticky pastries and strudels, as well as in recipes featuring sauerkraut or dumplings. There's a lot of fish, too – fish soup (*halászlé*) is one of the national dishes, a marvellously spicy *bouillabaisse* in the right hands – but it's worth remembering that landlocked Hungary's fish, such as the very bony carp and the more palatable catfish, all come from lakes and rivers – anything else will be imported. There's more on specific dishes in this book's glossary of **food and drink terms** (see p.231).

Traditionally, Hungarians take their main meal at **lunchtime**, when a growing number of restaurants offer a bargain set menu (*napi menü*) – some places call them business lunches. In the evenings, however, the majority of places are strictly à la carte. The menu (*étlap*) usually kicks off with **cold and hot starters** (*hideg* and *meleg előételek*), **soups** (*levesek*) and then the **main courses** (*főételek*) – sometimes divided into meat (*hús*) and fish (*hal*). These are followed by vegetables (*zöldségek*), salads (*saláták*) and sometimes pasta (*tészták*). Finally, there are the desserts (*édességek* or *desszertek*). Bread is provided automatically, on the grounds that "a meal without bread is no meal". **Drinks** are under the heading **italok** – or may be on a separate drinks or wine list (*itallap* or *borlap*). If you don't want a full meal, you might just order a filling soup, such as a fish or bean soup like *jókai bableves*.

13

fashionable end of the market, especially if you're really determined to eat somewhere in particular.

Opening hours Restaurants are generally open from 11am or noon to 10/11pm, though those that serve breakfast – of which there are an increasing number – will open around 8am. Most restaurants are open daily, though quite a few do close on Sundays; some of the top-end establishments, such as *Csalogány 26*, also close on Mondays.

Menus It's unusual now to find any establishment that doesn't have a menu in English, although dishes chalked up on a blackboard may not have a translation. Menus should clearly state whether there is a service charge (*szervízdíj*; typically ten or twelve percent) or not, but if you're not

sure, ask before ordering. If you're with children it's always worth asking whether there's a kids' menu, or whether they're able to knock up a small portion (*kisadag*).

Smoking The smoking ban that came into being in 2012 is strictly enforced indoors. Now it is the terraces and garden areas that are the haunts of smokers.

A warning The days of waiters in Budapest overcharging or making "mistakes" with your bill are largely gone. However, you should still be on your guard; avoid any establishment that doesn't display its prices (either food or drink), and don't be at all shy about querying the total amount if you think it looks suspect. One particularly annoying practice is waiters touting for business, which is a highly conspicuous activity along Váci utca.

THE BELVÁROS

QUICK BITES

Belvárosi Disznótoros V, Károlyi Mihály utca 17 📞 0670 602 2775, 🌐 belvarosidisznotoros.hu; map p.40. Meat galore in the "Downtown Pig Feast", a stand-up retro lunch bar that's the perfect place to taste traditional Hungarian dishes such as pig's trotters (3000Ft) and tripe stew, as well as duck leg (1200Ft) and grilled chicken (1000Ft). It's modelled on an old-style butcher's shop – there's even a butcher's counter at the back – and even has old-style surly staff. They also have delicious sausages, black pudding and salads, but not the sort to lure in vegetarians. There's another branch at Király utca 1 in the Erzsébetváros that's open also on Sundays. Mon–Sat 7am–7pm.

★ **Jacques Liszt** V, Apáczai Csere János utca 7 📞 0630 428 2232, 🌐 bit.ly/jacquesliszt; map p.40. Small rough-hewn bakery/café near Vigadó tér that serves some of the best bread in town – the name is a joke: to a Hungarian it sounds like "bag of flour". Misi the baker leads an Italian team in producing delicious sandwiches, quiches, pastries and cakes, which you can take away or eat at the couple of tables. They serve coffee as well as caramel and chocolate milk. Mon–Fri 7am–7pm, Sat 7am–2pm.

Szimply V, Károly körút 22 🌐 bit.ly/szimply; map p.40. Small, no-frills vegetarian place in the passageway that runs through to Semmelweis utca, where the food is simply delicious. The short menu, which includes gluten-free and vegan options, is divided into sweet and savoury sections, and includes all-day breakfasts that can also serve as lunch. Ask for coffee and you'll be directed to the café across the way. Dishes 1500–2200Ft. Mon–Fri 8am–4pm, Sat 9am–4pm.

RESTAURANTS

★ **Al-Amir** V, Petőfi Sándor utca 18 📞 1 266 0662, 🌐 al-amirbudapest.com; map p.40. This highly popular Syrian restaurant has been moving round the city over the years, but the current incarnation is as good as ever. One of the best places for vegetarians in the city, with its range of salads and fresh ingredients; there's also a wide range of Middle Eastern meat dishes, all at very moderate prices. Mains from 1800Ft. No alcohol. Daily 10am–11pm.

★ **Gerlóczy** V, Gerlóczy utca 1 📞 1 501 4000, 🌐 gerloczy .hu; map p.40. Atmospheric Parisian-inspired corner café on quiet Károly Kammermayer tér that gets packed at lunchtime with office staff popping in for a quick bite. The two-course (2390Ft) and three-course (2990Ft) set lunch menus are good value, but it's equally enjoyable for breakfast or a steaming cappuccino. Daily 8am–11pm.

Trattoria Toscana V, Belgrád rakpart 13 📞 1 327 0045, 🌐 toscana.hu; map p.40. On the Danube riverfront near Szabadság bridge, and with appealing faux-Tuscan surroundings, this is a favourite spot for authentic Italian cuisine at reasonable prices. The atmosphere is relaxed despite the smart business clientele. Mains 3000–5600Ft. Daily noon–midnight.

Vapiano V, Bécsi utca 5 📞 1 411 0864, 🌐 vapiano.hu; map p.40. Fast food Italian-style, and what style it is: excellent pizzas, pastas and salads made with fresh ingredients before your eyes. Collect a card as you enter, place your order at the counter and the meal will appear in minutes; your purchases are recorded on the card which is then handed to the cashier as you leave. Pasta and pizzas 1290–2390Ft, salads 900–2200Ft. Mon–Thurs & Sun 11am–11pm, Fri & Sat 11am–midnight.

LIPÓTVÁROS AND ÚJLIPÓTVÁROS

QUICK BITES

Briós V, Pozsonyi út 16 📞 1 794 6262, 🌐 bit.ly /brioskavezo; map p.50. Early birds should pay a visit to this sweet little neighbourhood café for its cracking

breakfast menu (660–1900Ft): temptations include American pancakes, French toast with ham and cheese, and their "omelette for hangovers" with bacon, sausage and cheese. If visiting later in the day, try a duck breast

13

BREAKFAST OF CHAMPIONS

A nation of early risers, Hungarians traditionally have a calorific **breakfast** (*reggeli*). Commonly, this includes cheese, eggs or salami together with bread and jam, washed down with coffee; in rural areas it's often accompanied by a shot of *pálinka* (brandy) to "clear the palate" or "aid digestion". While we're not suggesting that you should start the day with a brandy, quite a few city-centre restaurants offer breakfast menus, from the standard coffee-and-croissant option to French toast with ham and cheese, or Viennese sausages with mustard. For the best caffeine hit try the new-wave coffee bars (see p.170), where superb coffee with good pastries is an irresistible combination.

Sunday brunch remains popular, offering an all-you-can-eat buffet for a fixed price: many of the top hotels lay on a spread, and most of these also have staffed children's play areas. It is advisable to book. At the *Continental Hotel Zara* (see p.153), the magnificent spread costs 7500Ft, and the price includes a swim in the rooftop pool. Brunch usually starts around 11am and lasts till about 3pm; booking is advisable.

TOP 5 FOR BREAKFAST

Briós see p.160	**KicsiZso** see p.167
Delibaba see below	**Két Szerecsen** see p.165
Gerlóczy see p.160	

baguette (1500Ft). Those with children will love this place as there's a dedicated kiddies' menu and a small play area upstairs, so you might be able to drink your coffee in peace. Daily 7.30am–10pm.

★**Delibaba** V, Nádor utca 19 ☎0630 250 5169, ⓦdelibaba.hu; map p.50. You can find some of the most delectable sandwiches in town in *Delibaba*, whose inventive baguettes and rolls (990–1290Ft) are filled with *caponata* (grilled aubergine), grilled squash or duck liver, while the radish and rosewater salad is not to be missed. The desserts are fabulous too and all the ingredients are carefully sourced – as are the beers and coffee. Mon–Fri 8am–5pm.

Hummus Bar V, Október 6 utca 19 ☎1 354 0108, ⓦhummusbar.hu; map p.50. You'll find *Hummus Bar* outlets in at least thirteen places in central Budapest, two of which are completely vegetarian. This is the flagship branch, serving up plates of falafel (1600Ft as a main course) and hummus and fresh salad (1500Ft), as well as meaty versions with chicken breast or chicken liver (1600Ft). Mon–Fri 11.30am–10pm, Sat & Sun noon–10pm.

RESTAURANTS

Babka XIII, Pozsonyi út 3 ☎1 789 9672, ⓦbit.ly /babkabudapest; map p.50. Relaxed restaurant/café/bar – you can lounge on a sofa or sit at a table – at the Pest end of the Margít bridge, on the edge of the buzzing district of Újlipótváros, serving Middle Eastern dishes (five meze for 2600Ft) as well as interesting takes on Hungarian cuisine, such as confit duck leg with roasted gnocchi (2400Ft). Mon–Wed 11am–midnight, Thurs 11–1am, Fri & Sat 8–1am, Sun 8am–midnight.

★**Borkonyha** V, Sas utca 3 ☎1 266 0835, ⓦborkonyha.hu; map p.50. The third Budapest restaurant to earn a Michelin star, and the most appealing

of the three. You're greeted by the sight of a beautiful, gleaming bar stacked high with bottles of excellent Hungarian wine: more than two hundred are on offer, with just shy of fifty varieties sold by the glass. The food is no less exciting – expect the likes of suckling pig carpaccio, rabbit with rosemary and savoy cabbage, and lemon cake with gorgonzola ice cream. Mains 4000–8000Ft. Mon–Sat noon–midnight.

★**Café Kör** V, Sas utca 17 ☎1 311 0053, ⓦcafekor.net; map p.50. Local favourite round the corner from the Bazilika, with tightly packed tables but a very relaxed feel. Its grilled meats (predominantly chicken, but also turkey and duck) are excellent, as are the salads and specials of the day – the roasted pike-perch in garlic is always a favourite – and the wine list is reliably strong. Moreover, this place has retained its traditionally high standards of service. Mains 2000–4300Ft. Booking advised. Cash payment only. Mon–Sat 10am–10pm.

Csarnok V, Hold utca 11 ☎1 269 4906, ⓦcsarnok vendeglo.hu; map p.50. Down-to-earth Hungarian restaurant that used to serve the workers at the market a few doors along; despite a slightly more upmarket clientele these days, its unpretentious feel is still very much in evidence, with faded wood-panelled walls and red-and-white-check tablecloths. The food, too, is honest-to-goodness fare, such as veal paprika stew and pickled shank of smoked pork (2100Ft). Daily 10am–10pm.

Firkász XIII, Tátra utca 18 ☎1 450 1118, ⓦfirkasz.hu; map p.50. Done up like a journalists' haunt from the turn of the last century – witness the walls covered in newspaper cuttings and the rows of empty wine and *pálinka* bottles – *Firkász* serves decent traditional Hungarian dishes along the lines of crispy roast pork and goose leg with cabbage. The resident pianist tinkles his way into action nightly at

13

TOP 5 FOR FINE DINING

Borkonyha see p.161
Café Kör see p.161
Csalogány 26 see p.167
Mák Bistro see below
Zeller Bistro see below

7pm. Lunch menu 1550Ft, mains 2500–6000Ft, plus an all-day, all-you-can-eat-and-drink menu for 12,700Ft. Daily noon–11pm.

Govinda V, Vigyázó Ferenc utca 4 ☎1 473 1310, ⓦ govinda.hu; map p.50. This Hare Krishna vegetarian restaurant has been serving up its dhals and pakoras for twenty years. The inexpensive set meals range from 1200 to 2000Ft, all accompanied by the whiff of soporific incense. The sister restaurant *Govinda* at V, Papnövelde utca 1 near Ferenciek tere is vegan. Mon–Sat noon–9pm.

Hilda V, Nádor utca 5 ☎0631 782 9099, ⓦ bit.ly /hildabudapest; map p.50. There's a welcoming glow in this delightful lunch spot with its high arched interior, blue tiles and golden-yellow walls. The speciality here is the succulent grilled chicken and duck (2550Ft for half a bird), which come from a free-range farm in eastern Hungary. The desserts and coffee are also delicious, plus a good range of breakfasts. Daily 9am–5pm.

★**Kispiac** V, Hold utca 13 ☎1 269 4231, ⓦ kispiac.eu; map p.50. Small and very popular bistro right by the market hall behind the US embassy. The short menu, displayed on blackboards, is meat-dominated (mains 2500–4000Ft), and the grill is kept busy: there's duck, steak and sea bass, or tripe for the adventurous. They make their own breads and jams too, and the wines are from small Hungarian producers. There are a few outside tables. Booking essential. Mon–Sat noon–10pm.

★**Mák Bistro** V, Vigyázó Ferenc utca 4 1 ☎0630 723 9383, ⓦ mak.hu; map p.50. The high, vaulted bare-brick interior lends *Mák* ("poppy seed") a suitable grandeur that matches the whole dining experience. With its smooth service, creative menu and fine wines, this is one of the top places to eat in the city. Two-course lunch 3200Ft, six-course tasting menu 16,000Ft or 24,000Ft with wine. Booking advised. Tues–Sat noon–3pm & 6–11pm.

Pomo d'Oro V, Arany János utca 9 ☎1 302 6473, ⓦ pomodorobudapest.com; map p.50. An established fixture on the Budapest dining scene, this split-level trattoria also rates highly among the city's Italian community. The wood-burning oven turns out excellent pizzas from 1900Ft, and the pastas and risottos (2600–5000Ft) are also exceptional, although if you're only here once, seek out the charcoal grill (3000–6000Ft). A surprisingly varied selection of wines rounds things off beautifully. Daily 9am–midnight.

Pozsonyi Kisvendéglő XIII, Pozsonyi út 18 ☎1 787 4877, ⓦ bit.ly/kispozsonyi; map p.50. Atmospheric local joint with filling Hungarian dishes. The tables are in booths, which makes for a very cosy feel, and there's a small terrace on the pavement in the summer. Booking advisable on Friday evenings – the only day they serve *sólet*, and you need to book that too. Mains 1600–2700Ft, lunch menu 950Ft. Mon–Fri 9am–midnight, Sat & Sun 10am–midnight.

Stand 25 V, Hold utca 13 ☎0630 961 3262, ⓦ stand25 .hu; map p.50. The brainchild of Széll Tamás, who received one of the top awards for European chefs in 2016, *Stand 25* is one of the new crop of stylish mini-restaurants that are springing up in the market halls – this is in the Belvárosi, behind the US embassy. Its small menu, just three or four dishes for each course, always includes the Hungarian specialities goulash and *rakott krumpli* – layered potato with egg and sausage. Two course lunch 3900Ft (for some dishes you pay extra). Booking for lunch essential. Mon 8am–5pm, Tues–Fri 8am–6pm, Sat 11am–4pm.

★**Zeller Bistro** V, Hercegprímás utca 18 ☎0630 651 0880, ⓦ bit.ly/zellerbistro; map p.50. Boho-chic meets rustic simplicity in this superb and very popular restaurant. There's an appealing thoughtfulness behind the place: guests are welcomed with elderflower champagne, and this and much of what you eat and drink is from the family farm in Badacsony, by Lake Balaton. The enticing seasonal menu is Hungarian with a twist, such as the roasted lamb with smoked cheese polenta. It's a great place for families too – pencils and papers await on all tables and there's a children's corner with books and toys. Mains 2900–5500Ft. Booking essential. Tues–Sat noon–3pm & 6–11pm.

TERÉZVÁROS AND ERZSÉBETVÁROS

QUICK BITES

★**Beszálló** VII, Madách út 1 ⓦ bit.ly/beszallo; map p.40. "Eat well, travel often" is the motto over the door of this food bar near Deák tér: a small but slick place, with fast, friendly service. It's led by chef Krisztián Huszár, who has worked in some of Budapest's top restaurants; he took a break travelling round Asia, and it shows in the fantastic combinations he produces here, such as the Laos-style

papaya salad. On the menu the name of each dish is more like a list of the main ingredients, and the way these are combined is full of surprises. No bookings. Mains 2000–2800Ft. Daily noon–10pm.

Bors VII Kazinczy utca 10 ⓦ bit.ly/borsgasztro; map p.60. Delicious soups, pastas and baguettes at the "Pepper" gastrobar next to the Szimpla. The soft drinks come in appealing combinations, too, such as mint and raspberry.

13

VEGETARIAN BUDAPEST

Compared to yesteryear, **vegetarians** are much better catered for these days – you're much less likely to get told that noodles with bacon is okay because bacon is not real meat. There is a growing number of exclusively *vegetárianus* (sometimes "*vega*") and even vegan (*vegán*) **restaurants** in Budapest, such as *Vegan Love* (see p.168) with its street-food-style burgers, *Govinda* (see p.162) with its Indian food, and the *Hummus Bar* (see p.161) chain. The appearance of Thai and Vietnamese restaurants has also broadened the once limited palette, alongside the Middle Eastern cuisine found in *Al Amir* (see p.160), *Dobrumba* (see p.165) and *Babka* (see p.161).

Most restaurants now include one or two **vegetarian options** on the menu – most popularly *sült zöldségek* (roasted vegetables). It's only in the more traditional places your choice might be restricted to a diet of cheese or vegetables fried in breadcrumbs: *rántott gomba* (mushrooms), *rántott karfiol* (cauliflower), or *rántott sajt* (cheese). *Gomba paprikás* (mushroom paprika stew) is also fine, though check if it has been cooked in oil rather than in lard. Alternatively there are eggs – fried (*tükörtojás*), soft-boiled (*lágy tojás*) or scrambled (*tojásrántotta*). Hungary has traditionally been poor for salads, despite the excellent produce you see in the markets, but even that is changing in most restaurants.

The queues can be long here, and there are no tables – just a handful of seats round the walls. Baguettes start at 670Ft. Cash only. Daily 11.30am–9pm.

Igen VII, Madách út 5 🖥 bit.ly/igenpizza; map p.40. The shopfront of *Igen* ("yes" in Hungarian) on the edge of the Seventh District is so small you could easily walk straight past it. It's tiny inside too, with room for only a handful of customers and no seating, but the pizzas are probably the best in town. Served whole or by the slice, there are around eight kinds of thin, Neapolitan-style pizza, from the basic margherita to courgette and squash, truffle and mushroom, and spinach, walnut and Gorgonzola (from 420Ft a slice). Tues–Thurs noon–midnight, Fri & Sat noon–2am, Sun noon–10pm.

Kádár Étkezde VII, Klauzál tér 9 ☎1 321 3622; map p.60. Local stalwart in the heart of the old Jewish quarter, with its red-and-white-checked tablecloths and autographed photos on the walls. The menu has traditional (non-kosher) specialities such as roast goose leg with red cabbage and "broken" potatoes and – on Saturdays – *sólet*. Mains from 1800Ft. You pay at the door as you leave – tips should be given directly to the waitresses. Tues–Sat 11.30am–3.30pm; closed mid-July to mid-Aug.

★**Montenegrói Gurman** VII, Rákóczi út 54 ☎0670 673 0585, 🖥 mnggurman.com; map p.60. Fans of the traditional Balkan grill should make this place their first port of call. Gut-busting portions of succulent *čevapčiči* (spiced mincemeat rissoles) and *pljeskavica* (hamburger style patty) served with spicy paprika and *lepinja* (doughy bread), and all washed down with a bottle of Slovenian Laško beer. It's open around the clock, so just the job for post-drink munchies. It has another branch at Hercegprímás utca 2, near the basilica. Daily 24hr.

PizzaMe VI, Király utca 20 ☎1 266 0444, 🖥 pizzame .hu; map p.60. *La Pizza di Mamma Sofia*, as it's still called

on the sign outside, was the first branch of the successful *PizzaMe* chain, which now has five outlets in the city. It's right by the Goszdu udvar, and is always full of partygoers waiting for a slice (from 300Ft) on their way to and from the nearby bars. The range of toppings may be small but includes nutella (450Ft a slice), and the bases are wonderfully thin. Hardly enough room to swing a pizza dough, let alone sit down. Mon, Tues & Sun 11am–4am, Wed–Sat 11am–6am.

Sonkapult VII, Rumbach Sebestyén utca 7 ☎0630 943 7073, 🖥 sonkapult.hu; map p.40. Start your day at the "Ham Counter" breakfast spot, where the emphasis is on quality. Sandwiches (from 720Ft) are made with local produce and the soft drinks are organic. It also sells craft beers, wine and stronger stuff. Pride of place is a shiny red 1972 ham slicer in the corner – there is room for that and a couple of armchairs, and that is about it. Mon–Thurs 7.30am–7.30pm, Fri & Sat 7.30am–9.30pm, Sun 9am–2pm.

RESTAURANTS

Café Bouchon VI, Zichy Jenő utca 33 ☎1 353 4094, 🖥 cafebouchon.hu; map p.60. A real neighbourhood stalwart, and popular with the nearby opera-going crowd, *Café Bouchon* is a cracking place. The Art Deco furnishings look fab, the Hungarian/French-fused cuisine – Tokaj grape salad with walnuts and camembert, or Hungarian sausage with goose-liver pâté – is first class, and the place is serviced by friendly, knowledgeable staff. Mains 2400–5500Ft. Mon–Sat 11am–11pm.

Dang Muoi VI, Nagymező utca 51 ☎1 951 7369, 🖥 vietnamietterem.hu; map p.60. Small and very appealing Vietnamese bistro with an authentic feel, created by Dang and Muoi, a Vietnamese couple who met in Budapest. They work to their own recipes of *pho* noodle soup, the national dish of their homeland. Soups from 1000Ft. Perfect place for the reviving snack after a late-night drinking session. Mon–Sat 10am–10pm, Sun 11am–10pm.

Dobrumba VII, Dob utca 5 ☎ 0630 194 0049, ⓦ bit.ly /dobrumba; map p.60. The cool vibe of the design-shabby interior and recycled furniture give few clues to Dobrumba's Mediterranean cuisine. Presenting food from the Atlas to Ararat, the menu offers a delicious selection of meze (five for 3800Ft), including superb hummus and muhammara (a spicy pepper dip). Booking advisable. Mon–Thurs 11am–midnight, Fri & Sat 11am– 2am, Sun noon–midnight.

Fausto VII, Dohány utca 5 ☎ 1 269 6806, ⓦ fausto.hu; map p.60. Chef Fausto DiVora has unfailingly maintained standards at his elegant Italian restaurant in Dohány utca for more than twenty years. You can choose between the bistro (three-course lunch menu 3200Ft, five-course tasting menu from 7500Ft) on one side, and the more formal restaurant on the other, where you'll find a mean monkfish with courgette cream and tarragon (8500Ft). Mon–Sat noon–11pm.

★**Félix Hélix** VII, Kazinczy utca 52/b ☎ 0630 416 6959, ⓦ bit.ly/felixhelix; map p.60. It's is easy to miss this small bar, located on the walk between Kazinczy utca and Holló utca, as it doesn't shout about itself. That's partly the appeal of the place, squeezed in amid the brash bars in the middle of Seventh District partyland. The Irish-Egyptian duo behind it turn out a marvellous range of foods that you won't get anywhere else, such as cucumber soup with goat's milk and Moroccan-style beef with couscous. There is folk music of different kinds on Thursdays – details online – and you'll find backgammon boards up in the gallery. Two-course lunch 900Ft. Daily 11am–midnight, until 2am in summer.

Frici Papa VII, Király utca 55 ☎ 1 351 0197, ⓦ fricipapa .hu; map p.60. The plastic-covered tables give a fair indication of what to expect, and this no-nonsense place (which includes the waiters) certainly won't win any awards for refinement, but if it's cheap, no-frills grub you're after, look no further. A menu of grilled or fried chicken with chips, beef and mushroom goulash, and not much else, almost all for under 1000Ft. Daily 11am–10pm.

★**Funky Pho** VI, Mozsár utca 7 ☎ 0670 508 0658, ⓦ funkypho.hu; map p.60. Set up by András and Éva after they worked out east and learned from top chefs in Vietnam, Funky Pho is a rarity in Budapest. Unlike most other places it serves up food from South Vietnam, as well as other Asian cuisines, and has won awards for its sustainability. The menu is MSG-free (there is some in a jar on the counter if you are hankering after it) and the delicious food appeals to a younger Vietnamese generation – try their pho and summer rolls. Mains from 1090Ft. Mon–Sat 11.30am–10pm.

TOP 5 CHEAP BITES

Bors see p.162
Delibaba see p.161
Funky Pho see below
Montenegrói Gurman see p.164
Vapiano see p.160

★**Kazimír** VII, Kazinczy utca 34 ☎ 1 798 5747, ⓦ kazimir.hu; map p.60. Popular, large café-bar in the middle of the Seventh District that is welcoming throughout the day. They serve very good breakfasts (from 10am; omelettes start at 1090Ft) and a two-course lunch menu for 1250Ft. Specialities include duck leg (3390Ft) and the popular Jewish dish sólet (2890Ft). There is a courtyard terrace, and live music on Tuesday and Friday evenings. Daily 10am–4am.

★**Két Szerecsen** VI, Nagymező utca 14 ☎ 1 343 1984, ⓦ ketszerecsen.com; map p.60. Buzzy place nicely secreted away just off Andrássy út, that's good for coffee and breakfast (8–11am) or full-blown supper. The most appealing aspect, though, is the tapas menu (veg, meat and seafood), which can be taken individually or as an assortment. A varied mains menu includes salmon steamed in white wine, and a Thai green curry. Mains 2300–5000Ft. Terrace in summer. Mon–Fri 8am–midnight, Sat & Sun 9am–midnight.

Kis Parázs VII, Kazinczy utca 7 ☎ 0630 733 7760, ⓦ parazspresszo.com; map p.60. At last you can get authentic Thai food in Budapest, and at a very reasonable price. Delicious curries and pad Thai served up in a small restaurant across the road from the Szimpla bar. There are two other branches, one close by at VII, Király utca 53. Mains 1600–2100Ft. Mon, Tues & Sun noon–11pm, Wed–Sat noon–3am.

Klassz VI, Andrássy út 41 ☎ 1 413 1545, ⓦ klassz etterem.hu; map p.60. Klassz means "super", which describes this strikingly decorated restaurant-cum-wine-bar to a tee. Typical staples include pork tenderloin with sweet potato purée and roast mangalica (a fatty Hungarian pork) with gratin potatoes – while links with the Budapest Wine Society ensure a choice of top Hungarian vintages, most of which are available by the glass. It's small, extremely popular and does not take reservations. Mains 3200–5500Ft. Daily 11.30am–11pm.

Köles VII, Kertész utca 41 ☎ 1 400 8967, ⓦ koleshonyha .hu; map p.60. Gluten-free restaurant – the name means "millet" in English – down the road from the Music Academy serving burgers in gluten-free buns (1200Ft), grilled chicken (1400Ft) and vegan and lactose-free dishes. The cakes are delicious too. Friendly staff can help if you have any allergy questions. Mon 9am–8pm, Tues–Fri 9am–10pm, Sat 11am–10pm.

13

Kőleves VII, Kazinczy utca 41, ☎1 322 1011, ⓦ kolevesvendeglo.hu; map p.60. This relaxed restaurant in the heart of the Jewish quarter (the building used to be a kosher sausage plant) is named "Stone Soup" in reference to the fairytale about making soup in a time of scarcity. Instead you'll find classic Central European Jewish dishes, as well as Hungarian specialities. There is a terrace at the back, and a garden bar, *Kőleveskert*, next door for summer nights. They do breakfasts, too. Mains 2200–5000Ft and a daily set menu at 1100–1250Ft. Booking advisable. Daily 8am–midnight.

★**Krizia** VI, Mozsár utca 12 ☎1 331 8711, ⓦ ristorantekrizia.hu; map p.60. All the pasta at this refined Italian restaurant is made on the premises, as is the delicious prosciutto, resulting in a long list of well-thought-out creations like fettuccine with porcini mushrooms and prawns or tortelloni stuffed with goose liver and truffle sauce. There's also a daily "From the Market" menu, sourcing local ingredients, and tasting menus. The three-course lunch menu is good value at 1500Ft. Mains 2800–7000Ft. Mon–Sat noon–3pm & 6.30pm–midnight.

★**M** VII, Kertész utca 48 ☎0631 783 0161, ⓦ metterem.hu; map p.60. This small boho-style bistro is just the spot for a low-key evening dalliance. The small menu changes daily and can throw up some surprises: rabbit kidneys, as well as the more enticing duck breast with wild mushroom risotto, and shoulder of rabbit in garlic and thyme with ratatouille are what you can expect. Mains 2200–4400Ft. Booking essential. Cash only. Tues–Sun 6pm–midnight.

Menza VI, Liszt Ferenc tér 2 ☎1 413 1482, ⓦ menzaetterem.hu; map p.60. Few places on this lively square merit much consideration – at least where food is concerned – but *Menza* is one of them. The stylish retro decor, and very affordable retro-influenced Hungarian dishes, such as *hagymás rostélyos* (braised steak piled high with onions) and *kolozsvári töltött káposzta* (stuffed cabbage) seem to evoke nostalgic memories among the locals. The two-course lunch menu is good value at 1290Ft. Mains 2300–4900Ft. Daily 10am–1am.

Spinoza VII, Dob utca 15 ☎1 413 7488, ⓦ spinozahaz .hu; map p.60. In the heart of the old Jewish quarter, this popular restaurant has a very cultured feel – not least because the small theatre at the back has performances and readings every night, including a Jewish evening of music and food on Fridays. It has a big menu, including salads and sandwiches, alongside Hungarian favourites such as goose leg with red cabbage and potatoes (3450Ft), and on the soft drinks menu are elderflower and lavender lemonades. Lunch menu 1190Ft. Daily 8am–11pm.

Il Terzo Cerchio VII, Dohány utca 40 ☎1 354 0788, ⓦ ilterzocerchio.hu; map p.60. The Third Circle of Dante's hell was full of gluttons, and this handsome Florentine-run pizzeria has its share. Pizzas aside (from 1900Ft), there's superb risotto (3950Ft) and pasta, where seafood is a speciality – try the pennette with a spicy octopus sauce (2900Ft) or tagliolini with sea bass and prawns (3950Ft). It's popular with Italian visitors, which must be a good sign. Daily noon–11.30pm.

JÓZSEFVÁROS AND FERENCVÁROS

QUICK BITES

Butter Brothers IX, Lónyay utca 22 ☎0630 456 4019, ⓦ butter-brothers.com; map p.78. A congenial place to start the day, *Butter Brothers* is a small, bright café-shop with a couple of tables and a few stools, and a cheery team serving coffee and excellent pastries (curry and peach croissant or broccoli and cheese pastry; 390–490Ft), as well as sandwiches (790Ft). They also bake their bread, and their milk is delicious. Mon–Fri 7am–7pm, Sat 8am–1pm.

Caffé Torino VIII, Bródy Sándor utca 2 ☎0630 303 9466, ⓦ bit.ly/caffetorino; map p.78. Just across the road from the National Museum, the *Torino* is a very Italian basement café bar serving panini, quiches, pasta (from 890Ft), as well as cheesecake and other cakes. Mon–Fri 8am–5pm, Sat 9am–3pm.

RESTAURANTS

★**Borbíróság** IX, Csarnok tér 5 ☎1 219 0902, ⓦ borbirosag.com; map p.78. The marvellous "Wine Court" offers one of the city's most affordable and enjoyable introductions to modern Hungarian cuisine. The menu is by

---

INTO THE HUNGARIAN KITCHEN

Budapest's **cookery courses** are not just about how much paprika to add to your *halászlé*, and when is a goulash not a *gulyás*. They're also a primer in Hungarian culture. Courses often begin with a visit to a market to give an insight into the main pillars of the Hungarian kitchen – their love of pickling everything and how to use every inch of a pig – before the cooking proper begins, followed by a sit-down meal to enjoy it. You will also learn what wines go with what – and that Hungarian reds are often best served chilled. One of the best courses is Chef Parade (☎1 210 6042, ⓦ chefparade.hu), which has well-equipped kitchens and an informal, fun attitude.

no means exhaustive, but that doesn't detract from what is an exceptional medley of dishes; start with the Hortobági pancake (filled with mincemeat in a creamy paprika sauce), followed by grilled duck liver with caramelized fruits – and if there's still space, get stuck into a portion of cottage cheese dumplings. The wine list, on the other hand, will leave you completely spoilt for choice, with some of Hungary's finest vintners represented. Mains 2400–5000Ft. Mon–Sat noon–11.30pm.

Fülemüle VIII, Kőfaragó utca 5 ☎1 266 7947, ⓦfulemule.hu; map p.78. Popular and relaxed family-run restaurant a few minutes' walk from Rákóczi út, serving typical dishes of middle-class secular Jewish Budapest: *sólet*, goose soup with matzo dumplings, and duck leg with cabbage and "broken" potato. Mains 2900–5900Ft. Mon–Thurs & Sun noon–10pm, Fri & Sat noon–11pm.

★**Kék Ló** VIII, Víg utca 28 ☎0670 631 1623, ⓦbit.ly /keklopub; map p.78. The bohemian "Blue Horse", behind the Rákóczi tér market hall, recalls its former life as a ruin pub with hippyish walls, recycled furniture and eclectic clothing for sale. It has live experimental music in the evenings, often jazz, but it also serves up great food, mainly vegan – such as

the mushroom stew and delicious apple pie. Its coffee and craft beer also win plaudits. Two-course lunch menu 950Ft. Mon–Sat noon–midnight, Sun 4–11pm.

Múzeum VIII, Múzeum körút 12 ☎1 267 0375, ⓦmuzeumkavehaz.hu; map p.78. This grand nineteenth-century restaurant, adorned with Lotz ceiling frescoes and Zsolnay tiles, is an old-school venture working hard to retain standards in the face of stiff competition. For the most part, it succeeds, with a line-up of core Hungarian classics like breaded *mangalica* pork chops with mashed potato, and grilled goose liver with Tokaji Aszú cream. Mains 3300–7000Ft. Mon–Sat noon–3pm & 6pm–midnight.

Rosenstein VIII, Mosonyi utca 3 ☎1 333 3492, ⓦrosenstein.hu; map p.78. Don't be put off by the dingy location, in an anonymous side-street near Keleti Station: the family-run *Rosenstein* offers a most satisfying dining experience. Give yourself plenty of time to digest the menu, where you'll discover dishes as diverse as wild boar ragout with forest mushrooms, leg of wild hare, and breaded calf's foot with tartar sauce and chips. Mains 3000–6500Ft. Booking advised. Mon–Sat noon–11pm.

THE VÁR, CENTRAL BUDA AND THE TABÁN

QUICK BITES

Finomító Kantin II, Varsányi Irén utca 33 ☎0630 871 9588, ⓦfinomito.com; map p.90. Friendly little burger bar that has a big local following, lying in a quiet street running down from Széll Kálmán tér. All the ingredients are carefully sourced – these are burgers made with care. Also serves vegetarian burgers, three different soups, sandwiches and home-made lemonade. Burgers from 1100Ft. Mon–Sat 11.30am–8pm.

Gusto's II, Frankel Leó utca 12 ☎1 316 3970; map p.90. Near the Buda end of the Margít híd, this charming little bar has been going for more than 25 years – it's now under new management but hopefully they can maintain standards. Serving salads and cold dishes, but you can put together your own plateful from a range of hot dishes in the Daily Deal (990Ft). The bar is famed for its tiramisu (690Ft). Mon–Sat 8am–11pm.

KicsiZso II, Frankel Leó utca 11 ☎0620 200 2009, ⓦbit.ly/kicsizso; map p.90. Cosy breakfast joint at the Buda end of Margít híd, where you squeeze past the locals to get to your table. Ham and eggs (900Ft), baguettes (from 1300Ft), and a daily lunch menu (1500Ft). Breakfast available all day – the coffee is excellent. Weather permitting, you can sit at the long table outside. Mon–Fri 7.30am–4.30pm, Sat 7.30am–3pm.

RESTAURANTS

21 I, Fortuna utca 21 ☎1 202 2113, ⓦ21restaurant .hu; map p.93. Perhaps the pick of the restaurants in the Vár, the *21* has an elegant and modern feel (and a

wonderful terrace) while the food is fresh, contemporary Hungarian fare superbly cooked and beautifully presented. Mains 3000–5800Ft. Booking advised. Daily noon–midnight.

Alabárdos I, Országház utca 2 ☎1 356 0851, ⓦalabardos.hu; map p.93. The *Alabárdos* has been a feature in the Vár, close to the Mátyás church, for more than fifty years, and it is still winning awards. It serves up new-wave takes on Hungarian classics in delicate portions, such as trout with beans and smoked apple jus (6500Ft). It's not one for budget travellers. Four-course meal 13,500Ft. Mon–Fri 7–11pm, Sat noon–3pm & 7–11pm.

★**Csalogány 26** I, Csalogány utca 26 ☎1 201 7892, ⓦcsalogany26.hu; map p.90. Notwithstanding the very ordinary location and occasionally muted atmosphere, this is undoubtedly one of Budapest's finest restaurants. It's neither showy nor prohibitively expensive, and the small menu, which changes regularly according to the whim of the chef, contains some wonderfully executed dishes: expect creations like glazed rabbit leg with veg ragout, scallop with corn risotto and rice pudding with red-fruit ice cream. Mains are 4000–6500Ft – the portions aren't that big, but the three-course lunch (2500Ft) offers a cheaper way to enjoy their excellent cooking; there's also an eight-course tasting menu for 16000Ft. Booking advised. Tues–Sat noon–3pm & 7–10pm.

Mandragora II, Kacsa utca 22 ☎1 202 2165, ⓦmandragorakavehaz.hu; map p.90. Cosy, family-run restaurant tucked away in a quiet but accessible corner of Buda. You get the sense that care has been taken, both in

13

sourcing the ingredients – beef from rare breeds farmed on the Hungarian plain and cheese from the Bükk Hills – and putting them together to create a menu with a difference, with dishes such as courgettes stuffed with rice and mushrooms. The desserts and lemonades both earn high praise. Small terrace and friendly staff. Lunch menu 1750Ft, mains from 3000Ft. Mon & Tues 11am–11pm, Wed–Sat 11am–midnight.

GELLÉRT-HEGY

RESTAURANTS

★**La Nube** XI, Bartók Béla út 41 ☎0670 907 6882, ⒲lanubecafe.com; map p.109. Tapas bar with a bohemian air, run by a Spanish-Hungarian couple and offering authentic Iberian flavours, with hams, sausages, wines and beers and other Spanish ingredients; tapas start at 690Ft. It has a spacious, laidback feel and a shabby chic interior with a counter resting on books, and there are more books on the shelves. There's a kids' corner, sofa, books to read, bits to buy – and specially sourced coffee. The

Vár: A Speiz I, Hess András tér 6 ☎1 488 7416, ⒲varaspeiz.hu; map p.93. Just across the road from the *Hilton* hotel, the distinguished "pantry" has a homely yet smart feel, with half a dozen huge hams (from Spain, Italy and Hungary) dangling temptingly near the entrance. The schnitzels here are outstanding – there is a special breadcrumbed section of the menu. Mains 3300–5000Ft. Daily noon–11pm.

entrance is on Ménesi út. Mon–Thurs 9am–8pm, Fri 9am–10pm, Sat 10am–4pm.

Vegan Love XI, Bartók Béla út 9 ☎0630 597 5949, ⒲veganlove.hu; map p.109. The bright, smart interior may not be what you'd expect from a vegan burger bar, especially one with a hippy-sounding name like this – but don't let that put you off. The menu includes burgers made from sweet potato, tofu or lentils, and there are tofu hot dogs too (from 1500Ft), all proving that street food can be vegan and tasty. Mon–Sat 11am–8pm, Sun noon–8pm.

ÓBUDA

RESTAURANTS

Kéhli III, Mókus utca 22 ☎1 368 0613, ⒲kehli.hu; map p.116. One hundred years ago this was the favourite haunt of one of Hungary's great gourmands, the turn-of-the-century writer Gyula Krúdy, and today the *Kéhli* still serves the dishes he loved, such as beef soup with bone marrow on garlic toast. Set in one of the few old buildings in Óbuda to survive the 1960s planning blitz, it's a big place and does attract large groups, but there are plenty of local regulars, too; eat your fill to the accompaniment of a lively Hungarian Gypsy band (Tues–Sun). Mains 2000–5000Ft. Daily noon–midnight.

Kerék III, Bécsi út 103 ☎1 250 4261, ⒲kerekvendeglo .hu; map p.116. There is an unchanging feel to the "Wheel", a small 100-year-old restaurant in southern Óbuda. It serves traditional Hungarian food, such as

bableves füstölt csülökkel (bean soup with smoked pork knuckle) and *vasi pecsenye* (pork marinated in garlic and milk) at very reasonable prices. No haute cuisine here, just locals out for a meal. *Srámli* (accordion) music is provided by a couple of old musicians (Mon–Sat from 6pm), and there's outside seating in summer. Lunch menu 890Ft, mains 1200–2700Ft. Daily noon–10pm.

Stelázsi III, Nagyszombat utca 3 ☎1 631 3624, ⒲stelazsietterem.hu; map p.116. Chic yet cosy restaurant with an arty touch, located right by the ruined amphitheatre in Óbuda – and it's worth the trip up there. Family friendly, with a small children's corner upstairs. The menu adds a special touch to its home-cooked Hungarian favourites, such as chicken breast in red pesto with rocket and risotto, and is also good for vegetarians. Two-course lunch menu for 1190Ft. Daily noon–11pm.

THE BUDA HILLS

RESTAURANTS

Alessio II, Pasaréti út 55 ☎1 275 0049, ⒲cafealessio .hu; map p.123. Elegant local Italian restaurant and pizzeria, some 10min out from Széll Kálmán tér on the #5 bus. The chicken breast with goat's cheese is superb, as is the veal *saltimbocca*. The excellent pizzas start from 1600Ft – they also deliver food. Mains 2700–5900Ft. Daily 9am–midnight.

★**Vendéglő a KisBíróhoz** XII, Szarvas Gábor út 8/d ☎1 376 6044, ⒲vendegloakisbirohoz.hu;

map p.123. The "town crier restaurant" plays on the name of the wizard chef, Lajos Biró, but there's no playing around when it comes to the food. A 15min ride on bus #155 up from Széll Kálmán tér, the *KisBiró* produces Hungarian food with a modern twist, such as lamb in a nettle sauce or duck breast with ginger and kohlrabi. It doesn't come cheap but it is worth the journey out: the portions are huge and the wines – from the Bock vineyard, in Villány, and elsewhere – are superb. Mains 3700–6400Ft. Tues–Sun noon–11pm.

CÉNTRÁL KÁVÉHÁZ

Cafés and patisseries

Daily life in Budapest has long been punctuated by the consumption of strong black coffee and the city's coffee houses (*kávéház*) rival those of Prague and Vienna for sheer grandeur and deferential service. The days of writers, journalists and the odd revolutionary using them as unofficial "offices" has long gone, but they are still full of character and a hit with locals and tourists alike. The global trend towards artisan coffee (*kézműves kávé*) and hip baristas has also arrived with a vengeance. New-wave coffee bars have sprung up across the city, in designer premises – and often with English names. Tea-lovers won't be short-changed either, with several fine teahouses around the city.

14

The Hungarian passion for coffee can be seen in the number of new bars offering exceptional coffee – the up-and-coming thoroughfare of Pozsonyi út in Újlipótváros has three alone – and their (usually English) names often have coffee references, such as *Tamp & Pull* or *9 Bar*. The demand for novelty means you can get coffee bars themed with books, cats, clothes, prints, even flowers. Nor should visitors omit a trip to the grand old stalwarts of the coffee-house world which preserve a sense of the old traditions, such as the *Centrál Kávéház* and *Gerbeaud*.

Another tradition that has been caught up in the artisan craze is **bread**: not so long ago Hungarian bread was always white, but now small bakeries are springing up all over the city offering enticing seeded brown loaves and sourdough specialities. Most coffee houses also have counters stocked with scrumptious, beautifully crafted **cakes and pastries** like brightly coloured macaroons alongside local specialities such as *dobos torta*, *rétes* and *flódni*. Otherwise head straight to the nearest **patisserie** (*cukrászda*) for a delicious helping of sugar and carbs. Hungarians love their **ice cream**, too, and there are more and more excellent parlours dotted around the city, vying with each other to produce unusual flavours.

THE BELVÁROS

★**Centrál Kávéház** V, Károlyi Mihály utca 9 ☎1 266 2110, ⓦcentralkavehaz.hu; map p.40. In its heyday, the decades around World War I, this large coffee house was a popular venue in Budapest's literary scene. After many years as a dowdy university club, it was restored to its former grandeur and today stands as the city's most sophisticated café. To the left as you enter you'll find good coffee (690–1190Ft) that is cheaper than at many other places in the Belváros, and an immaculate selection of cakes. They also have a full menu for meals in the restaurant to the right. Daily 8am–midnight/1am.

Fekete V, Múzeum körút 5 ☎1 787 7503, ⓦfeketekv .hu; map p.40. Just down from the Astoria junction, "Black" is typical of the hip *kézműves* bars, with equal emphasis on design and good coffee. Building on the success of its excellent flat whites, lattes and delicious hot chocolate, it has expanded from a hole in the wall into a larger room behind, filling the courtyard when the weather permits. They have also expanded their menu, offering a full range of breakfasts (750–1250Ft) and cakes. Mon–Fri 7.30am–6.30pm, Sat 9am–4pm.

Gerbeaud V, Vörösmarty tér 7 ☎1 429 9000, ⓦgerbeaud.hu; map p.40. A Budapest institution, *Gerbeaud* has been a fixture on this square since 1858. The gilded salon is magnificent, though most people park themselves outside on the massive terrace, one of the best in the city. But be warned, this is very much tourist-central, with prices that reflect this; coffee will set you back 1050–1590Ft. Daily 9am–9pm.

LIPÓTVÁROS

Artizán V, Hold utca 3 ☎0630 856 5122, ⓦartizan.hu; map p.50. Superb patisserie behind the National Bank that produces great breads, coffees and sandwiches. Their loaves include pumpkinseed bread and a dill-and-feta creation. Mon–Fri 7am–7pm, Sat 8am–4pm.

★**Damniczki** V, Hercegprimás utca 17 ☎1 0620 919 3548, ⓦdamniczkibudapest.hu; map p.50. Balázs Damniczki brought more than 25 years of experience as a confectioner in the town of Székesfehérvár when he opened up shop in Budapest. His award-winning ice creams include exotic flavours such as wild garlic, poppy seed and a revelatory beetroot. *Damniczki* are also proud of their cakes, coffee, lemonade and hot chocolate. Mon–Fri 8am–8pm, Sat & Sun 11am–8pm.

★**Espresso Embassy** V, Arany János utca 15 ☎0620 445 0063, ⓦespressoembassy.hu; map p.50. One of the larger of the new-wave coffee bars – the interior, with its bare brick vaulting, is by the same team that designed two of the city's new metro stations. The coffee is exquisite – several members of the barista team have won awards – and don't miss the cheesecake and pastries, either. Mon–Fri 7.30am–7pm, Sat 9am–6pm, Sun 9am–5pm.

COFFEE PRICES

In the city's small coffee bars, expect to pay 400–450Ft for a basic one-shot **espresso**; the price range goes up for macchiatos, cortados and cappuccinos, and a latte will set you back around 750Ft. **Pastries** will cost 390–600Ft. Note that you'll always pay a bit more in places popular with tourists, such as *Centrál* and *Gerbeaud*.

Europa V, Szent István körút 7 ☎1 312 2362, ⓦ europakavehaz.hu; map p.50. Large and perennially busy coffee house a short stroll from the Pest end of the Margít híd. Both the coffee and cake are first-rate, though nothing tops the generously sliced *rétes* or *flódni*. Daily 9am–8pm.

Gelarto Rosa V, Hercegprimás utca 3 ⓦ gelartorosa .com; map p.50. Delicious ice creams beautifully presented as little roses at this successful place down the road from the Basilica. (The other branch by the Basilica at Szent István tér 3 has much longer queues.) You can choose ice creams or sorbets, and they offer a selection of vegan, lactose-free and diabetic flavours. The mango is heavenly, or the more adventurous can try pumpkin or wasabi hazelnut. Daily 10am–10pm.

Madal XIII, Hollán Ernő utca 3 ☎0620 281 9691, ⓦ madalcafe.hu; map p.50. New-wave coffee bar with a spiritual side – it was inspired by the Indian philosopher Sri Chimnoy, whose childhood name was Madal. Coffee aficionados will feel at home here: the friendly capped baristas take their beans very seriously and occasionally run workshops on making the perfect filter coffee. You

TOP 5 FOR COFFEE
9 Bar see below
Cube see below
Espresso Embassy see p.170
Kelet Kávézó see p.173
Szerelmes Levél see p.173

14

can also get vegan chocolate and macaroons. In summer there's a terrace in the pedestrianized street out front. It has also opened branches at Ferenciek tere 3 in the Belváros and Alkotmány utca 4. Mon–Fri 7.30am–8pm, Sat 9am–11.30am.

Smuz V, Kossuth Lajos tér 12 ☎0630 922 0850, ⓦ smuz.viragneked.hu; map p.50. A former florist that has now turned into a very successful café selling flowers on the side, *Smuz* is all a bit over the top, with its design aspirations, but it is in a handy spot, next to the Parliament Visitor Centre, as is reflected in the prices. Even if the service can be slow, the coffees (from 550Ft) are good, and you can also get salads (from 1690Ft) and sandwiches (from 1590Ft). Daily 10am–9pm.

TERÉZVÁROS AND ERZSÉBETVAROS

★9 Bar VI, Lázár utca 5 ☎1 400 9821, ⓦ bit .ly/9barbudapest; map p.60. Superb coffee from the barista team in a quiet road near the Basilica. They offer espressos, filter, Aeropress and more, with a choice of classic Italian style or the artisan coffee with its lighter roasts. You can also buy the full range of coffee-making equipment. Sandwiches, lemonades and cakes are on offer too – the gluten-free brownies are recommended. Mon–Fri 8am–6pm, Sat 9am–4pm.

Cirkusz VII, Dob utca 25 ☎1 786 4959, ⓦ cirkuszbp.hu; map p.60. Stylish, airy café in the old Jewish quarter with high ceilings and a spacious feel. They roast their own beans and have a champion barista, so the coffee is excellent, and there is a good range of breakfasts to go with it (1200–1900Ft). Mon–Thurs 9am–10pm, Fri & Sat 9am–11.45pm, Sun 9am–5pm.

★Cube VI, Hunyadi tér 8 ☎0630 233 3015, ⓦ cubecoffeebar.hu; map p.60. Anikó and László's friendly – and environmentally friendly – coffee bar marks the continued revival of this pleasant square just off Andrássy út. Everything here is chosen with care: the milk and yoghurt come from a local farm, the jam and cakes are home-made and they roast their own coffee. Salads, wraps and wine – from small producers – available for lunch. Mon–Thurs & Sat 8am–5pm, Fri 8am–9pm, Sun 9am–4pm.

Eco Café VI, Andrássy út 68; ☎0620 367 1500, ⓦ ecocafe.hu; map p.60. Welcoming organic café with sweet countrified tables and cushioned seating, serving up a small selection of very reasonably priced sandwiches,

salads and cakes; it also does a nice line in freshly baked breads. Mon–Fri 7am–7pm, Sat & Sun 8am–7pm, till 8pm in summer.

Fragola VI, Nagymező utca 7b ☎0630 341 5050, ⓦ fragolafagylaltozo.hu; map p.60. Fantastic range of ice cream: flavours include camembert, After Eight and cheesecake, alongside the more usual ones and some sugar-free options. They must be doing something right as they have opened several more branches, near the Astoria at Károly körút 3, at Ráday utca 1–3 and elsewhere. Daily 11am–8pm.

Fröhlich VII, Dob utca 22 ☎1 266 1733, ⓦ frohlich .hu; map p.60. Kosher patisserie, a 5min walk from the Dohány utca synagogue, with wrought-iron garden-bench-like seating and red- and orange-painted walls. Specialities include the best *flódni* in the city. Mon–Thurs 9am–6pm, Fri 9am–2pm, Sun 10am–6pm; closed Jewish holidays.

Hisztéria Cremeria VI, Jókai tér 4 ☎0630 210 5625, ⓦ bit.ly/hiszteria; map p.60. The Ipacs family have been making ice creams in the countryside for around thirty years. This is the second shop they have opened in the city, close to the Oktogon on the corner of Andrássy út, and – in spite of the strange name – their experience shines through in their ice creams: try the ricotta and caramelized fig or the cream, toffee and pine nut flavours. Daily 10am–9pm.

London Coffee Society VII, Dohány utca 27 ☎0630 567 0044, ⓦ bit.ly/londoncoffeesoc; map p.60. Family-run bolthole on the edge of the Seventh District, with a

> **TOP 5 FOR ICE CREAM**
> **Damniczki** see p.170
> **Fragola** see p.171
> **Gelarto Rosa** see p.171
> **Hisztéria Cremeria** see p.171
> **Levendula** see p.173

14

small gallery and a couple of tables on the pavement in front. The chatty barista learned his trade in London – and that is also where their coffee is roasted. All-day breakfast, and a delicious array of cakes – try the rosemary and olive oil cake. Daily 8.30am–6pm.

Magvető VII, Dohány utca 13 ☎1 205 3395, ⓦcafe .magveto.hu; map p.60. Culture meets coffee in this appealing café run by a publishing house – go through the door at the back and you come out in the Fókusz bookshop at Rákóczi út 14. In a nod to the literary traditions of the Budapest coffee houses, local writers get a discount in return for writing a piece of prose or verse. You can lounge around on the large steps up one side of the café. Holds regular literary events and occasional music evenings. Mon 3–10pm, Tues–Sat 8am–10pm, Sun 8am–3pm.

Mai Manó VI, Nagymező utca 20 ☎1 269 5642, ⓦbit .ly/maimano; map p.60. One of the more agreeable spots in the theatre quarter, this small café underneath the Mai Manó Photography Museum retains a cutesy interior with patterned tables and images splayed across the walls, as well as a convivial outdoor terrace. A great

place to stop, either for a pastry and breakfast or a late-night drink. Daily 8am–1am.

Művész VI, Andrássy út 29 ☎1 343 3544, ⓦmuveszkavehaz.hu; map p.60. There's an air of faded grandeur in this coffee house that's as notable for its decor – deep leather seating, chandeliers and gilt – as it is for its coffee (from 590Ft) and cakes. Mon–Sat 8am–9pm, Sun 9am–9pm.

New York Café VII, Erzsébet körút 9 ☎1 886 6167, ⓦnewyorkcafe.hu; map p.60. This opulent coffee house was a popular haunt of writers in the early 1900s. Restored as part of the *Boscolo* hotel, it has lost none of its magnificence, and the service is first class, but exorbitant prices (coffees start at 1200Ft) mean it has struggled to win back its place among today's impoverished intelligentsia. Daily 8am–midnight.

Podma Café VI, Podmaniczky utca 14 ☎1 720 1028, ⓦpodmacafe.hu; map p.60. Tea is finally catching on in Budapest, but this unassuming, two-floored café made a good head-start. Row upon row of teas from around the world are lined up in old-fashioned tins on the lovely mahogany shelves, and while you're here, you may as well grab a home-made cookie too. Daily 8am–10pm.

Sock's VII, Dohány utca 1b ☎0630 858 1858, ⓦbit.ly /sockscoffee; map p.60. Despite the unlikely name for a coffee bar – it was the owner's nickname from his taxi-driving days – the barista knows his stuff, and the cakes are delicious. Stands right across the road from the big synagogue, so very handy for sightseeing. They also have lactose- and gluten-free cakes. Daily 8am–8pm.

JÓZSEFVÁROS AND FERENCVÁROS

Múzeum Café & Bistro VIII, Múzeum körút 10 ☎1 338 4415, ⓦbit.ly/muzeumcafe; map p.78. Handy hangout that's a good spot to rest up for a coffee after digesting the nearby National Museum, or when you have been partying into the early hours. Daily 24hr.

Nandori IX, Ráday utca 53 ☎1 215 8776, ⓦnandori .hu; map p.78. Founded in 1957, the family-run *Nandori* is an institution that locals come to for their favourite pastries. Nothing new-wave here, this is a place of tradition, where you can buy reliable classics such as *beigli* or *rétes*, or ice creams. Mon–Sat 7.30am–7pm.

Rengeteg RomKafé IX, Tűzoltó utca 22 ☎0620 321 0229, ⓦbit.ly/rengeteg; map p.78. Congenial cellar café in a former glass factory underneath the *Élesztő* beer bar (see p.179) and near the Corvin negyed. The teddy bears,

sewing machines and bric-a-brac covering the brick walls and every surface give the place a very homely feel, and you can relax in armchairs. There's a huge range of teas, as well as coffee and hot chocolate, all fairly sourced, and home-made biscuits and savoury snacks. Daily 10am–10pm.

Tamp & Pull IX, Czuczor utca 3 ☎0630 456 7618, ⓦtamppull.hu; map p.78. Students at the university across the road flock to this minute craft-coffee bar, where the expert baristas serve superb "third-wave" coffee – they also run courses on making and tasting the stuff. The board on the wall tells you about the beans of the day: where they are from, who grew them and at what altitude. The pastries and sandwiches are delicious too. Mon–Fri 7am–7pm, Sat 9am–5pm, Sun noon–4pm.

THE VÁR AND CENTRAL BUDA

Artigiana Gelati XII, Csaba utca 8 ☎1 212 2439, ⓦbit.ly/Artigiana; map p.90. A couple of minutes from Széll Kálmán tér, this parlour has been concocting fine ice cream for more than twenty years. A magical assortment of wondrous flavours, such as beetroot,

cherry and chilli, and lavender and rosemary, are served up in cones or cups. It also has lactose- and sugar-free *gelati*. March & April Tues–Sun 11am–7pm; May–Sept daily 11am–7.30pm; Oct to mid-Dec Thurs–Sun 11am–6.30pm.

Auguszt II, Fény utca 8 ☎1 316 3817, ⓦauguszt cukraszda.hu; map p.90. Five generations have been continuing the *Auguszt* patisserie tradition since 1870, with mainly the women of the family at the helm. They certainly produce some of Budapest's finest cakes, and you can enjoy them upstairs or on the terrace out the back. The branch at V, Kossuth Lajos utca 14–16 in the Belváros is open Monday too. Tues–Fri 10am–6pm, Sat 9am–6pm.

Budai Pékség XII, Maros utca 23–25 ☎1 375 5284, ⓦbit.ly/budaipek; map p.90. A great bakery with a couple of tables that serves sandwiches, pastries, coffees and surprisingly delicious milk. It is also handy for picnics in the hills – the bread is very good, as are the cakes. The sister outlet, *Budai Pékség II*, just below Széna tér at Vársányi Irén utca 21, also sells delectable ice cream. Mon–Fri 7am–6pm, Sat 8am–1pm.

Levendula II, Fény utca 6 ⓦlevendulafagylaltozo.hu; map p.90. This popular parlour chain serves fabulous ice cream, including nutella, coconut, lavender (*levendula* in Hungarian), and more intriguingly, camembert. You'll also find outlets at V, Vámház körút 6, opposite the Great Market Hall, and at V, Szent István körút 21, near the Margít híd. Daily 11am–9pm.

Ruszwurm I, Szentháromság utca 7 ☎1 375 5284; map p.93. Near the Mátyás Church in the Vár, this diminutive Baroque coffee house can be so packed that it's almost impossible to get a seat in summer. Still, it's definitely worth seeking out for its coffee and cakes, the pick of which is its mouthwatering *rétes*. Daily 10am–7pm.

Steamhouse I, Batthyány tér 5–6 ⓦbit.ly /steamhouse; map p.90. This first-floor café in the cavernous former market hall offers a grandstand view over the Danube to the Parliament. The service can be a little lax but the speciality coffee is superb – the chief barista has won awards for his craft. Mon–Fri 8am–7pm, Sat 9am–3pm.

> ## TOP 5 FOR CAKES
> **Auguszt** see opposite
> **Daubner** see p.174
> **London Coffee Society** see p.171
> **Normafa Rétes** see p.174
> **À Table** see below

Szelence Café I, Pauler utca 1b ☎1 201 4335, ⓦszelencecafe.hu; map p.90. A family-friendly café with a rather quaint homely feel, near the Krisztina tér end of the tunnel under the Vár. The salads and soups on the menu are mainly gluten- and lactose-free, and they have vegetarian and vegan dishes as well. Mon–Fri 11am–7pm, Sat 11.30am–6pm.

★**Szerelmes Levél** I, Lövőház utca 7 ☎0630 742 3045, ⓦpekmuhely.hu; map p.90. "Love Letter", named after a traditional jam pastry, is a great place to start the day. Tucked away by the entrance to a bank in the side of the Mammut Mall, it is a member of the *Pékműhely* chain, one of the city's best *kovászos* (sourdough) bakeries. Besides their range of breads they do pastries – with common fillings like *túró* and plums or cocoa, and less usual ones such as pepperoni or gorgonzola. They have a few seats where you can sit and enjoy their fine coffee and freshly squeezed orange juice. Mon–Fri 8am–7pm, Sat 8am–2pm.

À Table II, Retek utca 6 ⓦatable.hu; map p.90. One of a chain of French-style cafés that are an excellent place to start the day – this branch is next to the Mammut mall. Delicious coffees, sandwiches and pastries – the pistachio croissants are mouthwatering – and you can also get delectable bread for picnics. Order from the counter before you sit down. Other branches are in V, Arany János utca 16, and at Wesselényi utca 9, behind the Dohány utca synagogue. Mon–Fri 7am–7pm, Sat–Sun 8am–6pm.

14

GELLÉRT-HEGY

Arnoldo XI, Bartók Béla út 46 ☎0670 338 7001, ⓦgrossarnold.com; map p.109. Doubling as a gallery of works by the popular graphic artist Arnold Gross, this is one of several places on this road giving the Újbuda (New Buda) district a real buzz. The excellent coffee is from the *Lumen* bar in Pest, and the sandwiches and cakes are delectable. Tues–Sat 10am–9pm.

★**Kelet Kávézó** XI, Bartók Béla út 29 ☎0620 456 5507, ⓦbit.ly/keletkavezo; map p.109. With books lining every inch of the walls (you can swap books), there is a strong literary theme in this warm café. The name "East" is part joke: the early twentieth-century writers' group called West used to meet in a café across the road – and students and writers certainly look very at home here today. The eastern theme is picked up in the food:

sandwiches include Indonesian peanut butter, curry and smoked catfish. Speciality coffees and a great range of teas, as well as wines and beers. Mon 3–10pm, Tues–Sat 8am–10pm, Sun 8am–3pm.

★**Tranzit Art Café** XI, Bukarest utca 3 ☎1 209 3070, ⓦtranzitcafe.com; map p.109. Friendly alternative café in the fabulous Modernist former bus station behind Kosztolányi Dezső tér. It's a very relaxed space where you can lounge around on sofas, with a children's play area in one corner. They have salsa evenings and film screenings outside in summer. You can get a lunch menu for 1390Ft, and they serve toasted sandwiches, tortillas and salads throughout the day, both meat and vegetarian. Mon–Fri 9am–11pm, Sat 10am–10pm.

ÓBUDA

Cziniel III, Nánási út 55 ☎1 240 1188, ⓦcziniel cukraszda.hu; map p.116. Large, popular café just north of the Roman ruins at Aquincum, with excellent ice creams and *gesztenye puré*. A good place to bring children too, as it has its own play area, and handy if you've been on the riverbank enjoying the bars and restaurants on the Rómaipart or want to head further out from Aquincum. Daily: May–Sept 8am–10pm; Oct–April 9am–8pm.

Daubner III, Szépvölgyi út 50 ☎1 335 2253, ⓦdaubnercukraszda.hu; map p.116. It is a trek to get to this patisserie in Óbuda, but the place is always crowded, especially at weekends, when people will patiently queue up for its delicious cakes, such as the plum slipper (*szilvás papucs*) or pumpkin-seed scone (*tökmagos pogácsa*). Mon–Sat 9am–7pm.

THE BUDA HILLS

Normafa Rétes XII, Eötvös utca 59, Normafa ⓦnormafaretes.hu; map p.123. The *Rétes Büfé* hut at the top of the Buda Hills by the old tree where Bellini's aria was sung (see p.122) has been a place of pilgrimage since 1978 for families, walkers and (in winter) skiers who flock to the area. You can expect to queue for the excellent *rétes* on fine days. The same crowd run the *Rétes Kert* across the road at no. 50 and the *büfé* at the top of the Libegő. Daily: March & April 10am–6pm; May–Aug 10am–7pm; Sept–Oct 10am–5pm; Nov–Feb 10am–4pm.

SZIMPLAKERT, ERZSÉBETVAROS

Bars and clubs

Trendy, traditional or bohemian – whatever you're after in Budapest, you're likely to find it. Rather than being focused on one central zone, the drinking scene is fairly diffuse, albeit heavily skewed towards Pest. Party central is the VII district, where you'll find the pick of the ruin bars, Budapest's home-grown drinking trend. In the Belváros, Erzsébet tér has leapfrogged Liszt Ferenc tér as the in-place to meet and hang out, while the outdoor bars in the Városliget and at various spots along the Danube do a roaring trade in the summer. For a slightly more chilled night, head for the area around the Károly kert or into the Palace Quarter behind the National Museum, and beyond in the VIII district.

Budapest's **ruin bars** (*romkocsma*; see box, p.10) have been a firm favourite with visitors for several years: *Szimplakert* and *Anker't* have turned into very established enterprises. Once a deserted series of courtyards between Király and Dob utca, **Gozsdu udvar** is now heaving with places to eat and drink and is the top destination for British stag groups. The more laidback VIII district has a distinctly bohemian feel at places like *Lumen* and *Csiga*, while the bars along the new **Corvin Sétány** offer a more modern vibe. For alfresco boozing you'll find several **outdoor summer bars** at the southern end of Margít-sziget and a couple of successful ones at the Városliget, though the renovations in both places have forced the bars to move around. Up the Danube on the Buda side at the Római-part, the *Fellini Római Kultúrbisztró* offers a more relaxed vibe.

The **wine bar** (*borozó*) scene has changed markedly recently, as the growing interest in provenance, backed by a passionate belief in promoting Hungarian wine, has led to the emergence of sophisticated bars with clued-up staff. *Doblo* and *Kadarka* are fine examples, but you can still find the more traditional Hungarian wine bars that are mainly working-men's watering holes offering humble snacks such as *zsíros kenyér* (bread and dripping with onion and paprika).

Beer has long lived in the shadow of wine in Hungary. However, the emergence of microbreweries has sparked a new curiosity in the humble hop and specialist beer bars (*söröző*) such as *Élesztő*, *Jónás* and *Monyó* are attracting a new generation of discerning drinkers.

Budapest's **club** scene is especially varied in the summer, when it expands into several large outdoor venues, and there are also regular events held in the thermal baths such as the old Turkish Rudas and the big outdoor Széchenyi, or in sites further out of town (advertised via promotional posters). DJs to look out for include Budai and Mango and anything with the Tilos Rádió stamp on it.

ESSENTIALS

Opening hours Most places open around lunchtime and stay open until well after midnight, unless otherwise stated, though bars in residential areas have to close their terraces at 10pm. Summer-only bars usually announce their openings (generally in May) via a Facebook page.

Costs Note that the warnings about rip-offs in restaurants (see p.160) apply equally to bars. Many bars do not take credit cards, although that is changing rapidly. Expect to pay 600–1200Ft upwards to get into a club.

Transport There is a good network of night buses (see p.26) that can help you make your way home, taxis are easy to flag down, and the streets are generally safe.

Smoking The smoking ban is strictly enforced indoors, but generally you can smoke on terraces and in garden areas.

THE BELVÁROS

Akvárium VII, Erzsébet tér 12 📞0630 860 3368, 🌐akvariumklub.hu; map p.40. The steps down into the great big hole in the middle of this central square are a very popular meeting-place day and night. The bar at the bottom, the *Akvárium*, is a heavily promoted venue that gets some top gigs – you'll understand the name when you see the light filtering through the lake that forms its roof. Mon & Tues noon–1am, Wed–Sun noon–4.30am.

★**Csendes Társ** V, Magyar utca 18 📞0630 727 2100, 🌐bit.ly/csendestarsbar; map p.40. With a small terrace across the road by the entrance of the delightful Károlyi

---

BOTTOMS UP!

Hungarian has a variety of tongue-twisting ways to **toast** fellow drinkers. *Egészségedre!* ("Your health") is the most common, but it's usually said to one person whom you know well. To a group, you might use *Egészségetekre!*; if your acquaintance is more formal, it would be *Egészségére!* To a friend, a simple *Szia!* is fine.

Clinking glasses of **beer** used to be frowned upon, as it was said that this was how the Austrians celebrated the execution of the Hungarian generals in 1849; the "right" Hungarian way was to bang your glass on the table before raising it to your lips. These days, though, people say that there was a 150-year time limit on that taboo, and clinking beer-glasses is back.

kert, *Csendes Társ* is a wine bar with a rather romantic feel. The bar itself is minute, but it benefits from sharing the kitchen and large wine cellar of its sister bar round the corner. There's nothing better than a quiet afternoon under the trees here, moving gently from coffee to the basil and strawberry lemonade and finally on to a little *pezsgő* as the candles are lit. Daily 10am–11pm.

★**Csendes Vintage Bar** V, Ferenczy Isván utca 5 ☎ 0630 727 2100, ✺ bit.ly/csendesbar; map p.40. Just down the road from Astoria junction, this bar's wacky decoration, chandeliers and bare brick walls have made it a popular destination for students at the university across the road (attracted in part by its vast range of spirits). You can also get reasonable meals here (mains from 1890Ft). Mon–Fri 10am–2am, Sat 2pm–2am, Sun 2pm–midnight.

TOP 5 OUTDOOR VENUES
Csendes Társ see p.176
Jonás see p.179
Kertem see p.179
Pántlika see p.179
Fellini Római Kultúrbisztró see p.181

Ibolya V, Ferenciek tere 5 ☎ 1 788 1944, ✺ ibolyaespresso.hu; map p.40. An old favourite with local students, the *Ibolya* preserves a wonderfully retro feel with its neon street sign, plastic seats and surly waiters. Even the snacks have stayed the same – *melegszendvics* (toasted sandwiches) and peanuts. Football matches are regularly screened. Mon–Thurs 8am–1am, Fri 8am–3am, Sat 11am–3am, Sun noon–1am.

LIPÓTVÁROS

Drop Shop V, Balassi Bálint utca 27 ☎ 0630 345 3739, ✺ dropshop.hu; map p.50. An excellent wine bar at the Pest end of the Margít bridge. The stock is dominated by more expensive foreign bottles, but there is also a good range of Hungarian fine wines too. You can lounge around on the sofas tasting the delicious snacks – or you can buy to take out, as the slightly strange name implies. Not as cheap as the relaxed interior might suggest. Daily 11am–midnight.

Tokaji Borozó V, Falk Miksa utca 32 ☎ 1 269 3143, ✺ bit.ly/tokajibor; map p.50. Inexpensive old-style cellar wine-bar serving wines from the Tokaj region in northeast Hungary – though this is not top-end stuff – as well as snacks such as *lepcsánka* (potato pancakes) and *zsíros kenyér* (bread and dripping). Mon–Fri 1–10pm.

TERÉZVÁROS AND ERZSÉBETVÁROS

Amigo Bar VII, Hársfa utca 1 ☎ 1 352 1424, ✺ amigobar.hu; map p.60. A fun time is guaranteed at this rockabilly haunt, with three floors crawling with 1950s nostalgia, right down to the bartenders with their pompadour quiffs. Live music (Sept–May) takes place down in the cellar bar, which otherwise has a fabulous jukebox and three immaculate red-clothed pool tables. Mon–Fri 3pm–3am, Sat 6pm–4am.

Anker't VI, Paulay Ede utca 33 ☎ 0630 360 3389, ✺ bit.ly/ankert; map p.60. Tucked away near the Opera House, *Anker't* has that distinctive ruin-pub cocktail of small and large spaces and courtyards that make a perfect party place. Three bars, DJs, burgers and a great atmosphere. Monthly Sunday vegan and flower market, and they also have cultural events here. Daily 3pm–3am.

Castro VII, Madách Imre tér 3 ☎ 0630 214 6466, ✺ castrobistro.hu; map p.40. Located at the entrance to the Gozsdu party zone, this casual, cheery bar with a misleadingly Cuban name nevertheless draws a mixed crowd of Hungarians and foreigners. It's nothing particularly fancy, but the boho decor, good beer, and Serbian-style meats keep people coming back. Mon–Thurs & Sun 11am–midnight, Fri & Sat 11am–1am.

Csak a Jó Sör VII, Kertész utca 42 ☎ 0630 251 4737, ✺ csakajosor.hu; map p.60. Small bar that is more of a shop with a few tables, but it's a must for craft ale lovers as the name "only good beer" suggests. As it's run by a true devotee, Gergely, you'll find six beers on tap, Hungarian and imported, and more than four hundred by the bottle. Mon–Sat 2pm–9pm.

Doblo VII, Dob utca 20 ☎ 1 20 398 8863, ✺ budapestwine.com; map p.60. Classy though far from pretentious wine bar, which looks all the better for its exposed brickwork. Some two hundred varieties of Hungarian wine are available by the glass, each costing between 950–2700Ft – and the meat and cheese plates are delicious. Wine-tasting sessions (45min) from 4950Ft. Live music Wed and Thurs. Mon–Wed & Sun 2pm–2am, Thurs–Sat 2pm–4am.

Fekete Kutya VII, Dob utca 31 ☎ 0620 580 3151, ✺ bit.ly/feketek; map p.60. The arcade in front of this dog-friendly Seventh-district gastrobar just off Kazinczy utca gets packed out as the evening draws on. The crowds are attracted by the draught Czech and craft beers, Hungarian tapas such as prunes wrapped in bacon and the relaxed vibe. In the daytime they do full-scale brunches and a two-course lunch menu – with enticing dishes such as Moroccan cauliflower soup or fennel risotto – for 1490Ft. Mon–Sat 9am–2am, Sun 9am–midnight.

Kadarka VI, Király utca 42 ☎ 1 266 5094, ✺ bit.ly/kadarkabar; map p.60. Taking its name from the distinctive Hungarian grape, this colourful, modern wine

15

15

TOP 5 RUIN BARS

Anker't see p.177
Kisüzem see below
Pótkulcs see below
Rácskert see below
Szimplakert see below

bar has a youthful appeal. It has mainly Hungarian wines on offer, and at reasonable prices; you can also buy bottles to take away. Their food is as good as the wine, with *pogácsa* (50Ft), ciabattas (1390Ft), as well as plates of cheese and meats (from 2290Ft). Big seating area out on the pavement in summer. Daily 4pm–midnight.

Kiadó VI, Jókai tér 3 ☎1 331 1955, ⓦbit.ly /kiadokocsma; map p.60. The polar opposite of the type of bar to be found across Andrássy út on Liszt Ferenc tér, *Kiadó* has few pretensions, with its laidback feel, small tables and cosy gallery. Full bar menu available too. Mon–Fri 10am–1am, Sat & Sun 11am–1am.

★**Kisüzem** VII, Kis Diófa utca 2 ☎1 781 6705, ⓦbit .ly/kisuzem; map p.60. Small bohemian bar on the corner of Klauzál tér, that stands out from the Seventh-district crowd with its unpretentious feel, avant-garde art, good music and delicious cheap food (a bowl of chili con carne for just 1000Ft). Live music on Thurs, silent movies on Sun. Mon–Wed & Sun noon–2am, Thurs–Sat noon–3am.

Központ VII, Madách Imre út 5 ☎1 783 8405, ⓦbit .ly/kozpontbar; map p.40. Stylish bar at the entrance to the Seventh district that is a favourite meeting place for media folk. In the daytime the "Centre" feels more like a relaxed café with its big window seats, but it turns livelier later as the music and the crowds arrive. Good salads and sandwiches. Mon–Thurs 8am–1am, Fri 8am–3am, Sat noon–3am, Sun noon–10pm.

Kuplung VI, Király utca 46 ☎0630 755 3527, ⓦbit.ly /kuplungbar; map p.60. This one-time motorcycle repair shop (the name means "clutch") is accessed via a graffiti-splattered corridor leading into a concrete courtyard masked with weirdly painted murals. A lime-green-coloured bar runs the length of one side, while the remaining space is taken up with simple wooden bench seating, table football (*csocsó*) and ping-pong. Daily 3pm–5am.

Mazel Tov I, Akácfa utca 47 ☎0670 626 4280, ⓦmazeltov.hu; map p.60. There's a strong touch of Tel Aviv in the *Mazel Tov* ruin bar, with its Middle Eastern food, fancy design and lively atmosphere. There's regular live music and a garden courtyard – but don't expect quick service. This street is party central, lying next door to the even bigger complex of the *Instant/Fogas Ház* ruin bar. Mon–Fri 4pm–2am, Sat–Sun noon–2am.

Mika Tivadar VII, Kazinczy utca 47 ☎0620 965 3007, ⓦmikativadarmulato.hu; map p.60. One of the

busiest bars on Kazinczy utca, with a large summertime garden next door, good food, and music on the stage at the back. The name comes from the owner of the factory that once stood here. Mon–Wed 4pm–midnight, Thurs 4pm–2am, Fri & Sat 4pm–5am.

Most VI, Zichy Jenő utca 17 ☎0670 248 3322, ⓦmostbisztro.hu; map p.60. A gentrified ruin bar centring around a lounge with a 1950s concrete and glass arched ceiling, to the side of which is a small bar and stage, where there is regular live music. In May the brick wall at the back is ceremonionally knocked down, opening up an enormous gravel-bedded garden. *Most* is a bar with a reputation for its food, and is especially popular for its breakfasts and brunches (1980Ft). Two-course lunch menu from 1290Ft. Mon–Wed & Sun 10am–2am, Thurs–Sat 10am–1am.

★**Pótkulcs** VI, Csengery utca 65b ☎1 269 1050, ⓦpotkulcs.hu; map p.60. There's not much by way of a sign on the tatty metal door of the "Spare Key", but go through and you'll find yourself in a verdant yard, with the bar straight ahead, and a room with sofas and table football off to the left. This is a laidback kind of place with a reputation built largely on the strength of its live music programme, ranging from klezmer and Roma bands to underground, folk and jazz. Mon–Wed & Sun 5pm–1.30am, Thurs–Sat 5pm–2.30am.

Rácskert VIII, Dob utca 40 ☎0670 428 1517, ⓦbit .ly/racskert; map p.60. One of the newer ruin bars, behind the railings (*rács*) of an old car park that hopes to recapture the iconoclastic spirit of the late 1990s. Run by the man behind the first "ruin garden" in the city, the much mourned *Ráckert*. On Fridays, two worlds collide as a traditional folk band plays to the cool kid – but they also have events on other nights. Mon & Tues noon–midnight, Wed & Thurs noon–2am, Fri & Sat noon–4am.

Szimplakert VII, Kazinczy utca 14 ☎0620 261 8669, ⓦszimpla.hu; map p.60. Occupying a former stove factory, this is the granddaddy of ruin bars, spawning ever more successful spin-offs. The darkened corridor feeds a warren of graffiti-strewn, junk-filled rooms, beyond which is the main, partially canopied, courtyard with bars on three sides and an old Trabant for seating. There's free live music (jazz, rock, retro, funk, folk) most nights of the week, exhibitions and films. Although there's a fair old din here at night, it makes a delightful refuge by day. Farmers' market held here every Sunday. Mon–Sat 10am–4am, Sun 9am–5am.

★**Szociális Helyiség** VII, Kazinczy utca 52c ☎06 20 913 4343, ⓦbit.ly/szocialis; map p.60. If the Seventh District party scene gets a bit raucous, the small gay-friendly bar is a bit of a refuge. You can sit out on the terrace all year round – it is heated in winter, and they serve light food such as pancakes and stuffed tortillas. Tues–Sat 5pm–1am.

THE VÁROSLIGET

Dürer Kert XIV, Ajtosi Dürer sor 19–21 ☎0670 459 4135, ⓦdurerkert.com; map p.71. One of the big party venues that Budapest seems to excel in, attracting a young crowd with its concerts and DJs, and indoor and outdoor dancefloors; there's also table football and big screens for big matches. It's been going for ten years and has so far resisted attempts to move it out. Daily 5pm–5am.

★**Kertem** XIV, Olaf Palme sétány ☎0630 225 1399, ⓦkertemfesztival.hu; map p.71. Close to the Olaf Palme House in the middle of the Városliget, "My Garden" is a great place to lounge away the summer. It's popular with families by day, with children playing around on the grass, while at night it is always packed. Friendly service, cheap drinks, good music and a very busy grill produces the perfect accompaniment for those long lazy evenings. During the construction work in the park *Kertem* may be relocated – check the website. Note also that by the end of the summer the grassy expanse gets pretty dusty. May–Sept daily 11am–4am.

Pántlika XIV, opposite Hermina út 47 ☎0670 376 9910, ⓦpantlika.hu; map p.71. Lying on the far side of the Városliget from the city centre, *Pántlika* offers a touch of Hungarian nostalgia in its 1970s pavilion building, red-and-white-checked table covers and retro decorations. After a day at the baths or the zoo, you can sit under the trees and enjoy a *fröccs* while the children slurp on a *szörp*. There is also food: Hungarian classics such as *gulyás* and stews or a range of burgers. Cash only. April–Sept daily noon–10pm.

JÓZSEFVÁROS AND FERENCVÁROS

Corvintető VIII, Blaha Lujza tér 1–2 ☎0630 751 5200, ⓦcorvinteto.hu; map p.78. For some of the best night-time views of Budapest, head on up to this inspired rooftop bar atop the Communist-era Corvin department store (the entrance/lift up is on Somogyi Béla utca). A 30m-long bar keeps happy folk going until the very early hours, while the floor below hosts DJs and the occasional band. Daily 6pm–6am.

Csiga VIII, Vásár utca 2 ☎0630 613 2046, ⓦbit .ly/csigabar; map p.78. An artsy, mellow atmosphere prevails at the appealing *Csiga* corner café, which remains the drinking venue of choice in the increasingly hip area around Rákóczi tér. Stripped wood flooring, mezzanine seating and big windows set the scene for a daytime or evening chillout. The food is excellent too – the two-course lunch menu is 1300Ft. Daily 9am–midnight.

★**Élesztő** IX, Tüzoltó utca 22 ☎0670 336 1279, ⓦelesztohaz.hu; map p.78. Housed in a former glass factory near the Corvin negyed, "Yeast" is one of the best places in town to try Hungarian artisan beers, with no less than twenty on tap, as well as a grill bar where you can soak up the booze. There's seating out in the courtyard, ruin-bar style, a wine and tapas bar, brewing school – and ambitious plans for further developments here make this a place to watch. Daily 3pm–3am.

Grund VIII, Nagytemplom utca 30 ☎0620 583 6712, ⓦagrund.hu; map p.78. Occupying the whole of a derelict house just off the booming Corvin sétány, the *Grund* is a huge party place where you can count on something happening most nights of the week, with DJs, live acts and football screenings. The focal point of the complex is a slick, bare-brick bar with side rooms and sofas, outside of which lies a neatly landscaped terrace with grass and gravel walkways. There is an outdoor grill at the back, and even an excellent children's playground by the entrance. Daily 10am–4am.

★**Jedermann** IX, Ráday utca 58 ☎0630 406 3617, ⓦjedermann.hu; map p.78. *Jedermann*, at the bottom of Ráday utca, scores top marks on all counts: it's a relaxed bar, has good food (two-course lunch for 990Ft), and puts on excellent music, mainly jazz but also world music, on Fri, Sat and other days. It's popular with local students for its cheap breakfasts (coffee 350Ft) and you can lounge about on the terrace at the back. As a bonus, it's attached to the Goethe Institute, which has a lively cultural programme. No credit cards. Daily 8am–1am.

★**Jonás** IX, Bálna building, Fővám tér 11–12 ☎0670 930 1392, ⓦbit.ly/jonasbeer; map p.78. Craft beer bar at the southern end of the "Whale" on the Pest riverbank. Eight beers on tap, craft *pálinka*, wine, hot chocolate, a range of interesting soft drinks – lavender, rose and mint – and a burger bar. The terrace (note no table service here) has great views over the river, and staff are friendly and informed. Mon–Thurs & Sun 10am–midnight, Fri & Sat 10am–2am.

★**Lumen** VIII, Mikszáth Kálmán tér 3 ☎1 781 5156, ⓦlumenkave.hu; map p.78. A wonderfully bohemian little bar with craft beers on tap, freshly roasted coffee (it was the first place in town to roast its own) and mainly vegetarian salads, soups and sandwiches – though the service can be a bit too cool. The terrace spreads out into the popular square. If plans to move to larger premises nearby come off, they will regain their live music and gallery – watch the website for details.

15

TOP 5 FOR CRAFT BEER
Csak a Jó Sör see p.177
Élesztő see above
Jonás see above
Lumen see above
Monyó see p.180

Mon–Fri 8am–midnight, Sat 10am–midnight, Sun 10am–10pm.

Monyó IX, Kálvin tér 7 ☎ 0670 415 7835, ⓦ monyo.hu; map p.78. Small bar with friendly staff who will enthusiastically lead you through their stock of Hungarian craft beers, both on tap and by the bottle, many of them from their own brewery in the Kőbánya district. Light

snacks only. Mon–Wed noon–midnight, Thurs & Fri noon–2am, Sat 5pm–2am.

Trapéz IX, Imre utca 2 ☎ 1 210 2541, ⓦ trapezkocsma .hu; map p.78. Down the road from the Great Market Hall, *Trapéz* is a popular student hangout – the Corvinus university is across the street. One of the attractions is the very reasonably priced food served in generous portions,

HUNGARIAN WINE

Hungary's **wines** have come a long way in recent years, though they are still under-appreciated in the global market. In general, the country's climate favours whites, especially crisp and floral varieties, but its reds are also delicious and offer more complexity and variation.

Many of the grape varieties used in Hungarian wines will be familiar, even if their Hungarian names are less so, but there are also some indigenous grapes that are worth trying. Among **reds**, alongside the well-known Cabernet Franc and Cabernet Sauvignon and others, the Kadarka yields a light, spicy, cherry-coloured wine that has undergone a revival in the past decade. It is a common ingredient in **Bikavér**, the well-known Hungarian **Bull's Blood wine** from Eger and Szekszárd. Alongside the familiar **whites** of Sauvignon Blanc and Olaszrizling (Italian Riesling) are Irsai Olivér, which produces a floral, aromatic wine, and Cserszegi Fűszeres, which has a slightly smoother, spicier flavour, as well as the crisp dry Furmint and Hárslevelű (lime or linden leaf), which produce some of Hungary's finest bottles in Tokaj and Somló. Another grape found in Somló is Juhfark, "sheep's tail", said to have desirable results if drunk on your wedding night. Hungary's **rosés** have improved markedly in recent years, benefiting from a good balance of fruit without being too sweet.

Although Hungary has twenty-two official wine regions, the best producers are concentrated in a few areas. Alongside the big established vintners, it is the smaller cellars (*pince*) that are producing the most exciting wines. Below is a brief introduction to the main regions and a few of the top names (★).

Lake Balaton to the southwest of Budapest has five different regions where whites dominate. ★Huba Szeremley, Jásdi, Otto Légli and Mihály Figula.

Eger is one of the big wine regions, in the north. ★Vilmos Thummerer, St. Andrea, Nimród Kovács, Bolyki and Tamas Pók.

Etyek-Buda is a smaller region that produces mainly white wines. It is perhaps best known for its sparkling wines in the Budafok cellars. Etyek, lying 30km west of Budapest, has some excellent wines and is easy to visit. Four times a year crowds flock out to its wine and food festival (ⓦ etyekipiknik.hu has details of how to get there). ★Törley (for sparkling), Etyeki Kúria and Nyakas Pince.

Szekszárd is strong on reds, especially Kadarka. ★Ferenc Vesztergombi, Takler, Tamás Dúzsi, Péter Vida, Németh János, Zoltán Heimann, and Adrian Bösz.

Somló is the smallest region, based around a hill west of Balaton whose volcanic soil produces fascinating results, just as it does around Tokaj; this is a crisp yet rich wine with a mineral character, and it found favour with Queen Victoria. ★Béla Fekete, Imre Györgykovács, Kolonics.

Tokaj is famed for its incredibly sweet Aszú wines, but the drier Furmint and the fragrant Hárslevelű (lime or linden leaf), less cloying than the Aszú, are the real surprise. ★Royal Tokaj, Disznókő, Oremus and Szepsy (whose wines are brilliant but very pricey), Gizella pince, Erzsébet pince, Kikelet, Vayi and Berger Zsolt. Look out also for wines from two Mád wineries, the ★Első Mádi Borház and Holdvölgy, which are distributed abroad too.

Villány, near the Croatian border, was the first region to make its name after 1989. It is strong on reds, but its rosés are also good. ★József Bock, Attila Gere and Tiffán, Vylyan and Sauska, and the smaller names, Jackfall, Ruppert and Balázs Hárságyi.

TOP 5 WINE BARS

Csendes Társ see p.177
Doblo see p.177
Kadarka see p.177

Palack see p.181
Szalonspicc see p.181

but it also has a very agreeable vibe, with sofas to lounge on. You can watch major sporting fixtures on the large screen upstairs, and they have regular quizzes for those who fancy their Hungarian knowledge. Daily 10am–10pm.

THE VÁR AND CENTRAL BUDA

★**Bambi** I, Frankel Leó utca 2–4 ☎1 212 3171, ⓦbit.ly/bambibudapest; map p.90. One of the few surviving Socialist-Realist bars, complete with stern waitresses and old men chatting and playing dominoes on red plastic-covered tables. The beers and wines are nothing fancy, and that's part of the joy. It's all straight honest fare, omelettes and toasted sandwiches, and none of your fancy coffee, either: it just comes black, or with milk/cream. Daily 7am–10pm.

Lánchíd Söröző I, Fő utca 4 ☎1 214 3144, ⓦlanchidsorozo.hu; map p.93. Handily placed at the Buda end of the Lánchíd, this chilled bar is a quiet place in daytime, frequented by tourists and the odd regular, but by sundown the mood is more animated. It has expanded its restaurant but the bar remains much the same. The owner is a serious music fan, as testified by the randomly scattered instruments, gig posters and photos of him with Robert Plant, B.B. King et al on the walls. Daily 11am–1am.

Szalonspicc II, Lövőház utca 17 ☎0630 861 9006, ⓦszalonspicc.hu; map p.90. Excellent wine, friendly staff and tasty mini-burgers at this small bar on a buzzy pedestrianized street close to Széll Kálmán tér. The pavement terrace is standing-room-only in summer. Mon–Sat noon–midnight, Sun 4–10pm.

GELLÉRT-HEGY AND THE TABÁN

Libella XI, Budafóki út 7 ☎1 950 4994, ⓦbit.ly/libellabar; map p.109. Friendly, agreeably down-at-heel spot near the Danube which is popular above all with the student crowd from the nearby technical university. Bar snacks, chess and draughts seem to keep those that pop by satisfied. Mon–Fri 8am–1am, Sat 4pm–1am.

★**Palack** XI, Szent Gellért tér 3 ☎0630 997 1902, ⓦpalackborbar.hu; map p.109. Lying across the square from the *Gellért Hotel* in southern Buda, *Palack's* classy interior, great tapas and superb selection of wines make it Buda's top drinking hole. The staff can offer useful guidance round the mysteries of Hungarian wine, and you can also buy bottles to take away – it's not the cheapest place in town, but the quality is assured. Mon noon–11pm, Tues–Sat noon–midnight, Sun noon–10pm.

Szatyor XI, Bartók Béla út 36 ☎1 279 0290, ⓦszatyorbar.com; map p.109. A typical Budapest mix here of bar and culture, colourfully exotic decoration, settees to lounge on in the gallery, good Hungarian fare on a full menu, and a strong student presence from the nearby technical university. Mon–Fri noon–1am, Sat & Sun 2pm–1am.

ÓBUDA AND MARGÍT-SZIGET

Fellini Római Kultúrbisztró III, Kossuth Lajos üdülőpart 5, Római-part ☎1 279 0290, ⓦfellini romai.hu; map p.116. The best of the string of open-air bars lining the riverbank north of Óbuda. You can sit along the shore on deckchairs enjoying the regular live music, films and other cultural programmes. Take the HÉV train from Batthyány tér to Rómaifürdő and it's a 15min walk down to the river. May–Sept: Thurs, Sat & Sun 10am–midnight.

Raktár Beach XIII, Margít-sziget ☎0630 718 6629, ⓦraktarbeach.hu; map p.120. While the northern end of the island has the grand hotels, the southern end has the summer bars. In the changing scene, one of the newer arrivals is *Raktár*, down to your left as you walk onto the island from the Margít bridge, offering burgers, drinks and dancing till dawn. There are other bars to the right around the old casino building a short way up the island to the right. May–Sept, Thurs–Sat 8pm–4am.

15

LISZT MUSIC ACADEMY

Arts and entertainment

Hungary's cultural pedigree is strong, and this is reflected in both the diversity of performers and quality of productions available on any given night in Budapest. Music is a Hungarian forte, and there's a huge depth of talent, particularly in classical, folk, jazz and world music. Its rhythms and vigour make Hungarian folk music very accessible, and you can catch its different forms, played by skilled bands in venues large and small, accompanying large ensembles on the big stage, or in the more informal setting of the *táncház* ("dance house"). The city also boasts some magnificent concert halls, cinemas and theatres, many worth visiting for their architecture alone. The Spring Festival in March (see p.30) and the Café Budapest Contemporary Arts Festival in October (see p.31) showcase some of the finest in both Hungarian and international cultural talent.

ESSENTIALS

Concert season The season for the main opera, theatre and concert halls runs from mid-September to the end of May. During the summer most concerts are in open-air venues (see p.184).

Tickets and reservations The best place for tickets is at the venues themselves, as you'll avoid paying booking fees on top. Otherwise try Ticketportal at VI, Bajcsy Zsilinszky út 49 (Mon–Fri 10am–6pm; ☎1 302 2942, ⓦticketportal.hu); Rózsavölgyi record shop ticket office at V, Szervita tér 5 (Mon–Sat 10am–10pm; ☎1 266 8337); Broadway ticket offices at VII, Károly körút 21 (Mon–Fri 10am–6pm; ☎1 780 0780, ⓦbroadway.hu) and XIII, Hollán Ernő utca 20 (Mon–Fri 10am–6pm; ☎1 340 4040, ⓦbroadway.hu); or the online ticket services ⓦjegymester.hu and ⓦjegy.hu.

Prices Attending any kind of performance in Budapest needn't cost an arm and a leg. A decent seat at the opera or for a classical music concert will set you back anywhere between 2500Ft and 14,000Ft, although you can bank on paying double that for the big international names. Theatre and dance performances are slightly cheaper at 2000–4000Ft. Rock or pop concerts range from 1000Ft for local bands up to 30,000Ft for stadium gigs by superstars, while

a gig at the *Budapest Jazz Club* will cost 1400–2500F. Cinema tickets typically cost 1500–1900Ft, with cheaper prices on a cinema's discount day (*kedvezményes nap*).

Listings The best online listings are provided by ⓦxpatloop.com (though sections such as Activities for Kids are hopelessly out of date), ⓦfunzine.hu, ⓦest.hu and ⓦmuzsikalendarium.hu, the latter covering classical music events in English. The last three all publish free magazines: the listings magazine *Funzine*, which can be found in bars, and the Hungarian freebie magazine *Pesti Est*, which has well laid out listings, and the free monthly *Koncert Kalendárium*, available from ticket offices. Many gigs and concerts by both local and international bands are publicized on posters around town – particularly around Deák tér, Ferenciek tere and the Astoria underpass. The most comprehensive cinema listings appear in the *mozi* section of *Pesti Est* – they also have a good section on films in English on their website. Note that in some publications the times of shows are cryptically abbreviated: *n8* or *1/4 8* – short for *negyed 8* – means 7.15pm; *f8* or *1/2 8* (*fél 8*) means 7.30pm; and *h8* or *3/4 8* (*háromnegyed 8*) means 7.45pm. "*Mb*." indicates the film is dubbed – as many are – and *fel.* or *feliratos* means that it has Hungarian subtitles.

16

ARTS AND CULTURAL CENTRES

The venues listed below are used for a variety of **concerts** and other **entertainment events**. Bear in mind that many arts centres close for the summer.

Jurányi Ház II, Jurányi utca 1 ☎0670 777 2533, ⓦjuranyihaz.hu; map p.90. Alternative cultural centre in a former school building just down the road from Széll Kálmán tér, presenting exhibitions, theatre and dance. The café is recommended for its laidback feel. Performances Sept–May, though the centre and its café are open all year. Box office Sept–May Mon–Fri 4–8pm, Sat & Sun open 2hr before performances start.

Millenáris Park II, Kis Rókus utca 16–20 ☎1 336 4000, ⓦmillenaris.hu; map p.90. Cultural centre and park near Széll Kálmán tér which may host music, theatre and dance shows once the reconstruction of its buildings is finished. In summer, concerts are held on the park's outdoor stages.

★ **Palace of Arts (Művészetek palotája – Müpa)** IX,

Komor Marcell utca 1 ☎1 555 3000, ⓦmupa.hu; 15min on tram #2 from Vigadó tér; map p.78. This substantial complex on the riverbank in southern Pest has one of the best concert halls in Europe, as well as a theatre and museum. As the shop window for the capital's culture scene, it sees a superb range of concerts, attracting the top international classical, jazz and world music orchestras and acts. Box office daily 10am–6pm.

Trafó IX, Liliom utca 41 ☎1 215 1600, ⓦtrafo.hu; map p.78. A dynamic contemporary arts centre in a former transformer station, pulling in full houses with its strong roster of dance, theatre and music, by Hungarian and foreign artistes. Contemporary art gallery and a good bar too. Closed July & Aug. Box office daily 4–7pm.

MUSIC FESTIVALS

Budapest stages several terrific music festivals (see p.29) throughout the year. The big one is the week-long **Sziget festival** (ⓦsziget.hu/fesztival), held in mid-August on Óbudai (or Hajógyári) sziget north of Margít-sziget. Now established as one of Europe's largest and most vibrant music events, it draws the very biggest names in rock, pop and world music. It's great value, too, with day-tickets costing around €70, and weekly tickets €325 (with reductions if bought in advance). Going by public transport, you take the HÉV from Batthyány tér to the Filorigát stop and follow the crowds across the bridge to the island. Slightly less crowded is the bus from Deák tér and the boats from Batthyány tér or Jászai Mari tér, at the Pest end of the Margít híd.

CHURCH AND OPEN-AIR CONCERTS

Quite a few places of worship in Budapest regularly host concerts, among them the church on **Kálvin tér** (map p.40); the **Lutheran Church** on Deák tér (see p.47), where the programme includes free performances of Bach before Easter, details of which are posted by the church entrance; and the **Dohány utca synagogue** (see p.65). The **Mátyás Church** on Várhegy (see p.91) stages choral or organ recitals on Fri and Sat between June and Sept (from 8pm), and less frequently the rest of the year.

There is a summer season of concerts at open-air venues, including the outdoor stage on Margít-sziget (see p.120); the courtyard of the **Pest County Hall** (Pesti Vármegyeház; V, Városház utca 7; map p.40); the garden of the **Óbuda Music Society** (see below); and the **Vajdahunyad Castle** in the Városliget (see p.74).

CLASSICAL MUSIC, OPERA AND BALLET

The city offers a wide variety of performances, with several **concerts** most nights, especially during the Budapest Spring Festival and the Contemporary Arts jamboree in the autumn, when you can bank on a roll-call of world-class artists pitching up. Most opera productions are in Hungarian, a custom introduced by Gustav Mahler when he was director of the Opera House, which remains Budapest's principal venue. One genre that has long appealed to the Hungarian spirit is **operetta**, with Hungarians making a major contribution to the turn-of-the-century Viennese tradition through composers such as Ferenc Lehár and Imre Kálmán. Lehár's *The Merry Widow* and Kálmán's *The Csárdás Princess* still draw the crowds with their combination of grand tunes, extravagant staging and romantic comedy in the suitably over-the-top Operetta Theatre.

16

★**Bartók Memorial House (Bartók Emlékház)** II, Csalán utca 29 ☎1 394 2100, ⊛bartokmuseum.hu; map p.123. Concerts – not just of the music of Bartók – are held in the villa where the composer used to live, often on Thurs at 6pm but also on other days. Tickets are either included in the entry fee or are up to a modest 2500Ft. Tues–Sun 10am–5pm or until start of concert.

Bartók National Concert Hall (Bartók Béla Nemzeti Hangversenyterem) IX, Komor Marcell utca 1 ☎1 555 3000, ⊛mupa.hu; 15min on tram #2 from Vigadó tér; map p.78. The home of the Hungarian National Philharmonic Orchestra has superb acoustics and attracts world-class performers, not just in the classical arena.

Budapest Music Center IX, Mátyás utca 8 ☎1 216 7894, ⊛bmc.hu; map p.78. Great acoustics in this chamber music venue just south of the Great Market Hall, one of the exciting recent additions to the Budapest music scene. Box office Mon–Fri 9am–9pm, Sat 10am–9pm, Sun open 2hr before concerts start.

Budapest Operetta Theatre (Budapesti Operettszínház) VI, Nagymező utca 17 ☎1 312 4866, ⊛operett.hu; map p.60. The magnificently refurbished home of Hungarian operetta, where you can enjoy works by Lehár and Kálmán, as well as modern musicals. Box office Mon–Fri 10am–7pm, Sat & Sun 1–7pm.

Erkel Theatre (Erkel Színház) VIII, János Pál papa tér 30 ☎1 332 6150, ⊛opera.hu; map p.78. Large concert hall with magnificent 1950s interior fresh from a major

restoration, that presents opera and ballet on its vast stage. Box office daily 10am–8pm, or until first interval of evening performances.

★**Music Academy (Zeneakadémia)** VI, Liszt Ferenc tér 8 ☎1 321 0690, ⊛zeneakademia.hu; map p.60. The Liszt Music Academy – founded by Ferenc Liszt in 1875 – has recently undergone a total refurbishment, restoring the original look of the interior and vastly improving the acoustics, air-conditioning and seats (which no longer creak). The magnificent gold-covered Nagyterem (Great Hall) and the smaller Sir Georg Solti Chamber Hall have regular concerts of a very high standard. Box office daily 10am–8pm, or until first interval of evening performances.

Óbuda Music Society (Óbudai Társaskör) III, Kiskorona utca 7 ☎1 250 0288, ⊛obudaitarsaskor .hu; map p.116. Small concert hall in the shadow of the housing estates south of the Árpád híd in Óbuda. The quality of performance is impressive, and big local ensembles such as the Liszt Chamber Orchestra, Budapest Strings and Auer String Quartet are based here. Also stages some jazz concerts, as well as outdoor concerts in the garden in summer. Box office daily 9am–7pm.

Old Music Academy (Régi Zeneakadémia) VI, Vörösmarty utca 35 ☎1 322 9804, ⊛lisztmuseum.hu; map p.60. Performances by young musicians every Sat morning at 11am, in the concert hall of the Liszt Memorial Museum (see p.64).

Opera House (Magyar Állami Operaház) VI, Andrássy út 22 ☎1 353 0170, ⊛opera.hu; map p.60.

Home to both the Hungarian State Opera and Hungarian National Ballet, this is one of the grandest venues in town, with its gilded frescoes and three-tonne chandeliers. The productions don't always live up to the setting, though the singers and orchestra can be scintillating. With tickets at 600–15,000Ft for most shows, and up to 25,000Ft for the best ones, you're almost guaranteed a good-value night out. The box office is inside the main doors or, if they are closed, round on the left-hand side of the building in Dalszinház utca. Box office daily 10am–8pm, or until first interval of evening performances.

Pesti Vigadó V, Vigadó tér 1 ☎ 1 328 3340, ⓦ vigado .hu; map p.40. Another fabulously decorated hall, dating from 1865, this is the oldest of the major concert venues: Liszt, Brahms and Debussy all played here. It is open again after a long and costly restoration, and no expense will be spared to make sure big names perform here again. Box office daily 10am–6.30pm.

POP, ROCK AND JAZZ

Budapest is one of the main stops in Central/Eastern Europe for touring international **bands**, while every Hungarian band worth its amplifiers will play the capital. A number of bars (see pp.175–181) host live music, including *Akvárium, Auróra* and *Kisüzem*, and performances are also held at the cultural centres (see p.183).

A38 XI, Pázmány Péter sétány ☎ 1 464 3940, ⓦ a38.hu; map p.78. Housed on a boat that was reputedly given to Hungary in return for writing off the Ukrainian debt and is moored on the Buda side of the river, just below Petőfi híd. One of the best venues in Budapest, it has a separate admission charge for each of its three decks, where top international and Hungarian performers play rock, folk, world music and jazz – it is strong on experimental free jazz.

★**Budapest Jazz Club** XIII, Hollán Ernő utca 13 ☎ 1 798 7289, ⓦ bjc.hu; map p.50. The high quality of acts ensures a terrific atmosphere at Budapest's premier jazz club. There are regular themed jazz evenings and free late-night jam sessions on Fri and Sat. Mon–Thurs 10pm–midnight, Fri & Sat 10am–2am, Sun times vary.

Budapest Park IX, Soroksári út 60 ☎ 1 434 7800, ⓦ budapestpark.hu; map p.78. The largest outdoor venue in the city, just beyond the Palace of Arts in southern Pest, attracting big Hungarian and international acts. April–Sept. Booking office Mon–Sat 1–8pm, or until end of concerts.

Gödör Klub VII, Central Passage, Király utca 8 ☎ 0620 201 3868, ⓦ godorklub.hu; map p.40. Alternative cultural centre that plays host to jazz, folk, Hungarian pop and Roma acts. Mon–Wed 6pm–2am, Thurs–Sat 6pm–4am, generally closed Sun.

IF Kávézó IX, Ráday utca 19 ☎ 1 299 0694, ⓦ ifkavezo .hu; map p.78. *IF* offers a particularly exciting programme of jazz, and you can count on something happening most nights of the week. Daily 11am–11.45pm.

Jedermann IX, Ráday utca 58 ☎ 0630 406 3617, ⓦ jedermann.hu; map p.78. Popular venue where the jazz is often avant-garde. Concerts on Fri, Sat and some other days, including monthly appearances by the masterful Mihály Dresch, all under the watchful eye of Hans, the saxophonist who runs the place. No credit cards. Daily 8am–1am.

★**Kobuci** III, Fő tér 1, Óbuda ☎ 0670 205 7282, ⓦ kobuci.hu; map p.116. Located in the large yard of the Zichy kastély that dominates one side of the square, this popular summer venue hosts folk, rock, blues and world music concerts, as well as films, but it is also a good place to come for a drink. It's a good atmosphere, the drinks are not too pricey – and then there's the *kobuci*: a fancy sausage sandwich. April–Sept: Mon–Fri 4pm–4am, Sat & Sun 11am–4am.

★**Opus Jazz Club** V, Mátyás utca 8 ☎ 1 216 7894, ⓦ opusjazzclub.hu; map p.78. Part of the new arts venue, the Budapest Music Center, the *Opus* is a brilliant venue with two levels: the lower level, for performers and connoisseurs, and the upstairs section, where you can chat quietly. The acoustics are highly praised, and the food isn't pricey. Concerts Wed–Sat from 9pm. Booking office Mon 11am–10pm, Tues–Fri 11am–midnight, Sat 6pm–midnight.

16

BUDAPEST JAZZ

When it comes to **jazz** (or *dzsessz*, as it is sometimes becomes in Hungarian), don't be fooled by the small number of regular venues in Budapest. The country boasts some brilliant jazz musicians, such as the pianist Béla Szakcsi Lakatos, the sax player Tamás Ladányi and the extraordinary young singer Cintia Horváth, who brings a freshness to the classics. It is worth looking out for the **Harmonia Jazz Workshop** (**Harmonia Jazz Műhely**), which holds regular sessions on Fridays at the **Budapest Jazz Club** (see above). There are also occasional jazz concerts in the *kert* bars.

FOLK MUSIC AND DANCE

Hungarian **folk music** and dancing underwent a revival in the 1970s, drawing inspiration from Hungarian communities in Transylvania, regarded as pure wellsprings of Magyar culture. The **táncház** movement (see p.221) still exists today, and there are regular sessions at the venues below, as well as in *Kobuci* (see p.185) and at ruin bars such as *Rács Kert* and *Szimplakert* (see p.178); see ⓦtanchaz.hu for more. There is also the big *táncház* gathering in the Budapest Spring Festival (see p.30). The *táncház* idea has also been extended to other cultures – you'll see adverts for Greek (*görög*), Slav, Irish and other dance houses. Apart from the places detailed below, folk music features at arts venues and cultural centres (see p.183), including the Music Academy and the Palace of Arts, and in pop and rock venues (see p.185).

Aranytíz Cultural Centre V, Arany János utca 10 ☎1 354 3400, ⓦaranytiz.hu; map p.50. The dancefloor is packed on Saturday nights from late September through to early June, with dance teaching from 7pm; the children's session begins at 5pm. As the evening rolls on, a jamming session often develops with other bands joining in. The cultural centre's programme includes Hungarian and international theatre performances and jazz concerts, too.

★**Fonó Music Hall (Fonó Budai Zeneház)** XI, Sztregova utca 3 ☎1 206 5300, ⓦfono.hu; four stops south of Móricz Zsigmond körtér on tram #18 or #47; map p.109. The best place in the city to catch regular folk music, this is a lively international folk and world music venue. There's a dance house every Wed evening. Box office opens 1hr before performances.

Hungarian Heritage House (Hagyományok Háza) I, Corvin tér 8 ☎1 225 6049, ⓦwww.heritagehouse.hu; map p.90. Just down the road from Batthyány tér, with folk dance on the big stage, performed by the state ensemble.

CINEMA

Hollywood blockbusters dominate Budapest's mainstream **cinemas**, though the city has a small chain of art-house cinemas that specialize in the latest releases and obscure European films – *angol* indicates a British film, *lengyel* Polish, *német* German, *olasz* Italian, and *orosz* Russian. In the summer, the best places to watch films **outdoors** are the Várkert Bazár (see p.112), Budapest Park (see p.185) or bars such as *Fellini Római Kultúrbisztró* (see p.181) and *Corvintető* (see p.179).

Cirko-gejzir V, Balassi Bálint utca 15–17 ☎1 269 1915, ⓦcirkofilm.hu; map p.50. One of the best alternative cinemas, with a regular selection of movies from around the globe. They have English subtitles for some Hungarian films. Cheaper tickets on Mon and Tues.

HUNGARY ON FILM

Hungarians have an impressive record in film, and many of the Hollywood greats were **Hungarian émigrés**: Michael Curtiz, Sir Alex Korda, George Cukor, and actors Béla Lugosi, Tony Curtis and Leslie Howard to name but a few. In the Communist years Hungarian film continued to make waves, with Miklós Jancsó, Károly Makk, István Szabó, Márta Mészáros and others directing films that managed to say much about the oppressive regime in spite of its restrictions. Now the main constraint on film-makers is chronic underfunding, but this has never been too great an obstacle to Magyar creativity.

Two Hungarian films to win Oscars in recent years are *Son of Saul*, the debut feature film by László Nemes, which won many awards for its searing portrayal of the Holocaust; and *Sing* (*Mindenki*), a short film by Kristóf Deák about a new girl who joins a winning school choir. Alongside established names such as Béla Tarr, the master of the slow, stark and very long take; and Ildikó Enyedi, who has just made a comeback with *On Body and Soul*, younger directors who have attracted international recognition include Kornél Mundruczó, with his *White God* (*Fehér Isten*), Reisz Gábor (*For Some Inexplicable Reason*) and Szabolcs Hajdú. Two young female directors to look out for are Virág Zomborácz and Orsi Nagypál.

Budapest is a popular **location** both for its looks and its cheapness. Harrison Ford was holed up in the former TV building on Szabadság tér when Ryan Gosling found him in the *Bladerunner* sequel, and *Spy* was all filmed in Budapest and around – Lake Balaton served as the sea. The city has also served as Buenos Aires in *Evita*, as Berlin in *The Boy in the Striped Pyjamas*, as Moscow in *A Good Day to Die Hard* and as Paris in the *Maigret* TV series, where the view towards the Basilica down Lázár utca behind the Opera House acts as the view of the Sacré-Coeur. But Budapest also serves as itself: the American documentary *Divan* by Pearl Gluck captures some of the characters and atmosphere of the old Jewish quarter in its interviews.

16

Corvin Budapest Film Palace (Corvin Filmpalota) VIII, Corvin köz 1 ☎1 224 5650, ⓦcorvin.hu; map p.78. This glitzy multiplex near the Corvin negyed metro is a good place to catch the latest foreign releases, and it also hosts the Hungarian Film Festival. Cheaper tickets on Wed.

Puskin V, Kossuth Lajos utca 18 ☎1 224 5650, ⓦartmozi.hu; map p.40. Complex of three cinemas in the centre of town, with a large café attached. The coffered ceiling of the turn-of-the-century main screen is magnificent. Cheaper tickets on Mon.

★Toldi V, Bajcsy-Zsilinszky út 36–38 ☎1 224 5650, ⓦartmozi.hu; map p.50. Next door to Arany János utca

metro station, the two-screen Toldi is one of the more dynamic alternative cinemas in town. Decent bar too. Cheaper tickets on Thurs.

Uránia National Film Theatre (Uránia Nemzeti Filmszínház) VIII, Rákóczi út 21 ☎1 486 3400, ⓦurania-nf.hu; map p.78. With its magnificent Venetian-Moorish decorations, this might seem a strange choice of location for Budapest's main showcase of Hungarian films. But it was in this cinema, built in the 1890s as a dance hall, that the first Hungarian feature film was shot in 1901. While its programme is international, it places special emphasis on local films, and is the principal venue for the annual Titanic film festival. Cheaper tickets on Mon.

THEATRE AND CONTEMPORARY DANCE

Hungarians show great sophistication when it comes to building theatres: take the splendid mass of the **Vígszínház** up the road from Nyugati Station, or the **New Theatre** near the Opera House. The strange design of the **National Theatre** attracted heavy criticism when it opened in 2000, though it may yet be lauded; productions here tend to be either uninspiring and old-fashioned, however, while anything avant-garde serves to alienate its core conservative audience. The provincial Hungarian companies are often more exciting: the Szombathely Theatre, led by Tamás Jordán, continues to arouse interest. **Alternative theatre** is well worth seeking out, however – particularly for visitors, as music and dance play a greater part than language here. One Hungarian group that has received considerable acclaim abroad is Krétakör, a theatre company led by the visionary Árpád Schilling that has transformed itself into a community forum. Scallabouche have been winning plaudits for their English-language performances for some years – catch them at the Jurányi or the Atrium. Other names to look out for are Pál Göttinger, László Hudi, Pál Frenák, Béla Pintér, Viktor Bodó and the Hoppart company. Two exciting names in **dance** are Réka Szabó, who runs the Tünet (Symptom) group, and Krisztián Gergye. And finally, Hungary has a strong puppet tradition and the shows in the two **puppet theatres** will appeal to adults and children alike. The **Trafó** and **Jurányi** (p.183) also host dance and theatre.

Átrium II, Margít körút 55 ☎1 317 9338, ⓦatriumfilmszinhaz.hu; map p.90. Fabulous 1930s cinema that is now a venue for theatre – including some performances in English – and dance. The café in the foyer is a great place to people-watch. Box office daily 10am–8pm.

Budapest Puppet Theatre (Budapest Bábszínház) VI, Andrássy út 69 ☎1 342 2702, ⓦbudapest -babszinhaz.hu; map p.60. The puppet theatre has a lot of shows for adults – masked grotesqueries or renditions of Bartók's *The Wooden Prince* and *The Miraculous Mandarin* and Mozart's *Magic Flute*. Box office daily 9am–4pm.

Katona József Theatre V, Petőfi Sándor utca 6 ☎1 266 5200, ⓦkatonajozsefszinhaz.hu; map p.40. The best of the established theatres, with a talented company and good productions. Box office Mon–Fri 11am–7pm, Sat & Sun 4–7pm, open till 9pm when shows are running.

Kolibri Pince VI, Andrássy út 77 ☎1 353 4633, ⓦkolibriszinhaz.hu; map p.60. Puppet shows and live performances for adults as well as children at two venues (see p.205 for the other two); this is the best one for grown-up performances. Closed early June–Aug.

MU Színház XI, Kőrösy József utca 17 ☎1 209 4014, ⓦmu .hu; map p.109. Alternative theatre venue that is particularly strong on dance, and also hosts the odd jazz concert.

National Theatre (Nemzeti Színház) IX, Bajor Gizi park 1 ☎1 476 6868, ⓦnemzetiszinhaz.hu; map p.78. The proud flagship of Hungarian theatre. Some shows are in English, put on by local troupes. Box office Mon–Fri 10am–6pm, Sat & Sun 2–6pm.

Szkéné Színház XI, Műegyetem rakpart 3 ☎1 463 3839x, ⓦszkene.hu; map p.109. A small theatre housed in the main building of the Technical University near the *Gellért Hotel*, this has been an alternative venue for many years, dating back to the bad old days of Communism. Box office opens 1hr before performances.

16

Shopping

The capital's streets have been transformed in recent years by the mushrooming of international chain stores and the opening of modern shopping malls. However, there are numerous small retailers that preserve local crafts and traditions, as well as backstreet shops recently colonized by young fashion designers. Budapest also has a set of distinguished market halls (*vásárcsarnok*) dating from the late nineteenth century, where the displays of cured meats and paprika are a fine introduction to the national cuisine. You can also spend a happy afternoon stocking up on Tokaj and Bull's Blood at the city's growing number of wine sellers. The city's cultural strengths are also reflected in its many bookshops and music shops.

17

One feature of old Budapest that has survived is its **artisan shops**: small jewellery workshops such as Wladis, the quirky brush shop in Dob utca and the old craftsmen and workshops in the backstreets inside the Nagykörút. Look out also for the growing number of **young designers** whose work is deservedly attracting attention; there are homegrown designer shops on Király utca in the Seventh District, and names of note include Je Suis Belle, Daige and Tomcsanyi, whose clothes range from the trendy to the avant-garde and the eccentric. One event worth catching is the Wamp design market (ⓦwamp.hu); taking place every month on Erzsébet tér, it showcases the work of emerging Hungarian designers, with some one hundred vendors selling everything from clothes and jewellery to home decor.

It has taken a while, but at last there is a far wider choice of **souvenirs** to take home from Budapest that extends beyond the folk tat sold in the Vár. You can find some chic Hungarian accessories and clothes in Rododendron, Printa or Insitu; and the city's market halls, as well as small shops such as Hecserli and Szalamibolt, offer excellent local produce – jams, sausages, honey and the like. Or head for one of the many alternative markets sprouting up, such as the weekly organic Bio-piac, the farmers' market in *Szimplakert* or the vegan and craft market *Anker't*.

ESSENTIALS

Shopping areas The biggest concentration of glamorous and expensive shops, as well as popular Western stores (and plenty of tourist tat), lies south of Vörösmarty tér in central Pest, particularly around pedestrianized Váci utca. The main streets radiating out from the centre – Bajcsy-Zsilinszky út, Andrássy út and Rákóczi út – are other major shopping focuses, as are the Nagykörút (especially between Margít híd and Blaha Lujza tér) and the Kiskörút. The smaller streets in between hold the more interesting shops – such as in the old Jewish quarter between Andrássy and Rákóczi út. Shops in the Vár are almost exclusively given over to providing foreign tourists with folksy souvenirs such as embroidered tablecloths, hussar pots and fancy bottles of Tokaj wine.

Opening times Most shops are open Monday to Friday between 10am and 6pm, and Saturday until 2pm or even 4pm, with food stores generally operating from 8am to 6 or 7pm. Some city-centre shops have extended hours on Saturdays, while the malls are open roughly 10am to 8pm Mon to Sat, but close around 6pm on Sunday. However, quite a few places are closed at weekends, so it is worth checking beforehand. The sale of tobacco is now restricted to "national tobacco shops" (*nemzeti dohánybolt*), which have frosted glass windows that make them look like pornography outlets. "Azonnal jövök" or "Rögtön jövök" signs on shop doors both mean "back shortly".

MARKETS

Anker't VI, Paulay Ede utca 33 ☎0630 360 3389, ⓦbit.ly/ankert; map p.60. Monthly vegan and craft market in the popular ruin bar near the Opera House, with a range of stalls selling jams, juices, pottery, soaps, jewellery and flowers. They also have small producer markets once or twice a month. Second Sun of the month 10am–6pm.

Belvárosi (Hold utca) V, Hold utca 13 ⓦbit.ly /belvarosi; map p.50. Right behind the US embassy, this fine nineteenth-century market hall still has some stalls selling produce, but many have been turned into trendy mini-restaurants such as *Stand 25* (see p.162), where street food meets fine dining. Mon 6.30am–5pm, Tues–Fri 6.30am–6pm, Sat 6.30am–4pm.

★**Bio-piac** XII, Csörsz utca 18 ⓦbit.ly/biopiac; map p.90. Organic market spreading around the Mom Cultural Centre (Mom Művelődési Központ), up the road from the Mom Park Mall. Great range of produce, especially in summer – the peaches, tomatoes and peppers are so much

better than supermarket fare. There is also a playground for children. Sat 6.30am–1pm.

Fény utca II, Lövőház utca 12 ⓦfenyutcaipiac.hu; map p.90. Popular market that has survived a transfer to a modern setting. Fruit and veg stalls on the street-level floor, and meat and cheese counters on the top floor, alongside one of the best *lángos* kiosks in town – a popular stand-up snack of fried dough eaten with garlic, sour cream, cheese or all three together. The nearby café serves excellent coffee Mon–Fri 6am–6pm, Sat 6am–2pm.

Great Market Hall (Nagycsarnok) IX, Vámház körút 2 ⓦbit.ly/greatmarkethall; map p.78. By the Szabadság híd at the bottom end of Váci utca, this is the largest and finest market hall of them all, as well as being the most expensive. Fruit, veg, meat and cheese counters galore, as well as bakers, confectioners and endless paprika stalls, though it's all rather hammered up for the tourists. Mon 6am–5pm, Tues–Fri 6am–6pm, Sat 6am–3pm.

17

★Hunyadi tér Market Hall (Vásárcsarnok) VI, Hunyadi tér 4 ⓦbit.ly/hunyadite; map p.60. The most atmospheric and the smallest of the old market halls, in a delightful refurbished square – but the *csarnok* itself has survived gentrification so far. Its stalls are full of colourful produce and spill out into the square in front. Good dairy and bread stalls inside. Mon 7am–5pm, Tues–Fri 7am–6pm, Sat 7am–2pm.

Lehel csarnok XIII, Lehel tér; map p.50. Large, popular market housed in an ugly, if wacky, building designed by the former dissident László Rajk. Its ship-like exterior has earned the nickname of the Barge, but inside it's a lively place with lots of small stalls selling veg, honey and sausages, with bars and *büfés* on the top floor. The only one of the main markets to open on Sundays. Mon–Fri 6am–6pm, Sat 6am–2pm, Sun 6am–1pm.

★Rákóczi tér Market Hall (Vásárcsarnok) VI, Rákóczi tér 7 ⓦbit.ly/rakocziter; map p.78. Another magnificent renovated old structure, which has the feel of a market for locals and still attracts a few small producers – look out for the fine cheese stall. Fri and Sat are the best days. Mon 6am–4pm, Tues–Fri 6am–6pm, Sat 6am–1pm.

Szimplakert VII, Kazinczy utca 14 ⓦszimpla.hu; map p.60. The weekly farmers' market in the ruin bar courtyard has a particularly villagey feel, with the stallholders and shoppers exchanging banter. You can get sausages, cakes, bread, honey, jams, cheeses – with cheese making and other workshops – and maybe a hen or two. But it is still the *Szimpla*, so there is music too. Sun 9am–2pm.

FLEA MARKETS

Ecseri market (Használtcikk piac) XIX, Nagykőrösi út 156 ☎1 348 3200; bus #84E from the Határ út metro stop on the blue line, or bus #55 from Boráros tér by Petőfi híd; map p.5. On the southeast edge of the city, this has become a well-known spot for tourists – and for ripping them off (you'll need to bargain hard). Stalls sell everything from bike parts and jackboots to peasant clothing and hand-carved pipes, with a few genuine antiques among the tat. The food on offer is fairly basic. Mon–Fri 8am–4pm, Sat 6am–3pm, Sun 9am–1pm.

Gardrób Second Hand and Vintage Clothing VII, Király utca 8 ⓦgardrobkozossegivasar.hu; map p.40. The idea behind this "community market" in the Central Passage outside the *Gödör Klub* is that anyone can take a table and sell off their old clothes, bags and accessories. Join the locals and spot those gems. Sat 11am–4pm.

MALLS

Mammut II, Lövőház utca 2–6 ☎1 345 8020, ⓦmammut.hu; map p.90. Close to Széll Kálmán tér, and next to Fény utca market, this is actually two malls linked by a pedestrianized bridge. Amid the 330 shops, there's a cinema, fitness centre, squash courts, children's play area and nappy-changing room. Mon–Sat 10am–9pm, Sun 10am–6pm.

Mom Park XII, Alkotás utca 53 ☎1 487 5500, ⓦmompark.hu; tram #61; map p.90. One of the more relaxed Buda malls, up the road from Déli Station and with more than seventy shops, a cinema, playhouse and fitness centre. Mon–Sat 10am–8pm, Sun 10am–6pm.

WestEnd Center VI, Váci út 1–3, next to Nyugati Station) ☎1 238 7777, ⓦwestend.hu; map p.50. Past the grand indoor waterfall cascading down at the southern entrance, you'll find the city's busiest mall, with over 400 shops (including lots of familiar brand-name stores), cinema and a huge food court. Mon–Sat 10am–9pm, Sun 10am–6pm.

ANTIQUES

Running south off Szent István körút, near the Pest end of the Margít híd, **Falk Miksa utca** is Budapest's "Street of Antiques", with the city's biggest collection of **antique stores** and galleries. Three or four times a year the street holds an evening festival of music, entertainment and, of course, antiques. Most specialists should be able to advise on what you can export from the country and how to go about it. Several shops organize **auctions**; the best months for these are April, May, Sept and Dec – check the free hotel magazine *Where Budapest* for dates. Flea markets (see above) are another good source of antiques, though you should be wary about parting with large sums of money, as stallholders can charge hugely inflated prices.

BÁV V, Bécsi utca 1–3 ☎1 429 2066, ⓦbav.hu; map p.40. The most central of numerous BÁV outlets in the city, this store specializes in jewellery. BÁV is primarily an auction house, and it holds regular auctions here. Mon–Fri 10am–7pm, Sat 10am–2pm.

Budapest Poster Gallery VI, Paulay Ede utca 20 ☎0630 855 1914, ⓦbudapestposter.com; map p.60. Superb stock of original vintage posters from between 1885 and 1990, with some fine Communist-era propaganda posters, such as one for the 1955 Tractor Day;

GREAT MARKET HALL (P.189) >

17

there are some choice film and commercial ones too. Prices from 10,000Ft. Open by appointment only.

Judaica VII, Wesselényi utca 13 ☎1 784 1047, Ⓦjudaica.hu; map p.60. Down the road behind the Dohány utca synagogue, and offering Jewish books, pictures and artefacts. It also organizes

occasional auctions. Mon–Thurs 10am–6pm, Fri 10am–3pm.

Sóos Foto VII, Wesselényi utca 10 ☎1 460 0036, Ⓦsoosfoto.hu; map p.60. An excellent place to pick up some fine junk and secondhand photographic goods. Mon–Fri 9am–5pm, Sat 10am–1pm.

ART AND PHOTOGRAPHY

★**Deák Erika Galéria** VI, Mozsár utca 1 ☎1 201 3740, Ⓦdeakgaleria.hu; map p.60. Contemporary Hungarian art gallery off Andrássy út. Wed–Fri noon–6pm, Sat 11am–4pm.

Knoll VI, Liszt Ferenc tér 10 ☎1 267 3842, Ⓦknoll galeria.hu; map p.60. Run by the Viennese gallery owner Hans Knoll, this was the first private gallery in the city when it opened in 1989. Since then, it has built up a strong reputation, with shows by Hungarian and foreign contemporary artists. Tues–Fri 2–6.30pm, Sat 11am–2pm.

★**Mai Manó Galéria** VI, Nagymező utca 20 ☎1 473 2669, Ⓦmaimano.hu; map p.60. Located on the first floor within the Hungarian House of Photography, this delightful little gallery shop stocks contemporary and old Hungarian photographs, cards and books. Mon–Fri 2–7pm, Sat & Sun 11am–7pm.

Várfok Galéria I, Várfok utca 11 ☎0630 562 2772, Ⓦvarfok-galeria.hu; map p.90. The best known of the three small galleries just off Széll Kálmán tér, this was founded in 1990 and displays work by the younger generation of Hungarian avant-garde artists. Tues–Sat 11am–6pm.

BOOKS AND MAPS

Hungarians are a literary bunch and Book Week, held in the capital each June, is a long-awaited event (see p.30). If it's old books and prints you want, one of the best places to head for is Múzeum körút, where there are numerous **secondhand bookshops** (*antikvárium*) clustered opposite the Hungarian National Museum. Larger stores often have a café attached and sell a range of English-language titles.

★**Bestsellers** V, Október 6 utca 11 ☎1 312 1295, Ⓦbestsellers.hu; map p.50. Budapest's best English-language bookshop has been serving the city for more than 25 years. It has thousands of titles: English and Hungarian literature, travel and reference, academia and children's books, as well as newspapers and magazines. Staff are friendly and can order books in. Mon–Fri 9am–6.30pm, Sat 11am–6pm, Sun noon–6pm.

Fókusz Könyváruház V Rákóczi út 14 ☎1 411 2400, Ⓦbit.ly/fokuszbooks; map p.60. One of three big bookshops in a row (Libri at no.12 also has a good range of English books), Fókusz has English books as well as records and DVDs upstairs. The *Magvető* café (see p.172) is through the passageway at the back. Mon–Fri 9.30am–8pm, Sat 10am–6pm.

★**Fuga** V, Petőfi Sándor utca 5 ☎1 266 2395, Ⓦfuga .org.hu; map p.40. The best place for books on the buildings of Budapest – hardly surprisingly, since this is the bookshop of the Budapest Centre for Architecture – with handy guides to buildings as well as serious architecture studies. It is a pleasant space to sit and browse, and you can get tea, coffee and cakes to keep you going. The centre also hosts exhibitions and concerts. Daily 10am–9pm.

★**Írók Boltja** VI, Andrássy út 45 ☎1 322 1645, Ⓦirokboltja.hu; map p.60. On the premises of the prewar *Japán* coffee house, the beautiful "Writers'

Bookshop" has a wide range of Hungarian fiction in translation in the gallery upstairs, and a good selection of photography and art books and Hungarian DVDs in the main part of the shop. You can drink coffee and read at the tables in the front or in the gallery. Mon–Fri 10am–7pm, Sat 11am–7pm; Sat 11am–3pm in July & Aug.

Központi Antikvárium V, Múzeum körút 13–15 ☎1 317 3514, Ⓦkozpontiantikvarium.hu; map p.40. Large secondhand bookshop with some antiquarian books and prints, plus maps. Also hosts auctions. Mon–Fri 10am–6pm, Sat 10am–2pm.

★**Massolit Books** VII, Nagy Diófa utca 30 ☎1 788 5292, Ⓦbit.ly/Massolit; map p.60. Peaceful secondhand bookshop/café where you can relax over your favoured tome. The café, which has eco friendly coffee and tea and good brownies, opens out onto a courtyard garden at the back. Strong on – but not restricted to – foreign-language literature and Jewish studies. Hosts exhibitions and readings. Mon–Fri 8.15am–7.30pm, Sat & Sun 10am–7.30pm.

Térképkirály VI, Ó utca 3 ☎1 221 9707, Ⓦmapking .hu; map p.60. The very kind gentleman can guide you through his range of maps and guidebooks, just across the road from Arany János utca metro station. There is another map shop round the corner at Bajcsy-Zsilinszy út 37, Földgömb-Térkép, if you can't find what you want here. Mon–Fri 10am–6.30pm.

17

CLOTHES AND SHOES

Emilia Anda V, Galamb utca 4 ☎ 0630 933 9746, ⓦ andaemi.com; map p.40. One of the most highly regarded Hungarian couturiers, Anda designs classy day and evening wear for women, and a range of jewellery including chunky rings and beautiful pendants. Mon–Fri 11am–6pm, Sat 11am–2pm.

Garden Studio VI, Paulay Ede utca 18 ☎ 0630 848 6163, ⓦ bit.ly/thegardenstudio; map p.60. The old Jewish quarter has more than just places to party: it also has some excellent fashion outlets, such as the Garden Studio, where you can find clothes by Tomcsanyi, scarves by VYF and cool jewellery by The Mama Kin. Mon–Sat 10am–8pm.

Hababa Design Store V, Feher Hajó utca 8-10 ☎ 0620 391 3218, ⓦ hababa.hu; map p.40. You can find the work of a number of leading Hungarian names in the Hababa Design Store, such as clothes by the creative Je Suis Belle or the Roma-inspired Romani. Daily 10am–9pm.

Ludovika VII, Rumbach Sebestyén utca 15 ⓦ bit.ly /Ludovika; map p.40. Vintage and modern women's clothes and bags by a variety of Hungarian designers, in a friendly setting on the edge of the VII district. Mon–Fri noon–8pm, Sat noon–6pm.

Manier VI, Dalszínház utca 10 ☎ 1 483 1140, ⓦ manier .hu; map p.60. Up on the first floor down the side of the Opera House, with zany, appealing clothes by Anikó Németh; the designs have calmed down from the Baroque early days but they retain plenty of inventiveness. Mon–Fri 10am–6pm.

Nanushka V, Bécsi utca 1–3 ☎ 0670 394 1954, ⓦ nanushka.hu; map p.40. The Hungarian-born designer Sandra Sandor stands up well against the big international names round the corner on "Fashion Street". Mon–Sat 10am–8pm, Sun noon–6pm.

Retrock VI, Anker köz 2 ☎ 0630 472 3636, ⓦ retrock .com; map p.40. An extensive collection of clothes and jewellery, both vintage and new, as well as by young Hungarian designers, just off Deák tér. Mon–Sat 11am–9pm.

Tisza Shoes VII, Károly körút 1 ☎ 1 266 3055; map p.60. This Hungarian brand of trainers is an unlikely survivor of the Communist era, and the shop at the Astoria junction, Tisza Cipő, has won an international reputation for the hipness of the shoes. Mon–Fri 10am–7pm, Sat 10am–4pm.

Valéria Fazekas V, Váci utca 50 ☎ 1 337 5320, ⓦ valeriafazekas.com; map p.40. One of the more creative places on the lower part of Váci utca, this small shop produces delightful hats, some wacky and some very wearable, as well as clothes – the silk jackets look great. Mon–Fri 10am–6pm, Sat 10am–4pm.

Vass V, Haris köz 2 ☎ 1 318 2375, ⓦ vass-shoes.com; map p.40. The most established of several fine shoemakers along this street, this traditional outfit, just behind Ferenciek tere, has been producing handmade shoes ready-to-wear and to order since 1978. Mon–Fri 10am–6pm, Sat 10am–4pm.

JEWELLERY AND SOUVENIRS

Brush Shop VII, Dob utca 3; map p.60. A wonderful little place: every kind of brush you can think of in this very traditional artisan's shop. Mon–Fri 10am–6pm.

Fian I, Fortuna utca 18 ☎ 1 224 0454, ⓦ fian.hu; map p.93. Fian is one of the new-wave Hungarian design shops that specialize in Budapest-inspired souvenirs, perfect if you want to avoid the folksy tat. It has two outlets in the Castle District, with works by at least eighty local designers – the nearby branch at Úri utca 26–28 is more tourist-oriented, with designs on mugs, bags and clothes. Daily 10am–6pm.

Herend VI, Andrássy út 16 ☎ 1 374 0006; ⓦ herend .com; map p.60. One of Hungary's best-known exports, very fancy – some would say twee – and expensive porcelain, from the Herend factory in western Hungary, as collected by the likes of Queen Victoria. Mon–Fri 10am–6pm, Sat 10am–2pm.

★ **Holló Folk Art Gallery** V, Vitkovics Mihály utca 10 ☎ 1 317 8103; map p.40. This beautiful early nineteenth-century shop near the Astoria is a very pleasant place in which to browse wares such as intricately iced gingerbread figures, as well as wooden furniture, boxes, eggs and

candlesticks, all hand-painted with bird, tulip and heart folk motifs. Ring bell to enter. Mon–Fri 10am–1pm & 1.30–6pm, Sat 10am–2pm; in Aug only open Tues, call ahead for appointments on other days.

Insitu V, Múzeum körút 67 ☎ 1 266 3080, ⓦ insitu.hu; map p.40. In the courtyard of the beautiful Unger Ház, Insitu is a design shop full of clever ideas, and has some souvenirs with a difference, such as T-shirts bearing the Hungarian alphabet. Mon–Fri 10am–7pm, Sat 10am–3pm.

Magma V, Petőfi Sándor utca 11 ☎ 1 253 0277 & I, Úri utca 26–28 ☎ 0630 960 4672; ⓦ magma.hu; maps p.40 & p.93. Wide range of stock by local designers, including funky bags and cushion covers decorated with Hungarian rare breeds – puli dogs and longhorned cattle – and with Budapest-related designs; the outlet in the Castle District is more souvenir-oriented. Mon–Fri 10am–7pm, Sat 10am–3pm.

Ómama Bizsúja V, Szent István körút 1 ☎ 1 312 6812, ⓦ omamaantik.hu; map p.50. A tiny treasure-trove of a shop crammed full of jewellery; it's at the Pest end of the Margít híd, on the left as you walk in from the street. In

17

among the more glitzy costume jewellery are some fine Deco-style pieces and good-quality paste. They have a larger shop with more clothes at the Buda end of the bridge at XII, Frankel Leó 7. Mon–Fri 10am–6pm, plus every other Sat 10am–1pm.

★**Printa** VII, Rumbach Sebestyén utca 10 ☎0630 292 0329, ⊚printa.hu; map p.40. Printa ticks a lot of the right boxes: it is eco-friendly, using a lot of recycled material, its appealing designs both on clothes and paper have a strong Budapest theme, it has great coffee and the staff are friendly. It also runs silkscreen printing courses. Mon–Sat 11am–7pm.

MUSIC AND FILM

Kodály Zoltán Zeneműbolt V, Múzeum körút 21 ☎1 317 3347, ⊚bit.ly/kodalyzoltan; map p.40. Scores of CDs and secondhand Hungarian classical records, opposite the Múzeum Cukrászda. Good jazz and folk section, and they sell sheet music too. Mon–Fri 10am–6pm, Sat 10am–2pm.

MesterPorta I, Corvin tér 7 ☎1 486 1189; map p.90. The outlet for Etnofon Records, one of the most active publishers of Hungarian and other folk music, with a great range of CDs, instruments and sheet music. The other half of the shop is given over to folk crafts to fill your case with pots and embroideries. You'll find it a tram stop down from Batthyány tér. Tues–Sat 10am–6pm.

TOYS

Fabatka V, Haris köz 3 ☎0620 934 9120, ⊚bit.ly/fabatka; map p.40. Toys, puzzles and wooden implements, delightfully shaped boards, bowls and more – all made of wood in this miniscule shop, presided over by a wizened old bloke. Daily 10am–7pm.

★**Fakopáncs** VIII, Baross utca 46 ☎1 337 0992, ⊚fakopancs.hu; map p.78. A massive array of wooden puzzles, toys and models, and sweet little cotton finger puppets, in the wonderful "Woodpecker" shop, near the junction of Baross utca and the Nagykörút. It has smaller outlets at József körút 50 and Erzsébet körút 23. All open Mon–Fri 10am–6pm, Sat 9am–1pm.

FOOD, WINE AND PÁLINKA

Bio ABC V, Múzeum körút 19, ⊚bioabc.hu; map p.40. Stacks of great organic products in this large store opposite the National Museum: natural oils, organic fruits, juices and teas, pastas, pulses and herbal medicines. Mon–Fri 10am–7pm, Sat 10am–2pm.

★**Bortársaság** V, Vécsey utca 5 ☎1 269 3286, ⊚bortarsasag.hu; map p.50. The largest branch of what's become the major distributor of Hungary's leading producers, with excellent wines and knowledgeable staff. There are three more outlets in the centre: Batthyány utca 59 (up the hill from Széll Kálmán

★**Rododendron** V, Semmelweis utca 19 ☎0670 419 5329, ⊚rododendronart.com; map p.40. Books, toys and accessories by thirty local artisans, such as a delightful design on T-shirts and bag with a pyramid of Hungarian rare breeds. Mon–Fri 10am–7pm, Sat 10am–5pm, Sun 11am–3pm.

Wladis Galéria V, Falk Miksa utca 13 ☎1 354 0834, ⊚wladisgaleria.hu; map p.50. Founded by a lecturer at the Applied Arts College, the workshop here produces very appealing chunky silver jewellery at a price: rings from 20,000Ft and earrings from 29,000Ft. Mon–Fri 10am–6pm, Sat 10am–2pm.

★**Rózsavölgyi Music** V, Szervita tér 5 ☎1 318 3500, ⊚bit.ly/Rozsavolgyi; map p.40. Long-established record shop near Vörösmarty tér, with a knowledgeable staff. Classical music on the ground floor, rock and folk downstairs. It has a concert ticket office at the back, and is good for sheet music as well. Mon–Sat 10am–10pm.

★**Wave** VI, Révay köz 1 ☎1 269 0754, ⊚wave.hu; map p.60. Cool, independent shop off the bottom of Bajcsy-Zsilinszky út, with wall-to-wall vinyl and racks of CDs; mainly indie-rock, but strong on underground, folk and Roma too. It also sells tickets to concerts. Mon–Fri 11am–7pm, Sat 11am–3pm.

★**Játékszerek anno** VI, Teréz körút 54 ☎1 302 6234, ⊚jatekanno.hu; map p.60. Gorgeous little shop with beautifully made reproductions of toys and games from the turn of the last century, including wooden tops, kaleidoscopes, and a spectacular wind-up duck on a bicycle. Mon–Fri 10am–6pm, Sat 9am–1pm.

Játék Udvar VII, Nagy Diófa utca 24 ☎1 215 6864; map p.60. The three small rooms of this toyshop are packed with models, books, puzzles, puppets, craft activities and games – mainly secondhand, but also some new. Mon–Fri 10am–6pm.

tér), Lánchíd utca 5 and Ráday utca 7. Mon–Fri 10am–8pm, Sat 10am–7pm.

★**Hecserli** V, Szerb utca 15 ☎0620 354 5676, ⊚hecserli.hu; map p.40. The perfect place to pick up presents, with a wide selection of Hungarian produce – sausages, oils (the pumpkin oil is spectacular), honey, jams and more. You can also have a bite to eat in their café. Mon–Fri 9.30am–8pm, Sat 9.30am–2.30pm.

Kóser Piac V, Dohány utca 36 ☎0670 632 2771, ⊚bit.ly/koserpiac; map p.60. Kosher grocery on the edge of the Jewish quarter, one of the few wholly kosher shops in the city selling both Hungarian and imported food and wines. Mon–Thurs 7am–7pm, Fri 7am–2.30pm, Sun 10am–4pm.

Magyar Pálinka Háza VIII, Rákóczi út 17 ☎0630 421 5463, ⓦmagyarpalinkahaza.hu; map p.58. A vast and dazzling range of flavours going far beyond the conventional pear and apricot *pálinkas* to include elderflower, quince, paprika and many more. Mon–Sat 9am–7pm.

Malatinszky V, József Attila utca 12 ☎0620 969 4170, ⓦmalatinszky.hu; map p.50. Tucked away just off the main street, this delightful small shop has a concentrated selection of excellent wines from Villány and Tokaj. Mon–Sat 10am–6pm.

★**Rózsavölgyi Chocolates** V, Királyi Pál utca 6 ☎0630 814 8929, ⓦrozsavolgyi.com; map p.40. Flavoured with plum *pálinka*, chestnut honey, smoked wood, lavender, the chocolates from this little shop just off Egyetem tér both look and taste fantastic. Owners Zsolt and Katalin have close contacts with the farmers they buy directly from in Venezuela and Madagascar. Mon–Fri 10.30am–1pm & 1.30–6.30pm, Sat noon–6pm.

★**Szalamibolt** IX, Ráday utca 24/A ☎1 337 1195, ⓦbit.ly/Szalamibolt; map p.78. A superb range of hams and sausages are crammed into this friendly little family-run shop. All the products are from small producers in the region, and you can find jams from Transylvania, spreads from the south, hams from the Mediterranean, craft beers and *pálinkas*. Mon–Fri 9am–7pm, Sat 10am–6pm, plus April–Oct Sun 10am–6pm.

Tasting Table VIII, Bródy Sándor utca 9 ☎0630 720 8197, ⓦtastingtablebudapest.com; map p.78. Stocked with wines from Hungarian small producers, and manned by knowledgeable staff, this is a great place to both try and learn about Hungarian wine. The evening tasting sessions offer eight kinds of wine (16,500Ft per head, 20,000 with plate of charcuterie and cheese), or they do a weekly dinner with wine (9900Ft per head). Daily noon–8pm.

Veritas VII, Dohány utca 58–62 ☎1 413 0002, ⓦborkereskedes.hu; map p.60. Friendly store close to Blaha Lujza tér, with an excellent range of wines, including a beautiful Baroque cabinet stocked with some vintage bottles of Tokaj. Mon–Fri 9am–8pm, Sat 10am–6pm.

ICE-SKATING IN THE VÁROSLIGET

Sports and activities

Hungarians are passionate about sport and the country possesses a far greater sporting pedigree than most people appreciate. The Olympics, above all, have been a source of outstanding triumph, which is all the more surprising given the country's size. The government's plan to host the 2024 Games has been dropped, but a bid for 2028 could be in the making. Budapest's major annual sporting event, bar none, is the Formula 1 Grand Prix, with the other main spectator sports being football and, to a lesser degree, horse racing – though years of underfunding and mismanagement have brought the last two nearly to their knees. Another activity popular with visitors are the "escape rooms", a boom which started in Budapest, where the challenge is to find the series of clues that will help players get out of a locked room.

The government's fixation with sport means that no expense is spared in its new **sporting facilities**, and it has embarked on a programme for building more than twenty new stadiums around the country, including the Puskás Stadium and the Honvéd club's stadium in Budapest. Football has not been the only beneficiary: the hosting of the World Aquatics Championships in 2017 required huge investments in facilities in Budapest: on the Margít-sziget and elsewhere, and around Lake Balaton.

FOOTBALL

18

Hungary's great footballing days are long past – the golden team of the 1950s that beat England 6–3 in 1953 and reached the World Cup Final in 1954 with stars such as Ferenc Puskás and József Bozsik is a world away from today's national squad. However, the football-obsessed Prime Minister Viktor Orbán dreams of turning the nation's fortunes round, and is pumping money into the sport. The Puskás Ferenc Stadium is being rebuilt at huge expense to host matches in the 2020 Euro Championships, and new stadiums are springing up across the country – including in the village of Orbán's birth, Felcsut, where a population of 1800 now has a 3500-seater stadium, a folly that was opened with great splendour in 2014. In spite of his efforts, the national team shows little sign of improvement, while the domestic league is terribly weak, with clubs struggling along with little or no money, and their best players continuously sold off to clubs in other countries. Club football in Budapest revolves around the turf of five main teams (listed below), while the big teams in the countryside are Debrecen Videoton (Székesfehérvár) and DVTK (MIskolc). The **season** runs from late July to late Nov and late Feb to mid-June. Most **matches** are played on Saturday afternoons, with tickets costing 1200–4500Ft; you can find fixtures online.

Ferencváros (aka FTC or Fradi) IX, Üllői út 129 ☎ 1 910 0210, ✆ fradi.hu; Népliget metro. Fradi is the biggest club in the country and almost a national institution, though success has been harder to come by in recent times. Its supporters, dressed in the club's colours of green and white, are the loudest presence at international matches too. The club has long had right-wing ties: this was the fascists' team before the war, and some of its supporters preserve its reputation for thuggishness and anti-Semitism. It plays at the newly redeveloped 24,000-capacity Groupama Aréna next to the road towards the airport.

Honvéd XIX, Puskás Ferenc utca 1–3 ☎ 1 357 6738, ✆ honvedfc.hu; six stops on bus #42 from Határ út metro station. Founded as Kispest in 1909, they assumed the mantle of the army team in 1949, and their name was changed to Honvéd. Playing in red and black, their glory days of the 1950s owed much to having the likes of Puskás, Kocsis and Bozsik (the backbone of the Mighty Magyars) in their side. The 1980s was another hugely successful decade, and in 2017 they returned to winning form, crowned league champions in the last match of the season. Honvéd play at the 10,000-capacity Bozsik József Stadium, southeast of the centre, though matches will be held at MTK's stadium while the Bozsik is turned into a top-spec UEFA venue.

MTK VIII, Salgótarján utca 12–14 ☎ 1 333 8368, ✆ mtkhungaria.hu; tram #37 from Blaha Lujza tér. Fradi's big local rival, "Em-tay-kah" – as it is popularly known – has traditionally had strong support among the Jewish community, and was banned during World War II. Second only to Ferencváros in terms of the number of domestic league titles won, these days MTK are struggling to survive. MTK's Hidegkuti Nándor Stadium (capacity 12,700) was the setting for scenes in the film *Escape to Victory*.

Újpest IV, Megyeri út 13 ☎ 1 231 0088, ✆ ujpestfc.hu; four stops on bus #30 from Újpest Központ metro station. Formed in 1885, Újpest have traditionally been one of the powerhouses of Hungarian football, enjoying particularly golden periods in the 1930s – when they supplied half of the Hungarian national team that were runners-up in the 1938 World Cup – and the 1970s, when they dominated the domestic league and reached the semifinals of the European Cup in 1974. Known as the Lilák (Purples) after the club colours, Újpest play at the 13,000 all-seater Szusza Ferenc Stadium north of the city.

Vasas XIII, Fáy utca 58 ☎ 1 450 0165, ✆ vasasfc.hu; a short walk from Forgács utca metro station. The Ironworkers' team was founded in 1911 and plays in a red and blue kit. It had the distinction in 1957 of winning the first championship after the defeat of the 1956 revolution. That marked the start of the club's apogee, winning the championship five times in the next nine years. It is enjoying a revival at present. Vasas play at the 9000-capacity Illovszky Rudolf Stadium, north of the centre.

TOP 5 HUNGARIAN SPORTS STARS
Aladár Gerevich (fencing)
Tamás Kásás (water polo)
Katalin Kovács (kayaking)
László Papp (boxing)
Ferenc Puskás (football)

HORSE RACING

Horse racing was introduced from England by Count Széchenyi in 1827 and flourished until 1949, when flat racing (*galopp*) was banned by the Communists. For many years punters could only enjoy trotting races, but in the mid-1980s flat racing resumed. **Betting** operates on a tote system, where your returns are affected by how the odds stood at the close of betting. The different types of bet comprise *tét*, placing money on the winner; *hely*, on a horse coming in the first three; and the popular *befutó*, a bet on two horses to come in either first and second or first and third. Winnings are paid out about fifteen minutes after the end of the race.

18

Kincsem Park X, Albertirsai út 2–6 ⓦkincsempark.hu; Pillangó utca on the red metro, and then either walk or catch #100 bus. Flat racing takes place here on Sundays from April to November; trotting – *ügető*, where the horse is harnessed to a light carriage – is all year round, mostly on Sat.

Races are advertised in *Fortuna* magazine. Both types have a devoted and excitable following, which makes attending the races entertaining; the atmosphere at the tracks is informal, but photographing the racegoers is frowned upon, since many attend unbeknown to their spouses or employers.

FORMULA ONE

The **Hungarian Grand Prix** usually takes place at the end of July or beginning of August at the purpose-built Formula One racing track, the Hungaroring, at Mogyoród, 20km northeast of Budapest. First held in 1986, it has managed to retain its place on the lucrative F1 calendar ever since, and has been guaranteed the event until 2026. **Tickets** (book far in advance) are available from Ostermann Forma-1, V, Deák Ferenc utca 3–5 (☏ 1 266 2040, ⓦgpticketshop.hu). A day-pass starts at €80, with a weekend pass costing anything between €90 and €500. You can reach the track by special buses from the Árpád híd bus station; trains from Keleti Station to Fót, and then a bus from there; or by HÉV train from Örs vezér tere to the Szilasliget stop, which is 1800m northeast of Gate C.

ACTIVITIES

Canoeing Taking a canoe or kayak (from around 1700Ft/day) out on the Danube can be exhilarating. The Béke Boathouse (Béke Csónakház) is a 10min walk from the Rómaifürdő HÉV station (or take bus #34 to the door from the Árpád híd station) at III, Római-part 51–53 (April to mid-Oct; ☏ 1 388 9303, ⓦbit.ly/bekecanoes).

Caving Óbuda offers the opportunity to explore a couple of fascinating cave systems (see p.118). You can walk round them without any special equipment, or you can go on more adventurous visits with Caving under Budapest (☏0620 928 4969, ⓦbarlangaszat.hu). The group leads 2–3hr tours – you don't need caving experience, but you do need to be fit and fairly agile, as you'll be climbing on walls and squeezing through passageways. You are given helmets, headlights and overalls. English-speaking tours (6000Ft) are on Mon, Wed and Fri afternoons and start at the Pálvölgyi Stalactite Cave. The Hungarian Speleological Society at the Szemlőhegyi Cave (☏0670 881 1477, ⓦbarlang.hu) can put you in touch with groups exploring caves in the Buda Hills and elsewhere in Hungary.

Escape rooms Budapest's dilapidated apartment blocks have spawned an unusual craze: locking people in a room and leaving clues and challenges for them to work out how to escape in sixty minutes. Luckily help is at hand if you can't work it out. There are several venues for this kind of slightly warped fun, including the first of the breed, Parapark, at VIII, Vajdahunyad utca 4 (☏0620 986 9196, ⓦparapark.hu); as well as Trap, VI, Paulay Ede utca 20 (☏0630 739 7067, ⓦtrap.hu); and Claustrophilia, VII, Erzsébet körút 8 (☏0630 724 2274, ⓦclaustrophilia.hu).

Fitness centres and gyms Most of the larger hotels and some of the shopping malls have gyms, which are properly regulated (unlike some of the backstreet ones), and are open to non-residents.

Ice-skating During winter, there's skating at the City Park ice rink by Hősök tere in the Városliget (mid-Nov to Feb Mon–Fri 9am–1pm & 4–8pm, Sat & Sun 10am–2pm & 4–8pm; ⓦmujegpalya.hu); entry costs 1000–2000Ft, depending when you go, and skates can be rented. Or there's the Buda Ice Rink (Budai Jégpálya) at Széna tér in Buda (Oct–April daily 8am–10pm; ☏0670 335 2553, ⓦbudaijeg.hu); entry is 1400Ft, and skates can be rented.

Skiing If it's a snowy winter, you can ski at Normafa in the Buda Hills, best reached on bus #21A from Széll Kálmán tér. Equipment can be rented from Suli Sí by the entrance of the Császár Komjádi pool at II, Árpád Fejedelem utca 8 (Mon–Fri 3–6.30pm, Sat 9am–1pm, Sun 10am–1pm; ☏0670 361 7615, ⓦsulisi.hu), or Bikebase at VI, Podmaniczky utca 19 (daily 9am–7pm; ☏0670 625 8501, ⓦbikebase.hu), where the friendly staff can also advise on places to ski.

Squash (Fallabda) Try City Squash Club at II, Marczibányi tér 13 (☏ 1 336 0408, ⓦsquashtech.hu; court rental 2500Ft/hr), 5min walk from Széll Kálmán tér; or Mammut Squash, on the fourth floor of the nearby Mammut Mall I (☏ 1 345 8093, ⓦmammutsquash.hu; court rental 2500Ft/hr).

Tennis Courts can be booked all year round at the Városmajor Tennis Club in Városmajor Park, near Széll Kálmán tér (☏ 1 202 5337, ⓦteniszbudapest.hu), and at the Tabáni Tennis Centre at Krisztina körút 101 (☏ 1 212 7205, ⓦtabantenisz.hu). Racquets are available for rent at both.

GELLÉRT BATHS

Baths and pools

With more than a hundred springs offering an endless supply of hot water at temperatures of up to 76˚C, Budapest is deservedly known as a spa city, and visiting one of the many baths is an unmissable experience. Housed in some of Budapest's finest buildings, the baths are impressive in their own right, while the thermal waters are reputed to cure myriad ailments – and of course there's the swimming itself. The baths are an important social hub too. As you admire the light filtering through the dome in the Rudas, watch chess players ponder strategies in the outdoor pool of the Széchenyi or peer through the mists in the steam rooms of the Gellért, there's a real sense of being part of a tradition that has lasted centuries. That history of indulgence has been given a new twist in recent years with the advent of night-time parties at the baths.

There are three types of bath: *gyógyfürdő*, a **thermal bath** in its original Turkish form, as at the Rudas and Király, or the magnificent nineteenth-century settings of the Gellért and Széchenyi; *uszoda*, a proper swimming pool such as the Sport; and *strand*, a lido in a verdant setting, such as the Palatinus. Most baths are divided into a **swimming** area and a separate section for **steam baths** (*gőzfürdő* or the *gőz*, as they are popularly known). The smaller Rudas, Veli Bej and Király baths are first and foremost steam baths, with saunas and pools fed by thermal springs. In the larger baths, such as the Gellért and Széchenyi, you can alternate between brisk dips in the swimming pool and leisurely soaks in the steam section.

The Budapest bathing experience can be a little daunting, as little is written in English once you are inside – though in baths that are popular with tourists such as the Széchenyi, many of the attendants speak English and are well-equipped to guide lost tourists through the system. However, the basic system of attendants and cabins is the same in most steam baths and swimming pools, and once you get the hang of the rituals, a visit to the baths becomes most rewarding. The website ⒲spasbudapest.com has general information on all the main baths. At present **night-time parties** take place on Saturdays in the Széchenyi (May–Sept) and Lukács Baths (Oct–April), where you can enjoy laser discos, music and occasionally films in a most unusual setting (⒲spartybooking.com; tickets €45–75). The partygoers are mainly young, foreign and male – but if you like bopping away in an alcohol-fuelled crowd of swimmers, this is for you. The night-time swimming on Fridays and Saturdays at the Rudas is a very different affair, a place to relax, without music and flashing lights.

The thermal baths are not recommended for **children under 14**, and the Király, Rudas and Veli Bej will not allow them in. Similarly, indoor baths insist that only potty-trained (*szobatiszta*) babies are allowed in the water.

A ROUGH GUIDE TO BATHING

Tickets A standard ticket purchased from the ticket office (*pénztár*) gets you into the pools as well as the sauna and steam rooms; you'll often have the choice between changing in a communal room and using a locker (*szekrény*), or a slightly more expensive cubicle (*kabin*) – the latter gives you more privacy and, in the mixed-sex baths, this allows couples to change together. At the *pénztár* you also pay for any other treatments, such as massages and pedicures, that you want during your visit.

Costs The baths are not a cheap entertainment, and ticket prices can be mystifying. In some baths children only get a discounted rate if they have a student card. Entrance prices are 3300–4900Ft on weekdays, though expect to pay 200–400Ft more at weekends; cabins cost around 400Ft more; individual prices are given under each bath listing. There are also discounts in most places if you go before 8am or after 5pm. Everything you need can be rented at all baths – costs are typically: swimsuit (1500Ft), bathrobe (2000Ft), towel (1000Ft), sheet (1000Ft) and hat (500Ft – though it is cheaper to buy one if you go more than once); baths such as the Gellért and Rudas charge more. You have to pay deposits of between 1500 and 10,000Ft for each item. It's usual to tip the attendant a couple of hundred forints. Supplementary tickets will buy you a massage (*masszázs*), a soak in a private tub (*kádfürdő*) or a mud bath (*iszapfürdő*) – a list by the office will detail the available services. You

can buy tickets with credit cards, but will need cash for deposits, such as for locker keys.

What to bring In all baths bring flip-flops if you have them, as well as your own soap and shampoo; in the steam baths, you don't need a towel as you're given a sheet to dry yourself with. In many pools, bathing caps (*uszósapka*) are compulsory: in the Széchenyi, they're only required in the middle of the three outdoor pools (the one reserved for swimming proper); go in without a cap and you'll be whistled at by the attendant and told to get out. The best advice is not to take valuables to the baths, but in practice that is not always possible. Most baths do have safes (*értékmegőrzés*), but in some, such as the Lukács, these are small and will not hold a handbag.

Getting changed Most – though not all – baths have the same system for entry and getting changed. Bath staff are now much more helpful – especially at places such as the Széchenyi – in showing foreign visitors what to do and telling them treatments are available. At the *pénztár* you'll be given tickets for any treatments and a plastic "wrist watch" that lets you through the turnstile into the baths and also locks your locker or cabin (don't lose it or you'll need to cough up 2000Ft). At the changing room (*öltöző*), an attendant will direct you to a cabin or locker (though not all pools have both); in the steam baths on single-sex days, they'll give you a *kötény* (a small loincloth for men or an apron for women) which offers a vestige of cover, and you

BATHHOUSE BACKGROUND

Even though the sulphurous content of Budapest's waters mean that they don't always smell very pleasant, their therapeutic qualities have long been exploited. The earliest remains of baths here date back to the Bronze Age, and a succession of invaders have since capitalized on the medicinal benefits of the waters. The **Romans**, who appreciated a good bath, set up camp along the banks of the Danube – you can see the ruins of their bathhouses in Óbuda (see p.118). After their arrival from the east, the **Hungarian tribes** also recognized the value of the thermal springs, as testified by the remnants of a hospital bathhouse from 1178 found near the Lukács.

During their occupation, the **Ottomans** played a vital role in the development of Budapest's baths – the precept, under Islamic law, for washing five times a day before prayers is thought to have engendered a popular bathing culture here. The oldest baths that survive today are the Turkish baths on the Buda side of the river: built in the late sixteenth century, the Király and the Rudas baths have preserved their original layout, with a central bathing pool surrounded by smaller pools that lie below the old Turkish cupolas.

The next **golden age of bathing** occurred in the late nineteenth and early twentieth centuries, as a fashion for spas swept across Europe. Budapest's existing baths were dressed up in a new magnificence, and splendid buildings such as the neo-Baroque Széchenyi Baths in the Városliget and the Art Nouveau Gellért Baths were erected. During the **Communist era**, the baths were as popular as ever – a place to meet and gossip in the murky mists – but they suffered prolonged neglect. In recent years, however, major investments have seen the buildings restored and their facilities upgraded by way of new features such as whirlpools – Budapest's baths are now far more salubrious places to visit. And it's not just people who have benefited from the thermal waters. The success of the hippopotamus-breeding programme at Budapest Zoo is thought to be partly due to the constant supply of hot water from the Széchenyi Baths across the road – the hippos clearly benefit from wallowing in lovely thermal pools. The hot springs also saved them during the bitter winter siege of the city in 1944–45, when most of the zoo's other animals died in the freezing temperatures.

choose a cubicle to change in. Once you've changed, lock your door with your "wrist watch" and make note of your cabin number, taking with you any supplementary tickets. Note that swimwear is compulsory where there is mixed-sex swimming.

In the baths The best way to enjoy the steam baths is to go from room to room, moving on whenever the heat gets too much. A popular sequence is: sauna (dry steam – often divided into three rooms, the furthest being the hottest), cool pool, steam room, cold plunge (if you can bear it), hot plunge (this makes your skin tingle wonderfully, but don't stay in for long), followed by a wallow in the larger, warmer pools that are usually at the centre of the baths. Most people then repeat the whole thing again, but the sequence you choose is entirely up to you. When you're completely finished, take a sheet from the pile to dry yourself and relax in the rest room if you feel exhausted – certainly don't plan on anything too strenuous afterwards.

THE BATHS

Császár Komjádi Uszoda II, Árpád fejedelem útja 8 ☎1 212 2750, ⓦcsillaghegyistrand.hu; map p.90. Hungary's national swimming stadium is a large, modern pool complex just north of Margít híd on the Buda side – the entrance faces the river. The large outdoor swimming pool (bathing caps compulsory) is covered over in winter. As it's one of the major water-polo venues in Budapest, one of its pools may be given over to the players on weekdays. Daily 6am–7pm; 1800Ft.

Gellért Gyógyfürdő XI, Kelenhegyi út 4 ☎1 466 6166, ⓦgellertfurdo.hu; map p.109. The most popular of the city's baths, and also one of the oldest (although nothing remains of the medieval buildings), the Gellért has it all: a magnificent main pool for swimming, hot pools for sitting

around in both inside and outside on the terrace, fabulous Art Nouveau steam baths, and a large outdoor area, including a wave machine in the main pool (May–Aug) and shaded terraces. To enjoy the waters you must first reach the changing rooms by a labyrinth of passages. At the far end of the pool are steps leading down to the thermal baths, with their ornate plunge pools. The Gellért attracts a lot of foreigners, and many of the attendants speak German or English. Daily 6am–8pm; Mon–Fri 4900ft with 5300ft with locker, 5500Ft with cabin; Sat & Sun 5500ft with locker, 5900Ft with cabin.

★**Hajós Alfred Sport Uszoda** XIII, southern end of Margít-sziget ☎1 450 4200; map p.120. One of the city's nicest places for proper swimming, this is a beautiful 1930s lido renovated for the 2001 European water-polo championships. There's a small sauna, and two large outdoor pools against a backdrop of trees; one is normally given over to water polo. In the winter you can swim out along a channel to the larger of the pools without walking outside. Daily 6am–6pm; 1800Ft.

Király Gyógyfürdő II, Fő utca 84 ☎1 202 3688, ⓦkiralyfurdo.hu; map p.90. Fabulous Turkish baths, in the Víziváros in Buda, easy to spot thanks to the four copper cupolas. This was formerly the most popular of the steam baths with the gay community, but is now mixed-sex every day (swimwear compulsory). The main pool under the cupola is surrounded by smaller – hotter and cooler – pools, with doors leading off to the steam massage rooms. Daily 9am–9pm; 3500Ft with locker, 3800Ft with cabin; you get 1100Ft back if you leave before noon.

★**Lukács Gyógyfürdő** II, Frankel Leó út 25–29 ☎1 326 1695, ⓦlukacsfurdo.hu; map p.90. This spa complex just north of the Margít híd in Buda has four small but delightful open-air pools, as well as mud baths and a medical treatment section – its waters are said to be good for rheumatism, arthritis and other complaints. The open-air facilities, including a thermal pool, a cooler and smaller swimming pool, and a bubbling pool with whirling currents, are in two intimate courtyards. Enter via the folly-like drinking hall (where you can take a sample) and head to the left (past plaques declaring gratitude from those who have benefited from the medicinal waters), following the signs for the *uszoda* (pool). The swimming pool and adjacent baths are mixed. Daily 6am–1pm; Mon–Fri 3500ft with locker, 3900Ft with cabin; Sat & Sun 3700ft with locker, 4100Ft with cabin, with reductions daily before 8am and after 6pm. If you stay for less than 2hr, you can get a 1000Ft refund.

Palatinus Strand XIII, Margít-sziget ☎1 340 4500, ⓦpalatinusstrand.hu; map p.120. Set among a sprawling park halfway up the island on the west side, the Palatinus is the city's most popular pool, with a large outdoor set of pools, including a wave pool and children's pools, all set in a big expanse of grass. Other facilities include football pitches and volleyball courts, as well as snack bars. The sunroof above the changing rooms is something of a gay centre. Note that parts of the lido are now open year-round. Daily 8am–8pm; Mon–Fri 2800ft with locker, reductions after 5pm.

Rudas Gyógyfürdő I, Döbrentei tér 9 ☎1 356 1322, ⓦrudasfurdo.hu; map p.109. One of the city's original

Turkish baths, at the Buda end of the Erzsébet híd, this is at its best when the sun shines through the holes in the dome to light up the beautiful interior. The steam baths were for many years a male preserve, but women now get a day to themselves (Tues). There's an apron system in the steam section on single-sex days, but swimming costumes are compulsory on mixed days (Fri night, Sat & Sun). The "Wellness" section at one end of the complex has a rooftop pool offering great views across the Danube. There is also a nineteenth-century swimming pool, open to both sexes, to the left of the main entrance. Swimwear is compulsory in mixed-sex areas. Baths: daily 6am–8pm, plus Fri & Sat night swimming 10pm–4am; Mon–Fri 3300Ft (2600Ft 9am–noon); Sat & Sun 3700Ft; Fri & Sat night 4800Ft; Wellness section: daily 6am–10pm; from 3100Ft.

Széchenyi Gyógyfürdő XIV, Állatkerti körút 11 ☎1 363 3210, ⓦszechenyifurdo.hu; map p.71. A magnificent nineteenth-century complex in the Városliget (main doors are opposite the entrance to the Budapest Circus). There are sixteen pools in all, including the various medicinal sections, but you'll probably use just the three outdoor ones: the hot pool where people play chess (bring your own chess set if you want to play); a pool for swimming (bathing caps compulsory); and a whirlpool. Across the far side of the hot pool from the changing rooms is a mixed sauna with a maze of hot and cold pools. Go before 8am if you want to avoid the tourist rush. Staff speak good English, guide you through the locker and cabin system and also tell you about treatments you can get, such as fish pedicures. Daily 6am–10pm; Mon–Fri 4900Ft with locker, 5400Ft with cabin; Sat & Sun 5100Ft with locker, 5600Ft with cabin; reductions before 8am and after 5pm.

★**Veli Bej Fürdő** II, Árpád fejedelem útja 7 ☎1 438 8587; map p.90. The sixteenth-century Veli Bej, the city's oldest Ottoman spa, has finally been restored in a pleasantly simple fashion. The large central cupola is surrounded by four smaller pools, with adjacent modern steam chambers, saunas and jacuzzis. The spa is run by a religious order, the Irgalmasok, and the presence of their hospital in the complex is a reminder of the very medicinal role of the thermal waters. Only eighty people are allowed into the bath at any one time. It gets full at weekends, but on weekday mornings you might have the place to yourself. Children under 14 not allowed in. Daily 6am–noon & 3–9pm; 2800Ft entry.

19

BUDAPEST ZOO

Kids' Budapest

Budapest offers a healthy range of activities for kids, from adventure and roller-skating parks to indoor play centres and state-of-the-art playgrounds. Moreover, the zoo – always a sure-fire hit with the little ones – is one of the most impressive in the region. There's plenty by way of artistic entertainment, too, and the capital retains a strong tradition of children's theatre – particularly puppetry – and dance. Don't expect anything too high-tech, however, as a lack of cash dogs many of the facilities; however, many of the city's playgrounds have been refurbished in recent years, and plenty of places have activities specifically for children, from the Palace of Arts, which has events most weekends, to the Millenáris Park with its regular workshops. Concessions for under-14s are available at most attractions.

Budapest's public transport – under-6s travel free – will keep children happily entertained. **Trams** are an endless source of fun, the best ride being along the embankment in tram #2. Across the water, the **Sikló** (see p.103) is a great experience, rising up above the rooftops from the Lánchíd to the Royal Palace. The new **green metro line** (#4) is driverless – so you can peep through the window at the front and watch the lights of the next station approach. A popular way for families to spend an afternoon in the Buda Hills is to go on the "railway circuit": the **Cogwheel Railway**, the **Children's Railway** and the **chairlift** – but note that the chairlift can be unnerving for smaller children. From April to October there's the added thrill of **boat rides** on the Danube – either short tours of the city up to Margít-sziget and back, or further afield to Szentendre and on to Esztergom – though for young children, boredom is less likely to kick in on the shorter rides. Throughout the summer there are lots of **craft activities** and children's entertainment at the Open-Air Museum in Szentendre, and many of the summer **festivals** (see p.29) also have craft stalls and activities for children, such as the August 20 festivities around the Royal Palace.

PLAYGROUNDS, PARKS AND THE ZOO

Budapest Eye V, Erzsébet tér ☎ 0670 636 0629, ⓦ oriaskerek.com. The giant Ferris wheel has been a regular feature of the central Pest skyline in recent years. 1500Ft for children, 2400Ft for adults. March–Oct daily 10am–midnight.

Caves Underground Buda is good fun for children who aren't scared of the dark. The caves under the Várhegy (see p.97) offer some underground exploration, while the Pálvölgyi and Szemlőhegyi caves (see p.118) display dramatic geological formations. Note that Pálvölgyi doesn't admit children under 5.

Csillebérc adventure playground (Kalandpálya) XII, Konkoly Thege Miklós út 21 ☎ 0620 584 0381 ⓦ kalandpalya.com; map p.123. Up in the Buda Hills and offering some of the city's best in outdoor fun, this is a real woodland adventure, where children over 100cm in height can go on ropewalks and swing from tree to tree. Safety is paramount, with all children taught how to use harnesses. Plenty of shade, so good on hot days. To get here, take the Children's Railway to Csillebérc Station, or catch the #21 bus from Széll Kálmán tér. Entry 3000Ft for a child for a 2hr session. It is also worth renting gloves (400Ft). April–Oct daily 10am–6pm; Nov–March Sat & Sun 10am–4pm, depending on weather.

Görzenál Skatepark III, Árpád fejedelem útja ☎ 1 250 4799 ⓦ gorzenal.hu; map p.116. Space to rollerblade, skateboard and cycle, with ramps and jumps, all to your heart's content. You can get here by taking the Szentendre HÉV to Timár utca. Day-ticket is 500Ft on weekdays, 900Ft at weekends. Mon–Fri 2–7pm, Sat & Sun 9.30am–7pm.

Kids' Park (Kölyökpark) II, Mammut Mall 2 (shop 328), Lövőház utca 1–5 ☎ 1 345 8512; map p.90. Indoor play area (for ages 1–11) in a city mall that comes into its own on wet days. You pay 880Ft for half an hour's use of slides, climbing walls and more – parents can leave the

kids here while they go shopping. Mon–Sat 10am–9pm, Sun 9am–9pm.

Margít-sziget This island in the Danube (see p.119) is a great open space where you can rent bikes, pedaloes and electric cars (from the northern end of the island, though it is worth asking on the island, as the hire points move around). The Palatinus lido (see p.202) has a wave machine and lots of small pools for kids. The petting zoo across on the eastern side has been vastly improved, and the varied scenery and open areas for frisbee and ball games all create a very pleasant atmosphere.

Playgrounds There are a lot of playgrounds in the squares and parks, such as the Károlyi kert, with the longest sandpit in town (see p.42), Szabadság tér (see p.51), Szent István park (see p.57), Klauzál tér (see map, p.160), on the Margít-sziget (see p.119) and at several locations in the Városliget (see map, p.71), one of the best being near Dembinsky utca. In Buda you can find them on the Gellért-hegy and at the Feneketlen tó (see map, p.109), and at the Millenáris Park near Széll Kálmán tér (see map, p.60), where there is the Green Peter (Zöld Péter) playground, inspired by a Hungarian fairytale.

Tropicarium You can get close to the sharks, feed stingrays and experience the rainforests in this huge aquarium-terrarium in southern Buda (see p.128).

Városliget The park (see p.74) has the largest concentration of activities and attractions for children. The Széchenyi Baths (see p.202) are popular with bigger children – especially the large outdoor hot pool and the whirlpool – but it's not a great place for splashing around in as the old ladies don't want their hairdos messed up. For those who prefer to stay above water level, there are playgrounds, the zoo and a circus, as well as rowing in summer and ice-skating in winter (see p.74) on the lake by Hősök tere.

46556666

Zoo (Állatkert) Under its visionary director, Budapest's zoo (see p.75) gets better every year, and there is lots for children to do: as well as the animal displays and an excellent playground, kids can stroke animals in the petting farm, ride ponies or go on the grand old Carousel. In addition, new activities are being developed in the old stable blocks at the eastern end of the zoo, and there are regular special children's events, as well. Daily 9am–8pm.

MUSEUMS

Aeropark Next to Terminal 2B at the main airport ⓦaeropark.hu; map p.5. Aircraft lovers can board planes that have been in public service in Hungary in the past sixty years. At weekends you can try flying planes on the flight simulator (it is worth checking in Nov–March if the simulator is operating). Tickets adults 1900Ft, children 900Ft. April, May, Sept & Oct daily 9am–6pm; June–Aug Mon–Thurs 9am–6pm, Fri–Sun 9am–8pm; Nov–March Sat & Sun 10am–6pm.

Center of Scientific Wonders (Csodák Palotája/ Csopa) This great interactive playhouse now operates in two venues, the Csopa Campona in Campona Mall (see p.128), an interactive "play-house" where activities such as the bed of nails and square-wheeled car serve as a back-door way of explaining scientific principles; and the Csopa Playbar in Óbuda (III, Bécsi út 38–44; daily 10am–8pm; ☎1 814 8060, ⓦcsopa.hu/csopa-playbar; adults 2500F, children 1900Ft), aimed at children aged 10 and up, and adults too. The games here are more electronic, and well-informed guides are on hand to show you round a series of exhibitions – though some displays, such as the one on birth, are a bit graphic. It also has interactive tables, a 9-D cinema (only for those over 130cm tall) and science-themed escape rooms. Good explanations in English.

Hospital in the Rock With gory waxworks, spooky Cold War bunkers and an excellent guided tour, the Hospital (see p.97) could be great fun for kids – but unfortunately you can't run around or touch anything and admission charges are steep.

Houdini Museum I, Dísz tér 11 ☎1 951 8066, ⓦhouseofhoudinibudapest.com; map p.93. Compact but informative display centred on the life (and death) of this Hungarian legend. It's full of Houdini memorabilia, all presented by enthusiastic hosts. The visit is rounded off with a show by a magician. Adults 2500Ft, children under 11 1900Ft. Daily 10am–7pm.

Hungarian Open-Air Museum Children's programmes every weekend, a playground and frequent folk-craft and folk-dancing displays in this museum outside Szentendre (see p.134).

Natural History Museum Full of colour and activity, the museum (see p.86) boasts interactive games and lots to look at, plenty of it at child height. Well thought out, it certainly grabs children's attention, but make sure you take snacks – if the café is closed, there is not much else nearby. Across the road is the Botanical Garden (see p.86).

Railway History Park Strong child appeal here: lots of big old engines and carriages, and in summer you can even drive an engine yourself (see p.127).

Telephone Museum A hands-on museum (see p.93), which is a rarity in Budapest; children enjoy sending faxes and calling one another on vintage phones.

Transport Museum The old museum was demolished in 2017 during the rebuilding of the Városliget, but will reappear at a new location in a couple of years; visit ⓦkozlekedesimuzeum.hu for updates.

20

DANCE, THEATRE AND CREATIVE FUN

The fact that successful music ensembles such as the Budapest Festival Orchestra and the folk group Muzsikás hold regular events designed specifically for **children** says a lot about Hungarian attitudes to young people. Budapest also has a strong tradition in **puppetry**, and many big Hungarian writers have contributed to its children's repertoire. There are some English-language performances, but again, puppet shows are good visual entertainment even without the language. Morning and matinée performances are for kids. Tickets are also available from the city's ticket offices (see p.183).

Budapest Festival Orchestra Cocoa Concerts III, Selmeci utca 14–16, Óbuda ☎1 489 4330, ⓦbfz.hu; map .116. Hour-long concerts for children aged 5–12, where the musicians introduce the music and the instruments – and give out a cup of cocoa, too. The concerts are usually every other month on either a Saturday or a Sunday at 2.30pm and 4.30pm, Sept–May (check the website to confirm); tickets cost 2700Ft.

Budapest Puppet Theatre (Budapest Bábszínház) VI, Andrássy út 69 ☎1 342 2702, ⓦbudapest -babszinhaz.hu; map p.60. One of the most established puppet theatres (see p.187), it also does shows for adults.

Kolibri Theatre (Kolibri Színház) VI, Jókai tér 10; **Kolibri Nest (Fészek)** VI, Andrássy út 74 ☎1 311 0870, ⓦkolibriszinhaz.hu; map p.60. Both venues have shows for children of all ages, but those at the Fészek theatre are usually better for smaller children. Both close early June to Aug.

Millenáris Park Some exhibitions and shows in the various buildings around the site (see p.106), including the unmissable Invisible Exhibition, an hour-long exploration of the world of the blind (for children aged 7 and over), and

Plaster Age (Mon–Fri 2–8pm, Sat & Sun 10am–8pm; from 1600Ft; ☎0670 518 1602, ⓦgipszkorszak.hu), with workshops for children to paint mugs, plates and assorted shapes. For younger children the large indoor play centre in the Fogadó building, Millipop (daily 10am–8pm; children 2500Ft, adults 900Ft; ☎0620 504 5511, ⓦmillipopjatszo .hu), has activities for all ages: a big complex of tunnels, slides and climbing frames, plus interactive and electronic games, Rubik's cubes and puzzles. Good café on the mezzanine too.

Muzsikás Children's Dance House TEMI Fővárosi Művelődési Háza, XI, Fehérvári út 47 ☎1 203 3868, ⓦmuzsikas.hu; map p.109. While members of the Muzsikás folk band play, dancers take children (and their parents) through some basic steps, chanting Hungarian children's songs and rhymes – don't worry, non-Hungarian children will enjoy the dancing anyway. The venue is two stops beyond Móricz Zsigmond körtér on trams #47 and #56. Most Tuesdays at 5.30pm Sept–May; 400Ft for children, 700Ft for adults.

20

LGBT+ Budapest

Of all the cities in the former Eastern bloc, Budapest perhaps has the most active LGBT+ scene, albeit still very underground compared to its Western counterparts. The annual Pride event here is one of the most established and well attended in the region and equality is formalized by law – the age of consent is 14 for homosexuals and heterosexuals alike, and in 2009, Parliament passed a bill allowing registered partnerships for same-sex couples. There has been a distinct chill since 2010, as the popular conservative government pushes the idea that the good Hungarian is straight and God-fearing; a constitutional amendment to allow same-sex marriage was rejected in 2015. The ruling party's hostility to the LGBT+ community has offered some encouragement to the more homophobic elements in the capital. Nonetheless, Budapest's rise as a party city has meant that more venues are welcoming LGBT+ visitors.

21

It is worth remembering, however, that outside of the venues listed here, Budapest is still a conservative city in terms of social mores. While there seem to be few limits to displays of heterosexual affectiona in public, the same behaviour between same-sex couples is much less tolerated, and even holding hands on the street can provoke a verbal reaction.

LGBT+ **venues** are mostly to be found on the Pest side and within the **Nagykörút**. The major event in the LGBT+ calendar is **Budapest Pride** (see p.30), a well-established week-long festival taking place in late June and culminating in the colourful Pride March at the weekend. The threat of disruption by right-wing groups means that the march now takes place between barriers along a carefully policed route, but the participants are determined not to let this dampen their spirits. At the big Sziget festival in August (see p.183) there is an LGBT+ tent, the Magic Mirror. LIFT (Lesbian Identities Festival) is a small event in the autumn organized by Labrisz (see below), while the annual LGBTQ+ film festival has become part of the Pride festival.

Budapest's LGBT+ scene is very **male-dominated**. That's true both in the bars listed below and in the parties organized around the city by groups such as Omoh (⊕bit.ly /omohbudapest), Garçons Budapest (⊕garconsbudapest.com) and Hellopartybp (⊕bit.ly/hellopartybp). The best spots for **lesbians** are venues such as *Club 93*, *Gastro Bistro*, *Why Not?* and the LGBT+-friendly bar *Szocialis Helyiség* (see p.178), which don't have an expensive price-tag attached. It is also worth checking online to see if the legendary *Eklektika* bar has found a new home. There are a couple of active lesbian **groups:** Labrisz (☎0630 295 5415, ⊕labrisz.hu/english) holds regular events in the Közkincs Könyvtár, a community library with an extensive range of English books at VIII, Rákóczi út 11, first floor (☎0630 278 1976, ⊕kozkincskonyvtar.com); Labrisz also stage monthly games evenings in the *Gastro Bistro* (see below), and a film club on the first Saturday of the month in the Zöld Macska Diákpince at IX, Üllői út 95, near Klinikák metro station, named after Hilda Gobbi, one of the great Hungarian postwar actresses and a lesbian icon. Another group, Ösztrosokk (⊕bit.ly/osztrosokk), arranges parties at various venues, usually on the second Saturday of every month, while the lobby bar of the Toldi cinema at V, Bajcsy Zsilinszky út 36–38 hosts a Women-on-Women (WoW) party once a month (⊕bit.ly/womenwomen).

As far as **accommodation** is concerned, the *Casati* hotel (see p.153) in the centre of town is LGBT+-friendly, and its *TukTuk* cocktail bar is a popular LGBT+ venue; while next door is the popular *Anker't* (see p.177), an LGBT+-friendly ruin pub. All the major hotels should welcome LGBT+ guests, however, or you can go through the website ⊕gaystay.net, which handles flats.

ESSENTIALS

Information The largest LGBT+ organization in town is Hattér, which runs a helpline (daily 6–11pm; ☎1 329 3380, ⊕hatter.hu) offering advice and information on events – although some of the operators only speak Hungarian.

Listings and websites You can find listings for places and events in English in the freebie magazine

found at most LGBT+ venues – it's called *Humen* in its latest reincarnation. This is the best place for up-to-date listings (the magazine is available online too, at ⊕humenonline.hu); or try pan-European LGBT+ sites such as ⊕travelgayeurope.com. It's also worth looking at ⊕budapestpride.hu, though it's not always up to date on events.

CAFÉS AND RESTAURANTS

Same-sex couples are unlikely to face discrimination in the cafés and restaurants of this cosmopolitan city. The places listed here are explicitly welcoming to same-sex groups.

★**Club 93** VIII, Vas utca 2 ⊕club93pizza.hu; map p.78. Simple, cheap pizzeria halfway between Astoria and Blaha Lujza tér just off Rákóczi út that's popular with the LGBT+ community. The gallery and

window seating make it a good place to people-watch. Daily 11am–midnight.

Gastro Bistro V, Belgrád rakpart 18 ☎0670 579 0719, ⊕gastrobar.hu; map p.40. The appeal of the riverfront setting worked for the *Why Not?* bar up the road, so the owner Olivér has expanded his empire by opening an LGBT+-friendly restaurant, with an appealing mix of Hungarian and Mediterranean dishes on the menu. It has a small terrace overlooking the river. Mon–Fri 5.30pm–midnight, Sat & Sun noon–midnight.

★**Why Not?** V, Belgrád rakpart 3–4 ☎0670 557

2727, Ⓦwhynotcafe.hu; map p.40. Relaxed small café-bar with terrace near the Pest end of the Szabadság híd, with great views across to the Gellért hegy. Its clientele is mixed in the daytime, turning more LGBT+-oriented in the evening. Serves drinks, snacks and sandwiches, and has karaoke sessions Tues and Sun. Daily 10am–4am.

DRINKING AND NIGHTLIFE

Some of the bars listed here levy an **entry fee** or set a minimum consumption level – the LGBT+ scene in Budapest is expensive. Such venues give you a card when you enter, on which all your drinks are written down; you pay for your drinks and the entry fee as you leave. Be warned that if you lose the card, you'll have to cough up a hefty penalty. Otherwise, be on the lookout for overcharging.

Action V, Magyar utca 42 ☎1 266 9148, Ⓦaction.gay.hu; map p.40. The most hardcore of the gay bars, full of young men looking for one-night stands. Dark room, video room and live shows on Friday (1000Ft entry). Minimum consumption 1000Ft Fri and Sat only. The entrance is hard to find – it's 15m along from the big "A" sign on the door. Daily 9pm–4am.

Alterego VI, Dessewffy utca 33 ☎06 70 565 1111, Ⓦalteregoclub.hu; map p.60. Perhaps the best-known LGBT+ club in town, *Alterego* has been going for more than ten years and attracts quite a mixed crowd. Drag shows, karaoke and dark room (though this may still be men only). Entry 1000Ft before midnight, 1500Ft after. Fri 10pm–5am, Sat 10pm–6am.

CoXx VII, Dohány utca 38 ☎1 344 4884, Ⓦcoxx.hu; map p.40. One of the popular gay bars in town, this men-only venue is a friendly place to meet. The ground floor is a gallery; downstairs holds a dancefloor, video rooms and numerous other spaces. Regular themed party nights. Free entry, minimum consumption 1000Ft. Daily 9pm–4am.

Habroló V, Szép utca 1 ☎1 950 6644, Ⓦbit.ly/habrolo; map p.40. Taking its name from a cream horn pastry, this friendly pre-clubbing bar close to the Astoria junction attracts quite a mixed crowd. Karaoke nights Thurs and Sun. Daily 6pm–2am.

BATHS

The once famed gay activity in the public **steam baths** (see pp.199–202) is far less widespread today. The Király (see p.202) has gone mixed (prompted in part by an undercover TV programme about gay sex there) and the Rác has become entombed in a luxury hotel that is still waiting to open; there is some action at the Rudas but it is all very discreet. One reason for this decline is that gays can meet elsewhere – cruising bars, or in private saunas such as Magnum that offer dedicated facilities to gay visitors. However, the sun terrace at the Palatinus strand and the roof terrace at the Széchenyi remain popular meeting places.

Magnum Szauna VIII, Csepreghy utca 2 ☎0630 844 6864, Ⓦmagnumszauna.hu; map p.78. Budapest's first private gay bath (it's near the Corvin negyed metro stop), with a steam room and dry sauna, gym, lounge, dark rooms and cabins. "Dark and Naked" parties take place on Fri at 10pm, as well as other regular events. 2100Ft for 18–24s, 2700Ft for 25–29s, 3900Ft for over-30s, discounts on Tues for under-30s and on

Wed for over-50s. Mon–Thurs 1pm–midnight, Fri 1pm–4am, and open continuously Sat 1pm–Sun midnight.

Szauna 69 IX, Angyal utca 2 ☎1 210 1751, Ⓦgay sauna.hu; map p.78. Finnish sauna, jacuzzi and private rooms, as well as a bar. 2200Ft for under-25s, 3200Ft for over-25s. Mon–Thurs & Sun 1pm–1am, Fri 1pm–2am, Sat 1pm–4am.

STATUE OF MÁTYÁS CORVINUS ON THE MÁTYÁS FOUNTAIN

Contexts

211 History

220 Music

225 Books

228 Hungarian

236 Glossary of Hungarian terms

History

Although Budapest has only formally existed since 1873, when the twin cities of Buda and Pest were united, the city has loomed large in European history. Besieged and invaded by Roman legions, Turkic nomads, Nazi stormtroopers and Soviet tanks, it retains a strong identity of its own and remains "Janus faced", looking both east and west. What follows is the briefest sketch of a complex and fascinating past – the history titles in our book recommendations (see p.225) offer a deeper analysis.

In 35 BC the Danube Basin was conquered by the **Romans** and subsequently incorporated within their empire as the province of Pannonia, whose northern half was governed from the town of **Aquincum** on the west bank of the Danube. Ruins of a camp, villas, baths and an amphitheatre can still be seen today in Óbuda and Rómaifürdő. Roman rule lasted until 430 AD, when Pannonia was ceded to **Attila the Hun**. Attila's planned assault on Rome was averted by his death on his wedding night, and thereafter Pannonia was carved up by **Germanic tribes** until they were ousted by the Turkic-speaking **Avars**, who were in turn assailed by the **Bulgars**, another warlike race from the Eurasian steppes. Golden torques and other treasures from Hun, Goth and Avar burial sites – now on display in the National Museum – suggest that they were quite sophisticated rather than mere "barbarians".

The coming of the Magyars

The most significant of the invaders from the east were the **Magyars**, who stamped their language and identity on Hungary. Their origins lie in the Finno-Ugric peoples who dwelt in the snowy forests between the Volga and the Urals, where today two Siberian peoples still speak languages that are the closest linguistic relatives to Hungarian; along with Finnish, Turkish and Mongolian, these languages make up the Altaic family. Many of these Magyars migrated south, where they eventually became vassals of the Khazar empire and mingled with the Bulgars as both peoples moved westwards to escape the marauding Petchenegs.

In 895 or 896 AD, seven Magyar tribes led by Árpád entered the Carpathian Basin and spread out across the plain, in what Hungarians call the "**landtaking**" (*honfoglalás*). They settled here, though they remained raiders for the next seventy years, striking terror as far afield as France (where people thought them to be Huns), until a series of defeats persuaded them to settle for assimilating their gains. The runic-style writing the Magyar tribes used is increasingly visible today – often used by hardline nationalists to underline their Hungarianness. According to the medieval chronicler, known today simply as Anonymous, the clan of Árpád settled on Csepel-sziget, and it was Árpád's brother, Buda, who purportedly gave his name to the west bank of the new settlement.

8000 BC	35 BC	895	1000
Homo sapiens appeared in Budapest area	Danube Basin conquered by Romans	The seven Hungarian tribes enter the Carpathian Basin under Árpád	Pope Sylvester II sends a crown for King Stephen's coronation

The Árpád dynasty

Civilization developed gradually after Árpád's great-grandson **Prince Géza** established links with Bavaria and invited Catholic missionaries to Hungary. His son **Stephen** (István) took the decisive step of applying to Pope Sylvester for recognition, and on Christmas Day in the year 1000 AD was crowned as a Christian king. With the help of the Italian Bishop Gellért, he then set about converting his pagan subjects. Stephen was subsequently credited with the **foundation of Hungary** and canonized after his death in 1038. His mummified hand and the crown of St Stephen have since been revered as both holy and national relics, and are today some of Budapest's most popular tourist attractions.

Despite succession struggles after Stephen's death, a lack of external threats during the eleventh and twelfth centuries enabled the **development of Buda and Pest** to begin in earnest, largely thanks to French, Walloon and German settlers who worked and traded here under royal protection. However, the growth in royal power caused tribal leaders to rebel in 1222, and Andrew II was forced to recognize the noble status and rights of the **nation** – landed freemen exempt from taxation – in the Golden Bull, a kind of Hungarian Magna Carta.

Andrew's son **Béla IV** tried to restore royal authority, but the **Mongol invasion** of 1241 devastated the country and left even the royal palace of Esztergom in ruins. Only the timely death of Ghengis Khan spared Hungary from further ravages. Mindful of a return visit, Béla selected the **Vár** as a more defensible seat and encouraged foreign artisans to rebuild Buda, which German colonists called "*Ofen*" after its numerous lime-kilns (the name Pest, which is of Slav origin, also means "oven").

Renaissance and decline

After the Árpád dynasty expired in 1301, foreign powers advanced their own claims to the throne and for a while there were three competing kings, all duly crowned. Eventually **Charles Robert** of the French Angevin (or Anjou) dynasty triumphed. Peacetime gave him the opportunity to develop the gold mines of Transylvania and northern Hungary – the richest in Europe – and Charles bequeathed a robust exchequer to his son **Louis the Great**, whose reign saw the population of Hungary rise to three million, and the crown territories expand to include much of what are now Croatia and Poland. The oldest extant strata of the Buda Palace on the Vár date from this time.

After Louis' demise, the throne was claimed by **Sigismund of Luxembourg**, Prince of Bohemia, whom the nobility despised as the "Czech swine". His failure to check the advance of the Turks through the Balkans was only redeemed by the Transylvanian warlord **János Hunyadi**, whose lifting of the siege of Belgrade caused rejoicing throughout Christendom. Vajdahunyad Castle in the Városliget is a romantic nineteenth-century replica of Hunyadi's ancestral seat in Transylvania.

Hunyadi's nephew, **Mátyás Corvinus**, is remembered as the **Renaissance king** who, together with his second wife Beatrice of Naples, lured humanists and artists from Italy to their court. Mátyás was an enlightened despot, renowned for his fairness, but when he died in 1490, leaving no legitimate heir, the nobles took control, choosing a pliable successor and exploiting the peasantry. However in 1514 the peasants, led by **György**

1458	1541	1556	1686
Mátyás Corvinus accedes to the throne, ushering in a golden age	Ottoman armies occupy Budapest	Rudas Baths constructed on the orders of Pasha Sokoli Mustafa	Habsburg armies capture Budapest from the Turks

Dózsa, rebelled against the oppression. The savage repression of this **revolt** (over seventy thousand peasants were killed and Dózsa was roasted alive) and subsequent laws imposing "perpetual serfdom" alienated the mass of the population – a situation hardly improved by the coronation of the 9-year-old **Louis II**, who was barely 16 when he had to face the full might of the Turks under Sultan Süleyman "the Magnificent".

The Turkish conquest: Hungary divided

The Battle of **Mohács** in 1526 was a shattering defeat for the Hungarians – the king and half the nobility perished, leaving Hungary leaderless. After sacking Buda, the Turks withdrew to muster forces for their real objective, Vienna. To forestall this, Ferdinand of Habsburg proclaimed himself king of Hungary and occupied the western part of the country, while in Buda the nobles put János Zápolyai on the throne. Following Zápolyai's death in 1541, Ferdinand claimed full sovereignty, but the Sultan occupied Buda and central Hungary and made Zápolyai's son ruler of Transylvania, which henceforth became a semi-autonomous principality – a tripartite division known as the **Tripartium**, formally recognized in 1568. Despite various truces, warfare became a fact of life for the next 150 years, and national independence was not to be recovered for centuries afterwards.

   Turkish-occupied Hungary was ruled by a Pasha in Buda, with much of the land either deeded to the Sultan's soldiers and officials, or run directly as a state fief. The towns, however, enjoyed some rights and were encouraged to trade, and the Turks were largely indifferent to the sectarian bigotry practised in Habsburg-ruled Hungary. The Habsburg **liberation of Buda** in 1686 was actually a disaster for its inhabitants, as the victors massacred Jews, pillaged at will and reduced Buda and Pest to rubble. The city's Turkish baths and the tomb of Gül Baba were among the few surviving buildings.

Habsburg rule

Habsburg rule was a bitter pill, which the Hungarians attempted to reject in the **War of Independence** of 1703–11, led by Prince **Ferenc Rákóczi II**. Though it was unsuccessful, the Habsburgs began to soften their autocracy with paternalism as a result. The revival of towns and villages during this time owed much to settlers from all over the empire, hence the Serb and Greek churches that remain in Pest and Szentendre. Yet while the aristocracy commissioned over two hundred palaces, and Baroque town centres and orchestras flourished, the masses remained all but serfs, mired in isolated villages.

   Such contradictions impelled the Reform movement led by **Count István Széchenyi**. His vision of progress was embodied in the construction of the Lánchíd (Chain Bridge) between Buda and Pest, which proved an enormous spur to the development of the two districts. The National Museum, the Academy of Sciences and many other institutions were founded at this time, while the coffee houses of Pest became a hotbed of radical politics. Széchenyi's arch-rival was **Lajos Kossuth**, small-town lawyer turned member of parliament and editor of the radical *Pesti Hirlap*, which scandalized and delighted citizens. Kossuth detested the Habsburgs, revered "universal liberty", and demanded an end to serfdom and censorship. Magyar chauvinism was his blind spot, however, and the law of 1840, his greatest pre-revolutionary achievement, inflamed

1800	1848	1849
Beethoven plays in Budapest	Crowds gather in front of the National Museum on March 15, marking the start of the second War of Independence	Opening of István Széchenyi's Lánchíd, the first permanent bridge between Buda and Pest

dormant nationalist feelings among Croats, Slovaks and Romanians by making Hungarian the sole official language.

When the empire was shaken by revolutions that broke out across Europe in **March 1848**, local radicals seized the moment. Kossuth dominated Parliament, while **Sándor Petőfi** mobilized crowds on the streets of Pest. A second war of independence followed, which again ended in defeat and Habsburg repression, epitomized by the execution of Prime Minister Batthyány in 1849, and the construction of the Citadella atop Gellért-hegy, built to intimidate citizens with its guns.

Budapest's belle époque

Gradually, brute force was replaced by a **policy of compromise**, by which Hungary was economically integrated with Austria and, as Austrian power waned, given a major shareholding in the Habsburg empire, henceforth known as the "Dual Monarchy". The compromise (*Ausgleich*) of 1867, engineered by **Ferenc Deák**, brought Hungary prosperity and status, but tied the country inextricably to the empire's fortunes. Buda and Pest underwent rapid expansion and formally merged. Pest was extensively remodelled, acquiring the Nagykörút (Great Boulevard) and Andrássy út, a grand approach to the Városliget, where Hungary's millennial anniversary celebrations were staged in 1896, marking a thousand years since the arrival of the Hungarian tribes in the Carpathian Basin. (In fact they arrived in 895 but preparations were late, so the official date was adjusted to 896.) New suburbs were created to house the burgeoning population, which was by now predominantly Magyar, though there were still large German and Jewish communities. Both elegance and squalor abounded, café society reached its apogee, and Budapest experienced a **cultural efflorescence** in the early years of the twentieth century to rival that of Vienna. Today, the most tangible reminders are the remarkable buildings by Ödön Lechner, Béla Lajta and other masters of Art Nouveau and National Romanticism – the styles that characterized the era.

The Horthy years

Dragged into **World War I** by its allegiance to Austria and Germany, Hungary was facing defeat by the autumn of 1918. The Western or Entente powers decided to dismantle the Habsburg empire in favour of the "**Successor States**" – Romania, Czechoslovakia and Yugoslavia – which would acquire much of their territory at Hungary's expense. In Budapest, the October 30 "Michaelmas Daisy Revolution" put the Social Democratic party of Count **Mihály Károlyi** in power, but his government avoided the issue of land reform, attempted unsuccessfully to negotiate peace with the Entente and finally resigned when France backed further demands by the Successor States.

On March 21, 1919, a **Republic of Councils** (*Tanácsköztársaság*) was proclaimed led by **Béla Kun**, which ruled through local Soviets. Hoping for radical change and believing that "Russia will save us", many initially supported the new regime, but enforced nationalization of land and capital and attacks on religion soon alienated the majority. After 134 days, the regime collapsed before the advancing Romanian army, which occupied Budapest.

1873	1896	1898	1905
Buda, Pest and Óbuda are united to form Budapest	The Underground Railway is inaugurated as part of the Millennial celebrations in Budapest	Sisi, Empress Elizabeth, is assassinated in Switzerland	St Stephen's Basilica is completed after 54 years' work

Then came the **White Terror**, as right-wing gangs moved up from the south killing "Reds" and Jews, who were made scapegoats for the earlier Communist "Red Terror" – especially in Budapest, the Bolshevik capital. **Admiral Miklós Horthy**, self-appointed regent for Karl IV, who had been exiled by the Western allies ("the Admiral without a fleet, for the king without a kingdom") entered what he called the "sinful city" on a white horse, and ordered a return to "traditional values". Meanwhile, at the Paris Conference, Hungary was obliged to sign the **Treaty of Trianon** (July 4, 1920), surrendering two-thirds of its historic territory and three-fifths of its total population (three million in all) to the Successor States. The bitterest loss was **Transylvania** – a devastating blow to national pride. Horthy's regency was characterized by gala balls and hunger marches, revanchism and growing **anti-Semitism**, enshrined in law from 1925. Yet Horthy was a moderate compared to the **Arrow Cross** Fascists waiting in the wings, whose power grew as **World War II** raged, and the Hungarian Second Army perished at Stalingrad.

Anticipating Horthy's defection from the Axis in October 1944, Nazi Germany staged a coup, installing an Arrow Cross government, which enabled them to quicken the pace of the Holocaust in Hungary and begin the massacre of the **Jews** of Budapest. It was only thanks to the valiant efforts of foreign diplomats like Wallenberg and Lutz that half of them survived, when ninety percent of Hungary's provincial Jews perished. In late December, the Red Army smashed through the defensive "Attila Line" and encircled the capital, held by German troops. During the seven-week **siege of Budapest**, citizens endured endless shelling amid a bitter winter, as street-fighting raged. In January the Germans withdrew from Pest, blew up the Danube bridges and holed up in Buda, where the Vár was reduced to rubble as the Red Army battered the Wehrmacht into submission. Aside from the Jews in the ghetto – for whom it meant salvation from the Arrow Cross – the city's **liberation** on February 13, 1945 brought little joy to Budapestis, as the Red Army embarked on an orgy of rape and looting, followed by a wave of deportations to Siberia.

The Communist takeover and the 1956 Uprising

As Budapestis struggled to rebuild their lives after the war, the Soviet-backed **Communists** took control bit by bit – stealthily reducing the power of other forces in society, and using the threat of the Red Army and the **ÁVO secret police**, who took over the former Arrow Cross torture chambers on Andrássy út. By 1948 their hold on Hungary was total, symbolized by the red stars that everywhere replaced the crown of St Stephen, and a huge statue of Stalin beside the Városliget, where citizens were obliged to parade before Hungary's "Little Stalin", **Mátyás Rákosi**.

The power struggles in the Moscow Communist Party leadership that followed the death of Stalin in 1953 were replicated in the other Eastern European capitals, and in Hungary Rákosi was replaced by **Imre Nagy**. Nagy's "New Course" allowed Hungarians an easier life before Rákosi struck back by expelling him from the Party for "deviationism". However, society had taken heart from the respite and intellectuals held increasingly outspoken public debates during the summer of 1956. The mood came to a head in October, when 200,000 people attended the funeral of László Rajk (a victim of the show trials in 1949) in Kerepesi Cemetery, and Budapest's students decided to march to the General Bem statue near the Margít híd.

1912	1919	1920	1944
The magnificent Elephant and Giraffe houses are unveiled in Budapest's Zoo	Admiral Horthy enters Budapest, marking the start of the anti-Semitic White Terror	The Treaty of Trianon carves up the old Hungarian kingdom	A ghetto is established in Budapest's Jewish quarter

On October 23, demonstrators chanting anti-Rákosi slogans crossed the Danube to mass outside Parliament. As dusk fell, students demanding access to the Radio Building were fired upon by the ÁVO, and a spontaneous **1956 Uprising** began, which rapidly took hold throughout Budapest and spread across Hungary. The newly restored Nagy found himself in a maelstrom, as popular demands were irreconcilable with realpolitik – independence and withdrawing from the Warsaw Pact were anathema to the Kremlin. It was Hungary's misfortune that the UN was preoccupied with the Suez Crisis when the Soviets reinvaded on November 10, crushing all resistance in six days. An estimated 2500 Hungarians died and some 200,000 fled abroad; back home, hundreds were executed and thousands jailed for their part in the uprising.

"Goulash socialism" and the end of Communism

After Soviet power had been bloodily restored, **János Kádár** gradually normalized conditions, embarking on cautious reforms to create a "**goulash socialism**" that made Hungary the envy of its Warsaw Pact neighbours and the West's favourite Communist state in the late 1970s. Though everyone knew the limits of the "Hungarian condition", there was enough freedom and consumer goods to keep the majority content. Decentralized management, limited private enterprise and competition made Hungary's economy healthy compared to other Socialist states, but in the 1980s it became apparent that the attempt to reconcile a command economy and one-party rule with market forces was unsustainable. Dissidents tested the limits of criticism, and even within the Party there were those who realized that changes were needed. Happily, this coincided with the advent of Gorbachev, which made it much easier for the reform Communists to shunt Kádár aside in 1988.

The **end of Communism** was heralded by two events the following summer: the ceremonial reburial of Imre Nagy, and the dismantling of the barbed wire along the border with Austria, which enabled thousands of East Germans to escape to the West while "on holiday". In October 1989, the government announced the legalization of other parties as a prelude to free elections, and the People's Republic was renamed the **Republic of Hungary** in a ceremony broadcast live on national television. Two weeks later this was eclipsed by the fall of the Berlin Wall, closely followed by the Velvet Revolution in Czechoslovakia and the overthrow of Ceaușescu in Romania on Christmas Day.

The post-Communist era

Hungary's first **free elections** in the spring of 1990 resulted in a humiliating rejection of the reform Communists' Hungarian Socialist Party (MSzP), and the installation of a centre-right coalition government dominated by the **Hungarian Democratic Forum** (**MDF**) under Premier **József Antall**. Committed to a total break with Communism, the MDF aimed to restore the traditions and hierarchies of prewar Hungary and its former position in Europe.

After Antall's premature death in 1993, his successor failed to turn the economy around and the 1994 elections saw the **Socialists** (under the **MSzP**) return to power. To allay fears of a Communist return to power, they included the **Free Democrats** (SzDSz)

1945	1949	1953	1956
Soviet troops capture Budapest from the Nazis	Budapest's first trolleybus line, #70, is inaugurated on Stalin's seventieth birthday	Hungary's football team demolishes England 6–3	The Hungarian Uprising breaks out on October 23

in government, and reassured Hungary's foreign creditors with austerity measures that angered voters who had expected the Socialists to reverse the growing inequalities in society. It soon became obvious that they were riddled with corruption; some party members became millionaires almost overnight.

The 1998 elections were narrowly won by the **Fidesz-Hungarian Civic Party** of **Viktor Orbán**, a figure of undeniable charisma who repositioned his party to the right, stressing the need to revive national culture and using the buzzword *polgári* (meaning "civic", but redolent of bourgeois middle-class values) to appeal to a broad constituency. The youngest prime minister in Hungarian history, the Oxford-educated Orbán promoted a conservative Christian agenda with an acute understanding of national and religious symbolism.

With an expanding economy, falling inflation and low unemployment levels – plus the achievement of steering Hungary into NATO – Orbán anticipated victory in the parliamentary elections of 2002. Instead, after a vitriolic campaign, his Fidesz–MDF coalition was ousted, the electorate preferring a return to the centre-left alliance of Socialists and Free Democrats, whose most important achievement was to preside over Hungary's accession to the **European Union** in 2004.

In August 2004, the premiership passed to the sports minister and millionaire businessman **Ferenc Gyurcsány**, who revitalized the jaded Socialists by appointing a cabinet of fellow millionaires who got rich during the privatization of state assets in the 1990s. Like previous governments, however, they faced the dilemma that Hungary was living beyond its means – its budget deficit of ten percent of GDP was the highest in the EU – while voters opposed further belt-tightening or reforms of the health system. By promising better welfare while secretly running up deficits, Gyurcsány managed to delay a reckoning long enough to win the **April 2006 election** – the first time a government had been re-elected since democracy was restored.

In September 2006, however, national radio broadcast a **tape-recording** of him telling his cabinet that austerity measures were inevitable "because we fucked up. Not a little, a lot… We lied in the morning, we lied in the evening." While both the context of the speech and the leaking of the tape have aroused much debate, a furore ensued, with weeks of demonstrations outside Parliament led by Fidesz and the MDF. On October 23, **rioting** erupted, protesters battling police around Kossuth tér and Nyugati Station. In a throwback to 1956, they waved Hungarian flags with a hole cut out, and even managed to activate an old Soviet tank from a museum (which stalled before it reached Parliament).

Gyurcsány clung to office but the government was robbed of all authority. Even after he resigned in 2009, the Socialists were a broken force, and in the **elections of 2010** Fidesz, led by a resurgent Orbán, stormed to a massive victory, securing more than two-thirds of the vote. Orbán promptly announced that a **national declaration** "May there be peace, freedom and unity" be posted in every building, an act which soon had the press cynically dubbing him the "Dear Leader".

An even clearer sign of the change in Hungarian politics was the success of the far-right **Jobbik (Movement for Better Hungary)**, which received sixteen percent of the vote, coming third. The rise of this media-savvy group under Gábor Vona was based on its appeal to younger Hungarians – anti-Semitic nationalism is no longer the preserve of old embittered Magyars. Jobbik proudly waved its flags bearing the "Árpád stripes"

1958	1978	1989	1990
Imre Nagy is executed for his role in the 1956 revolt	St Stephen's crown is returned to Hungary from Fort Knox	The Iron Curtain is dismantled	First free elections after the fall of Communism

of the Arrow Cross and openly flaunts its links with the banned Magyar Gárda (Hungarian Guard), the paramilitary group that parades through villages in eastern Hungary "restoring order" – ie terrorizing Gypsy villagers.

Back to the future

Orbán's determination – and there is no doubt that everything his government does stems from him – to shape a new Hungary, transforming its economy and culture, has required a pugnacious, centralized and **interventionist state**. A legal avalanche – some nine hundred laws were drafted between 2010 and 2014 – swept any opposition aside. When independent bodies such as the Constitutional Court voiced criticism, they were stripped of powers; stuffed with government supporters, as at the National Bank; or simply abolished. Checks and balances, Orbán said, were an American invention unsuited to European politics. Government money poured into the coffers of its business supporters with the declared aim of building a right-wing entrepreneurial class, arousing claims of corruption. Much of the media is Fidesz-controlled (state TV news is the propaganda arm of government) or in the hands of friendly oligarchs; Fidesz also handed back control of numerous schools and hospitals to the churches, hoping they would regain their prewar role as the moral backbone of the nation.

Come the **2014 elections**, Fidesz was helped by the lack of a credible alternative, with the opposition on the left riven by divisions. Fidesz's share of the vote fell to 43 percent, but in a reformed electoral system (critics said it was designed to benefit the government) it still won a two-thirds majority in parliament. The far-right **Jobbik** party increased its share of the vote to twenty percent, closing in on the Socialists.

The new Kadarism?

In response to the growing strength of Jobbik, the prime minister increasingly adopted its nationalist rhetoric. In 2014 Orbán said Hungary should become an "**illiberal state**", following the model of Russia, China and Turkey. He put this into practice as he became closer to Vladimir Putin, signing a major deal to build a new nuclear reactor at Paks and taking his cue from the Russian leader in attacking the Central European University and foreign-funded NGOs, which he accused of undermining his government. Like Putin, Orbán developed an obsession with the Hungarian-born financier George Soros, the founder of the CEU, and has accused all his critics of being Soros puppets.

Most significantly, Orbán used the **refugee crisis** to present himself as the true defender of Hungary, indeed of Christian Europe, against the Muslim "hordes" threatening to overrun the country. His speeches talked of Europe belonging to the Europeans, and of Hungarians needing to maintain their homogenous culture. Encouraged by the Brexit vote and Donald Trump's victory, Orbán redoubled his anti-EU rhetoric, with a flow of anti-Brussels propaganda – paradoxical in the country that from 2008 was among the biggest beneficiaries per capita of EU grants. Orbán's ambitions have met some setbacks, however. His plan to create a new golden era in Hungary's **football**, pumping money into stadiums and training across the country, was mocked by the team's defeat by Andorra in 2017; while the country's bid to host the 2024 Olympics was dropped when a national petition revealed the strength of

1999	2001	2002	2004
Hungary joins NATO	*Gresham Palace* hotel is restored to its 1907 glory	National stadium renamed after Ferenc Puskás, the legendary Hungarian footballer	Hungary joins the EU

opposition to the idea. Nonetheless, the continued construction of facilities suggests that a bid for 2028 remains on the cards. The enthusiasm for sport perfectly illustrates Orbán's bread-and-circuses approach which, to his critics, is reminiscent of **Kadarism**, where people are allowed to enjoy themselves while the government maintains a strong grip over many aspects of society, such as the press and schools.

As campaigning began for the 2018 elections, Fidesz was ahead in the polls, helped by Orbán's appeal to national pride in a country that sees itself as being on the losing side in so much of its history. This stance has taken very practical forms, such as cutting the fees charged by foreign-owned utility companies and so defending Hungarians against outside interests. However, Jobbik gained a new ally in 2017: one of Orbán's oldest sparring partners, the businessman turned media mogul **Lajos Simicska**, who fell out with the prime minister in 2014, became increasingly supportive of the right-wing party – a combination that Orbán was at pains to upset. Another potential threat was the **Momentum** party that grew out of the campaign against the Olympics in 2017 (a debacle that showed Orbán was vulnerable), which aims to emulate the victory of the French president Emmanuel Macron.

The view from Budapest

In **Budapest**, while national governments came and went after 1990, **Mayor Gábor Demszky** steered the city gently forwards for twenty years, finally securing state funding for the **fourth metro line** from Keleti Station in Pest to Etele tér in Buda. However, he stepped down at the 2010 elections before he was engulfed by the Fidesz tide – and by allegations of corruption that threatened his administration. His successor, **István Tarlós**, an engineer by trade, ran as an independent with Fidesz backing. He immediately stamped his mark on the city by changing **street names** (the park in front of the Lukács baths in Buda became Elvis Presley Park), and also vowed to make Budapest a cleaner place in part by banning homeless people from the city centre (this was later overturned by the courts).

The city's intellectuals viewed Tarlós with suspicion: his attempt to ban a gay stall at the Sziget festival in 2001 when he was mayor of Óbuda did little to endear him to them. Their fears seemed confirmed by some of the new mayor's actions, but generally Tarlós' time as mayor has seen the city spruced up. Streets and major junctions have been made more pedestrian- and cyclist-friendly, the gleaming new metro line is running smoothly and **restoration projects** have transformed public buildings from the Music Academy to the Várkert Bazár. There is an undeniable buzz about the place , albeit tinged by a palpable political edginess as Hungarians remain deeply divided. However, Tarlós has been increasingly squeezed out of the inner circle of Fidesz, limiting his influence and access to funding. The former Belváros mayor, **Antal Rogán**, is now far closer to Orbán, and Tarlós looks likely to be discarded when his term ends in 2019.

2010	2014	2016	2017
Viktor Orbán leads Fidesz to crushing electoral victory	Orbán re-elected with large parliamentary majority	Orbán's anti-refugee campaign sees a fence built on Hungary's southern border	Hungary's football team lose 0-1 to lowly Andorra

Music

Hungarian classical music enshrines the trinity of Liszt, Bartók and Kodály: Liszt was the founding father, Bartók one of the greatest composers of the twentieth century, and Kodály (himself no slouch at composition) created a widely imitated system of musical education. When you also take into account talented Hungarian soloists like András Schiff and ensembles such as the Budapest Festival Orchestra, it's clear that this small nation has made an outstanding contribution to the world of classical music. After classical, the musical genres most readily associated with Hungary are folk and Gypsy, both of which have some excellent exponents, the former led by Muzsikás and the wonderful singer Márta Sebestyén, and the latter by the likes of the cimbalom player Kálmán Balogh. Meanwhile, Hungarian popular music, while not exactly cutting-edge, is becoming more adventurous as a new generation of DJs and bands exchange ideas with Western European and American artists.

Classical music

Franz Liszt (1811–86), who described himself as a "mixture of Gypsy and Franciscan", cut a flamboyant figure in the salons of Europe as a virtuoso pianist and womanizer. His *Hungarian Rhapsodies* and other similar pieces reflected the "Gypsy" side to his character and the rising nationalism of his era, while later work like the *Transcendental Studies* (whose originality has only recently been recognized) invoked a visionary "Franciscan" mood. Despite his patriotic stance, however, Liszt's first language was German (he never fully mastered Hungarian), and his expressed wish to roam the villages of Hungary with a knapsack on his back was a Romantic fantasy.

That was left to **Béla Bartók** (1881–1945) and **Zoltán Kodály** (1882–1967), who began exploring the remoter districts of Hungary and Transylvania in 1906, collecting peasant music. Despite many hardships and local suspicion of their "monster" (a cutting stylus and phonograph cylinders), they managed to record and catalogue thousands of melodies, laying down high standards of musical ethnography – still maintained in Hungary today – while discovering a rich source of inspiration for their own compositions.

Bartók created a personal but universal musical language by reworking the raw essence of Magyar and Finno-Ugric folk music in a modern context – in particular his six string quartets – although Hungarian public opinion was originally hostile. Feeling misunderstood and out of step with his country's increasingly pro-Nazi policies, Bartók left Hungary in 1940, dying poor and embittered in the United States. Since then, however, his reputation has soared, and the return of his body in 1988 occasioned national celebrations, shrewdly sponsored by the state.

Kodály's music is more consciously national: Bartók called it "a real profession of faith in the Hungarian soul". His *Peacock Variations* are based on a typical "Old Style" (to use Bartók's terminology) pentatonic tune and the *Dances of Galanta* on the popular music played by Gypsy bands. "Old Style" tunes also form the core of Kodály's work in musical education: the "Kodály method" employs group singing to develop musical skill at an early age. His ideas made Hungarian music teaching among the best in the world.

The classical tradition was continued by two of the leading avant-garde composers of the late twentieth century, **György Ligeti** and **György Kurtág**. Both were born in Transylvania, and both were strongly influenced by their time in the West in the late 1950s. Ligeti never returned, and completely embraced the experimental techniques around him, while Kurtág returned to Budapest to develop his very individual style that retains a strong Bartokian influence.

Folk music

Hungarian folk music (*Magyar népzene*) originated around the Urals and the Turkic steppes over a millennium ago, and is different again from Gypsy or Roma music. The haunting rhythms and pentatonic scale of this "Old Style" music were subsequently overlaid by "New Style" European influences – which have been discarded by more modern enthusiasts in the folk revival centred around **táncház**. This "Dance House" movement was born in the 1970s when folk musicians in Budapest began to re-create the rural dance gatherings that were still part of everyday life in Hungarian villages in Transylvania. It struck a chord with the urban middle classes, who were left cold by the official version of Hungarian folk music and attracted by the forbidden fruits of Hungarian culture. Official disapproval (the dance houses were tolerated but were carefully monitored by the authorities) lent them an underground thrill, and their popularity spread – the musicians noted that even the police informers couldn't resist joining in. Since then, the shouting, whistling and slapping of boots and thighs has continued unabated, and has managed to survive the official embrace that the Fidesz government has predictably flung round the folk movement – folk now has its own kitsch talent show, *Fölszállt a Páva*.

The two biggest names to emerge from the *táncház* movement were **Muzsikás** and **Márta Sebestyén**, who have been regular collaborators for years. A four-piece ensemble comprising bass, violin and flute, Muzsikás (pronounced *Mu-zhi-kash*) started out in the early 1970s by exploring the musical archives of village folk music, from which they derived their own distinctive repertoire, combining traditional Hungarian music with the sounds of Transylvania, across the border in Romania – while their recorded output is not that prolific, they do tour regularly, both at home and abroad.

Unquestionably Hungary's finest folk singer, and one of the best in Europe, Sebestyén's gorgeous and distinctive voice has seen her become firmly established on the world music scene in recent years, a reputation that was sealed after she featured on the soundtrack to the film *The English Patient*. Aside from her regular appearances with Muzsikás, Sebestyén has also sung with **Vujicsics**, a seven-strong ensemble from Pomáz near Szentendre who specialize in Serbian and Croatian folk melodies. As both of these bands grow older, they have spawned a second generation of groups: two of the top new ensembles are the **Buda Folk Band** and **Söndörgő**, formed respectively by the sons of Muzsikás and Vujicsics members.

Two dance house specialists that play regularly in the city are the **Ökrös** and **Tükrös** bands, while others upholding folk traditions are **István "Szalonna" Pál** and his band, **Róbert Lakatos and the Rév** – Lakatos's viola (*brácsa*) gives the music a wonderfully mellow sound – and three Roma ensembles from Transylvania, the **Szászcsávás** and **Magyarpalatkai Band** bands and the brilliant violinist **Kis Csipás** and his band. The **Csík Ensemble** has moved away from its folk roots towards folk-style cover versions of pop songs – though they alienated some followers by backing the Fidesz electoral campaign.

Three artists to look out for are **Miklós Bóth**, a guitarist who sounds like Jimi Hendrix jamming with Muzsikás; the American violinist **Bob Cohen**, whether with the Budapest klezmer outfit **Di Naye Kapelye** or in other configurations; and perhaps the best known of the three, **Félix Lajkó**, a Hungarian virtuoso violinist and zither player from the Vojvodina region of Serbia, whose eccentric fusion of folk, Gypsy and jazz inspires a devout following.

The new generation of female singers is a very strong one: **Bea Palya**, who spans Hungarian, Roma and Jewish music traditions; **Ági Szaloki**, who has sung with the Ökrös Band as well as performing solo; **Ági Herczku**, **Éva Korpás** and **Szilvi Bognár**, who sing with a range of bands.

Gypsy music

Played on anything from spoons and milk jugs to guitars, **Gypsy** or **Roma music** ranges from haunting laments to playful wedding songs. The band that pioneered this sound in the 1980s was **Kályi Jág**, whose success transformed the way Roma communities played their own music. For a primer check out Tony Gatliff's excellent film *Latcho Drom*, which explores Roma music from India to Spain. The next generation of Hungarian Roma musicians includes the groups **Romengo**, **Vojasa**, **Parno Graszt** and the **Karaván Familia** – all of whom tour extensively and are the focal point of most Roma festivals in Hungary and abroad. Transylvanian dance house bands (see p.221) are from a different Roma tradition, but they are also worth catching. The distinctive voice of Mónika Juhász-Miczura, or **Mitsoura**, is featured on many CDs – she has also recorded albums as a solo artist.

Three of the best known Roma artists are **Kálmán Balogh**, one of the world's foremost exponents of the cimbalom, a hammer dulcimer (stringed instrument) played with little mallets, with a repertoire ranging from Gypsy tunes to Bach; the jazz guitarist **Ferenc Snétberger**; and the wizard violinist **Roby Lakatos**, who tours extensively around the world from his base in Brussels. A seventh-generation descendant of János Bihari (aka "King of the Gypsy Violinists"), Lakatos hails from the Romungro tradition of "Gypsy music" that you will see advertised at touristy restaurants, known in Hungarian as **Magyar nóta**. Consisting of a series of mid-nineteenth-century Hungarian ballads traditionally played by Roma musicians, Magyar nóta is usually performed by one or two violinists, a bass player and a guy on the cimbalom. The more famous restaurants boast their own musical dynasties, such as the Lakatos family, who have been performing this sort of music for over a century.

In recent years a decline in demand for Gypsy restaurant bands has sent younger Romungro musicians in new directions, such as **Roma jazz** – look out for tenor saxophonist **Gábor Bolla** in particular – or the cabaret-style music of **Budapest Bár**, led by Róbert Farkas.

Popular music and jazz

Budapest has undergone a **popular music** revival in the last few years: radio stations and music magazines have taken off and the city has become part of the international tour circuit – the Sziget Festival each August (see p.183) is now one of the premier music gatherings on the continent. This has all had a knock-on effect on local music. **Róbert Németh** turns out Magyar alt rock; **Punnany Massif** and **Hallott Pénz** do a pop/hip-hop crossover; and **Kiscsillag** is the new band around the popular singer **Lovasi**. **Ivan and the Parasol** and **Fran Palermo** are young retro rock outfits while **Quimby**'s Tibor Kiss is the Hungarian equivalent of Tom Waits. Two newer groups on the circuit are the rapping **Anna and the Barbies** and the alternative rock band **30Y**. Budai is the king of **DJ** scene, but look out too for Bahlzack and Chris Lawyer.

A popular crossover style blends pop with Hungarian folk or Thirties swing: **MagyarVista Social Club** (a play on the name of the famous Cuban outfit – Magyar Vista is the Hungarian name of a village in Romania) and **Tárkány Művek** combine jazz, rock and folk. The bands backing the gloriously clear voice of **Flóra Herczeg** combine folk, pop and jazz; **Bori Rutkai**'s pop-chanson style draws on many traditions; and **Cimbaliband** offer a world-music take on Roma music.

Jazz has a devout (but small) following in the country. As well the acts mentioned in this book's Arts and entertainment chapter (see p.185), it is worth checking out **Mihály Dresch**, a saxophonist who draws on folk traditions; and **Miklós Lukács**, a pupil of the cymbalomist Kálmán Balogh. **Péter Rozsnyoi** produces some fabulous fugues; and **Orbán György** is a bass player of flair. Four fine female performers are the singer-songwriter **Harcsa Veronika**; **Nikoletta Szőke**, who has won international awards; **Tamara Mózes**, a singer-pianist who sheds new light on the classics; and **Janka Vörös**, who has a passion for Janis Joplin.

Discography

An excellent online source for all CDs is the Hangvető website (⊚hangveto.hu). A full discography of the works of Liszt, Bartók and Kodály, conductors like Dohnányi and Doráti, and contemporary Hungarian soloists and singers would fill a catalogue, but look out for the following names: pianists András Schiff, Zoltán Kocsis (who died in 2016) and Dezső Ránki; the Liszt Ferenc Chamber Orchestra and the Budapest Festival Orchestra; conductors Iván Fischer and Tamás Vasáry; and singers Mária Zádori, Ingrid Kertesi, Andrea Rost, Adrienne Csengery, József Gregor and Kolos Kováts.

Folk and Gypsy music can be bought at all record stores – Fonó is the biggest label. Note that a CD with a picture of a Gypsy orchestra all dressed up in red waistcoats is of the "*nóta*" variety – listen before you buy to check this is the kind of Gypsy music you want. As well as the artists listed here, there are hundreds of great recordings in the above fields. The following simply offer an introduction; particular recommendations are marked with the ★ symbol.

INDIVIDUAL ARTISTS

★**Kálmán Balogh** *Kálmán Balogh and the Gipsy Cimbalom Band* (Fonó). A terrific collection of tunes from Hungary and the wider region, including the heart-rending version of the folk song *A csitári hegyek alatt*. Recorded with artistic director Romano Kokalo, *Gipsy Colours* (Fonó, Budapest) is a fabulous selection of Gypsy dance tunes from the region.

★**Félix Lajkó** *Remény*, *Félix* (both on Tilos), *Lajkó Félix and his Band* (Fonó). The best recordings so far of this Hungarian virtuoso violinist from Subotica in northern Serbia – *Remény* (*Hope*) features previously unreleased concert recordings alongside pieces from the soundtrack to *Othello*, while *Lajkó Félix and his Band* is a highly charged set of recordings made in the woods near his home. He also features with the Boban Markovic Orchestra, the fantastic Serbian Gypsy ensemble, on the CD *Srce Cigansko*, which combines typically rumbustious Serbian brass with Lajkó's busy violin.

★**Roby Lakatos** Earlier works include *Lakatos* (Deutsche Grammophon), which features new workouts of favourites by the likes of Brahms alongside traditional Hungarian folk songs; *Later with Lakatos* (Deutsche Grammophon) is a homecoming concert in Budapest's Thália Theatre from 1999. More recent albums (all on the Avanti label) are *Firedance*, a sizzling record exploring Gypsy themes from around the world; *Klezmer Karma*, a funky, Jewish-influenced recording featuring performances by Miriam Fuks and the Franz Liszt Chamber Orchestra; and *Roby Lakatos with Musical Friends*, an all-jazz project boasting some stellar guests such as Stephane Grappelli and Marc Fossett.

Bea Palya *Ágról ágra* (Orphea). Starting with a Hungarian folk prayer at dawn, Palya moves across borders to embrace Romanian and Persian songs with the same authority she brings to her own tradition.

Márta Sebestyén *Kismet* (Hannibal). On this wide-ranging album, Hungary's leading *táncház* singer draws upon various folk traditions, with Bosnian, Hindi and Irish songs, among others; otherwise, Sebestyén is best known for her recordings with the folk group Muzsikás (see p.221), while her international star has risen thanks to significant contributions to the Grammy-award-winning Deep Forest album *Boheme* and the film *The English Patient*.

GROUPS

★**Bazseva** *Első Bekezdés* (Fonó). Bazseva's six members got together in 2013 with the intention of ridding folk of the kitsch image of boots and hats and moustaches, and show what a life force it can be.

Béla Lakatos and The Gypsy Youth Project *Introducing* (World Music Network). Lively debut album from this talented outfit, with songs pertaining to rural Roma life. Wonderful vocals and some fabulous instrumental improvisation.

Besh o Drom Vibrant large ensemble that produces a feverish Balkan blend of dance music with its driving brass and whirling rhythms – perhaps at its rawest on their first album, *Macsó Hímzés* (Fonó).

★**Buda Folk Band** *Magyar Világi Népzene* (Fonó). The first recording by "Sons of Muzsikás" band – which includes Sándor Csoóri and Márton Éri – develops traditional Hungarian folk, drawing on its melodies and instrumentation.

★**Budapest Bar** *Budapest Bar 1* (EMI). The first album of the Robert Farkas cabaret band is their best, with the supreme opening song *Szivemben bomba van* (*There's a bomb in my heart*).

Csik Ensemble *Ez a vonat, ha elindult, Hadd menjen…* (Fonó). Rooted in the folk tradition, the band works with pop musicians such as Tibor Kiss of the band Quimby, to powerful effect.

★**Di Naye Kapelye** The band's three albums to date are the eponymous *Di Naye Kapelye*, *A Mazeldiker Yid* and *Traktorist* (all Oriente Musik), all terrific, and typically exuberant, klezmer recordings, which make for immensely enjoyable listening. *Traktorist* features a wonderfully jolly Communist-era ode to the Yiddish tractor.

★**Herczeg Flóra és a Például Igen** *Mi Jöhet még!* Very enjoyable collection of songs by this young singer from Eger and her group, led by trumpeter János Hámori.

★**Muzsikás** *The Bartók Album* (Hannibal). Featuring Márta Sebestyén and the Romanian violinist Alexander Balanescu, this manages to set the music of Bartók in its original context – three of Bartók's violin duos are presented alongside original field recordings and recordings of his transcriptions by Muzsikás.

★**Morning Star** (Hannibal). Another fine Muzsikás volume – interestingly, their record company recommended slight changes and a softening of edges for this foreign edition of *Hazafelé* (Hungaroton), the original Hungarian recording. Their latest release, 2004's *Live at the Liszt Academy of Music*, which again stars Sebestyén, is a compilation of recordings taken from successive appearances at the Budapest Spring Festival.

★**Lakatos Róbert és a Rév** *BrácsaTánc* (FolkEuropa). A pleasantly low-key CD by this group from Komarom in Slovakia, led by the mellow viola of Robert Lakatos. *Rév* means ferry, and the group moves happily between the different musics of the region – Lakatos himself is also at home in the classical tradition, playing Bartók.

Tükrös Ensemble Two of the best CDs by this established folk band present tunes from the Mezőség region of Transylvania (*A mi Mezőségünk*) and from the Szatmár region of eastern Hungary (*Szatmári népzene*, both FolkEuropa).

Vujicsics Ensemble *Serbian Music from South Hungary* (Hannibal). More complex tunes than most Magyar folk music, with a distinct Balkan influence. Two albums featuring Márta Sebestyén are *25 – Live at the Academy of Music* (R-E-Disc 005), a concert in Budapest celebrating the group's twenty-fifth anniversary, and *Podravina* (R-E-Disc 004), a selection of Croatian dance melodies.

COMPILATION ALBUMS

Magyar népzene 3 (*Hungarian folk music*; Hungaroton). A four-disc set of field recordings covering the whole range of folk music, including Old and New Style songs, instrumental and occasional music, that's probably the best overall introduction. In the West, the discs are marketed as *Folk Music of Hungary Vol.1*.

★**Rendhagyó Prímástalálkozó 1** (*Prímás Parade 1*; FolkEuropa). A fascinating supergroup that brings together folk musicians, a rock guitarist, a classical violinist, jazz saxophonist and more – but all rooted in Hungarian and Roma traditions of Transylvania. The result sparkles, never more so than when the electric guitar of Miklós Both plays the role of the violin *primás*. The follow-up CD struggles to match its sparkle.

Rough Guide to Hungary (World Music Network). The second Rough Guide to Hungarian music is an excellent introduction to the many wildly differing sounds of the country's music. It includes a bonus CD by Tarkány.

Rough Guide to the Music of Eastern Europe (World Music Network). Although most of the songs on this CD are from the Balkans, there is a healthy representation from Hungary, featuring songs by Márta Sebestyén, Vízöntő and Kálmán Balogh and the Gypsy Cimbalom Band.

Rough Guide to the Music of Hungarian Gypsies (World Music Network). All the big-hitters are here on this thoroughly comprehensive introduction to the many strands of Hungarian Gypsy music – the highlight is a ripping tune by Mitsoura performed with the brilliant Romanian band Fanfare Ciocarlia. Also worth checking are the *Rough Guide to Music of the Gypsies*, with Hungary represented by Kálmán Balogh and the Joszef Lacatos Orchestra, and the *Rough Guide to Klezmer Revival* (RGNET 1203), which features a track by Di Naye Kapelye.

Táncházi muzsika (*Music from the Táncház*; Hungaroton). An early double album of the Sebő Ensemble playing *táncház* music from various regions of Hungary. Wild and exciting rhythms by pioneers of the movement.

Táncház-Népzene (*Dance House – Folk Music*; Hagyományok Háza). An excellent series that has been going since 2003, produced by the Hungarian Heritage House.

Új élő népzene. The series *Living Village Music* has been going for twenty years, and its twenty albums feature a great mixture of dances, ballads and instrumental pieces by local artists from all over the Carpathian Basin.

Books

There is a wide range of books on Budapest available in the city, particularly architecture titles, photography collections or translations of Hungarian literature. Books tagged with the ★ symbol are particularly recommended. See p.192 for a list of Budapest's better bookshops, most of which can take orders.

ART, ARCHITECTURE AND PHOTOGRAPHY

Irén Ács *Hungary at Home*. Excellent collection of photos covering all walks of life in postwar Hungary. Her other books, including *Rendezvous*, are also worth looking out for in bookshops.

★ **Bruno Bourel & Lajos Parti Nagy** *Lightscapes*. One of the most interesting collections of photos available. Taken around the city by Bourel, a sharp-eyed French photographer who has lived there for many years, they are accompanied by words from a leading contemporary Hungarian writer.

Bob Dent *Budapest: A Cultural and Literary History*. A wide-ranging background to the city by an English journalist and long-term resident of Budapest.

Györgyi Éri et al *A Golden Age: Art and Society in Hungary 1896–1914*. Hungary's Art Nouveau age captured in a beautifully illustrated coffee-table volume.

★ **János Gerle** et al *Budapest: An Architectural Guide*. The best of the small new guides to the city's twentieth-century architecture, covering almost 300 buildings, with brief descriptions in Hungarian and English.

★ **Ruth Gruber** *Jewish Heritage Travel: A Guide to Central and Eastern Europe*. The most comprehensive guide to Jewish sights in Budapest and elsewhere.

Edwin Heathcote *Budapest: A Guide to Twentieth-Century Architecture*. A useful and informative pocket guide to the city, though with some curious omissions.

★ **László Lugo Lugosi** et al *Budapest – On the Danube; Walks in the Jewish Quarter; The Castle District; Jewish Budapest; Walks Around the Great Boulevard*. A series of small-format architectural guides – the last one is especially recommended.

Imre Móra *Budapest Then and Now*. A personal and very informative set of accounts of life in the capital, past and present.

Our Budapest A very informative series of pocket-size books: written in Hungarian and English by experts in their fields, and published by Budapest City Hall, they cover the city's architecture, baths and parks, and are very cheap, though unfortunately the standard of English varies.

Tamás Révész *Budapest: A City before the Millennium*. Excellent collection of black-and-white photographs of the city, though the text can be irritating.

Dora Wieberson et al *The Architecture of Historic Hungary*. Comprehensive illustrated survey of Hungarian architecture through the ages.

HISTORY, POLITICS AND SOCIETY

Robert Bideleux & Ian Jeffries *A History of Eastern Europe: Crisis and Change*. An excellent and wide-ranging history of the region.

Bryan Cartledge *The Will to Survive: A History of Hungary*. An excellent account of how the Magyars came to the Carpathian Basin and have since clung on to their small patch of territory through the ups and many downs of history.

Judit Frigyesi *Béla Bartók and Turn-of-the-century Budapest*. Placing Bartók in his cultural milieu, this is an excellent account of the Hungarian intellectual world at the beginning of the twentieth century.

Jörg K. Hoensch *A History of Modern Hungary 1867–1994*. An authoritative history of Hungary.

Paul Lendvai *The Hungarians: 1000 Years of Victory in Defeat*. Refreshing, readable and authoritative book on Hungary's complex and often tragic history, with particularly stimulating accounts of the Treaty of Trianon

and the subsequent Nazi and Communist tyrannies – there are some fascinating pictures, too.

Bill Lomax *Hungary 1956*. Still probably the best – and shortest – book on the Uprising, by an acknowledged expert on modern Hungary. Lomax also edited *Eyewitness in Hungary*, an anthology of accounts by foreign Communists (most of whom were sympathetic to the Uprising) that vividly depicts the elation, confusion and tragedy of the events of October 1956.

John Lukács *Budapest 1900*. Excellent and very readable account of the politics and society of Budapest at the turn of the century, during a golden age that was shortly to come to an end.

John Man *Attila the Hun*. A beautifully written biography of the Magyars' mythical ancestor, illuminating horsemanship and warfare as practised by the Seven Tribes that later colonized the Carpathian Basin.

★**Michael Stewart** *The Time of the Gypsies*. This perceptive book on Roma culture is based on anthropological research conducted in a Roma community in northern Hungary in the 1980s.

Tony Thorne *Countess Dracula*. An intriguing biography of the sixteenth-century "Blood Countess" Erzsébet Báthory, which argues that she was framed by her uncle to safeguard the Báthory fortune.

BIOGRAPHY AND TRAVEL WRITING

Magda Dénes *Castles Burning: A Child's Life in War*. A moving biographical account of the Budapest ghetto and postwar escape to France, Cuba and the United States, seen through the eyes of a Jewish girl. The author died in 1966, shortly before the book was published.

★**György Faludy** *My Happy Days in Hell*. A remarkable autobiographical account of Faludy's horrendous experience of both Nazi and Soviet repression, including starvation and torture in a labour camp, told with ironic good cheer. His *Selected Poems 1933–80* presents fiery, lyrical poetry with themes of political defiance and the nobility of the human spirit.

Edward Fox *The Hungarian Who Walked to Heaven*. A brief account of the life of Sándor Kőrösi Csoma, the Hungarian who went in search of the roots of the ancient Hungarians and got sidetracked into making the first Tibetan dictionary.

Paul Hoffman *The Man Who Loved Only Numbers*. Highly engaging biography of the Hungarian mathematical genius Paul Erdős. Includes a fascinating portrait of Budapest between the wars.

Ray Keenoy *Eminent Hungarians*. Everything you always wanted to know about Hungary's most renowned historical and contemporary figures – from Lajos Kossuth and Attila

József, to Harry Houdini and Ernő Rubik, creator of the Rubiks cube.

★**Patrick Leigh Fermor** *A Time of Gifts; Between the Woods and the Water*. In 1934 the young Leigh Fermor started walking from Holland to Turkey, reaching Hungary in the closing chapter of *A Time of Gifts*. In *Between the Woods and the Water* the inhabitants of the Great Plain and Transylvania – both Gypsies and aristocrats – are wonderfully evoked. Lyrical and erudite. Artemis Cooper's biography, *Patrick Leigh Fermor: An Adventure*, also sheds interesting light on his account.

Giorgio and Nicola Pressburger *Homage to the Eighth District*. Evocative short stories about Jewish life in Budapest, before, during and after World War II, by twin brothers who fled Hungary in 1956.

Ernő Szép *The Smell of Humans*. A first-rate but harrowing memoir of the Holocaust in Hungary.

★**Nick Thorpe** *The Danube: A Journey Upriver from the Black Sea to the Black Forest*. The BBC's Central European Correspondent, Thorpe (who lives in Budapest) has both the background knowledge and the journalist's eye to put together a fascinating volume that presents the living river in its historical setting.

LITERATURE

Hungary's fabulously rich **literary heritage** has been more widely appreciated in recent years thanks to the success of authors such as Antal Szerb, Sándor Márai and the Nobel Prize-winning Imre Kertész. A useful starting point is Babel Guides' *Hungarian Literature*, an informative guide to the best Hungarian fiction, drama and poetry in translation, with selected excerpts. There are also numerous collections of short stories published in Budapest, though the quality of translations varies from the sublime to the ridiculous. Works by nineteenth-century authors such as Mór Jókai are most likely to be found in secondhand bookshops (see p.192). The list of volumes published by Bloodaxe has done much to spread the word about Hungary's poets.

POETRY

Attila József *The Iron-Blue Vault*. József's powerful and arresting verse, which made him enemies on both the left and right, is some of the finest poetry ever written in Hungarian.

Miklós Radnóti *Forced March* (Enitharmon). There are several translations of Radnóti's sparse, anguished poetry. This collection of his final poems, found in his coat pocket after he had been shot on a forced march to a labour camp, translated by György Gömöri and Clive Wilmer, is an excellent place to start.

Zsuzsa Rakovszky *New Life*. Well-received volume translated by the Hungarian-born English poet George Szirtes.

FICTION

Tibor Déry *The Portuguese Princess*. Wry short stories by a once-committed Communist, who was jailed for three years after the Uprising and died in 1977.

Péter Esterházy *Celestial Harmonies*. Written by a descendant of the famous aristocratic family, this is a dense and demanding book, chronicling the rise of the Esterházys during the Austro-Hungarian empire and their downfall under Communism. It was also a glowing tribute to his father – but as the book was being published Esterházy was shocked to learn that his father had been an informer for the Communist secret police. Esterházy later published a revised edition with an extra section reassessing his relationship with his father.

Tibor Fischer *Under the Frog, A Black Comedy.* "Under a frog down a coalmine" is a Hungarian expression meaning "Things can't get worse", but this fictional account of the 1956 Uprising will have you in stitches. Fischer's parents fled to Britain in 1956.

★ **Imre Kertész** *Fateless.* Drawing from the author's own experiences as an Auschwitz survivor, this Nobel prize-winning author's book tells the tale of a young boy's deportation to, and survival in, a concentration camp. A brilliant translation by Tim Wilkinson.

Dezső Kosztolányi *Skylark.* A short and tragic story of an old couple and their beloved child by one of Hungary's top writers of the twentieth century, in a masterly translation by Richard Aczél. Kosztolányi's *Esti Kornél* is a Hungarian classic, a series of whimsical short tales that offers a wonderful portrait of prewar Budapest.

Gyula Krúdy *Adventures of Sinbad.* Stories about a gourmand and womanizer by a popular Hungarian author with similar interests to his hero.

Sándor Márai *Embers.* An atmospheric and moving tale about friendship, love and betrayal by one of Hungary's most respected pre-World War II writers; a

beautiful read, as is his early novel *The Rebels*, translated by George Szirtes.

Péter Nádas *A Book of Memories.* This translation of a novel about a novelist writing about a novel caused a sensation when it appeared in 1998. A Proustian account of bisexual relationships, Stalinist repression and modern-day Hungary in a brilliant translation by Iván Sanders.

Jenő Rejtő *The Blonde Hurricane.* Like Antal Szerb and Miklós Radnóti, Rejtő was a great Hungarian writer who was killed in the Holocaust for his Jewish descent: all three could have escaped, but they thought it would never happen in Budapest. He wrote a series of excellent romps – this translation succeeds better than Rejtő's *Quarantine in the Grand Hotel.*

★ **Antal Szerb** *Journey by Moonlight.* This Hungarian classic, written in 1937, tells the story of a Hungarian businessman on honeymoon in Italy who embarks upon a mystical and dazzling journey through the country. Len Rix's translation captures the atmosphere of the original beautifully. Two more brilliant Szerb novels are *The Pendragon Legend* and *Oliver VII*, one set in Wales and the other mainly in Venice, while his *Martians' Guide to Budapest* is a delightful portrait of the city.

FOOD AND WINE

Carolyn Bánfalvi *Food, Wine, Budapest.* A very useful primer on Hungarian cuisine and drink, with information about shopping, markets and restaurants. This first edition was printed in 2007, and a new edition is long overdue.

Susan Derecskey *The Hungarian Cookbook.* A good, easy-to-follow selection of traditional and modern recipes.

George Lang *The Cuisine of Hungary.* A well-written and beautifully illustrated work, telling you everything you need to know about Hungarian cooking, its history and how to do it yourself.

Zsófi Mautner *Budapest Bites.* Hungary's top food blogger has produced her first cookbook in English, an enticing showcase for Hungarian cuisine.

★ **Robert Smyth** *Hungarian Wine: A Tasting Trip to the New Old World.* An authoritative and up-to-date guide to Hungarian wine, region by region, introducing the grape varieties and picking out the winemakers to look for. Smyth also recommends places to eat and stay for those who want to visit the wineries.

Hungarian

Hungarian is a unique, complex and subtle tongue, classified as belonging to the Finno-Ugric linguistic group, which includes Finnish and Estonian. If you happen to know those languages, however, don't expect them to be a help: there are some structural similarities, but lexically they are totally different. In fact, some scholars think the connection is completely bogus and have linked Hungarian to the Siberian Chuvash language and a whole host of other fairly obscure tongues. Essentially, the origins of Hungarian remain a mystery and, although a few words of Turkish have crept in, together with some German, English and (a few) Russian neologisms, there's not much that the beginner will recognize.

Consequently, foreigners aren't really expected to speak Hungarian, and locals are used to being addressed in **German**, the lingua franca of Hungarian tourism. However, **English** is gaining ground rapidly, and is increasingly understood. That said, a few basic Magyar phrases can make all the difference. Hungarians are intensely proud of their language and pleased when foreigners make an effort to learn a few courtesies. Note that **signage** is mostly in Hungarian only, though multilingual signs can be found on the metro, in most museums and in many restaurants.

The Rough Guides' *Hungarian for Travellers* is a useful **phrasebook** and, if you're prepared to study the language seriously, the best available book is *Colloquial Hungarian* (Routledge). As a supplement, invest in one of the handy little *Angol–Magyar/Magyar–Angol Kisszótár* dictionaries, available from bookshops in Hungary.

BASIC GRAMMAR

Although its rules are complicated, it's worth describing a few features of **Hungarian grammar**, albeit imperfectly. Hungarian is an agglutinative language – in other words, its vocabulary is built upon **root-words**, which are modified in various ways to express different ideas and nuances. Instead of prepositions "to", "from", "in" etc, Hungarian uses **suffixes**, or tags added to the ends of genderless **nouns**. The change in suffix is largely determined by the noun's context: for example the noun "book" (*könyv*) will take a final "*et*" in the accusative (*könyvet*); "in the book" = *könyvben*; "from the book" = *könyvből*. It is also affected by the rules of vowel harmony (which take a while to get used to, but don't alter meaning, so don't worry about getting them wrong!). Most of the nouns in the vocabulary section below are in the nominative or subject form, that is, without suffixes. In Hungarian, "**the**" is *a* (before a word beginning with a consonant) or *az* (preceding a vowel); the word for "**a/an**" is *egy* (which also means "one").

Plurals are indicated by adding a final "k", with a link vowel if necessary, giving -ek, -ok or -ak. Nouns preceded by a number or other indication of quantity (eg, many, several) do not appear as plural: eg *könyvek* means "books", but "two books" is *két könyv* (using the singular form of the noun).

Adjectives precede the noun (*a piros ház* = the red house), adopting suffixes to form the comparative (*jó* = good; *jobb* = better), plus the prefix *leg* to signify the superlative (*legjobb* = the best).

Negatives are usually formed by placing the word *nem* before the verb or adjective. *Ez* (this), *ezek* (these), *az* (that) and *azok* (those) are the **demonstratives**.

PRONUNCIATION

Achieving passably good **pronunciation**, rather than grammar, is the first priority (see opposite for general guidelines). **Stress** almost invariably falls on the first syllable of a word and all letters are spoken, although in sentences the tendency is to slur words together. Vowel sounds are greatly affected by the bristling **accents** (that actually distinguish separate letters) which, together with the "double letters" *cs, gy, ly, ny, sz, ty* and *zs*, give the Hungarian **alphabet** its formidable appearance.

a o as in h**o**t

á a as in f**a**ther

b b as in **b**est

c ts as in ba**t**s

cs ch as in **ch**urch

d d as in **d**ust

e e as in y**e**t

é ay as in s**ay**

f f as in **f**ed

g g as in **g**o

gy a soft dy as in **d**ue

h h as in **h**at

i i as in b**i**t, but slightly longer

í ee as in s**ee**

j y as in **y**es

k k as in sic**k**

l l as in **l**eap

ly y as in **y**es

m m as in **m**ud

n n as in **n**ot

ny ny as in oni**on**

o aw as in s**aw**, with the tongue kept high

ó aw as in s**aw**, as above but longer

ö ur as in f**ur**, with the lips tightly rounded but without any "r" sound

ő ur as in f**ur**, as above but longer

p p as in si**p**

r r pronounced with the tip of the tongue like a Scottish "r"

s sh as in **sh**op

sz s as in **s**o

t t as in si**t**

ty ty as in **T**uesday

u u as in p**u**ll

ú oo as in f**oo**d

ü u as in the German "**ü**ber" with the lips tightly rounded

ű u as above, but longer

v v as in **v**at

w v as in "**V**alkman," "**v**hiskey" or "**W**C" (vait-say)

z z as in **z**ero

zs zh as in mea**s**ure

WORDS AND PHRASES

BASICS

Do you speak ...	beszél ...
... English	... angolul
... German	... németül
... French	... franciául
yes	igen
OK	jó
no/not	nem
and	és
or	vagy
I (don't) understand	(nem) értem
please	kérem
excuse me (apology)	bocsánat, or elnézést
excuse me (to attract attention)	legyen szíves
two beers, please	két sört kérek
thank you (very much)	köszönöm (szépen)
you're welcome	szívesen
hello/goodbye	szia (informal)
good morning	jó reggelt
good day	jó napot
good evening	jó estét
good night	jó éjszakát
goodbye	viszontlátásra (formal)
see you later	viszlát (more informal)
how are you?	hogy vagy? (informal)
how are you?	hogy van? (formal)
could you speak more slowly?	elmondaná lassabban?
what do you call this?	ennek mi a neve? or ezt hogy hívják?
please write it down	kérem, írja le
today	ma
tomorrow	holnap
the day after tomorrow	holnapután
yesterday	tegnap
the day before yesterday	tegnapelőtt
in the morning	reggel
in the evening	este
at noon	délben
at midnight	éjfélkor

QUESTIONS AND REQUESTS

Hungarian has numerous interrogative modes whose subtleties elude foreigners, so it's best to use the simple *van?* ("is there?"), to which the reply might be *nincs* or *nincsen* ("there isn't"/"there aren't any"). In shops or restaurants you will immediately be addressed with the one-word *tessék*, meaning "Can I help you?", "What would you like?" or "Next!" To order in restaurants, shops and markets, use *kérek* ("I'd like ...") plus accusative noun; *Kérem, adjon azt* ("Please give me that"); *Egy ilyet kérek* ("I'll have one of those").

I'd like/we'd like	Szeretnék/szeretnénk
Where is/are ...?	Hol van/vannak ...?
Which way is/are ...?	Merre van/vannak ...?
Hurry up!	Siessen!
How much is it?	Mennyibe kerül?
for one night	egy éjszakára
per week	egy hétre
a single room	egyágyas szoba
a double room	kétágyas szoba

hot (cold) water	meleg (hideg) víz	a one-way ticket to ... please	egy jegyet kérek ... -ra/ re csak oda
a shower	egy zuhany		
It's very expensive	Ez nagyon drága	a return ticket to ...	egy retur jegyet ... -ra/re
Do you have anything cheaper?	Van valami olcsóbb?	Do I have to change trains?	Át kell szállnom?
Do you have a student discount?	van diák kedvezmény?	towards	felé
		on the right (left)	jobbra (balra)
Is everything included?	Ebben minden szerepel?	straight ahead	egyenesen előre
I asked for ...	Én ... -t rendeltem	(over) there/here	ott/itt
The bill please	Fizetni szeretnék	Where are you going?	Hova mész/megy?
We're paying separately	Külön-külön fizetünk		(informal/formal)
what?	mi?	Is that on the way to ...?	Az a ... úton?
why?	miért?	I want to get out at ...	Le akarok szállni ... -on/ en
when?	mikor?		
who?	ki?	please stop here	itt álljon meg
		I'm lost	eltévedtem
SOME SIGNS		arrivals	érkező járatok (or érkezés)
entrance	bejárat		
exit	kijárat	departures	induló járatok (or indulás)
arrival	érkezés	to/from	hova/honnan
departure	indulás	change	átszállás
open	nyitva	via	át
closed	zárva		
push	tolni	**COMPUTER/TECHNOLOGY**	
pull	húzni	charger	töltő
free admission	szabad belépés	@	kukac (literally, worm)
women's toilet	női mosdó (or WC – "Vait-say")	mobile phone	mobil (telefon)
		plug	dugó
men's toilet	férfi mosdó	socket	konnektor
shop	bolt	website	honlap, weboldal
market	piac	wi-fi	wi-fi (pronounced vee-fee)
room for rent	szoba kiadó or Zimmer frei		
		DESCRIPTIONS AND REACTIONS	
hospital	kórház	nothing	semmi
pharmacy	gyógyszertár	perhaps	talán
(local) police	(kerületi) Rendőrség	very	nagyon
caution/beware!	vigyázat!/vigyázz!	good	jó
no smoking	tilos a dohányzás/ dohányozni tilos	bad	rossz
		better	jobb
no bathing	tilos a fürdés/fürdeni tilos	big	nagy
		small	kicsi
DIRECTIONS		quick	gyors
Which way is the ...?	Merre van a ...?	slow	lassú
campsite	kemping	now	most
hotel	szálloda/hotel	later	később
railway station	vasútállomás	beautiful	szép
bus station	buszállomás	ugly	csúnya
bus-stand	kocsiállás	Help!	Segítség!
(bus or train) stop	megálló	I'm ill	beteg vagyok
inland	belföldi		
international	külföldi	**NUMBERS AND MEASURES**	
Is it near (far)?	Közel (messze) van?	In shops and markets, items are priced per piece (*darab*,	
Which bus goes to ...?	Melyik busz megy ... -ra/ re?	abbreviated to *db*.) or per kilogram. Shoppers commonly	

request purchases in multiples of ten grams (*deka*); one hundred grams is *tíz deka*. The measure for fluids is the *deci* (decilitre, abbreviated to dl., equivalent to about 3.5 fl oz) – see "Drinks" (see p.235) for how this applies in bars and restaurants.

1	egy
2	kettő
3	három
4	négy
5	öt
6	hat
7	hét
8	nyolc
9	kilenc
10	tíz
11	tizenegy
12	tizenkettő
13	tizenhárom
14	tizennégy
15	tizenöt
16	tizenhat
17	tizenhét
18	tizennyolc
19	tizenkilenc
20	húsz
21	huszonegy
30	harminc
40	negyven
50	ötven
60	hatvan
70	hetven
80	nyolcvan
90	kilencven
100	száz
101	százegy
150	százötven
200	kettőszáz
300	háromszáz
400	négyszáz
500	ötszáz
600	hatszáz
700	hétszáz
800	nyolcszáz
900	kilencszáz
1000	egyezer
half	fél
a quarter	negyed
each/piece	darab (db.)
10 grams	egy deka
100 grams	tíz deka

TIME, DAYS AND DATES

Luckily, the 24-hour clock is used for timetables, but on cinema programmes you may see notations like 1/4, 3/4, etc. These derive from the spoken expression of time which, as in German, makes reference to the hour approaching completion. For example 3.30 is expressed as *fél négy* – "half (on the way to) four"; 3.45 – *háromnegyed négy* ("three quarters on the way to four"); 6.15 – *negyed hét* ("one quarter towards seven"), etc. However, " ... o'clock" is ... *óra*, rather than referring to the hour ahead. Duration is expressed by the suffixes –*től* ("from") and –*ig* ("to"); minutes are *perc*; to ask the time, say "*Hány óra?*"

Monday	hétfő
Tuesday	kedd
Wednesday	szerda
Thursday	csütörtök
Friday	péntek
Saturday	szombat
Sunday	vasárnap
on Monday	hetfőn
on Tuesday	kedden
on Wednesday	szerdán
on Thursday	csütörtökön
on Friday	pénteken
on Saturday	szombaton
on Sunday	vasárnap
day	nap
week	hét
month	hónap
year	év

HUNGARIAN FOOD AND DRINK TERMS

The **food categories** here refer to the general divisions used in menus. In cheaper places you will also find a further division of meat dishes: ready-made meals like stews (*készételek*), and freshly cooked (in theory) dishes such as those cooked in breadcrumbs or grilled (*frissensültek*). *Tészták* is a pasta-doughy category that can include savoury dishes such as *turoscsusza* (pasta served with cottage cheese and a sprinkling of bacon), as well as sweet ones like *somlói galuska* (cream and chocolate covered sponge). Two popular **snacks** which are nicer than they sound are *zsirós kenyér* (bread spread with lard and sprinkled with paprika; often sold in old-fashioned wine bars); and *lángos* (fried dough served with soured cream or a variety of other toppings, and available in markets).

BASICS

		cukor	sugar
borraváló	tip	ecet	vinegar
bors	pepper	egészségedre!	Cheers!

étlap	menu
jó étvágyat!	Bon appétit!
kenyér	bread
kifli	croissant-shaped roll
kovászos kenyér	sourdough bread
mentes	-free, as in *glutén-mentes* (gluten-free); *cukor-mentes* (sugar-free)
méz	honey
mustár	mustard
rizs	rice
sajtos or **vajas pogácsa**	cheese or butter scones
só	salt
tejföl	sour cream
tejszín	cream
vaj	butter
vega	vegetarian
vegán	vegan
zsemle or **péksütemeny**	bread rolls

COOKING TERMS

angolosan	(English-style) underdone/rare
comb	leg
főtt	boiled
főzelék	creamed vegetable dishes – better than it sounds
jól megsütve	well done (fried)
jól megfőzve	well done (boiled)
mell	breast
paprikás	in a paprika sauce
pörkölt	stewed slowly
rántott	deep-fried in breadcrumbs
roston sütve	grilled
sülve	roasted
sült/sütve	fried
töltött	stuffed

SOUPS (LEVESEK)

bakonyi betyárleves	"Outlaw soup" of chicken, beef, noodles and vegetables, richly spiced
csirke-aprólék leves	mixed vegetable and giblet soup
erőleves	meat consommé often served with noodles (*tésztával* or *metélttel*), liver dumplings (*májgombóccal*), or an egg placed raw into the soup (*tojással*)
gombaleves	mushroom soup

gulyásleves	goulash in its original Hungarian form as a soup, sometimes served in a small kettle pot (*bográcsgulyás*)
halászlé	a rich fish soup often served with hot paprika
hideg meggyleves	chilled sour cherry soup
húsleves	meat consommé
jókai bableves	bean soup flavoured with smoked meat
kunsági	chicken soup
lencseleves	lentil soup
palócleves	mutton, bean and sour cream soup
pandúrleves	seasoned with nutmeg, paprika and garlic
paradicsomleves	tomato soup
tarkonyos borjúraguleves	lamb soup flavoured with tarragon
ujházi tyúkleves	chicken soup with noodles, vegetables and meat
zöldségleves	vegetable soup

APPETIZERS (ELŐÉTELEK)

These comprise both hot (*meleg*) and cold (*hideg*) dishes.

füstölt csülök tormával	smoked knuckle of pork with horseradish
hortobágyi palacsinta	pancake stuffed with minced meat and served with creamy paprika sauce
körözött	a paprika-flavoured spread made with sheep's cheese and served with toast
libamáj	goose liver
rakott krumpli	layered potato casserole with sausage and eggs
rántott gomba	mushrooms fried in breadcrumbs, sometimes stuffed with sheep's cheese (*juhtúróval töltött*)
rántott sajt, Camembert/ karfiol	Camembert or cauliflower fried in breadcrumbs
tatárbeefsteak	raw mince mixed with an egg, salt, pepper, butter, paprika and mustard, and spread on toast

tepertő	crackling (usually pork, sometimes goose)
velőcsont fokhagymás pirítóssal	bone marrow spread on toast rubbed with garlic, a special delicacy associated with the gourmet Gyula Krúdy

SALADS (SALÁTÁK)

Salads are not Hungary's strong point; they are usually simple, and are often served in a vinegary dressing, although other dressings include blue cheese (*rokfortos*), yogurt (*joghurtos*) or French (*francia*).

csalamádé	mixed pickled salad
fejes saláta	lettuce
idénysaláta	fresh salad of whatever is in season
jércesaláta	chicken salad
paradicsom saláta	tomato salad
uborka saláta	cucumber; can be gherkins (*csemege* or *kovászos*) or the fresh variety (*friss*)

FISH DISHES (HALÉTELEK)

csuka tejfölben sütve	fried pike with sour cream
fogas	a local fish of the pike-perch family
fogasszeletek Gundel modra	breaded fillet of *fogas*
harcsa	catfish
harcsa paprikás	catfish in paprika sauce
kecsege	sterlet (small sturgeon)
nyelvhal	sole
pisztráng	trout
pisztráng tejszínes mártásban	trout baked in cream
ponty	carp
ponty filé gombával	carp fillet in mushroom sauce
rántott pontyfilé	carp fillet fried in breadcrumbs
rostélyos töltött ponty	carp stuffed with bread, egg, herbs and fish liver or roe
süllő	another pike-perch relative
sült hal	fried fish
tonhal	tuna

MEAT DISHES (HÚSÉTELEK)

baromfi	poultry
bécsi szelet	Wiener schnitzel
bélszin	sirloin
bélszinjava	tenderloin
csirke	chicken
fácán	pheasant
fasírt	meatballs
hátszin	rump steak
kacsa	duck
kolbász	spicy sausage
liba	goose
máj	liver
marha	beef
nyúl	rabbit
őz	venison
pulyka	turkey
sertés	pork
sonka	ham
vaddisznó	wild boar
vadételek	game
virsli	frankfurter
borjúpörkölt	closer to what foreigners mean by "goulash": veal stew seasoned with garlic
cigányrostélyos	"Gypsy-style" steak with *vadasmártásban* (see p.234) sauce
csikós tokány	strips of beef braised in bacon, onion rings, sour cream and tomato sauce
csülök Pékné módra	knuckle of pork roasted with potatoes and onions
erdélyi rakott-káposzta	layers of cabbage, rice and ground pork baked in sour cream (a Transylvanian speciality)
hagymás rostélyos	braised steak piled high with fried onions
pacal	tripe (usually in a paprika sauce)
paprikás csirke	chicken in paprika sauce
rablóhús nyárson	kebab of pork, veal and bacon
sertésborda	pork chop
sült libacomb tört burgonyával és párolt káposztával	grilled goose leg with potatoes, onions and steamed cabbage
töltött káposzta	cabbage stuffed with meat and rice, in a tomato sauce
töltött paprika	peppers stuffed with meat and rice, in a tomato sauce

vaddisznó borókamártással	wild boar in juniper sauce
vasi pecsenye	fried pork marinated in milk and garlic

SAUCES (MÁRTÁSOK)

bormártásban	in a wine sauce
ecetes tormával	with horseradish
fokhagymás mártásban	in a garlic sauce
gombamártásban	in a mushroom sauce
kapormártásban	in a dill sauce
meggymártásban	in a morello cherry sauce
paprikás mártásban	in a paprika sauce
tárkonyos mártásban	in a tarragon sauce
tejszínes paprikás mártásban	in a cream and paprika sauce
vadasmártásban	in a brown sauce (made of mushrooms, almonds, herbs and brandy)
zöldborsós	in a green-pea sauce
zöldborsosmártásba	in a green peppercorn sauce

ACCOMPANIMENTS (KÖRETEK)

burgonya	served with parsley
galuska	noodles (though *Somlói galuska* is different – see p.231)
gombóc	dumpling
hasábburgonya	chips, French fries
krokett	potato croquettes
petrezselymes	boiled potatoes
rizs	rice
zöldköret	mixed vegetables

VEGETABLES (ZÖLDSÉGEK)

bab	beans
borsó	peas
burgonya/krumpli	potatoes
fokhagyma	garlic
gomba	mushrooms
hagyma	onions
(vörös) káposzta	(red) cabbage
karfiol	cauliflower
kelkáposzta	savoy cabbage
kukorica	sweetcorn
lecsó	tomato and green pepper stew that's a popular ingredient in Hungarian cooking
padlizsán	aubergine/eggplant
paprika (édes/erős)	peppers (sweet/hot)
paradicsom	tomatoes
sárgarépa	carrots

spárga	asparagus
spenót	spinach
uborka	cucumber
zöldbab	green beans
zöldborsó	peas
zukkini	courgette
rakott krumpli	layered potatoes with egg and sausage
Sólet	a superior baked beans (a Jewish speciality)
spenót főzelék	a garlicky creamed spinach (often served with a fried egg)
tök főzelék	creamed marrow with dill

FRUIT AND NUTS (GYÜMÖLCSÖK ÉS DIÓK)

alma	apple
birsalma	quince
bodza	elderflower
citrom	lemon
dió	walnut
eper	strawberry
földi mogyoró	peanut
füge	fig
(görög) dinnye	(water) melon
körte	pear
málna	raspberry
mandula	almond
meggy	morello cherry
mogyoró	hazelnut
narancs	orange
őszibarack	peach
sárgabarack	apricot
szilva	plum
szőlő	grape
tök (sütőtök)	marrow (pumpkin/ squash)

CHEESE (SAJT)

Cheeses made in Hungary are a rather limited selection, the most interesting being the soft *juhtúró*.

füstölt sajt	smoked cheese
juhtúró	sheep's cheese
kecske sajt	goat's cheese
márvány	Danish blue cheese
trappista	rubbery, Edam-type cheese
túró	a cross between cottage and curd cheese

DESSERTS (ÉDESSÉGEK)

almás pite	apple pie
aranygaluska	golden dumpling cake

SPRITZERS

Most bars serve **spritzers** – wine mixed with soda water – on request and increasingly you can see them on menus too. Given the sometimes questionable quality of the wine in cheaper wine bars, it is a much nicer way to drink it, and very thirst-quenching. A popular drink among the younger generation is VBK, wine mixed with cola (see below).

Hungarians give their mixes curious names:

Kifröccs – small spritzer:	1dl. soda water, 1dl. wine
Fröccs – spritzer:	1dl. soda water, 2dl. wine
Hosszúlépés – long step:	2dl. soda water, 1dl. wine
Viceházmester – deputy janitor:	3dl. soda, 2dl. wine
Haziúr – landlord:	1dl. soda, 4dl. wine

diós metélt	pasta with walnuts	ásányvíz	mineral water
dobos torta	multilayered sponge and chocolate cake topped with caramel	bor	wine
		borsmenta teá	peppermint tea
		csapalt sör	draught beer
fánk	doughnut	édes bor	sweet wine
flódni	layered apple, walnut and poppy-seed pastry	fehér bor	white wine
		féledes bor	medium-dry wine
gesztenye puré	chestnut purée	gyümölcslé	fruit juice
gundel palacsinta	pancake with walnuts in a chocolate sauce	kávé	coffee (espresso)
		kézműves kávé	artisan coffee
mákos or diós beigli	poppy-seed or walnut roll	kézműves sör	artisan (craft) beer
mákos guba	poppy-seed pudding	koffeinmentes kávé	decaffeinated coffee
palacsinta	pancake	korsó	half-litre of beer
párolt alma	stewed apple	menta teá	mint tea
rétes	strudel	narancslé	orange juice
szilva gombóc	dumpling stuffed with a plum	pálinka	schnapps-like fruit brandy, in a range of flavours
túrógombóc	cottage cheese dumpling		
		pezsgő	sparkling wine

DRINKS (ITALOK)

The drinks list (*itallap*) is usually divided into wine, beer, spirits and soft drinks. **Wine** is often served by the *deci* (dl.), or 100ml, and may be charged as such, so that the sum on the drinks list may be multiplied by two or three times on the bill. To avoid ambiguity over glass sizes, you can specify *egy deci*, *két deci* or *három deci* (respectively, 100ml, 200ml or 300ml). **Pálinka** is a popular aperitif, distilled from apricots (*barackpálinka*), plums (*szilva*), William's pears (*Vilmoskörte*) or other fruit; and **Unicum** a dark, bitter digestif that Hungarians swear is good for the stomach. **Soft drinks** have expanded their presence on the menus as many places offer an increased range of *limonádé* (lemonade) and *szörp* (cordial) drinks. Due to Hungary's abundant thermal springs there are numerous local brands of **mineral water**; it's sold with colour-coded bottle-caps for easy recognition of still (*szénsavmentes* – pink caps), mildly fizzy (*enyhe* – green) or sparkling (*szénsavas* or *buborékos* – blue).

pohár	300dl. of beer, or a glass of wine
rosé	rosé wine
sima (csap) víz	ordinary (tap) water
sör	beer
száraz bor	dry wine
szódavíz	soda water
szörp	cordial
teá	tea
tejeskávé	coffee with milk
Traubiszóda	sparkling grape-flavoured soft drink
Unicum	a bitter medicinal digestif
üveg	bottle (of wine)
(csap) víz	(tap) water
vörös bor	red wine
vörösboros kola (VBK)	red wine mixed with cola

Glossary of Hungarian terms

ÁFA Goods tax, equivalent to VAT.
Állatkert Zoo.
Arrow Cross see Nyilas.
Áruház Department store.
ÁVO The dreaded secret police of the Rákosi era, renamed the ÁVH in 1949.
Barlang Cave.
Belváros Inner city.
Biedermeier Heavy nineteenth-century style of Viennese furniture that became very popular in Budapest homes.
Borkostoló Wine tasting.
Borozó Wine bar.
Botanikuskert Botanical garden.
Büfé Snack bar.
Cigány Gypsy/Roma (can be abusive).
Cigánytelep Gypsy settlement.
Cigányzene Gypsy music.
Csárda Inn; nowadays, a restaurant with rustic decor.
Csárdás Traditional wild dance to violin music.
Cukrászda Cake shop.
Diszterem Ceremonial hall.
Domb Hill.
Duna River Danube.
Egyetem University.
Erdély The Hungarian word for Transylvania, the region of Romania where a large Hungarian minority lives.
Erdő Forest, wood.
Étterem Restaurant.
Fasor Avenue.
Fogadó Inn.
Folyó River.
Forrás Natural spring.
Fürdő Public baths.
Gözfürdő Steam bath.
Gyógyfürdő Mineral baths fed by thermal springs with therapeutic properties.
Hajó Boat.
Hajóállomás Boat landing stage.
Halászcsárda/halászkert Fish restaurant.
Ház House.
Hegy Hill or low mountain.
HÉV Commuter trains running from Budapest.
Híd Bridge.
Hídfő Bridgehead.
Honvéd Hungarian army.
Ifjúsági szálló Youth hostel.
Iskola School.
Kápolna Chapel.
Kapu Gate.

Kert Garden, park.
Kerület (*ker.*) District.
Kiállítás Exhibition.
Kiáltó Lookout tower.
Kincstár Treasury.
Kirakodó vásár Fair, craft or flea market.
Kollégium Student hostel.
Korzó Promenade.
Köröd Circus (road junction, as in Piccadilly Circus).
Körtér Circus (as *köröd*).
Körút (*krt.*) Literally, ring road, but in Budapest refers to the main boulevards surrounding the Belváros.
Köz Alley, lane; also used to define narrow geographical regions.
Kulcs Key.
Kút Well or fountain.
Lakótelep High-rise housing estate.
Lépcső Flight of steps.
Liget Park, grove or wood.
Lovarda Riding school.
Magyar Hungarian (pronounced "*mod*-yor").
Magyarország Hungary.
MÁV Hungarian national railways.
Megálló Railway station or tram or bus stop.
Megye County; the county system was originally established by King Stephen to extend his authority over the Magyar tribes.
Mozi Cinema.
Műemlék Historic monument, protected building.
Művelődési ház/központ Arts centre.
Nádor Palatine, highest administrative office in Hungary in the Habsburg empire pre-1848.
Nyilas "Arrow Cross"; Hungarian Fascist movement.
Palota Palace; *püspök-palota*, a bishop's residence.
Pályaudvar (*pu.*) Rail terminus.
Panzió Pension.
Patak Stream.
Pénz Money.
Piac Outdoor market.
Pince Cellar.
Rakpart Embankment or quay.
Református The reformed church, which in Hungary means the Calvinist faith.
Rendőrség Police.
Repülőtér Airport.
Rév Ferry.
Rom Ruined building.
Roma The Romani word for Gypsy, preferred by many Roma in Hungary.
Romkocsma Bar located in a ruined building or courtyard.

Sétány "Walk" or promenade.

Skanzen Outdoor ethnographic museum.

Sor Row, as in *fasor*, row of trees, ie avenue.

Söröző Beer hall.

Strand Beach, open-air baths or any area for sunbathing or swimming.

Szabadtér Open-air.

Szálló or **szálloda** Hotel.

Szent Saint.

Sziget Island.

Szoba kiadó Room to let.

Tájház Old peasant house turned into a museum, often illustrating the folk traditions of a region or ethnic group.

Táncház Venue for Hungarian folk music and dance.

Temető Cemetery.

Templom Church.

Tér Square; *tere* in the possessive case.

Terem Hall.

Tilos Forbidden; *tilos a dohányzás* means "smoking is forbidden".

Tó Lake.

Torony Tower.

Türbe Tomb or mausoleum of a Muslim dignitary.

Udvar Courtyard.

Uszoda Swimming pool.

Út Road; in the possessive case, *útja*.

Utca (*u.*) Street.

Vár Castle.

Város Town.

Városháza Town hall.

Vásár Market.

Vásárcsarnok Market hall.

Vasútállomás Railway station.

Vendéglő Restaurant.

Verbunkos Folk dance, originally a recruiting dance.

Völgy Valley.

Zsidó Jew or Jewish.

Zsinagóga Synagogue.

Small print and index

239 Small print

238 About the authors

240 Index

ABOUT THE AUTHORS

Charles Hebbert fell in love with Budapest in 1982 and lived there for more than ten years. He regularly visits the city with his family when he isn't working as an editor in London, playing his accordion or updating Rough Guides in northern Italy.

Norm Longley has been visiting Budapest for the best part of twenty years, and has spent most of his working life in Central/Eastern Europe – he is also the author of Rough Guides to Slovenia and Romania; more recently he has turned his hand to home shores, contributing to the Scotland, Wales and Ireland guides. He lives in Somerset and can occasionally be seen erecting marquees on The Rec in Bath.

A ROUGH GUIDE TO ROUGH GUIDES

Published in 1982, the first Rough Guide – to Greece – was a student scheme that became a publishing phenomenon. Mark Ellingham, a recent graduate in English from Bristol University, had been travelling in Greece the previous summer and couldn't find the right guidebook. With a small group of friends he wrote his own guide, combining a contemporary, journalistic style with a thoroughly practical approach to travellers' needs.

The immediate success of the book spawned a series that rapidly covered dozens of destinations. And, in addition to impecunious backpackers, Rough Guides soon acquired a much broader readership that relished the guides' wit and inquisitiveness as much as their enthusiastic, critical approach and value-for-money ethos. These days, Rough Guides include recommendations from budget to luxury and cover more than 120 destinations around the globe, from Amsterdam to Zanzibar, all regularly updated by our team of roaming writers.

Browse all our latest guides, read inspirational features and book your trip at **roughguides.com**.

Rough Guide credits

Editor: Polly Thomas
Layout: Anita Singh
Cartography: Deshpal Dabas
Picture editor: Aude Vauconsant
Proofreader: Diane Margolis
Managing editor: Monica Woods
Assistant editors: Payal Sharotri, Shasya Goel

Production: Jimmy Lao
Cover photo research: Marta Bescos
Editorial assistant: Aimee White
Senior DTP coordinator: Dan May
Programme manager: Gareth Lowe
Publishing director: Georgina Dee

Publishing information

This seventh edition published January 2018 by
Rough Guides Ltd,
80 Strand, London WC2R 0RL
11, Community Centre, Panchsheel Park,
New Delhi 110017, India
Distributed by Penguin Random House
Penguin Books Ltd, 80 Strand, London WC2R 0RL
Penguin Group (USA), 345 Hudson Street, NY 10014, USA
Penguin Group (Australia), 250 Camberwell Road,
Camberwell, Victoria 3124, Australia
Penguin Group (NZ), 67 Apollo Drive, Mairangi Bay,
Auckland 1310, New Zealand
Penguin Group (South Africa), Block D, Rosebank Office
Park, 181 Jan Smuts Avenue, Parktown North, Gauteng,
South Africa 2193
Rough Guides is represented in Canada by DK Canada, 320
Front Street West, Suite 1400, Toronto, Ontario M5V 3B6
Printed in Singapore
© Rough Guides 2018
Maps © Rough Guides

A catalogue record for this book is available from the
British Library
ISBN: 978-0-24130-621-5
The publishers and authors have done their best to ensure
the accuracy and currency of all the information in **The
Rough Guide to Budapest**, however, they can accept
no responsibility for any loss, injury, or inconvenience
sustained by any traveller as a result of information or
advice contained in the guide.
1 3 5 7 9 8 6 4 2

MIX
Paper from
responsible sources
FSC
www.fsc.org   FSC™ C018179

Help us update

We've gone to a lot of effort to ensure that the seventh
edition of **The Rough Guide to Budapest** is accurate
and up-to-date. However, things change – places get
"discovered", opening hours are notoriously fickle,
restaurants and rooms raise prices or lower standards. If
you feel we've got it wrong or left something out, we'd like
to know, and if you can remember the address, the price,
the hours, the phone number, so much the better.

Please send your comments with the subject line
"**Rough Guide Budapest Update**" to mail@uk
.roughguides.com. We'll credit all contributions and send a
copy of the next edition (or any other Rough Guide if you
prefer) for the very best emails.

Acknowledgements

Charles Hebbert Thanks to Lőrincz Anna, Fazakas
Peter and Julia and Richard Lock for their generosity
and support; Rachel Appleby and Rozgonyi Zoltan for
their additional assistance; and to Biber Kriszta, Helene
Bienvenue, Jonathan Birchall, Bodrogi Bea, Bozoki András,
Bob Cohen, Csaba Mester, Csősz Anna, Dévényi Dalma,
Fenyő Krisztina, Rosie Jones, Kamilla Peksa, Máthé Elek,
Pallai Péter, Julia and Peter Sherwood, Michael Stewart,
Szervatiusz Lilla, Szöllősi Judit, Vágvölgyi András and

Jodi Wade; my co-author, Norm Longley; a big thanks to
Polly Thomas for attentive and patient editing, and finally
Caroline, Molly and Fergus Hebbert.

Norm Longley Thanks to Monica for getting the project
off the ground; Polly for her first-class editing; Charles;
and Tsvia Vorley and Monika Fodor at Danubius. Most
importantly, thank you to Christian, Luka, Patrick and
Anna.

Readers' updates

Thanks to all the readers who have taken the time to write in with comments and suggestions (and apologies if we've
inadvertently omitted or misspelt anyone's name):

Robin Dixon, John Hackett, Stephen Rothholz and Philip Starling.

Photo credits

All photos © Rough Guides, except the following:
(Key: t-top; c-centre; b-bottom; l-left; r-right)

Index

Maps are marked in grey

A

accommodation 150–157
addresses 25
admission charges 32
Aeropark 205
Agriculture Museum 75
airport 23
Alpár, Ignác 41, 47, 52
Ámos, Imre 102
Andrássy Gyula 54, 61
Andrássy út 61–65
Anker Palace 47
Anonymous statue 75
Antall, József 57, 83, 112, 216
apartments 151
Aquincum 117
Arany, János 42
Árpád, Prince 71
arrival 23
arts centres 183
Astoria Hotel 44
ÁVO secret police 54, 64, 65,
    79, 106, 110, 128, 147, 215

B

Baba, Gül 107
Bajcsy-Zsilinszky, Endre 51
Bajcsy-Zsilinszky út 51
ballet 184
Bandholtz, General 52
banks 35
bars 175–181
Bartók, Béla 64, 93, 124, 125,
    220, 224, 225
Bartók Memorial House 124
baths 13, 199–202
    Császár-Komjádi 107, 201
    Gellért 110, 201
    Hajós Alfred (Sport) 120, 201
    Király 105, 202
    Lukács 107, 202
    Magnum Szauna 209
    Palatinus Strand 120, 202
    Rudas 111, 202
    Szauna 69 209
    Széchenyi 76, 202
    Veli Bej 107, 202
Batthyány, Lajos 42, 54, 56, 83,
    105, 214
Batthyány monument 54
Batthyány tér 105

Bécsi kapu tér 94
Bedő House 54
Belváros 38–47
Belváros 40
Belváros Parish Church 45
Bem statue 105
Bem tér 105
Bershka store 41
bike rental 28
Blaha, Lujza 83
books 192, 225–227
bookshops 192
Botanical Garden 86
bridges
    Chain Bridge 104
    Erzsébet híd 45
    Lánchíd 104
    Margit híd 119
    Mária Valéria híd (Esztergom) ... 144
    Szabadság híd 110
Bródy Sándor utca 79
Buda Hills, The 121–125
Buda Hills, The 123
Budakeszi 124
Budapest 5
Budapest and around 130
Budapest Card 32
Budapest City Hall 42

Budapest Eye 204
Budapest Festival Orchestra
.... 205, 223
Budapest History Museum 102
Budapest Pride 208
Budapest Spring Festival 30
bus stations 24
buses 25
buses to Budapest 22

C

cafés 169–174
camping 157
car rental 28
Castle Hill 89–103
Castle Theatre 99
Cathedral of the Dormition 46
Cave Church 110
caves 198
Center of Scientific Wonders... 128
Centrál Kávéház 42
Chain Bridge (Lánchíd) 104
chairlift 124
children, travelling with 34
children's Budapest 203–206
Children's Railway 122
Church of St Anne 105
churches and cathedrals
    Basilica (Esztergom) 141
    Belgrade Church (Szentendre) 133
    Belváros Parish Church 45
    Blagovestenska Church
        (Szentendre) 131
    Cathedral (Vác) 147
    Cathedral of the Dormition...........46
    Cave Church...............................110
    Church of St Anne.....................105
    Franciscan Church (Ferenciek tere)
       44
    Lutheran Church 47
    Mátyás Church...........................91
    Požarevačka Church (Szentendre)
       134
    Preobraženska Church (Szentendre)
       134
    St Stephen's Basilica.....................51
    Servite Church...........................44
cinema 186
Circus 75
Citadella 111
city tours 28
city transport 24–28
civilian amphitheatre 118
Clark, Adam 81, 104
classical music 184, 220
climate 10
clubs 175–181
Cogwheel Railway 122
consulates 33
Contra-Aquincum 45
cookery courses 166
Coronation Regalia 57
Corvin Cinema 84

Corvin köz 84
Corvinus University 83
costs 32
crime 33
Császár-Komjádi Pool 107, 201
Csillebérc 122
Csontváry, Tivadar Kosztka
.... 100, 101
Csopa Playbar 205
Curtis, Tony 66
cycling 28

D

dance 187
dance music 186
Deák tér 46
Demszky, Gábor 219
disabled travellers 37
Dísz tér...................................... 98
Dob utca 68
Dohány utca 68
Dohány utca Synagogue 65
driving 27
driving to Budapest 22
Duna-korzó 45

E

Economics University 83
electricity 33
embassies 33
Empress Elizabeth 62, 112,
    124, 148, 149
Eötvös Loránd Science
    University 79
Erkel Theatre 81
Ervin Szabó Library 81
Erzsébet híd 45
Erzsébet lookout tower 124
Erzsébet tér 47
Erzsébetváros 65–69
Erzsébetváros, Terézváros and
.... 60
escape rooms 198
Esztergom 141–145
Esztergom 142
    Basilica 141
    Castle Museum 143
    Christian Museum 143
    Danube Museum 144
    Djami 143
    Mária Valéria híd...................144
Eternal Flame (Aulich utca) 54
etiquette 31

F

Farkasréti Cemetery..................125
Ferenc Hopp Museum 65

Ferenciek tere 42
Ferencváros 83–87
Ferencváros, Józsefváros and
.... 78
ferries 26
festivals.............................29–31
Fidesz 217
films 186
Fischer, Iván 223
Fisher-girl fountain 41
Fishermen's Bastion 15, 92
flat rental 151
flea markets 190
flights to Budapest.....................21
Fő tér (Óbuda) 115
Fő utca (Víziváros) 104
folk music 186, 221
food 159
football 197
Formula One 198
Foundry Museum 106
Fountain of Hungarian Truth.... 81
Fradi (FTC) 83, 197
Franciscan Church (Ferenciek
    tere) 44
Friar John Capistranus 96
Funerary Museum 82
funicular (Sikló) 103

G

gay Budapest 207–209
Gay Pride 30, 208
Gellért-hegy................. 109–111
Gellért-hegy and the Tabán
.... 109
Gellért Baths......................110, 201
Gellért Hotel 110
Geological Institute 76
Geological Museum 76
Gerbeaud patisserie 39
German occupation monument
.... 52
ghetto 66
Glass House Memorial Room ...53
glossary 236
Gödöllő.............................. 148
    Gödöllő Artists' Colony 101, 149
    Gödöllő Town Museum 149
    Royal Palace..........................148
Golden Eagle Pharmacy
    Museum 98
Goldmark Hall 67
Gozsdu-udvar 68
Grand Prix...................................198
grave of Abdurrahman 96
Great Market Hall 83
Great Synagogue................. 16, 65
Gresham Palace.......................... 49
Gül Baba's tomb 107
gypsy music................................222
Gyurcsány, Ferenc 217

H

Hajós Alfréd Swimming Pool 120, 201
Hárshegy 124
health 33
Hercules Villa 118
Heroes' Temple 67
HÉV trains 26
history 211–219
Holocaust 52, 66, 67, 79, 87, 133, 186, 215
Holocaust Memorial Centre 86
Holocaust memorials 55, 57, 67, 86, 133
horse racing 198
Horthy, Admiral 53, 81, 86, 97, 98, 110, 111, 145, 149, 214
Horthy, Miklós 52
Hősök tere 71–74
Hospital in the Rock 97
hostels 156
hotels 15, 150–156
Houdini Museum 205
House of Terror 16, 63
Hungária Baths 69
Hungarian Academy of Sciences 49
Hungarian cuisine 159
Hungarian House of Photography 62
Hungarian National Gallery 15, 99–102
Hungarian National Museum 80
Hungarian State Treasury ... 53
Hungaroring 198
Hűvösvölgy 124

I

II János Pál pápa tér 81
insurance 33
international bus station 24
internet 34
Invisible Exhibition 106
itineraries 18

J

János-hegy 124
Japanese Garden 120
jazz 185, 223
Jewish Archives 67
Jewish Cemetery (Kerepsesi) 83
Jewish Cemetery (New Public) 127

Jewish Museum 66
Jewish quarter 61, 65–69
Jews in Budapest ... 32, 53, 55, 57, 65–68, 86, 93, 94, 96, 103, 104, 133, 197, 213, 215
Jobbik 217
József, Attila 55, 83
József körút 81
Józsefváros 79–83
Józsefváros and Ferencváros 78

K

Kádár, János 81, 83, 97, 141, 216, 218
Kálmán statue 62
Kapisztrán tér 94
Károlyi, Mihály 42, 214
Károlyi Mihály utca 42
Károlyi-kert (garden) 42
Kassák Museum 117
Kazinczy utca 67
Keleti Station 23, 81
Kerepesi Cemetery 82
Kerepesi Cemetery 82
kids, travelling with 34
kids' Budapest 203–206
Kilián Barracks 84
Kilometre Zero 103
King Stephen 92, 141, 212
King Stephen, statue ... 92, 110, 143
Király Baths 105, 202
Király utca 67
Kiscelli Museum 119
Kisfaludi-Strobl, Zsigmond 111
Klotild Palaces 44
Kodály, Zoltán 61, 65, 124, 125, 220
Kodály körönd 64
Kodály Memorial Museum 65
Kolosy tér 118
Kossuth, Lajos 54, 55, 82, 103, 213
Kossuth Lajos utca 44
Kossuth tér 54–57
Kristóf tér 41
Kun, Béla 117, 128, 214

L

Lajta, Béla 44, 62, 82, 127, 214
Lánchíd (Chain Bridge) 104
language 228
language courses 34
laundry 34
Lechner, Ödön ... 53, 62, 76, 84, 127, 214
Lehel tér market hall 58

Leigh Fermor, Patrick 68
LGBT+ Budapest 207–209
Libegő 124
Liberation Monument 111
Lipótváros 48–58
Lipótváros and Újlipótváros 50
listings information 29, 183
Liszt, Ferenc (Franz) 41, 46, 63, 64, 81, 142, 220, 223
Liszt Ferenc International Airport 23
Liszt Ferenc tér 63
Liszt Memorial Museum 64
Liszt Music Academy 63, 184
Little Princess statue 46
living in Budapest 34
lost property 35
Lotz, Károly 51, 56, 63, 91, 101, 167
Ludwig Museum 87
Lukács Baths 107, 202
Lutheran Church 47
Lutheran Museum 47
Lutz, Carl 53, 67, 93, 215
Lutz monument 67

M

Madách sétány 68
Magyar conquest 211
Mahler, Gustav 46, 61, 184
Mai Manó House 62
mail 35
Makovecz, Imre 125, 140
maps 35
Március 15 tér 45
Margít híd 119
Margít körút 106
Margít-sziget 119
Margít-sziget 120
Margít-sziget, Óbuda and 116
markets 189
  Belvárosi 53
  Great Market Hall 83
  Lehel tér 58
  Rákóczi tér 81
Mary Magdalene Tower 94
Mátyás Church 91
Mátyás Fountain 102
media 29
Medieval Jewish Prayer House 94
Memento Park 15, 127
menu terms 231
metro 25
Miksa Róth Museum 69
Mikszáth Kálmán tér 81
military amphitheatre 118
military baths 118
Military Court of Justice 105
Military History Museum 96

Millenáris Park 106
Millennary Monument 71
Mindszenty, Cardinal.......... 51, 52, 141, 142
Mogyoród.................................198
money......................................35
Monument to the Uprising......74
Műcsarnok................................71
Munkácsy, Mihály........... 100, 101
Museum of Applied Arts..........84
Museum of Electrotechnology 68
Museum of Ethnography 57
Museum of Fine Arts........72–74
Museum of Trade and Tourism 117
museums
Aeropark....................................205
Agricultural Museum....................75
Aquincum Museum........................118
Barcsay Museum (Szentendre) ...131
Bartók Memorial House..............124
Budapest History Museum..........102
Castle Museum (Esztergom)........143
Center of Scientific Wonders 128
Christian Museum (Esztergom) 143
Csopa Playbar.............................205
Czóbel Exhibition (Szentendre) 133
Danube Museum (Esztergom) 144
Diocesan Treasury (Vác) 146
Ferenc Hopp Museum 65
Ferenczy Károly Museum (Szentendre).............................130
Foundry Museum 106
Funerary Museum........................82
Geological Museum......................76
Gödöllő Town Museum 149
Golden Eagle Pharmacy Museum 98
Holocaust Memorial Centre..........86
Hospital in the Rock....................97
Houdini Museum 205
House of Terror............................63
Hungarian House of Photography 62
Hungarian National Gallery 99
Hungarian National Museum.......80
Hungarian Natural History Museum 86
Hungarian Open-Air Museum (Szentendre)............................134
Ignác Tragor Museum (Vác) 145
Invisible Exhibition.....................106
Jewish Archives 67
Jewish Museum............................66
Kassák Museum............................117
Kiscelli Museum..........................119
Kodály Memorial Museum 65
Kovács Ceramic Exhibition (Szentendre)............................131
Liszt Memorial Museum..............64
Ludwig Museum 87
Lutheran Museum 47
Mai Manó House..........................62
Medieval Jewish Prayer House 94
Memento Mori (Vác)....................145
Memento Park..............................127
Miksa Róth Museum.....................69
Military History Museum...............96

Műcsarnok................................71
Museum Hall (Vác) 147
Museum of Applied Arts............84
Museum of Electrotechnology 68
Museum of Ethnography.............57
Museum of Fine Arts 72
Museum of Hungarian Art Nouveau 54
Museum of Trade and Tourism ...117
Music History Museum..................93
Nagytétényi Castle Museum.......128
Natural History Museum..............86
Óbuda Museum...........................117
Petőfi Literary Museum 42
Pinball Museum............................58
Police History Museum................82
Post Office Museum.....................65
Railway History Park....................127
Retro Design Center (Szentendre) 133
Robert Capa Contemporary Photographic Centre..................62
Royal Palace (Gödöllő) 148
Semmelweis Medical Museum....112
Serbian Ecclesiastical History Collection (Szentendre) 133
Szántó Memorial House and Synagogue..............................133
Telephone Museum 97
Underground Railway Museum ...47
Varga Museum.............................117
Vasarely Museum.........................117
music........................ 220–224
Music Academy..................63, 184
Music History Museum............93
Múzeum körút.............................79

Nagy, Imre............. 54, 71, 81, 105, 127, 215
Nagy statue 54
Nagymező utca 62
Nagytétényi Castle Museum... 128
names 35
Napraforgó utca housing estate 124
National Archives 94
National Bank............................52
National Pantheon....................127
National Széchényi Library 102
National Theatre 87, 187
Natural History Museum...........86
Neolog Judaism 65
New Public Cemetery 127
New Theatre 62
New York Palace........................69
Normafa...................................122
Nyugati Railway Station...........51

Óbuda 114–119
Óbuda and Margít-sziget ... 116

Óbuda Museum........................115
Officers' Casino 41
Oktogon....................................63
Old Father Danube statue........47
opening hours...........................35
opera..184
Opera House 61
Orbán, Viktor...........................217
Országház utca 97
Orthodox Synagogue 68
Ötvenhatosok tere 74
Outdoor Theatre......................120

Palace of Arts 87, 183
Palatinus Strand.............. 120, 202
Pálvölgyi Stalactite Cave 118, 198
Pantheon of the Working Class Movement.................................82
Papp László Sportaréna 76
Paris Department Store.............63
Párisi Udvar 42
Parliament.................................55
Paul Street Boys 84
Pest Theatre..............................41
Pesti Vigadó.......................46, 185
Petőfi, Sándor 30, 42, 46, 80, 83, 214
Petőfi Literary Museum.............42
Petőfi statue 45
Petőfi tér 45
phones 36
Pinball Museum.........................58
police 33
Police History Museum 82
pools ....see baths
pop music 185, 222
post...35
Post Office Museum...................65
Post Office Savings Bank, former 53
private rooms...........................151
public holidays 36
puppet theatres.......................205
Puskás, Ferenc 76, 197
Puskás, Tivadar 65, 97
Puskás Ferenc Stadium 76, 197

Radnóti statue 62
railway circuit..........................122
Railway History Park.........16, 127
railway stations 23
Rákóczi, Ferenc....................54, 213
Rákóczi tér..................................81
Rákosi, Mátyás 125

Raoul Wallenberg Memorial
Garden...................................67
Reagan, Ronald 53
religion 32
restaurants.................. 158–168
Rippl-Rónai, József......62, 72, 102
Robert Capa Contemporary
Photographic Centre.............62
Rómaifürdő 117
Ronay, Egon..............................44
Róth, Miksa 44, 49, 56, 69, 84
Royal Palace............. 98, 99–103
Rózsadomb.............................106
Rózsavölgyi Building.................44
Rubik, Erno...............................76
Rudas Baths 111, 202
ruin bars.....................10, 16, 178
Rumbach utca Synagogue.......67
Ruszwurm patisserie................93

S

St Stephen's Basilica 51
St Stephen's Crown.............56, 57
Sándor Palace 99
Semmelweis, Ignác 112
Semmelweis Medical Museum
....112
Servite Church...........................44
shopping 188–195
Sikló (funicular) 103
Sisi (Empress Elizabeth)............62,
112, 124, 148, 149
Soviet Army Memorial...............52
Sportaréna 76
sports 196–198
State Opera House.....................61
Statue Park.............................127
steam trains............................126
Stock Exchange (former)
....41, 52
study 34
Svábhegy................................122
swimming ....see baths
Szabadság híd 110
Szabadság tér 51
Szarvas tér..............................112
Széchenyi, István 49, 57, 103,
104, 213
Széchenyi Baths.................76, 202
Széchenyi István tér..................49
Széchenyi-hegy.......................122
Széll Kálmán tér......................106
Szemlőhegyi Cave..........118, 198
Szent István Park......................57
Szentendre................... 130–136
Szentendre 132
Art Mill..................................133
Barcsay Museum 131
Belgrade Church 133
Blagovestenska Church..........131
Czóbel Museum......................133
Ferenczy Károly Museum..........130

Fő tér 130
Hungarian Open-Air Museum.....134
Kovács Ceramic Exhibition..........131
Požarevačka Church 134
Preobraženska Church............134
Retro Design Center 133
Serbian Orthodox Ecclesiastical Art
Collection...........................133
Serbs in Szentendre................134
Szántó Memorial House 133
Szentendre Gallery 131
Templom tér 131
Szentháromság tér...................91
Szerb, Antal....................83, 94, 227
Szervita tér 44
Sziget festival 183
Szilágyi Dezső tér 104

T

Tabán 111–103
Tabán, Gellért-hegy and the
.... 109
Táncsics Mihály utca.................93
Tarlós István............................219
taxis 26
Telephone Museum...................97
telephones 36
Terézváros...................61–65
Terézváros and Erzsébetváros
.... 60
theatre.....................................187
ticket offices...........................183
time 36
Timewheel................................74
tipping......................................36
Tisza, István..............................54
Tóth Árpád sétány....................96
tour operators...........................22
tourist information....................37
tourist offices............................37
train stations 23
trains to Budapest.....................22
trams 13, 25
Transport Museum...................205
Trianon, Treaty of.........52, 81, 215
trolleybuses 25
Tropicarium 128
Turul statue...............................99

U

Újlipótváros..............................57
Underground Railway................41
Underground Railway Museum
....47
Uprising of 1956 215
Úri utca.....................................97

V

Vác 145–148
Vác 146
Cathedral 147
Diocesan Treasury...................146
Ignác Tragor Museum 145
Memento Mori 145
Museum Hall..........................147
Prison....................................147
St Michael's Church crypt 145
Triumphal Arch 147
Váci utca...................................41
Vajdahunyad Castle...................74
Vár, The 89–103
Vár, The 93
Vár and central Buda, The... 90
Varga, Imre..................67, 117, 128
Varga Museum 117
Várkert Bazár...........................112
Várkert Kioszk 113
Városliget 70–76
Városliget and the stadiums
.... 71
Vasarely Museum 115
Veli Bej Baths 107, 202
Vienna Gate 94
Vigadó tér.................................46
visas 33
Visegrád..................... 136–141
Visegrád 138
bobsleigh...............................139
Citadel..................................139
Fun Extreme Canopy 140
Royal Palace..........................138
Solomon's Tower 139
Visegrád Hills.........................139
Zsitvay lookout tower 139
Víziváros, The 104–106
Vörösmarty, Mihály.....39, 99, 102
Vörösmarty tér..........................39

W

Wallenberg, Raoul 53, 58,
67, 215
Wallenberg monument..............58
Weiss, Manfred 83
wine 180
work...34

Y

Ybl, Miklós.......47, 51, 61, 79, 112
Ybl Miklós tér 112

Z

Zoo....................................13, 75

Step inside!

Hilton Budapest
Danubius Hotel Helia

There are so many good reasons to pay us a visit. You can always get in touch with us by phone to request a great offer, but our beautifully restored hotels need to be seen to be believed!

Check out our contemporary event spaces and premium category rooms and discover why we're the perfect hosts for your big occasion.

Drop by any of our two refurbished city locations to see for yourself.

Let us be the difference that makes your day.

Map index

Budapest Book Map	5	Gellért-Hegy and the Tabán	109
Belváros	40	Óbuda and Margít sziget	116
Lipótváros and Ujlipótváros	51	Margít sziget	120
Terézváros and Erzsébetváros	60	Buda Hills	123
Városliget	71	Budapest and around	130
Jozsefváros and Ferencváros	78	Szentendre	132
Kerepesi Cemetery	82	Visegrád	138
The Vár and Central Buda	90	Esztergom	142
The Vár	93	Vác	146

Listings key

- ■ Accommodation
- ● Eating
- ■ Drinking/nightlife
- ● Shopping

City plan

The **city plan** on the pages that follow is divided as shown:

N

0   500
metres

Map symbols

Main road	⊠	Post office	✡	Synagogue	∩	Arch	
Minor road	ⓘ	Tourist office	◠	Cave	🏛	Monument	
Motorway	⊞	Hospital	⅄	Campsite	♉	Castle	
Pedestrianised road	P	Parking	▲	Peak	⚲	Church (regional map)	
Steps	◆	Point of interest	✈	International airport	⇨	Church (town map)	
Railway	@	Internet access	Ⓗ	Hév station		Building	
Funicular line	⊠	Gate	Ⓜ	Metro station	□	Market	
Path	⊙	Statue	★	Bus stop	◯	Stadium	
Wall	⊥	Garden	🏎	Formula 1 circuit	⋯	Park/forest	
Ferry route	⛵	Swimming pool	⚓	Ferry dock	⊞	Christian cemetery	
Chairlift	∴	Ruins	�½	Viewpoint	⊔	Jewish cemetery	
Bridge							

Hajós Alfréd
Pool

Margit
sziget

Millennial
Monument

River Danube (Duna)

IPOLY UTCA
GOGOL UTCA
PANNÓNIA UTCA
GOGOL UTCA
VISEGRÁDI UTCA
IPOLY UTCA
HEGEDŰS GYULA UTCA
THURZÓ UTCA
RÖNTGEN UTCA
ALIG UTCA
VÁCI ÚT

Lehel
csarnok

MASSA LAJOS UTCA

VICTOR HUGO UTCA

Lehel tér

Szent
István
Park

POZSONYI ÚT
HOLLÁN ERNŐ UTCA
TÁTRA UTCA
CSANÁDY UTCA
KRESZ GÉZA UTCA

CARL LUTZ RAKPART
ÚJPESTI RAKPART
RADNÓTI MIKLÓS UTCA
GERGELY G. UTCA
BALZAC UTCA

XIII

LEHEL
TÉR

LEHEL UTCA

VISEGRÁDI UTCA
CSANÁDY UTCA

DÓZSA UTCA
KATONA JÓZSEF UTCA
WALLENBERG UTCA

ÚJLIPÓTVÁROS

TELKA UTCA
GYÖNGYHÁZ UTCA
BALZAC UTCA

RADNÓTI MIKLÓS UTCA

FERDINÁND HÍD

MARGIT HÍD

BUDAI N. U.
TÁTRA UTCA
PANNÓNIA UTCA
HEGEDŰS GYULA UTCA
VISEGRÁDI UTCA
KRESZ GÉZA UTCA
KATONA JÓZSEF UTCA

Pinball
Museum

VÁCI ÚT

JÁSZAI
MARI TÉR

Budapest
Jazz Club

WestEnd
Center

SZENT ISTVÁN KÖRÚT

Vígszínház
Theatre

BORBÉLY UT

KÁDÁR UTCA

ID. ANTALL JÓZSEF RAKPART
SZÉCHENYI RAKPART
BÁLINT UTCA
BALATON U.
HONVÉD UTCA
BALATON UTCA

Olimpia
Park

Cirko-gejzir Cinema

FALK MIKSA UTCA
BALASSI
MARKÓ UTCA
HONVÉD TÉR
STOLLÁR B. UTCA
SZEMERE UTCA
NAGY IGNÁC UTCA
MARKÓ UTCA
BIHARI UTCA

P
Nyugati
Station

NYUGATI
TÉR

Eiffel
Tér

CSENGERY UTCA

Visitor
Centre

SZALAY UTCA
VAJKAY UTCA

SZALAY UTCA

Police
Station

BAJCSY-ZSILINSZKY ÚT

JÓKAI UTCA
PODMANICZKY UTCA
SZOBI UTCA
SZONDI UTCA
EÖTVÖS UTCA

TERÉZ KÖRÚT

Museum of
Ethnography

ALKOTMÁNY UTCA

LIPÓTVÁROS

VI

Parliament

KOSSUTH
LAJOS
TÉR

TÓZMA F. UTCA
HONVÉD UTCA
HOLD UTCA

KÁLMÁN IMRE UTCA

BÁTHORY UTCA

WEINER LEÓ UTCA
LOVAG UTCA
JÓKAI UTCA

NAGYMEZŐ UTCA

TERÉZVÁROS

Ministry of
Agriculture

VÉRTANÚK
TERE

Bedö
House

Glass
House
Memorial
Room

Ó UTCA

P

JÓKAI
TÉR

Kossuth
Lajos tér

GARIBALDI UTCA
VECSEY UTCA
AULICH UTCA

Belvárosi
Market
Hall

MÓZSAR UTCA

SZÉCHENYI RAKPART
NÁDOR UTCA
ZOLTÁN UTCA
SZABADSÁG
TÉR
PERCZEL M. UTCA
NAGYSÁNDOR J. UTCA

Hungarian
State Treasury

DESSEWFFY UTCA
ZICHY JENŐ UTCA
HAJÓS UTCA

Operetta
Theatre

Paris
Department
Store

AKADÉMIA UTCA
STEINDL I. UTCA
SZÉCHENYI UTCA
TÜKÖRY UTCA

KISS E. U.
HOLD UTCA

National
Bank

Toldi
Cinema

State Opera
House

Mai Manó
House

PAULAY EDE UTCA

Former
TV
Building

V

BANK UTCA

PODMANICZKY
TÉR

Arany
János
utca

DALSZÍNHÁZ UTCA

Opera

Aranytíz
Centre

ARANY JÁNOS UTCA

ARANY JÁNOS UTCA

LÁZÁR UTCA

Hungarian Academy
of Sciences

VIGYÁZÓ F. UTCA
NÁDOR UTCA
OKTÓBER 6 UTCA
SÁS UTCA
HERCEGPRÍMÁS UTCA

SZENT
ISTVÁN
TÉR

St Stephen's
Basilica

RÉVAY ÚT

New
Theatre

SZÉCHENYI
ISTVÁN
TÉR

CEU

ZRÍNYI UTCA

ANDRÁSSY ÚT

KÁLDY GYULA U.
PAULAY EDE UTCA
SZÉKELY M. UTCA
VASÁRI P. UTCA
KIS DIÓFA UTCA

Carousel

Széchenyi
Baths

KÓS KÁROLY SÉTÁNY

HERMINA UTCA
BETHESDA UTCA

VÁROSLIGETI KÖRÚT

Agriculture
Museum

PÁL LÁSZLÓ ÚT

Vajdahunyad
Castle

Városliget

ÓLOF PALME SÉTÁNY

ZICHY MIHÁLY ÚT

Olaf Palme ház

SÉTÁNY

Monument to
the Uprising

DVORÁK

Virgin
Mary
Church

DÓZSA GYÖRGY ÚT

NDY UTCA

MAREK JÓZSEF UTCA

ISTVÁN ÚT

CSERHÁT UTCA

MURÁNYI UTCA

RNÁD UTCA

TERFY SÁNDOR UTCA

GARAY UTCA

KÖS UTCA

Garay tér
Market

AJTÓSI DÜRER SOR

SAJÓ UTCA

ALPÁR UTCA

SZINVA UTCA

DÓZSA GYÖRGY ÚT

ISTVÁNMEZEI ÚT

SZÁZHÁZ UTCA

Police
Station

JOBBÁGY UTCA

MURÁNYI UTCA

VERSENY UTCA

THÖKÖLY ÚT

Keleti
Station

HORVÁT BOLDIZSÁR UTCA

Mexikói út

KOLUMBUSZ EDISON UTCA

EDISON KÖZ

AMERIKAI ÚT

ERZSÉBET KIRÁLYNÉ ÚTJA

UZSOKI UTCA

LAKY ADLER UTCA

HERMINAMEZŐ

AMERIKAI ÚT

KOLUMBUSZ UTCA

KORONG UTCA

PÁLMA UTCA

ERZSÉBET KIRÁLYNÉ ÚTJA

MEXIKÓI ÚT

FRANCIA ÚT

AMERIKAI ÚT

XIV

HUNGÁRIA KÖRÚT

KOLUMBUSZ UTCA

KORONG UTCA

GYARMAT UTCA

MIMÓZA UTCA

BÁCSKAI UTCA

Police
Station

AJTÓSI DÜRER SOR

VÁROSLIGETI KÖRÚT

HERMINA ÚT

IDA UTCA

ILKA UTCA

THÖKÖLY ÚT

STEFÁNIA ÚT

JÁVOR UTCA

ZICHY GÉZA UTCA

ILKA UTCA

GIZELLA UTCA

ARÉNYI UTCA

1250 UTCA

SZABÓ J. UTCA

Police
Station

STEFÁNIA ÚT

SEMSEY ANDOR UTCA

ILKA UTCA

CHÁZÁR ANDRÁS UTCA

ARÉNYI UTCA

THÖKÖLY ÚT

SZABÓ J. UTCA

SEMSEY ANDOR UTCA

Geological
Institute &
Museum

Kisstadion

ISTVÁNMEZŐ

XIV

Puskás
Ferenc
Stadion

DÓZSA GYÖRGY ÚT

4

KLAUZÁL TÉR

ERZSÉBETVÁROS

✡ **Museum of Electrotechnology**

New York Palace

RÁKÓCZI ÚT

Keleti Station Ⓜ

FIUMEI ÚT

Blaha Lujza tér Ⓜ

Erkel Theatre

II JÁNOS PÁL PÁPA TÉR

Uránia Cinema

BLAHA LUJZA TÉR

RÁKÓCZI ÚT

JÓZSEF KÖRÚT

NÉPSZÍNHÁZ UTCA

Il. János Pál pápa tér Ⓜ

Hungarian Radio

Rákóczi tér Market Hall

Rákóczi tér Ⓜ

Police Station

MÁTYÁS TÉR

VII

Hungarian National Museum

JÓZSEFVÁROS

Józsefváros Parish Church

BAROSS U

Fountain of Hungarian Truth

SZABÓ E. TÉR

Ervin Szabó Library

BAROSS UTCA

JÓZSEF KÖRÚT

HORVÁTH MIHÁLY TÉR

Magnum Szauna

Police Station

ÜLLŐI ÚT

IX

IF Kávézó

MARKUSOVSZKY TÉR

Paul Street Boys

PRÁTER UTCA

MOLNÁR

Corvin Film Palace

CORVIN KÖZ

Corvin Promenade

CORVIN SÉTÁNY

Museum of Applied Arts

Corvin negyed Ⓜ

Killian Barracks

Trafo Arts Centre

Holocaust Memorial Centre

Klinikák Ⓜ

St Francis of Assisi Church

FERENC KÖRÚT

Goethe Institute

FERENCVÁROS

FERENC TÉR

Nehru Part

Szauna 69

BORÁROS TÉR

Ⓗ *Boráros tér*

PETŐFI HÍD